DECISIVE AIR BATTLES
of the
FIRST WORLD WAR

Books by ARCH WHITEHOUSE

Wings of Adventure

Hell in the Heavens

Hell in Helmets

Crime on a Convoy Carrier

The Real Book of Airplanes

Fighters in the Sky

Years of the Sky Kings

Tank: History of Armored Warfare

Bombers in the Sky

Years of the War Birds

Combat in the Sky

Subs and Submariners

Adventure in the Sky

Squadrons of the Sea

Billy Mitchell

Action in the Sky

Legion of the Lafayette

Amphibious Operations

Decisive Air Battles of the First World War

DECISIVE AIR BATTLES
of the
FIRST WORLD WAR

by Arch Whitehouse

DUELL, SLOAN AND PEARCE

New York

First edition

Affiliate of
MEREDITH PRESS
Des Moines & New York

Library of Congress Catalogue Card Number: 63-10353

MANUFACTURED IN THE UNITED STATES OF AMERICA FOR MEREDITH PRESS

VAN REES PRESS   •   NEW YORK

To

the airmen of all ranks of all
Allied air services who fought
in World War I

Contents

Illustrations

Introduction

ONE DAY late in August of 1917 I inaugurated the aerial dogfight. The term "dogfight" has been used carelessly for more than four decades, and is applied loosely to any air combat in which three or four aircraft were engaged. This is entirely erroneous, and the point should be clarified. Therefore, to introduce this volume, I shall describe my own experiences and role in a World War I air battle that I honestly believe initiated such conflicts. I might add that as far as I can trace, only two more dogfights were fought before the Armistice brought an end to our sky-high adventures.

I was an aerial gunner, a so-called first-class air mechanic (machine gunner), with Number 22 Squadron, Royal Flying Corps. I had been flying as an N.C.O. since the previous March, having transferred from the Northamptonshire Yeomanry, a territorial regiment I had joined on the outbreak of the war. A short time before, we had turned in our old two-seater pushers and became one of the first R.F.C. squadrons to be equipped with the new Bristol Fighter, probably the finest fighter aircraft developed during that war.

I had just returned from a fourteen-day leave in London, following many exciting weeks of flying against the German Flying Circus. As a matter of fact, my period of service coincided almost to the month with that of Baron Manfred von Richthofen.

My leave had been most pleasant and refreshing, but I was shocked to learn on my return to Estrée-Blanche that my regular pilot, Captain R. G. Bush, had been shot down on the enemy side of the line. Ward Clement, my bosom pal from Kitchener, Ontario, met me as I stepped down from our transport tender, and from his expression I sensed instantly that something doleful had happened. He said nothing, but just stood looking at me.

"Bush has gone down," I said, reading the somber news in his eyes.

Ward's face was tragic. He nodded his head. "I'm sorry," he began. "We tried to get to him, but it was no use. He kept going in deeper."

"The same day I went on leave," I added.

"That same morning."

"What a shame! Why didn't they let him go on leave at the same time?"

"He'd had his leave," Ward grumbled.

"I could have gone on that early-morning patrol with him. The Boulogne bus didn't leave until eleven o'clock."

"Your pass began at six that morning," Ward reminded me. "And don't blame yourself. I was the one who told you to lie low. If you had gone, you might have gone down with him. You had done enough patrols."

"I would have brought him back."

"Okay, you might have brought him back. But he would've had to fly without you eventually, and our officer observers aren't worth their rations."

This was a classic example of how N.C.O. gunners of that era stuck together. We had to, because we were being exploited cruelly. We were all good machine gunners with a wealth of war experience, and once we had survived those first few weeks of wartime flying, we unquestionably were valued hands, regardless of our noncommissioned rank. Officer observers were out there simply to book fifty hours of patrol flying, after which they were relieved and sent to pilot-training schools. The aerial gunners flew on and on until the uncompromising law of averages exacted its toll.

"Bush was a good pilot," I reflected, "but he never knew where he was and if he took an inexperienced observer, God help him. He couldn't seem to absorb the details of the front."

"Well, there you are. That's what happened," Ward explained. "He had a new officer observer, some chump who had never been over the line before. I guess he never had a chance."

I believe that this was the first time the full impact of war flying hit me, and I realized that the catch phrase "Suicide Club" which had been applied to the R.F.C. might have some verity.

We went on to our tent, and I stretched out on my bed. The indistinct specter of Captain Bush sat beside me and kept saying, "I made a special bid for you the day I arrived here at Estrée-Blanche; so don't ever get chummy with anyone else. You may as well know now that I can't seem to figure out where I am when I'm in the air, and I shall rely on you to bring me home."

As we learned later, that was exactly what had happened. Captain Bush and his officer observer had lost the formation somehow and floundered around in the Jerry back area until they were shot down by half a dozen Albatros scouts led by Oberleutnant Erich Lowenhardt, who was to score fifty-three victories before he himself was killed.

But there was little time to mourn the loss of Captain Bush. Our Wing was concentrating on an enemy air base at Gontrode near Bruges. The bombers were trying to batter this Zeppelin-Gotha base in reprisal for the intermittent raids on London, and we were responsible for getting them there, and getting them back. These were hectic days, and we were thankful to have the Bristol Fighter.

Of the original C Flight, to which I had been assigned some six months before when the squadron was at Chipilly on the Somme, only Captain Carleton Clement (Ward's cousin) and I were left. Most of the new officer observers seemed to be uncertain and confused as they tried to get a grip on this frantic profession; and many of them, seeing my three hundred or more hours on the time board in the Recording Office, sought me out to learn my secret of longevity. I had little to offer, except to warn them never to become panicky—and to make sure they knew where they were at all times. This common-sense advice made little impression, for they were seeking some exclusive and magic formula.

My first patrol after my return from leave provided a much-needed tonic, for it turned out to be an epic. C Flight was slated for a midday escort mission—to Gontrode again—and according to the still-legible scrawlings in the notebook that lies beside me as I write this, my pilot was a young Lieutenant Youl, and we were flying a Bristol Fighter, Number A7624, taking off at 11:55 A.M. Captain Clement carried the leader's streamers, and probably because I was the senior gunner of the flight, we were given the post of subleader.

Lieutenant Youl was a tall, well-built Somerset lad who knew how to fly and fight—as long as his engine kept ticking over. But the Brisfit, as she was called, was new to him and he had not as yet fully mastered the fuel system of the Rolls-Royce engine. However, I knew I could cope with this, and I felt quite confident with him.

Prior to take-off we went over the general idea of the show, kneeling around a map spread out on the ground. I noticed that Captain Clement looked very tired, and that his voice had lost much of its cheerful boom; but he beamed when he spotted me in the group and said, "Did you have a good leave, Whitehouse?"

"Yes, sir," I answered, "but I was rather anxious to get back this time. . . ."

He smiled wistfully, possibly wishing he could arouse such enthusiasm again. "Good! I know what you mean, but don't worry. You and Ward will be going back soon for commissions and flight training. That's what you have in mind, eh?"

"Exactly, sir," I responded, but I remembered that I had been promised such a reward for the past four months.

"You both are on the book. In the meantime, don't forget you are the senior gunner, and I'm relying on you. We have some heavy work ahead over the next few weeks, and as the subleader's gunner you will be expected to take over—in any emergency. You like Mr. Youl?"

"Very much, sir. I've flown with him occasionally."

"Fine. You're both lucky. He likes you too. Let's go!"

The tone of the conversation was encouraging, but I didn't like Captain Clement's weary expression. I feared he was cracking up and was in need of a long rest. As things turned out, I was right.

We climbed in and rolled out to our positions on the field, for the

Bristol Fighter squadrons were now taking off in formation. This was usually a majestic sight. The biplanes stood throbbing wingtip to wingtip, their idling propellers glistening in the sunshine. Everyone's head was up, all eyes on the leader's cockpit. We saw Captain Clement's hand go up to "Alert" and the other pilots began to press their throttles. The leader's hand went forward, and the planes seemed to stiffen and crouch like greyhounds at the leash. The engines opened up full; the rudders waggled and their bold colors flashed. The observers in their brown leather cocoons snuggled down inside their Scarff-gun mountings and flicked impudent salutes to each other.

With these colorful preliminaries, the aircraft tore away in a great swirl of dust, and from the hangar apron only the trailing edges of their wings showed. Suddenly all six machines zoomed together, and earth-bound mortals caught the broad surfaces of the upper wings with their jaunty cockades and their identification letters. For an instant they presented the shimmering impression of a solid triangle composed of mottled greens and browns.

We turned carefully and climbed as we crossed over the field for our last glimpse of the hangars and for any final orders. I saw a strip letter signal laid out—the letter L—which informed the leader that all was well and that no last-minute order had been received to cancel the patrol.

I quickly realized that Lieutenant Youl now flew well and seemed much at home in our tight formation. He was keen, alert, and never relaxed his vigil on the turns but glanced around now and then to make certain we two were co-operating in mind and deed.

Once we picked up the D.H.4 bombers over Ypres, as prescribed, we turned northeast for Roulers. There were twelve machines below; they seemed unusually sluggish, and I decided that they were carrying an extra-heavy load. So far, so good; but by the time we had adjusted our formation speed to their restrained performance and began to settle down in a spirit of professional security, our engine started to splutter.

I leaped to my feet and peered over Lieutenant Youl's shoulder to scan his instruments. I listened intently as he jiggled and reset his throttle adjustment, and decided that something was cluttering the fuel line. I snatched at the pressure-pump handle and rammed it up and down for a few strokes. The engine gradually picked up, but by that time we had lost considerable distance.

"Try to catch them," I scribbled in my notebook rather than yelling in his ear. In a situation like this I wanted no misunderstanding.

My pilot nosed down to pick up some speed and we made a good effort to rejoin our formation, but the engine spluttered again. Once more I tried the immediate action, and once more the Falcon engine picked up. Lieutenant Youl naturally was concerned, for Gontrode was about forty miles over the line and it was senseless to attempt the trip with a faulty engine. He looked at me for a suggestion. This is where an experienced gunner is expected to make a sensible decision. It was no time for the phony heroics of fiction flying, or attempting an impossible solution. I knew it was unwise to chance this continuing mechanical condition, so I yelled, "Get back to our side!"

Since the fuel-supply trouble had not been caused by gunfire, we had little or no idea what was wrong. There was no justification in trying to continue with the formation and add to our leader's responsibilities. Only fools accept risks that are not defensible.

I decided that we should return to our side of the line, work out the difficulty, and, once certain the trouble had been cleared, wait around near the line and time a second crossing that would enable us to rejoin our flight on its return. It was the only logical thing to do.

I continued to pump madly, forcing the tank pressure up, while Youl tried several throttle adjustments, but the Rolls-Royce still spluttered and complained until I suggested that we switch over to the emergency tank. By this time we were patrolling between Dixmude and Langemarck, with the water-logged fester of Flanders throbbing below. As we listened for a responsive even beat from our engine, I suddenly spun around, startled by the muffled roar of other engines, then breathed a deep sigh of relief. Six Belgian Spads were directly behind us, churning along in a very respectable formation; in fact, they were so close to our tail assembly that I could have tossed a drum of ammunition into the leader's propeller.

"Try your main tank again," I cried into Mr. Youl's ear.

He switched over, and after some hesitant spluttering the Falcon picked up some revs. Youl grinned, and as our power improved he stared at me with an inquiry of what course to take now. I pointed back at the Spads. He must have caught the suggestion in my eyes, and both of us smiled as we came to the same conclusion.

Back over the line we went with the single-seaters following cheerfully. To be sure, I had enticed them on with a wave of my arm; then a minute later I slapped Mr. Youl's shoulder and yelled, "Look at this! We've picked up a flight of S.E.5's now!"

No sooner had we reached Hooglede and started along the main road toward Roulers than six silver Nieuports joined us.

"We have nineteen planes in our parade," I yelled. "Now where's that Jerry Red Devil?"

Lieutenant Youl nodded pleasantly, and I was sure he had no idea what to do in an unscheduled situation like this. The armada had its points and possibilities, but I continued to listen to our engine until I was satisfied she was ticking over perfectly.

When I looked back again another flight of Spads had joined our circus and a formation of Sopwith Camels was coming up in our direction from over Courtrai.

Just what did one do in a case like this? My pilot was just as puzzled but was obviously pleased to be flight commander over such a militant flock. As I looked over our forces wondering how to employ them, I noticed the leader of the Camel flight firing a series of red lights as fast as he could load his Very pistol. I scanned the sky and discovered the reason for his anxiety. High above the oncoming Camels glinted the wings of a German formation, one as large as, probably larger than, ours.

I was not particularly concerned at first, for I was still wondering why all these scouts had selected us. Then I remembered Cap-

tain Clement's reference to our subleader's streamer. All these fighters had selected us for their leader and were gathering in circus
numbers with premeditated intent—and more were streaming in
from all sides.

My mind went out to the Bristols and D.H.4's on the Gontrode
show. They would have had a bad enough time over their target.
Some would be limping home; some already would have gone
down; and in all probability there would be wounded pilots and
gunners who needed double protection. This Jerry circus formation had to be taken out of their path. Here was a heaven-sent
opportunity.

Tapping a signal on Mr. Youl's shoulder, an order to turn in that
direction, I yelled, "Climb like hell! Go deep into enemy territory
and we'll pretend we haven't seen those Huns."

My pilot looked a trifle bewildered, but as he made the turn I
was relieved to see that the rest of our giddy formation followed.
We went in deep, almost as far as Thielt, before I swung the formation back, all the time watching the Germans and sensing somehow that their leader was not quite certain what our game was.

Finally I fired one signal cartridge, and before the Jerries could
interpret the situation, I led this pack of at least thirty fighters into
the center of the Hun circus.

This was the opening phase of the first dogfight of World War I,
and when I speak of a dogfight I mean an aerial engagement in
which at least fifty aircraft take an actual part, and the action must
be confined to the diameter of a few hundred yards—not miles! The
high speed of modern fighters makes this type of combat impossible. For instance, the air fighting of World War II and the Korean
conflict could not employ the combination of aircraft maneuverability and the 350-yard range of the 1914–18 machine gun. The
planes of 1939–45 had outranged the weapons, for it takes a modern
jet fighter, flying at combat speed, a distance of seven miles to
make a 360-degree turn. The .50-caliber gun or rocket pod does
not have the pepperbox effective range of the rifle-caliber weapon,
so that you cannot stage a prolonged duel with these modern war

machines. Air fighting under such conditions can be only a series of passes, short, hurried bursts, and the pull-out to clear—with the hope that the attack has been successful.

So here we were in a dogfight, and by the time Mr. Youl was firing I realized what a dreadful conflict I had set up. Eyewitnesses who later reported on this engagement stated that there were sixty-seven planes in the air at one time. I believed we had gone in with about thirty, but I could have been mistaken, for I was told afterward that at least ten more British single-seaters joined us a few minutes after the first burst was fired.

From that point on, insanity and pandemonium reigned. Aircraft were charging in from all angles, and were drawing a crazy-quilt design against the sky with their tracer rounds. Machines collided in midair, clutched each other for a few seconds, then tumbled earthward in slow, sweeping spins. The sky was littered with broken wings and struts that flashed and glinted like new rulers. Bundles of wreckage twisted and turned and trails of smoke scratched crayon marks down the azure walls. Human forms, all arms and legs, spread-eagled through the thunderous storm; one fouled the wingtip of a bright green Albatros.

I saw instantly that we had caught the Germans out of step when we had attacked from their side of the line, and our move forced many of them to turn to the hostile side, in Belgium. Naturally they wanted no part of that area, and in their frantic efforts to head toward the Homeland, some of them were forced into strange capers. Whatever formation they may have started with was soon scattered, and the more devastating part of the dogfight began.

Although we contributed our share of tight turns and rounds of ammunition, while quaking with fear, I did have a box seat from which to look on this fantastic combat. The Camels came down from above and cut the top-flight Albatroses to bits. I saw the Camel leader lose control of his mount; the snubby biplane rolled over on its side, slithered through the upper layer of aircraft and wreckage, and exploded in the middle of the pattern. A wing fluttered away with two yellow struts dangling from the spar sockets.

Mr. Youl came back and literally blasted his way through any opposition by pressing his gun trigger and fishtailing his rudder, hacking down everything in our path. I had to be content to wait until we had reached the center of operations before I could fire again.

The initial impact had been murder, and I must admit that the Belgian Spads had taken the brunt of it. Two collided in midair with a Fokker triplane. My pilot was skidding or banking through the aerial mixture, and I found myself firing down into the cockpit of a yellow Fokker. But before any decision could be reached there, Mr. Youl ripped up into a sharp climbing turn that gave me a chance to pour a number of hot bursts into another enemy formation. This seemed to split up this group of opposition, and we continued on and roared through the hole left by a triplane that had discarded its wings.

All this took place in a matter of seconds, although it takes minutes to write or read, but this is the form, spirit, and action of a dogfight. Nothing in any other chapter of warfare can compare with it. Even an old-time cavalry charge had more definite structure, pattern of movement, and certainly less immediate impact.

I saw a flight of S.E.5 pilots draw clear once and circle away to evade the debris. Mr. Youl dived on a mottled fuselage and shot it to bits before he realized it had no wings. The silver Nieuports circling above, waiting for an opening, suddenly came down in a compact vertical line to put a mass burst into a gaggle of two-seater Albatros machines. The German gunners were dividing up the scene in geometric patterns with tracer-bullet rulings.

An S.E.5 wriggled away in flames with the pilot climbing over the cockpit coaming to get out on the wing. I remember seeing him jerk his bus over into a sideslip and attempt to ride it down while the flames fluttered out at an angle just clearing the tail assembly. When next I looked, the burning S.E.5 had stalled, clawing at nothing, and there was no pilot standing on the wing root.

By this time the air was cluttered with wreckage and tumbling planes. Once we hit a fluttering red rudder with an interplane strut and the impact sounded like a howitzer shot, but we stumbled out of it and cleared as a warped fuselage screamed past our tail. The

Nieuports were taking a frightful beating from the German two-seaters whose gunners were sitting tight and firing from the outer fringes of the madness. The little French scouts seemed to be losing their vee struts whenever they turned to snarl at their tormentors—and a Nieuport without a vee strut, well, they had no pack-seat parachutes in those days.

How it ended, or when, I can't recall. There was no sane period of relaxation in which to jot down necessary notes. The last I remember of the action was when we were picking off a black and white Albatros. I saw it jerk in flight, and smoke, as I poured a long burst into it. The observer tried to scramble over into the pilot's cockpit, for some reason or other, and with that the whole aircraft went up in flames and screwed away from the melee. I turned to check our tail and saw that we were leading a mere handful of Camels, Spads, and Nieuports—a mere handful.

As we crossed the line, Lieutenant Youl turned and yelled, "You certainly started something, didn't you?"

I was too muscle-weary and mentally upset to answer.

"I'll bet there never was an air scrap like that before," he added.

"I wonder who won," I replied hollowly. "There won't be enough scouts left in France to stage a decent balloon show."

"One more like that ..." Youl observed grimly.

We both sensed that we were lucky to have scrambled out of that engagement, regardless of the outcome. Lieutenant Youl gave me credit for two flamers, and I discovered later that I had fired every round in the six drums of ammunition I had available.

I think it was about two thirty-five when we landed, for we had been in the air for two hours and forty minutes. We just sat there in our cockpits staring out at the dozens of slug holes in every section of the airplane. How we stayed in the air with that tangle of splintered spars and struts was a mystery. I can still see the half circle of mechanics standing peering at our battered Bristol. The prize line of the reaction was, "Coo! What a write-off!"

A short time later the rest of our original formation returned and rumbled up to the cabrank.

"Holy smoke!" Ward Clement ejaculated as he yanked off his

helmet after climbing down from his cockpit. "What happened?
You two trying for a Victoria Cross?"

Two days later, when some sketchy reports were in on that mass
engagement, it was indicated that about thirty planes had been
shot down—or lost in air collisions—eleven of them Allied aircraft.
My concept of war flying was tinged with a new quality of concern,
and I hoped that Captain Clement's promise of my being relieved
and sent to England for pilot training was substantially more than
an expression of encouragement.

A short time later I was awarded the Military Medal, for the
Royal Flying Corps was still the stepchild of the British Army, and
there were no distinctive aviation awards as such. Otherwise, I
would have been honored with the Distinguished Flying Medal.
The Royal Air Force was some eight months away and its aviation
decorations were not struck until late in April, 1918. Therefore those
of us who served in action between August 4, 1914, and April 1,
1918, could not gain awards that indicated our particular service or
role in the war.

My award appeared in orders, but there was no citation explaining why it was given, or whether it had been bestowed for any particular heroic or gallant action. The Orderly Room corporal just
showed me the official acknowledgment and handed me a piece of
the medal's ribbon to wear beneath my observer's wing. I did not
actually receive the award until some six months later when it was
presented before the R.F.C. Cadet Corps with the usual formality.
It was then that I discovered on the obverse of the medal the phrase
FOR BRAVERY IN THE FIELD—about as illogical a pronouncement as
one can conceive.

I was determined to learn more about single-seater machines, and
one day when Ward Clement had gone to London on leave, I wandered across our field and watched the mechanics working on the
sprightly S.E.5's of Number 56 Squadron. I had come to the conclusion that once I got to England I was going to volunteer for

single-seaters, rely on my own ability, make my own decisions, and
not be burdened with responsibility for another man. As I sauntered
around, peering into cockpits and checking on the gun controls and
sights, I was interrupted by a young officer who seemed to know
me, at least he knew my name.

"I suppose you'll want to fly one of these, eh, Whitehouse?" he
ventured with a pleasant smile.

Turning, I recognized Captain James McCudden, crack pilot of
the squadron. He had not as yet been awarded the Victoria Cross,
but he had the D.S.O. and Bar and the Military Cross; and what
was more interesting to me, he also wore the red, white, and blue
ribbon of the Military Medal, with which he had been honored
more than a year before while serving as an N.C.O. aerial gunner.

I wondered if I would ever catch up to him.

I agreed that my ambition was to fly scouts and, if my luck held,
to join Number 56 Squadron.

"When are they sending you home?"

"I don't know, sir. I volunteered under the impression that I'd
be sent back after logging fifty hours over the line."

"I hear you've done very well, though. How long have you been
flying?"

"I've done nearly four hundred hours as a gunner."

He scowled. "That's a long time in the back seat. Very unfair.
Someone ought to be shot."

"I hope it won't be me," I said grimly.

"Don't worry. You've been at it too long. You know when to pull
out of trouble, don't you?"

I grinned sheepishly. "I don't know, sir. I pulled into plenty the
other day. I'm afraid I was the one who started that big mess with
the Jerry circus."

Captain McCudden whistled. "I hear it was a howler. Don't tell
me you were in the middle of that. You mustn't do that too often,"
he warned.

I later learned that McCudden had run up his great score by his
lone-wolf tactics. He would take off aboard his S.E.5, climb to

about 18,000–20,000 feet, and hover there until an enemy formation came along. Then, getting up-sun, he would pounce, make his strike and zoom back to his safety zone, and await another victim.

"I'll never get into anything like that again," I answered, and quickly switched the subject.

Even after all these years, I realize today that I had experienced one of the war's greatest thrills. I have no idea how decisive it was, or how much it contributed to the eventual victory, but I present it here in the hope that its recording will assure my right to pen the rest of this volume, and its writing will be ratified by my many months of comparable experiences on the old Western Front.

All this took place at the end of August, 1917, and although I had been promised the reward of a commission and pilot training, I had to continue as an aerial gunner until January 18, 1918, before I was relieved. I saw Ward Clement die in a midair collision. Captain Clement was shot down in flames when his officer observer mistook a Vee-strut Albatros for a French Nieuport. When I finally left Estrée-Blanche for Britain, only Major L. W. Learmount, our C.O., was left of the original Number 22 Squadron I had joined almost a year before.

It is not to be assumed that all were victims of the Hun circus guns—not by a long sight. Some were lost on long-distance raids when their engines failed. Some went down under the physical strain and had to be relieved. Others were promoted to flight commanders or to command other squadrons. Some had the added misfortune to be taken prisoners of war. Only a few of the aerial gunners lived through their back-seat careers to go back to England for their ultimate rewards.

Since we were all volunteers, our treatment was inequitable and our rewards meager, but those of us who survived know that we have memories and accomplishments few others can enjoy.

This is how it was.

DECISIVE AIR BATTLES
of the
FIRST WORLD WAR

CHAPTER 1

The Birth of Air Power

The decision to use the airplane as a weapon was one of the most decisive moves of the Great War. Few generals or admirals had any respect for this noisy contraption. Few had any idea what made it fly or how its pilots controlled it in the air. Such a weapon threatened their staff positions and promised to place younger men in the posts of importance. The entrenched military minds were perfectly content with the status quo and believed nothing could replace their prancing cavalry for open warfare or scouting patrols. Aerial reconnaissance could just as well be carried out by hussars or dragoons in captive balloons. Hadn't the North used some such arrangement during America's Civil War? After all, where would such a complex flying machine fit into any major land campaign?

THE AIRPLANE GOES TO WAR

THE AIRPLANE was but eleven years of age when World War I erupted across Europe in the summer of 1914. Whether the two Dayton, Ohio, brothers had intended their invention to become a military weapon is difficult to decide, but on May 28, 1905, two years after their first successful flights, Wilbur Wright wrote to Octave Chanute, explaining that "We stand ready to furnish a practical machine for use in war at once, that is, a machine capable of carrying two men and fuel for a fifty-mile trip. . . . We have made a formal proposition to the British Government and expect to have a conference with one of its representatives at Dayton very soon."

America, the homeland of the Wrights, had ignored their continued success and efforts and was allowing European nations to take the lead in the development of the heavier-than-air craft for military purposes. Paradoxically, the first occasion on record in which the airplane was employed on a war mission was during the Mexican revolution of February 1911 when a government pilot is said to have flown over Ciudad Juárez to observe the position of the rebel forces. In September of the same year Italy is said to have used six aircraft for scouting work during her conflict with Turkey, and also employed airships for taking aerial photographs.

ACTION IN THE ITALIAN-TURKISH CAMPAIGN

One month later, on November 1, 1911, the first bomb was dropped from an airplane during the same Italian-Turkish war, which ended with the Italian annexation of Libya. The pilot of this plane was a Lieutenant Gavotti whose historical flight was the result of a personal desire to see the effect of explosive missiles dropped from the air. Carrying four bombs in a leather bag, he flew an Etrich monoplane, one that was powered by a six-cylinder, 130-horsepower Austro-Daimler engine, over the Turkish lines near Tripoli. The detonators were in his pocket, and on arrival over a Turkish encampment, at about six hundred feet, he took one of the bombs between his knees, fixed the detonator, and dropped the bomb over the side. Observing what he described as "disastrous results," he circled the camp and dropped the rest of his load.

All this was done in the face of a declaration that had been signed by forty-four nations in 1899, which outlawed the launching of projectiles or explosives from balloons or other "aerial vessels." Five years later when the pact came up for renewal at the Hague Convention it was ratified by only twenty-seven of the original signatories.

As the famous aerial strategist Giulio Douhet pointed out shortly after World War I, these aeronautics opened a new field of action, and in doing so naturally created a new battlefield; and since these early aircraft had many limitations, they of necessity were at first considered only as military equipment. They in no way could fill the bill for civil transportation, because they were limited in power, range, pay load, and certainly in human comfort. The airplane did have an element of speed, a freedom of movement through three dimensions, and gave great promise for military reconnaissance. As it proved itself in this phase, the idea of employing it as a range finder for the artillery was conceived; but other than some vague method of attacking the enemy behind his own lines by bombing or the distribution of free missiles, an offensive program was never considered seriously. Not until the need for countering enemy aerial operations was evident was the airplane armed for fighting in the air.

These demands were not discernible immediately, for once the airplane received sufficient power to provide city-to-city flights and over-water hops, and became structurally sound enough to perform exciting maneuvers, it was utilized chiefly as an exhibition vehicle and flown by daredevil pilots for the amusement of patrons of municipal fairs and expositions. Other flyers joined in thrilling point-to-point air races or attempted long-distance flights for prizes put up by the leading newspapers of the day. Between 1903 and 1913 the airplane became the playboy's toy, and hundreds of thrill-seeking sportsmen engaged in the pastime for their own pleasure.

It required a war to bring out the full potential of the heavier-than-air machine. Balloons of the lighter-than-air science had been used in military operations as far back as man could remember. History tells us that the Chinese used various forms of the balloon ages ago, but not for war purposes. In 1793 the French Army employed captive balloons for reconnaissance, and the next year these inflated platforms were used with considerable success against the Austrians at Maubeuge. The gas balloon was employed later at Charleroi and Fleurus. Another French balloon company was taken to Egypt by Napoleon but was disbanded at Abukir after it lost its portable apparatus for manufacturing hydrogen. The federal forces of the North used a captive balloon against the Confederates during the United States Civil War; but, as noted before, all were sent up for aerial reconnaissance only.

America lagged woefully in the development of the airplane as a military weapon, or in any employable form, until her entrance into World War I. Although it is generally considered to be a completely American invention, the two men who had given it to the scientific world were ignored in their homeland for years, and there were times when their claims were ridiculed. All this, despite their initial success at Kitty Hawk, the fact that they were flying regularly from a farm eight miles outside Dayton, and their amazing exhibitions that later electrified all Europe. Why they were so ignored has often been explained, and there is little point in flogging a dead horse; it is sufficient to state that when the Great War broke out, the United States had nothing that even resembled an air arm and had to beg or borrow equipment from the French and the British. America's most outstanding contribution to the air-war history was the Lafayette Escadrille, that valiant band of volunteers who served and fought with the French from early in 1916. Of them, more later.

FIRST WARTIME AIRMEN

But France, Great Britain, or Germany did not become air powers immediately, for the old die-hard elite cavalrymen still controlled the destinies of the military services, while the navies highhandedly refused to consider this noisy contraption, just as they had shunned the submarine and the torpedo. In Britain, for instance, although a number of civilian airmen had built and flown acceptable machines, it was not until 1912 that the War Office grudgingly granted £320,-000 (then $1,600,000) for the development of an air arm. They purchased thirty-six aircraft, only half of which were British-built, and a White Paper issued that same year contained these words:

In consideration of the difficult and hazardous nature of the flying service, H.M. King George V has granted the title "Royal Flying Corps." ...

Britain's Air Service thus not only gained the much-coveted "Royal" to its name, but also broke away from the ties of the Royal Engineers, who wielded control over this heterogeneous organization that had started simply as a balloon company. The first Royal Flying Corps was expected to assume both Army and Navy duties, and when its Central Flying School was established at Uphaven, provision was made to train ninety-one military, forty naval, and fifteen civilian pilots. The staff had only twenty-five aircraft for this bold project.

It was soon evident that this broad program could not be carried out, so a Military Wing was organized at Farnborough, and a Naval Wing at Eastchurch, after which a series of Military Trials, in which British manufacturers were invited to compete in order to develop airplanes suitable for these proposed military operations, was arranged. Later on, because of the shortage of British entries, the Military Trials had to be opened to all comers, since proposals were being considered for the formation of seven squadrons of twelve planes each. The balloons and airships were handed over to the Naval Wing.

These Military Trials proved to be an excellent idea, for in the 1912 program the British received a shock; only one British-built aircraft passed the simple tests. This was the Cody biplane, a monster that was designed and built by Colonel Samuel Franklin Cody, an Anglo-American pioneer from Fort Worth, Texas. In his early life Cody was associated with a cowboy troupe that traveled the world, and with the money he made he investigated a number of man-lifting kites. So successful were some of his experiences that he was employed by the War Office at Farnborough as a kite instructor in the balloon section, where he also took part in the designing and building of *Nulli Secundus*, Britain's first dirigible. He built his first airplane in 1908 and made his first short flight the following year. A few months later he made a world's record cross-country flight and won numerous money prizes, including $20,000 for the best military aircraft. He was flying this model with a passenger in

August, 1913, when it crashed and both he and his passenger were killed.

Cody's plane was big, ungainly, and ill-suited for military work, although it had taken first-prize money. British military men therefore had to revise their views and reconsider machines already built by Avro, Bristol, Farman, and Sopwith, and with the aid and co-operation of these manufacturers, the Royal Aircraft Factory was built to produce only military machines.

HOW MILITARY AIRCRAFT WERE DEVELOPED

It should be added here that some experiments were made during 1913 to equip certain aircraft with machine guns. In September a Maxim gun was mounted in the front seat of a Maurice Farman, but the weapon was too heavy and its recoil proved dangerous to the flimsy nacelle structure. In another experiment a volunteer gunner was furnished with a seat mounted on the axle of the landing gear and given a Lewis gun and two drums of ammunition. There are no reliable reports of how this Goldbergian contraption worked out. At any rate, the idea of providing aircraft with automatic weapons was dropped, and so far as is known, no aircraft of any nation went into the 1914 conflict so armed.

By February of 1914 the British Military Wing had 161 aircraft on its books, most of them the early B.E. (British Experimental) types from the Royal Aircraft Factory, and the Naval Wing had acquired sixty-two planes of various shapes and sizes. They were naval only in that some could take off from or alight on the water—if weather and sea conditions were most favorable. Among these were the Short, with a 160-horsepower Mono-Gnome engine, and a new Sopwith seaplane powered with a 200-horsepower engine and said to be armed with a 1½-pound, quick-firing gun; but again there are no reliable sources for this claim. Both Wings were experimenting with Bristol, Sopwith, and Martinsyde scouts, but none of these could be put into mass production until late in November, 1914, and none was available that fateful August.

On July 1, 1914, the Naval Wing made its break with the Royal

Flying Corps and became the Royal Naval Air Service, settling many Admiralty–War Office arguments.

Thus, on entering the Great War, Britain possessed the following inventory of flying equipment, many of which had to be shipped to France by surface vessels:

WARPLANES OF GREAT BRITAIN–1914

Type	Engine	Speed (mph)	Purpose
Avro	Gnome 80-hp	70	General
B.E.2	R.A.F. 90-hp	62	General
R.E.8	R.A.F. 90-hp	65	General
Farman Shorthorn	Renault 75-hp	58	Reconnaissance
Farman Longhorn	Renault 75-hp	55	Reconnaissance
Blériot XI	Gnome 80-hp	66	Reconnaissance
Sopwith Tabloid	Gnome 80-hp	84	Scouting
R.E.5	R.A.F. 90-hp	62	Reconnaissance
R.E.7	R.A.F. 90-hp	68	Reconnaissance
Bristol Scout	Gnome 80-hp	89	Escort
Short Seaplane	Sunbeam 200-hp	90	Bombing

The Imperial German Air Force was organized on paper as early as 1912, for German military officials had been among the first to appreciate what the Wright brothers had created and clearly saw the airplane as a potential war machine. When the European situation began to create serious war considerations, a sum approximating $20,000,000 was offered as prize money to encourage and finance the building of aircraft and engines; but little came of this, for the military staff was more interested in Count Zeppelin's famous dirigibles, which were establishing amazing passenger-carrying records all over Europe. Everyone wanted to invest in Count Zeppelin's miracle gasbags and few civilians saw any financial future in the limited range of the airplane.

It was not until 1911 that an Austrian inventor, Igo Etrich, produced a satisfactory military airplane—a model he tried to sell to his own government, but he was turned down. Later on a German

Secret Service agent got in touch with Etrich, and that resulted in his Taube design's being purchased outright by officials of the Rumpler factory at Berlin-Kichtenberg. The government ordered Rumpler's to turn out twenty Taubes at once, and sent Herr Etrich back to Austria, where little was heard of him from then on.

Taube is the German word for "dove," and Etrich's machines were so named because of the wing form and resemblance to a bird in flight, rather than to the boxy shape of the orthodox biplane. They were most efficient for early war work, and in time about twenty factories were producing various Taube types, powered by either Argus or Mercedes engines. The Rumpler model surpassed all others, and on July 9, 1913, Herr Linnekogel, chief pilot for the Rumpler factory, set a new altitude record of nearly 20,000 feet—an effort that was to have an important part in Rumpler's future plans, for the company designers concentrated on height and a rapid rate of climb, rather than forward speed. This was to make their photography and reconnaissance machines the most successful in the German inventory.

Germany actually had decided as early as 1900 that aircraft presented great military possibilities, but these considerations were based on the tethered balloon and the dirigible which in itself could be an offensive weapon. They were so obsessed with the lighter-than-air concept that one designer produced a winged balloon that was supposed to be loaded with bombs, carry a clockwork quick-release gear that would be set according to wind and drift, and at a specified time—presumably when the balloon was over its objective—the release gear would operate and down would go the balloon, bombs and all. In fact, this idea was tried out in October, 1914, but the test was unsatisfactory because the balloon refused to leave the ground. Some thirty years later the Germans released their first covey of buzz bombs on Britain, fulfilling their idea of a pilotless air weapon.

Fortunately for Great Britain, the German Naval Airship Service experienced a discouraging period of development and at one time seemed to be on the point of being disbanded after the loss of nearly all of its experienced officers in two Zeppelin disasters in 1913. Only the delivery of L.3 from Count Zeppelin's factory at Friedrichshafen in May, 1914, kept the lighter-than-air service in existence.

By the spring of 1913 the German High Command placed orders for additional aircraft, half of which were to be biplanes, and the rest monoplanes. The latter were practically all Taube types, and the biplanes were manufactured by Rumpler, Euhler, A.E.G., L.V.G., A.G.O., and D.W.F. Twelve months later, when Germany was making active preparation for war, an Army bill was passed granting $2,000,000, and what was left of the original design prize of $20,-000,000, to the Imperial Air Service. More aircraft were ordered and the old types were replaced. An additional clause in all contracts now specified that all new machines were to be of German manufacture and would have seats for a pilot and a passenger. In addition, they were to be provided with bomb racks and fittings for an aerial camera. No engines of less than 100-horsepower would be accepted, and a minimum top speed of 65 miles per hour, a ceiling of 8,000 feet, and a flight duration of at least four hours were mandatory.

When the August drums rolled, Germany's Air Force was well ahead of that of any other belligerent power. She had 38 Zeppelins or Schutte-Lanz dirigibles and more than 80 pilots to handle these giants. In heavier-than-air hangars she had the production of more than three years, totaling 1,954 aircraft built for military purposes. Allowing a certain percentage loss for crashes, wear and tear, and unserviceability, she must have had some 1,000 aircraft available at the outbreak of war. Of these, 36 were excellent seaplanes for use over coastal waters.

About 1,000 pilots had finished their training, and there were 487 skilled observers and additional personnnel of 2,600 men to fly and maintain these aircraft. In 1912 there were only twenty-eight airfields in Germany, but by the outbreak of the war this number had been more than doubled.

These figures may seem puny beside the numbers of later aerial armadas, but all situations and conditions are relative. All World War I aircraft are often looked on as "crates," to use a popular Hollywood or pulp-paper term; but they were the best that could be produced and were competing with aircraft of contemporary times, not against Spitfires, Hawks, Me.109's or Thunderbolts of another age. Most of them were not "crates" any more than the Hurricane or the Mustang is a crate compared to the modern jet fighter. World War I aircraft were in almost all instances built by skilled artisans; their engines were beautiful examples of the factory system that insisted on hand assembly and close-tolerance workmanship. True, they did not produce such power as later engines, but they simply were waiting for more rugged airframes, better fuel, and supercharged carburetor systems. Considering the power available, the progress of design, and the weapons carried, the airplanes produced through 1917–18 were possibly the most efficient fighting machines ever put into the air. Certainly no other fighter has equaled the records made by the 1917 Sopwith Camel.

CAVALRY OF THE CLOUDS

What drawbacks the early military planes disclosed may be found in man's concept of their employment. All military powers of that day rightfully looked on the airplane as just an adjunct to the cavalry to be used in scouting and reconnaissance; and these comparatively slow vehicles were ideal for such missions, as was proved during the first Battle of the Marne. Is it any wonder, then, that the top officials of the ground forces who had full say over the employment of aviation, did their best to limit their airmen to these early tactical duties? When the idea of bombing was broached, the artillerymen argued that their Long Toms and Jack Johnsons could do a much better job and deliver more explosive in a very short space of time, and contended that it would be better for the airmen to concentrate on accurate spotting for the gunners.

Of course the men who were doing the flying, coursing over the enemy lines day after day, realized eventually that there were many situations in which they could perform more spectacular work. If they could spot the grouping of enemy troops, why couldn't they interfere with their movement by dropping bombs along their line of march? If they could find enemy supply dumps or concentrations of troops, what was wrong with bombing the dumps or concentrations then and there? Also, they were able to find many important targets well beyond the range of the artillery.

PARIS IS RAIDED

This was most clearly outlined on August 13, 1914, less than two weeks after the opening of hostilities, when Lieutenant Franz von Hiddeson of the Imperial German Air Force flew to within a mile of the outskirts of Paris and dropped two four-pound hand bombs, then turned his Taube for home. No damage was done, but an idea was conceived and another seed of aerial bombing was planted. Jakob Werner, another German flyer, risked a flight to Paris and dropped a taunting message that read:

> People of Paris: Surrender! The
> Germans are at your gates. Tomorrow
> you will be ours.

For years this note—still on view at the Paris Museum—was credited to Max Immelmann, but since the Eagle of Lille did not join the German Air Force until November 12, 1914, he could not have participated in this memorable flight.

On September 2, Lieutenant von Hiddeson was shot down by a defense battery of antiaircraft guns near the Bois de Vincennes, but he was not the first airman to go down in this manner. On August 24 of that year a Sergeant Kausen who was scouting in an Aviatik was downed by British ground guns near Le Quesnoy, and another German, unnamed, was forced to land a Rumpler inside the British lines by Lieutenant H. D. Harvey-Kelley and his "gunner," a Sergeant Major Street. It should be explained that Street was armed only with a light automatic rifle that was mounted on a metal peg fitted to the front cockpit of a B.E. biplane. How he managed to fire such a weapon through the tangle of struts and bracing wires

that surrounded him has never been clearly explained, but the
Rumpler unquestionably went down and was captured. The crew,
however, somehow escaped.

Whether or not Lieutenant von Hiddeson's one-man raid on Paris
furnished the stimulus, the first raid on an enemy airdrome was
carried out on August 29 by a German Aviatik from which three
bombs were dropped on the R.F.C. field at Compiègne, and the
bomber eluded a flight of British machines sent up to overtake it.

With the opening of World War I the following types of aircraft
were available to the Imperial German Air Force:

WARPLANES OF GERMANY—1914

Type	Engines	Speed (mph)	Purpose
Albatros	Mercedes 100-hp	56	General
D.F.W.	Mercedes 100-hp	62	General
Gotha	Benz 100-hp	60	General
Goodekker	Mercedes 100-hp	60	General
Halberstadt	Mercedes 100-hp	68	General
Etrich	Argus 100-hp	56	General
Jeannin	Argus 100-hp	55	General
Rumpler	Mercedes 100-hp	70	General
Stahalz	Argus 100-hp	65	General
L.V.G.-B.2	Mercedes 100-hp	60	General
D.W.F.-C	Mercedes 100-hp	80	General
Friedrichshafen FF.17 *	N.A.G. 135-hp	62	General
Friedrichshafen FF.27 †	N.A.G. 135-hp	60	General
Sommer	Gnome 80-hp	70	General

* The Friedrichshafen FF.17 was a tractor seaplane.

† The Friedrichshafen FF.27 was a pusher seaplane.

French military aeronautics can be traced back to 1870, when
free balloons were used during the Prussian siege of Paris to fly out
important personages and dispatches, and even as an ammunition
airlift. In an attempt to overcome these escape routes, the Krupp
factory designed and produced the first high-angle gun that became
the basic weapon for all antiaircraft defenses.

Early in 1910 the Aero Club of France advised the War Cabinet that the airplane had great possibilities in warfare, and three weeks later the French Air Service was formed, its first flying officer being a Lieutenant Cameron who gained his "wings" on March 9, 1910. Balloons long had held the interest of the French military, and they had four Army balloon sections available. Heavier-than-air aviation did not get much attention until July 12, 1909, when the War Minister agreed to purchase a Wright biplane, but in the same breath demanded that a French machine be produced that would be adaptable for military use. As a result, the original order was revised for the purchase of not only the Wright machine but two Farman biplanes and one Blériot monoplane, and all four aircraft were delivered early in 1910—at about the time the Aero Club was drawing up a set of regulations for the issuance of pilots' licenses.

Events moved with creditable speed, and a number of military officers were assigned to flight training under Captain Lucas-Girardville, who had been taught by Wilbur Wright at Pau in 1908. Lieutenant Cameron was the first of this group of pilot students to gain his pilot's brevet, Aero Club certificate Number 33. The military brevet was not devised until March 18, 1911.

About a dozen aircraft of various types were available, but by late 1910 the Blériot monoplane was the most popular, probably because of its feat in crossing the English Channel the year before, and its continued successes in many French air races. The Henri Farman also had its share of followers, as it had proved its worth in several Military Trials in Europe and was most adaptable as a two-seater, general-purpose machine. The Wright biplane that had started all this activity never gained much success as a military vehicle, and never became important in Europe.

The French took to military flying with great enthusiasm and were soon experimenting with many types and ideas for the employment of the machine. In the summer of 1910 a Lieutenant Fequant, with a Captain Marconnet as his passenger, flew a Farman from Châlons to Vincennes, a distance of 145 kilometers, in two hours, forty minutes. During the trip Captain Marconnet took a number of aerial photographs that impressed the War Cabinet with their detail and reconnaissance value. This flight marked a turn in French aviation, for all pilots were immediately ordered to train for long cross-country flights and to carry skilled observers.

Later on, during Army maneuvers in Picardy, the Air Service pilots and observers outdid themselves, carrying out dozens of important patrols, some in most inclement weather. The speed with which they produced good photographs, maps, and reports of movements of the "enemy" forces impressed the Military Staff, and three complete aviation groups were established immediately. The reconnaissance work was stepped up and improved, and eventually motion-picture cameras were taken aloft to record the actual movement of troops and transport. In 1911 these air maneuvers were repeated on a larger and wider scale, and by that time the service had been given a certain degree of autonomy and was known as the Cinquième Arme, or Fifth Service. Thus France was the first military power to set up a unified air force. Its popularity was immediate, and a national subscription furnished funds for the development of new and more suitable aircraft.

Up to this time no specific requirements had been laid down for military aircraft; any plane with good performance, structural strength, and adaptability was suitable for these reconnaissance missions. But it was soon obvious—in France, at least—that the airplane had no offensive power; there was nothing with which to attack troops on the ground or other aircraft in the air.

A new Military Aircraft Competition was organized in which machines would have to fulfill the following requirements: they would have to be two-seaters capable of flying 186 miles, carrying a pay load of 660 pounds besides the crew, and be able to maintain a speed of at least thirty-seven miles per hour.

This and other competitions eventually weeded out the culls of the industry, and by August, 1914, the French Air Service, composed of twenty-one escadrilles of six two-seaters each, and four escadrilles of three single-seaters (reserved for the use of the cavalry), was ready, willing, and able. The aircraft concerned were the Blériot,

Henri Farman, Maurice Farman, Deperdussin, Bréguet, Voisin, Caudron, R.E.P., Nieuport, and Blériot single-seaters.

A considerable nucleus of the new arm had been undergoing
training in North Africa. Escadrilles had been formed in Algiers in
1911, where the training provided experience with desert, hot winds,
and sandstorms. One section based in western Morocco was com-
mitted to what in fact were military operations against Moroccan
nomads, including bombing attacks against these tribesmen. In one
of these sorties a Captain Hervé and his mechanic, named Roeland,
were forced down, captured and killed by the desert enemy, thus
becoming the first French military airmen to be killed in action.

GUN MOUNTINGS AND BOMB RACKS

Although the French devoted much time and study to the development of definite types, bombers, reconnaissance and chasse, or hunt-
ing, aircraft, we have little reliable information of what steps were
taken to provide weapons for their machines. Bombs they did
devise and deliver, but we find no evidence that any serious consideration was given to the arming of their aircraft, or producing a
so-called fighter airplane. In some instances we learn that the two-
seaters were equipped with automatic weapons, but these declarations do not indicate how or where these guns were mounted; but
we do know that early in the war a Corporal Pilot Stribick, accompanied by a passenger named David, attacked a German photography machine over French territory. Stribick is said to have
rested a Hotchkiss machine gun on the side of his cockpit, and sent
the enemy two-seater to the ground with a short burst. Both French
airmen received the Médaille Militaire for this feat, but we have
no more authority than this for the exploit.

How Roland Garros finally solved the problem of mounting a
machine gun so that it would fire bursts of bullets along its line of
flight between the whirling blades of the propeller, and thus produced the first true fighter plane, will be related in a later chapter.
Some historians have published photographs of Morane-Saulnier
single-seaters showing both Vickers and Hotchkiss guns mounted

behind the propeller, which they insist were assembled as early as 1913, but again, no reliable records are at hand to prove that this service arrangement was actually available. Certainly no such weapon appeared on the Western Front until Garros went out with his fixed-gun Morane-Saulnier monoplane on April 1, 1915. However, it should be pointed out that a number of pusher types, such as the Farmans and British F.B.5's (Vickers Gunbus), which had their engines mounted aft of the cockpit, were able to fire a gun forward; but the idea of using the airplane as a winged weapon, as Garros employed it, was not considered seriously until the war had been on many months.

France's inventory of military aircraft available at the opening of the war is listed as follows:

FRENCH WARPLANES—1914

Type	Engine	Speed (mph)	Purpose
Blériot 11	Mono-Gnome 80-hp	75	General
Blériot 39	Le Rhône 60-hp	68	General
Blériot 43	Mono-Gnome 80-hp	78	General
Astra C.M.	Renault 70-hp	56	General
Caudron G.2	Mono-Gnome 80-hp	76	General
Henri Farman	Renault 70-hp	58	General
Maurice Farman	Renault 70-hp	55	General
Morane-Saulnier	Mono-Gnome 80-hp	78	General
Nieuport	Le Rhône 60-hp	85	General
R.E.P.	Le Rhône 60-hp	70	General
Voisin	Canton-Unne 140-hp	68	General
Deperdussin	Gnome-Rhône 100-hp	65	General

Like the Germans and the British, the French went into the war with a catalogue of aircraft of multipurpose capability, but none was efficient for any one mission. Specialized mounts were slow in being developed, and France's first fighter was the Nieuport scout, in which a Lewis gun was mounted on the top plane to fire over the arc of the propeller—a primitive arrangement in its initial form, since the gun was fixed and so far away from the pilot that the ammunition drum could not be changed when expended. Various devices were tried later that enabled the pilot to tilt the weapon back to a position where he could change the empty drum, and eventually armorers of a British squadron invented what came to be known as the Cooper-Foster rail that contributed much to the arrangement and also allowed the pilot to tilt and fire the gun through an elevated angle at an enemy above him. In this the Nieuport gun, to some extent, became quite flexible. The scouts progressed from this through the various interrupter-gear systems, becoming true fighters, and remained in that configuration until the end of the war.

Italy had a minor role in the air war and contributed practically nothing in the equipment used, but as far back as 1908 Italian military men showed keen interest in the airplane and many of them flew as a hobby. A flying school was established at Centocelle for training of both civil and military airmen. Later on other schools were built at Cameri, Salussola, Bovolenta, Malpensa, Cortile, and Pordenone. Around this time Lieutenant Savoia made aviation history by flying a 50-horsepower Henri Farman biplane from Mourmelon, France, to Centocelle near Rome, and that created new interest in flying. By the end of 1910 Italy had thirty-eight licensed pilots.

Aviation progressed rapidly over the next few years, military maneuvers became an annual affair, and the airplane was introduced formally for observation duty. Italy's First Aeroplane Flotilla of Tripoli was sent to Libya, where the Italo-Turkish War was being fought, and a second aeroplane squadron was formed at Bengazi; but just what these services did has not been recorded officially.

By 1913 Italy had thirteen military training fields, and the chief equipment were Blériots, Maurice Farmans, Nieuport-Macchis and Savoia-Farmans. It must be assumed that the Nieuports were manufactured under the license at the Macchi plant and the Farmans at the Savoia works.

·When the war started in August, Italy had thirteen aviation squadrons and her airmen were specializing in long-distance cross-country flights. When Italy joined the Allies on May 24, 1915, her Royal Army Air Service could be considered to be in a state of readiness and her Naval Air Service, based on the Adriatic, had three airships, a number of flying boats, and assorted seaplanes, but none was in organized squadrons and they were of little actual value.

In the early days of the war Italy used a number of bombers, but had only one fighter squadron, the 8th, which employed Nieuports. Some artillery-spotting and reconnaissance work was attempted, but the Air Service was not reorganized and put on a true war footing until 1916, when more fighter squadrons were formed and some semblance of order obtained. Another reorganization was made in 1917 in which each army had its own air arm, and there was a so-called independent air service under the direct orders of the Supreme Command at Udine. The Italians were now using Spads, Hanriots, Macchi-Nieuports, Caudron G.IV's, F.B.A. flying boats, Nieuport fighters and S.A.M.L. aircraft. By August, 1917, fighter squadrons were predominant, many of them outfitted with composite equipment. Number 76 Squadron, for instance, had Nieuports, Hanriots, and Spads. By the time of the Armistice, Italy had sixty-eight squadrons available, but the British had to contribute four fighter squadrons and the French three to hold this organization together.

Forty-three Italian airmen made the "ace" list and five were credited with twenty or more victories.

BELGIUM'S AIR ARM

Belgium contributed considerably to the air war in 1914–18, and her aviation history is gallant and noteworthy. Since she was connected to France over so wide a border, she naturally absorbed much of the aviation pioneering France carried out in the early days. French airmen went into Belgian towns and exhibited many daring displays, with the result that Baron Pierre de Caters and Professor Émile Allard engaged in the sport as early as 1910 and became pilots. The Chevalier Jules de Laminne, a young well-to-do engineer, gained his wings at the Farman flying school at Mourmelon, and was the first airman to fly a royal passenger when he took Ferdinand of Bulgaria aloft at Kiewit, Belgium. De Laminne was to become the founder of the Belgian Air Force.

Two civilian airfields were established in Belgium in 1910, one at Kiewit, where de Laminne was housing his new Farman H.F.3. On a day in July of that year the War Minister, General Hellebaut, stopped at the Kiewit landing ground while on an inspection tour and became so much interested in the airplane that he returned a few days later and risked a flight. He was enthusiastic after his experience and decided then and there to form an air arm for the Belgian Army, asking de Laminne to train a number of military officers, which the young engineer agreed to do. This would have worked out well, except that other staff officers conceived new ideas of aviation training and decided that airplane pilots should come only from the ranks of the military balloon sections, and suggested a form of the powered glider as a basic training craft. So de Laminne's good intentions went for naught.

In the meantime two young officers, Lieutenants Baudouin de Montens d'Oostenryck and Alfred Sarteel, had taken up flying as a hobby at Baron de Caters' flying school at Antwerp, although they were supposed to be training under de Laminne. When General Hellebaut heard of it, he immediately ordered the purchase of an airplane and told de Laminne to establish the proposed military training. The general meant well but other generals still managed to delay the proceedings. Some young officers ignored regulation channels and hired de Laminne to train them at his Kiewit school, and all this soon put a bonfire under the Belgian military so that eventually normal training procedures were established, with officers being taught to be pilots, and enlisted men given courses in the mechanical features of the airplane.

The progress of military aviation in Belgium endured the misfortunes and hardships of all such pioneering, and over the years prior to the start of the war this advance was slow, but one interesting and historic incident was worth much of the tribulation.

In May, 1912, Colonel Isaac Newton Lewis, an American armament expert, was in Europe trying to interest some government in a new machine gun he had invented. As had been the case with the Wright brothers, he had been ignored at home, so he requested help in Belgium to display the weapon and explain how it might be used aboard an aircraft. No one saw much necessity for arming an airplane, but Colonel Lewis was permitted to have his gun taken aloft by a Lieutenant Nelis with a Second Lieutenant Stellingwerff acting as his gunner. A Farman F.20 Jero pusher was used, and in this model the gunner sat behind the pilot and the gun was mounted on a metal peg bolted to the side of the fuselage.

A white bed sheet was laid out on the ground for a target and held down at the corners with large stones. Lieutenant Stellingwerff was a good marksman, for after two or three runs over the target the sheet was cut to ribbons. The field quartermaster was enraged and demanded that the two flying men be court-martialed for destroying government property, but the field commandant arranged to have the sheet written off by the equipment officer, thus mollifying the quartermaster.

Colonel Lewis gained a small contract from the Belgian Government for the manufacture of his gun—a favor his own country would not concede—and a short time later Nelis and Stellingwerff flew their "battleplane" with its Lewis gun to Great Britain and staged another performance.

After two demonstrations, one at Hendon, another at Aldershot, the British were delighted with the displays and bought and adopted the American's weapon, with the result that they had a large number ready when war broke out. The Belgians, who had ignored the gun although they had renamed it the Belgian Rattlesnake, had none available and had to rely on British manufacturers for their supply when German troops violated their border.

In March, 1913, a new Minister for War, a M. de Broqueville, signed a decree making Kiewit a military airfield, and officers who volunteered for flying duty were given two months' leave with pay to take the course, and on completion of the training were presented with an additional allowance of 600 francs to cover incidentals. Later a royal decree set up a heavier-than-air division consisting of four squadrons, and it was hoped that two more could be added as fast as pilots could be trained. The competitions of Military Trials added more impetus to the growth, and practice reconnaissance patrols amazed the generals on the ground with their completeness and accuracy.

The Belgians were particularly adept in developing ground facilities, such as hangars, portable workshops, equipment trucks, spare-parts trailers, ambulances, and motorized vehicles that made for great mobility. On one occasion they experimented with wireless (radio) and primary arrangements for carrying the Hotchkiss gun. In a war exercise, with the Army divided into Red and Blue forces, the 1st and 2d Air Squadrons supported their moves, and, fearing wholesale aerial carnage, the War Ministry took great pains to warn the population of these aircraft being turned loose against each other, and added that when planes were about to land, everyone must "clear the area at the double!"

At the start of the war Belgium had one Depot Squadron and three service squadrons available, but only two of these could be considered at full strength. There were thirty-seven pilots with a mixture of aircraft, including Voisins, Farmans, Blériots, and Maurice Farman-14 biplanes. Eight civilian pilots brought their personal planes and volunteered their services, but in three days there was little left of the Belgian Air Service; much of the country and their airfields were overrun. When Namur was threatened, Number 2 Squadron flew to Buc near Paris to reorganize, and a month later moved up to Ostend just in time to encounter a storm of gale proportions that wiped out many of their aircraft.

Meanwhile Number 1 Squadron fought on with six Maurice Farmans and a Nieuport scout for its commander until France could re-equip them with Nieuport Baby scouts. Over the months and years eleven squadrons were organized by the Belgians who flew British Camels, Hanriots, Spads, Breguets, and various other types.

Second Lieutenant Willy Coppens was credited with thirty-seven aerial victories, Adjutant A. de Muelemeester downed eleven, and Second Lieutenant Edmond Thieffry became a ten-plane ace.

Russia's role in the 1914–18 air war affords few bright chapters or personal heroics. The young officers who were burdened with duty with the air arm went into the war believing that a victory over Germany would end the influence of German intrigue at the Russian court, and hoped that the Russians then would be allied more closely with democratic forms of government, such as they had seen in Britain and France. When early in the war they realized that they had been "betrayed" and that there was little hope for victory, apparently they lost interest in continuing to fight.

Actually, Russia had taken to the air as early as 1812, for Napoleon's troops found a form of observation balloon in General Mikhail S. Vorontsov's camp, and Russian balloon divisions were active at Port Arthur in the Russo-Japanese War ninety-two years later. Between that unfortunate campaign and 1914, Russia purchased airships from France and Germany and designed one or two of her own.

The airplane was adopted soon after it was available, and a military flying school was opened outside St. Petersburg as early as 1910, and later that year a naval flying school was established at Sevastopol. Young Russian officers were sent to Great Britain and France for pilot training.

A Military Trials meeting was held at Gatchina near St. Petersburg in 1911, where a series of contests indicated that the Russian airmen had learned well. Igor I. Sikorsky produced his S.5 biplane, and one of these aircraft won the 1911 trials when flown by a Lieutenant Alechnovich, who later was a test pilot for the Sikorsky firm. Russian military aviation got off to a good start, therefore, and enjoyed royal support, but from all accounts the renegade monk Rasputin, through his influence with the Tsarina, soon broke up this official co-operation. The Grand Duke Nicholas was removed from his command of the armed forces, and the Mad Monk was responsible for the almost permanent prorogation of the Duma (parliament). The resulting civil war destroyed every important feature of Russia's Air Service.

When the war broke out Russia had 224 airplanes, twelve airships, and forty-six kite balloons. One hundred and forty-five airplanes were with organized squadrons, and by February, 1917, when the Russian Government collapsed, 1,039 aircraft were available. It should be added that few of these were modern in the sense of the development up to that time, for most of them were 1914 models; many were imported or had been built under license.

Through their doleful months of warfare Russian aircraft factories were not able to maintain any worth-while production, and their French and British allies contributed what they could. They even had a few American Curtiss single-engined flying boats, but all this generosity and concern availed little in a country being swept by revolution. The Germans had practically no opposition in the air and did not waste first-class squadrons on the Russian front, with the result that there was comparatively little air fighting there, and few Russian aces are on record.

Staff Captain A. A. Kazakov was credited with seventeen victories, and in some records the figure has been raised to thirty-two. Captain P. V. d'Argueef downed fifteen, Lieutenant Commander A. P. de Seversky (today an American citizen) is credited with thirteen, and Lieutenant I. W. Smirnoff with twelve. About fifteen other Russian airmen are listed as aces.

AMERICA'S GREAT CONTRIBUTION

The United States, which did not enter World War I until April, 1917, could not produce the number of high-scoring aces that the other chief belligerent powers did, but considering the few months they were in action, their performances were most creditable. What America lacked was not willing and able airmen, but an imaginative and vital aerial organization to guide them and furnish aircraft for their activities.

To some extent the early history of American military aviation parallels that of Great Britain. Both powers ignored the value of the airplane, and jealous rivalry of the senior services almost denied both countries an air arm when one was most needed.

As is well known, the northern forces in the Civil War used the observation balloon to great advantage. The Confederates had but two of them, and these were employed early in the war, then were allowed to fall into discard. On the northern side, however, John La Mountain and Thaddeus S. C. Lowe, civilians attached to the Army, provided a first-class reconnaissance team until personal differences broke up their partnership. La Mountain was relieved of his post, and by September, 1861, Lowe became Chief of the Army of the Potomac's Balloon Corps, and by 1862 Lowe had seven various-sized balloons in almost constant use.

In 1863 internal problems within the Army, and the rule of assigning troops to operate the balloons under temporary arrangements instead of permanent duty, broke up the operations. Later, field commanders were not convinced of the value of aerial balloons and Lowe felt it necessary to resign; in a short time the Balloon Corps was disbanded.

Heavier-than-air operations received much the same treatment. Although the Wright brothers had given their country the first successful airplane, little use was made of the invention. The Wrights offered their machine to the U.S. Government on two occasions, and both times were turned down. In the meantime European powers gladly purchased and employed the Wright patents. Not until 1907, four years after their successful flight at Kitty Hawk, were their claims recognized. President Theodore Roosevelt then ordered the Board of Ordnance and Fortification to investigate and issue bids for the construction of a suitable military aircraft. The Wright Flyer was the first machine to fill all specifications and on August 2, 1909, the United States purchased its Army Aeroplane Number 1 for $30,000.

Lieutenants Frank P. Lahm, Frederick E. Humphreys, and Benjamin D. Foulois were trained by the Wrights at College Park, Maryland, but when this program had been completed, these pilots had nowhere to go—except back to the cavalry or to the engineers. A government flying school was not established at College Park until 1911, where routine "military" missions were attempted and some progress was made. By 1912 the school had grown to fourteen flying officers, thirty-nine enlisted men, and nine airplanes of the Curtiss, Wright, and Burgess manufacture.

During February, 1911, relations with Mexico became strained and Army forces were organized to meet any opposition made by the revolutionary General Victoriano Huerta, who had seized power. At the same time it was hoped that an air organization might aid military operations, and a provisional unit, the 1st Aero Squadron, was set up. However, hostilities did not materialize and little was accomplished beyond a few so-called cross-country flights.

By 1913 most military air operations had been shifted to San Diego, California, where a new Signal Corps Aviation School was established. There had been some twenty-eight aircraft available previously, but nine of these had been written off in crashes, and eleven pilots had lost their lives. As a result, the pusher-type airplane (Wright and Curtiss) was condemned, leaving the Army with but five airworthy mounts.

Glenn Curtiss had been experimenting with a sports plane that could be fitted with dual controls, and a short time later the Curtiss firm produced the Curtiss-J, or Curtiss Jenny. For reasons best known to the students who trained aboard her, Jenny won some strange affection, but compared with the trainers available to students in Britain and France she actually was a very doubtful performer.

By July, 1914, legislation authorized the Aviation Section of the Signal Corps with a strength of 60 officers and 260 enlisted men. The act also provided for flight pay and established the aeronautical ratings of Junior Military Aviator and Military Aviator. The Aviation Section expanded through 1915, and General Scriven hoped to organize a force of eighteen squadrons of twelve machines each; but such was not to be, for America, who had given the world the first successful airplane, had not kept pace with the technical development in Europe. She had nothing resembling a fighter plane and no aircraft capable of conversion for wartime missions.

More incidents along the Mexican border erupted in 1914 and 1915, and when Brigadier General John J. Pershing was ordered to raise a force of 15,000 men to capture Pancho Villa (dead or alive), the 1st Aero Squadron attempted to join the fray, but unfortunately the aircraft were incapable of flying over the 12,000-foot mountains or of withstanding the difficult air turbulence in that area. They were grounded most of the time by duststorms, high winds, and snow. By April, 1915, only two of the original eight machines of the squadron were left, and these were conveniently condemned, to evade flying them back to San Diego. This fiasco, more than anything else, needled Washington into realizing the shortcomings of America's air arm, and in August, 1916, Congress appropriated $13,000,000 for the expansion of military aviation. The National Defense Act of that same year also authorized an increase in the strength of the Aviation Section and established a reserve corps of officers and enlisted men.

When America entered the war in 1917, almost two years after the sinking of the *Lusitania*, she again realized how far behind she had lagged in the development of military aviation. She had nothing but the desire of a few young men to fly. Great Britain had produced the Sopwith Camel, the Bristol Fighter, the S.E.5, the D.H.9, and the Handley Page bomber. Germany was flying the Fokker, the Albatros, the Halberstadt, the Rumpler, and the Gotha. France had contributed the Nieuport, the Spad, the Breguet, the Hanriot, the Salmson, and the Caudron. All America had to offer was something called a "Jenny," and European trainees were using far better planes than the Jenny for primary flight training.

A gallant effort was made over the next nineteen months, but the initial lag proved to be too much to overcome. On entering the war America had 131 officers, 1,087 enlisted men, and fewer than

250 aircraft, none of which was suitable for any wartime mission. The two air officers on the General Staff in Washington had never seen a true fighting plane!

Proclamations were made, and astronomical figures flaunted in newspaper headlines indicating that America would soon be "over there" with vast fleets of military aircraft. Fortunes were spent on the development of the Liberty engine, when the Allies willingly would have furnished the blueprints for their Rolls-Royce, Sunbeam, Hispano-Suiza, and other tried-and-true power plants. But the discarded D.H.4 was adopted, loaded down with a Liberty engine and presented as a modern warplane. The French had experimented with the Nieuport-28 and discarded it when it was discovered that its wings were unreliable, but America took it over without question. With months of hard-won experience behind them, American volunteers who had served in the Lafayette Escadrille offered to transfer to their flag, but they were ignored and for weeks were left in the discard. Inexperienced American officers, straight from Washington, then presumed to teach these veterans of the Western Front how to fly, behave, and wear their uniforms.

Finally sage minds prevailed and American airmen were trained by Allied tutors and given Allied aircraft—not the best, but the best that was available. Some were taken into Allied squadrons and taught under the glare of battle; some climbed out of the Jennys and started all over again on French or British air training grounds until suitable tuition could be given by their own forces.

Despite their handicaps, these American candidates performed unusually well. Many were killed in the 289 aircraft lost, and the 48 balloons downed in action. In contrast, they shot down 781 planes and 73 balloons. They carried out 150 bombing raids, delivered 140 tons of bombs, and penetrated as deep as 160 miles inside the enemy lines. At the end of the war America had 45 combat squadrons on the front and 740 airplanes, 800 pilots and 500 observers. Captain Edward V. Rickenbacker was America's leading ace, with 26 confirmed victories. Lieutenant Frank Luke, the Arizona Balloon Buster, was next, with 21 victories; and Major Raoul Lufbery, who had scored all his successes with the Lafayette Escadrille, was third, with 17. He was a member of the U.S. 27th Squadron when he was killed on May 19, 1918. Four Americans were awarded the Medal of Honor, and many of their personal stories will be related in subsequent chapters. Their fighting spirit, teamwork, and traditions more than made up for the deficiencies of their bureaucratic leadership.

THE BIRTH OF THE GREAT TRADITION

This was the beginning of air power. This is how the various nations rated at the outbreak of World War I. What was to take place had never been envisioned before, not even by such imaginative writers as H. G. Wells or Jules Verne. Those who participated went into those early war skies with no precedent or instructors to guide them. There were no previous air heroes to emulate. This was a new military element and they had to set up their own guidelines and methods of procedure. In the beginning there were no fighter or bomber schools. There were no guns or bombs to speak of. Gunsights and bombsights had yet to be invented. Those of us who went into that early campaign were completely on our own, and we did the best we could with what we had; and out of this bewildering, glorious, deadly profession we created one undeviating standard.

The tradition of the skies . . .

And of that we are proud.

CHAPTER 2

Brickbats and Bombers

With the outbreak of war both sides found difficulty in getting their squadrons to the scene of operations. The Royal Flying Corps had to decide whether to risk flying across the English Channel or sending their war birds to the front in crates. On arrival they did as much fighting against irate farmers and peasants as they did against their opposite numbers in the air. The air crews assigned to early reconnaissance missions performed splendidly but had to watch their enemy carry out the same work unmolested, since neither side had the equipment to deny the other the air. Another decisive decision, completely unofficial, was to take carbines, pistols, and shotguns aloft, and when Lieutenant Waterfell was shot down and killed over Ath, Belgium, both sides realized that a new phase of gallantry had been brought to military operations.

COMIC-OPERA WARFARE

WORLD WAR I actually opened on July 30, 1914, when the Austrians, after declaring war on Serbia following the assassination of the Austro-Hungarian crown prince at Sarajevo, bombarded Belgrade. Russia made immediate plans to mobilize, and Germany, realizing the proximity of *Der Tag* and knowing how well France had fortified her Franco-German border, decided to "tear up" all previous treaties and invade Belgium, a move that gave access into France where no military defenses had been erected. The invasion took

31

place on August 3, and the next day at 11 A.M. Great Britain honored her commitments to both France and Belgium and declared war on Germany.

The Royal Flying Corps took to the skies, as did the Imperial German Air Service. France rallied her military escadrilles, and what Belgian squadrons could be organized were flown back to join the men who had come to her aid. How strong, or efficient, any air service was no one knew, for there were no standards for comparison. In 1914 it had been decided that excessive speed was unnecessary in any military plane, since it was expected to provide only a platform from which to observe the activities of the enemy.

Aviation history over these opening days is vague and confused, for no reliable reports of squadron activity appear to have been kept. There were no precedents and the administrative routine had to be devised as the war continued. We do know, however, that although the Royal Flying Corps was mobilized instantly for action, it was not able to assemble to go overseas until nine days later, August 13. The aircraft had to be flown across the Channel while the stores and motor transport followed by ship.

Only a few planes of Britain's four available squadrons could be flown across the twenty-three-mile-wide strip of water, although there are some reports that practically all made the over-water hop. At any rate, one crashed on take-off and Lieutenant R. R. Skene and Air Mechanic R. K. Barlow were killed, the first R.F.C. men to die in the war.

The mobilization and move to the front had some lively and humorous sidelights in spite of the seriousness of the situation. Each pilot carried a revolver, field glasses, spare goggles, a water bottle, a small stove, biscuits, a chunk of chocolate, and some soup cubes. All of this came in handy, for most of the airmen spent the next few days and nights huddled against French haystacks, picnicking alfresco as they awaited the arrival of transport and spare parts.

No one had any idea where the war was being staged, or what uniforms the enemy would wear. They had no military maps of France or Belgium until M. Michelin, the well-known tire manufacturer, furnished a few automobile road guides. These profusely illustrated sheets may have been interesting to vacationing tourists but were of little value to aviators. They had to do for weeks, however, until a London newspaper publisher obliged with a few copies of gaily colored "war maps" that were given away to subscribers as premiums.

The equipment assembly afforded some burlesque situations. Blériot tails were bolted to Avro fuselages; undercarriages intended for Morane Parasols were "bent a bit" and affixed to B.E.8 aircraft; engines provided for Farmans were blandly attached to R.E.2's. Amazingly, everything seemed to fly; what didn't was hauled over by Channel packet steamer, unloaded and towed through French streets to the nearest cow pasture, and eventually flown to the battle areas.

Number 2 and 4 Squadrons were equipped with B.E.2's. These machines were said to be Blériot-inspired—a dreadful slur on M. Blériot—and were registered as Blériot Experimental, but were manufactured at the Royal Aircraft Factory. Number 3 Squadron had a mixed covey of B.E.2's and Henri Farmans. Avros, Maurice Farmans, and B.E.8's (affectionately known as Bloaters) were the warplanes of Number 5 Squadron.

This comic-opera collection of aircraft took off at two-minute intervals, and most of them eventually arrived in France. One plane even got as far as its final destination, Amiens, the first night, and its pilot, Lieutenant H. D. Harvey-Kelley, received a severe reprimand for taking a short cut and arriving on French soil before his commander, Major J. C. Burke, formerly of the Royal Irish Regiment. Lieutenant R. N. Vaughn was forced down with engine trouble near Boulogne, arrested by French authorities, and kept in confinement for a week. It seems they had not been advised officially of the arrangements. At any rate, Number 2, 3, and 4 Squadrons left Amiens for Maubeuge by August 16, and four more casualties were experienced en route. Two Bloaters crashed.

Transport was composed mainly of borrowed furniture vans, commercial delivery vehicles, and one odorous tumbril that had been used for the collection of garbage. One bright-red truck, commandeered from a well-known provision firm, was used by Number 2 Squadron as its mobile service unit, and during the retreat from Mons this gaudy vehicle was better than any electronic guidance system—for both sides. It could be easily seen and could travel almost as fast as the military aircraft it was serving.

WHOSE AIRCRAFT IS THAT?

Aerial warfare, to some extent, was more hazardous during the opening days of the war than it was a year or so later. The early aircraft had no international markings, and since all types looked much alike to the unpracticed eye, they were fired upon by friend and foe. Forced landings in friendly areas were likely to be risky experiences, because civilians on both sides of the line asked no questions but attacked with pitchforks, hatchets, or shotguns. Airplanes landing anywhere near groups of infantry generally were fired on until the unfortunate crew could explain that they were indeed "on their side."

Realizing that steps had to be taken to have some form of recognition, the British daubed streaks of red, white, and blue on their wings or rudders. Since the French colors were the same, it became obvious that more distinctive markings would have to be devised; a few "battleplanes" had Union Jacks painted on them wherever there was space. Later this insignia was simplified by a red, white, and blue roundel that proved to be most satisfactory. The French adopted a like cockade, but reversed the sequence of colors by painting the outer circle red and the inner spot blue. Out of this original precautionary measure came the first military air insignia. Before 1914 ended the Germans selected their Iron Cross design.

Most of the flying personnel were basically sportsmen flyers who had been drawn into a fraternal association with this new flying arm, and when the call came, they simply doffed their reversed caps, sports jackets, and knickerbockers, donned the accepted military uniform, and dashed around on motorcycles until they could find a covey of aircraft. This was particularly true of the British.

Most of the airmen were the playboy types who had been deprived of their motorcar licenses because of frequent speed infringements, and had taken up flying to avoid the frowns of highway bobbies. Lieutenant W. B. Rhodes-Moorhouse, the first Britisher to win the Victoria Cross in the air, was such a culprit.

IF YOU CAN LOAD A GUN, YOU'RE AN AERIAL GUNNER

At first the observers and gunners were picked haphazardly from the ranks of mechanics, or Orderly Room officers who were not otherwise engaged that day. None had had air or gunnery training, their chief qualifications being the ability to load and fire a cavalry carbine, immunity to airsickness, large jacket pockets that would accommodate half bricks for dropping on enemy aircraft, and a general disregard for their own safety. One of Great Britain's finest war airmen, Major James McCudden, began his career in this manner. It seems that he knew how to start a rotary engine and fire a Parker shotgun.

This "winged cavalry" went to work in earnest, and their scouting had an important part in saving the combined Franco-British forces in the first few weeks of the war. As pointed out previously, there was no real air fighting, since none of the planes taken to the front was armed. A few boisterous characters conceived the idea of "having a go" at enemy aircraft with small-arms fire, but nothing deliberate or premeditated had been contemplated. A Maurice Farman biplane of Number 3 Squadron reportedly took to the war skies carrying a Hotchkiss machine gun—but not for shooting purposes. It was just an experiment in weight carrying.

MISSILES OF THE IRON AGE

By mid-September it was noticed that both sides were using many aircraft and the skies were becoming somewhat crowded, and with so many targets, a few pugnacious types began to take along duck guns, pistols, and even half bricks. In fact, Captain G. W. Mapplebeck of the Royal Flying Corps returned from one reconnaissance patrol with a German pistol bullet in his shoulder. But generally speaking, everyone went about his business, checking the movement of troops, photographing the farm country, and wondering what was burning down there. Whenever enemy machines passed by, the ill-mannered types thumbed their noses or shook belligerent fists.

But these Arcadian conditions could not last, since some uncouth oaf was certain to bespoil the sanctity of harmless patrols and interrupt the industry of others. A few half bricks were tossed, lengths of rusty chain were flung, large lead weights were dangled from lengths of wire with the idea of fouling some Rumpler's propeller. Another destructive type amused himself with firing a Webley pistol at passing Aviatiks. The Parker shotgun idea finally shattered the *entente cordiale*.

The Germans retaliated with rifle fire, and during this early belligerency Lieutenant Waterfell was shot down and killed over Ath, Belgium, the first such casualty of 7,589 who were to die in the British flying services during the next four years of air action.

It was no longer possible to ignore this situation and measures were considered for mounting regulation rifles to the cockpits of all aircraft. Engagements were being reported from all sectors, and in most cases the observers, who sat in the front seats of the biplane types, were handicapped in having to aim and fire through the network of struts, stays, flying wires, fluttering wingtips, and a whirling propeller. To hold a rifle in the slipstream also made sighting accuracy difficult.

Toward the end of September two Bristol Scouts were delivered, one to Number 3 and one to Number 5 Squadron, each of which was armed with a rifle mounted on a peg and limited in arc of fire to avoid shooting into the propeller blades. Whether they were ever used in action has not been related.

Rifles, shotguns, and carbines provided some small measure of satisfaction, but the German aircraft were so superior in gaining and maintaining altitude that it was almost impossible for British or French airplanes to get at them. German Rumplers would buzz over Allied areas while their observers drew maps, took photographs, or wrote out detailed reports undisturbed. Frustrated British airmen floundered about some three thousand feet below vainly shooting off carbines at the nosy Huns; but since they couldn't vent their wrath on the enemy above, they took it out on the ground troops below, and in firing single shots at groups of infantry they must be credited with establishing the groundwork for attack aviation.

On October 5 the observer of a French machine shot the pilot of an Aviatik stone dead from a range of one hundred yards. The next day a German claimed to have destroyed a Caudron by throwing a brick into its propeller.

Heavier-than-air bombing seems to have begun late in October when a squadron, known popularly as the Ostend Carrier Pigeons, was formed by the Germans at Ghistelles, and shortly after made what was considered a mass raid on Dunkirk. Later in December a plane from this squadron attempted a raid on Dover, but for some reason dropped its bombs into the sea instead. Another of the Carrier Pigeons appeared over Sheerness on Christmas Day, but a patrol of Royal Naval Air Service aircraft drove it off before any damage was done.

During these early days there were several variations of aerial bombs, the first being a streamlined canister of gasoline that was supposed to ignite on impact with the ground and was used often against German hangars and airship sheds. Another incendiary bomb was a can of explosive that was wrapped with coils of sticky tarred rope; the burning hemp was supposed to fly off in all directions and complete the arson job. There was also a treacherous melinite shrapnel bomb that actually was a converted French shell with an unpredictable nose striker. These would sometimes explode while being hung in the racks and eventually had to be discarded. Parachute-braked bombs were tried later on, and by delaying the fall the parachute would give the airman a chance to escape from the explosion and debris. Some shell bombs were tied to the upper longerons with common wrapping cord, and when the airman wished to release them over the target, he used his pocketknife to sever the string.

Britain's first real bombing raid was carried out against occupied Brussels early in the war. All available R.F.C. aircraft took part, with each plane carrying six twenty-pound bombs that were dumped over the Flemish city. Several of the airplanes were damaged by ground gunfire and had to land in Holland, but instead of being interned for the duration of the war, the air crews signed on as ships' firemen at Rotterdam and worked their way back to England.

The former Naval Wing, now the Royal Naval Air Service, had something of an edge over the Royal Flying Corps. In the first place, their aircraft were faster, higher-powered, and carried wireless sets, and of course, they generally were operating from home bases. On the outbreak of war the R.N.A.S. assumed many patrol duties along the coasts and escorted transports across the Channel, but once this routine work was well under way the General Staff detailed them to prepare for attacks against enemy airship sheds and landing fields, for Britain already could foresee the menace of the Zeppelins.

FIRST RAIDS ON ZEPPELIN SHEDS

Around the middle of September a colorful character, Wing Commander C. R. Samson, took his R.N.A.S. command over to Ostend to assist in the defense of Antwerp. While that city was being evacuated, Flight Lieutenant Marix and Squadron Commander Spenser Grey, flying Sopwith Tabloids, set out to bomb the Zeppelin sheds at Düsseldorf. When Commander Grey ran into bad weather, he dropped his bombs on the railroad station at Cologne, but Lieutenant Marix reached Düsseldorf and, going down to six hundred feet, dropped his load of twenty-pounders on a shed, scored a direct hit, set the hangar in flames, and the brand-new Zeppelin Z.9 went up with it.

But the defense fire was so heavy that Marix's Tabloid was shot up badly and he had to force-land about twenty miles from his base. Knowing the geographic situation and being a persuasive man, he swapped his Tabloid for a Belgian peasant's bicycle and pedaled to safety. Twenty-seven years later, almost to the day, Air Vice Marshal Marix bombed and sank a German vessel in the Norwegian harbor of Aalesund.

Wing Commander Samson became a particular thorn in the enemy's side, and at one time they put up a price of $50,000 for his capture—dead or alive. When he was not flipping about the war zone at hair-raising levels, he would be found roaring around the occupied areas in a Daimler touring car to which he had bolted slabs of boiler plate and a chattering Maxim gun. These armored-car antics gave an Admiralty official named Winston Spencer Churchill one of the first ideas for what eventually became the tank.

On the evacuation of Antwerp, the Royal Naval Air Service settled down at Ostend, still nurturing militant ideas concerning the Zeppelin sheds. As the main hangars were at Friedrichshafen, practically in Switzerland, they promoted the idea of using a French field at Belfort, and from there four Avro planes, flown by Samson's rowdies, took off to splather the dirigible hangars on Lake Constance.

"Get 'em where they build 'em and they'll never fly a war patrol" was Samson's motto, little knowing he was uttering one of the first rules of strategic aviation.

The attack was made on November 21, 1914; one Avro lost its tail while taxiing out and had to withdraw, the rest, led by a Commander Briggs, got away safely and, to respect Swiss neutrality, flew a crooked course that took them first to Mülhausen, then over the Black Forest to Schaffhausen. Here they turned southward for Lake Constance. They flew over the lake at a height of ten feet, but went to 1,200 feet on reaching the shed area. The total flight was about 125 miles, which was a stout effort for those days. Antiaircraft guns went into action immediately, but all three airmen, Commander Briggs, Flight Commander Babbington, and Flight Lieutenant Sipps, scored direct hits and inflicted severe damage.

Briggs was shot down. When he made his forced landing he was badly mauled by German civilians and had to be rescued, in a serious condition, by the military. Babbington and Sipps returned safely.

The fourth and last raid of that year was directed against the Zeppelin sheds at Cuxhaven. This was made on Christmas Day and on this occasion the formation consisted of both land and sea planes, with naval-destroyer and submarine escort. The object of the attack was not only to bomb the airship hangars, but to gain some information on the disposition of the German Navy at Wilhelmshaven and in the Schillig Roads. By 6 A.M. on that merry day the British force had reached a position twelve miles north of Helgoland; an hour later seven of the nine seaplanes were put over the side, and they took off. By 10 A.M. three of the British seaplanes had returned safely; the other four had been shot down, but three crews were rescued by the submarine E.11 as they floated close to the Norderney Gap.

All these proceedings were watched by the crew of a Zeppelin maneuvering to drop bombs where they would do the most good, but the missiles fell a few seconds after the last airman had been hauled aboard, and E.11 crash-dived to forty feet to escape. The fourth seaplane crew was picked up by a Dutch trawler, and was interned in Holland for some time.

Actually, the Cuxhaven sheds were not found, but the effort was not entirely wasted, for the R.N.A.S. observers returned with a comprehensive picture of the German harbor and roadsteads. Seven battleships, three cruisers, and a number of other warships were identified.

MACHINE GUNS AND HOW THEY WORK

Meanwhile on the Continent the Allied and German air forces were developing the rivalry and competition that were to mark their activities over the next four years. Musketry was exchanged at every opportunity and each day saw new variations of war in the air. Among the first British casualties was a Sergeant Major Jillings who was flying with a Lieutenant Noel at the time. Jillings was credited with downing an Albatros two-seater with a single rifle

Imperial War Museum

This aircraft, the 1914 Deperdussin, was typical of the types available to both sides at the outbreak of the war in 1914. It was not armed or capable of carrying bombs. It was powered with a 70-hp Gnome engine and carried a pilot and passenger. At one time this plane was known as the Thunderbug.

This shows an advance in design produced by the French in 1915. This Caudron G.III was used on the Western Front for more than two years. Powered with a 100-hp Anzani engine, it had a top speed of about 75 mph. It carried no guns, but the observer was provided with a rifle.

U.S. Air Force

Arch Whitehouse

While the fitting of machine guns was not evident until 1915, the British were equipping some of their biplanes with rockets intended for anti-balloon work. This shows a test of a pod of these missiles attached to the outer struts of an early B.E.12. There is one recorded instance of a German plane's being shot down by a salvo of these rockets.

This was Britain's earliest single-seater fighter, the D.H.2, which fought the early fixed-gun Fokkers all through 1915 and 1916. It had one semi-flexible Lewis gun fixed to fire forward (not shown in this picture). Powered with a 100-hp Mono engine, it had a top speed of 105 mph. The R.F.C.'s first fighter squadron, No. 24, was equipped with this aircraft and commanded by the famous Major Lanoe G. Hawker.

De Havilland Aircraft

A group of American volunteers who served with the French. Left to right: Walter Lovell, Edmond Genet, Raoul Lufbery, and James McConnell. They are checking out a new map-roller device.

The famous Quirk, Britain's B.E.2c biplane, which carried the brunt of reconnaissance and artillery spotting for about three years. Here she is shown in her early design with the observer displaying her only armament, a .303 Lee Enfield rifle. This particular model was powered with a 90-hp R.A.F.1a engine, and her top speed was 72 mph.

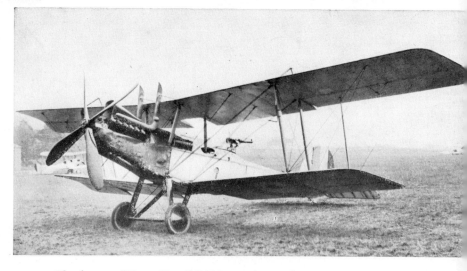

The famous "Harry Tate," R.E.8, another early two-seater reconnaissance biplane; this one is shown with a flexible Lewis gun on an early ring mounting. This had a 160-hp R.A.F.4a engine, which produced a speed of 102 mph. Although probably one of the worst aircraft produced by the British, it did a remarkable job despite enemy opposition.

The Morane Bullet, the first wartime aircraft equipped with a machine gun to fire through the propeller. The device was first perfected and flown on April 1, 1915, by the Frenchman Roland Garros, who with this mount destroyed five enemy aircraft in sixteen days—a score that become the standard of the "ace" designation. The Fokker interrupter gear did not appear until several months later.

The Fokker Eindekker Scout, Germany's first fixed-gun fighter, designed by Anthony Fokker, a Dutch engineer. In this the Spandau gun was synchronized mechanically to fire through the whirling blades of the propeller, an improvement over Garros' idea, which gave the German airmen a short period of air superiority.

An early two-seater fighter, the Caudron G.IV twin-engined reconnaissance machine, equipped with a Vickers gun and flexible mounting for the observer. This aircraft was also used for day bombing and, fully loaded, was capable of 82 mph. Many American airmen were trained on this type of machine.

The air-type Vickers gun shown mounted on a Spad-7. This was the model American volunteers in the Lafayette Flying Corps flew before America entered the war. It was equipped with Britain's Constantinesco interrupter gear, a hydraulic device invented by a Rumanian inventor named George Constantinesco, who had been living in England for several years. Later Spad models were equipped with two fixed guns.

The primitive gun mounting employed on early Nieuport scouts, in which a ground-type Lewis with infantry stock was set to fire over the tips of the propeller. In early models the gun was fixed and could not be reloaded once the pilot was in the air. Later a curved rail was adopted down which the weapon could be lowered to remedy stoppages and replace ammunition drums. The pilot in this picture is the famed Georges Guynemer.

The Lewis gun mounting on the British S.E.5 scout. This was the Cooper-Foster rail that allowed the pilot to draw the gun down to replace an empty drum. Some S.E.5 pilots also used this flexibility to fire up at an enemy, thus making the most of his blind spot. The S.E.5 also carried a fixed Vickers gun mounted under the engine cowling.

The Bristol Fighter, the classic two-seater fighter of World War I. This machine provided the backbone of Britain's fighter efforts through 1917 and 1918 and was capable of high speed and maneuverability down low for trench strafing or for high-altitude dog-fighting against all comers. Powered with the Rolls-Royce Falcon engine, it had a top speed of 125 mph and carried two or three machine guns. Unquestionably the finest all-around fighting machine of the war.

America's first Lafayette Escadrille ace, Raoul Lufbery of Wallingford, Connecticut, destroyed seventeen enemy aircraft before he was killed. A true soldier-of-fortune, he became one of the war's finest flight leaders.

Victor Chapman, an architecture student, was the first American to die in the Lafayette Escadrille. He had been a machine gunner in the Foreign Legion, and after three months of trench warfare was wounded in the leg. After convalescence he volunteered for the French aviation and was among the most determined airmen in the Allied services. In fact it was his determination that contributed to his death.

Dudley L. Hill of Peekskill, New York, one of the most popular members of the Lafayette Escadrille, began his career as a volunteer ambulance driver. Unspectacular and self-effacing, he nevertheless lived through the war and ended up as the C.O. 5th Group of the U. S. Aviation Service, refusing to admit he ever destroyed one enemy aircraft. He was never seen wearing the decorations he had been awarded.

U.S. Air Force

Lieutenant W. B. Rhodes-Moorhouse, first British airman to win the Victoria Cross. Flying an old Quirk (B.E.2c) biplane, he carried out a vital bombing mission over Courtrai, holding up a German attack, and he remained in the area long enough to complete a valuable reconnaissance although he was critically wounded. Instead of landing the minute he had crossed into the British lines, he continued on and landed at British Headquarters to deliver personally a full report. He died two days later.

Arch Whitehouse

Captain Albert Ball, the first of Britain's great aces. While an infantry lieutenant, he bought his own flying training and transferred to the Royal Flying Corps. Bold, impetuous, and yet bearing many characteristics of the schoolboy, Ball put on one of the wildest fighting careers of any service. He destroyed forty-three enemy aircraft before he himself was shot down by a machine gunner lurking in an old church tower.

Arch Whitehouse

Lieutenant W. Leefe-Robinson's claim to fame was that in September, 1916, he destroyed the first German Zeppelin shot down over British territory. Later he commanded a Bristol Fighter squadron and was himself shot down and taken prisoner. He died before the war ended because of a physical breakdown brought on by his treatment in an enemy prison camp.

Arch Whitehouse

Britain's unknown air-war hero, Captain A. W. Beauchamp-Proctor, a South African, who won practically every decoration the Empire could bestow. He was credited with fifty-seven enemy aircraft although he was not at first considered a reliable pilot. His score was racked up in less than four months of front-line flying and included many kite balloons.

Arch Whitehouse

Major Edward C. Mannock, Britain's leading ace, had only one eye. He had been interned early in the war by the Turks and then repatriated, since he was considered unfit for military service. Never a great pilot, but a valuable leader, Mannock destroyed seventy-three enemy aircraft before being shot down and killed.

Germany's Ace of Aces, Baron Manfred von Richthofen, who, before he was killed, had claimed eighty victories over British airmen. Many of these claims could not be substantiated, but he was a powerful figure in the Imperial German Air Service, and his exploits played a great part in the build-up of his country's flying service.

German Archives

Captain René P. Fonck, France's Ace of Aces, credited with seventy-five victories. A remarkable shot, a brilliant pilot, and a redoubtable leader, Fonck was one of the greatest airman to live through the war. After the war he went into politics and served as Inspector of Fighter Aircraft for many years. He died in 1953.

One of Ray Collishaw's all-black Sopwith Triplanes that created such havoc on the Western Front in 1917. Ignored by most Royal Flying Corps squadrons, it was finally adopted by the Royal Naval Air Service and proved to be superior to most enemy mounts of the day. Its specialty was its rate of climb and maneuverability at high altitude.

Canada's airman hero Major William A. Bishop, standing before his Nieuport scout, the mount with which he had so much success. He is credited with seventy-two victories although he began his war career as an observer and was wounded in one of his earliest patrols. In one period of twelve days he shot down twenty-five enemy aircraft, twelve of them in the last three days—all in a total flying time of thirty-six hours.

The classic fighter of them all, the Sopwith Camel, which in World War I destroyed 1,634 enemy aircraft, a record unsurpassed by any other machine in any war. Not meant for the novice pilot, but in skilled hands one of the finest fighting weapons designed on either side of the line.

One of Germany's finest fighters, the Pfalz D.12, which played an important role in the March, 1918, push. It was superseded by the Fokker D.7 the following summer, but many well-known German aces ran up much of their scores aboard this N-strut fighter. Some pilots found it hard to fly, and the mechanics objected to the complicated rigging and bracing systems that demanded much skilled labor.

Captain Eddie Rickenbacker, America's Ace of Aces, shown beside his Spad-13, the popular mount made available to the American service by the French in 1918. Rickenbacker was credited with twenty-six victories during a comparatively short career on the Western Front.

Section of the Howard Chandler Christie portrait of Captain Eddie Rickenbacker.

Frank Luke, the Arizona Balloon Buster, sometimes known as Peck's Bad Boy of the Air. Luke, a headstrong maverick, had a wild career while he lived and is credited by some historians with twenty-one victories. He was the first American airman to win the Medal of Honor.

Lieutenant George Vaughn ranks second to Captain Eddie Rickenbacker among our living aces of World War I. Vaughn put in much time with the British, flying Camels, and was then transferred to No. 17 Squadron. He ended the conflict with thirteen enemy aircraft to his credit.

bullet, but on the way home from this success someone on the ground took a shot at the sergeant major and hit him "where he sat down." Admittedly, Jillings had to be assisted from his cockpit, but he lived down the indignity and went on to glory, becoming a squadron leader and eventually winning the Military Cross.

Since guns and other weapons highlight much of this book, it may be well to examine what was available and how they were used. For instance, the Lewis gun was a light, automatic-fed weapon in which the ammunition was carried in a circular drum that rotated as each round was fired. As explained previously, it was the invention of Colonel Isaac Newton Lewis, an American, who had to go to Europe to find recognition. Another American, Hiram Percy Maxim, who also had to go abroad to commercialize his weapon, produced the Maxim gun. Benjamin Berkeley Hotchkiss, an inventor from Watertown, Connecticut, had to go to France to get support and financial backing for his weapons.

The original Lewis gun weighed 26½ pounds and was 50½ inches in length, but the bulky cooling jacket could be dispensed with in aerial combat. It was gas-operated and was actuated by the combination of a return spring and the gas pressure set up by the discharge of each cartridge. It had a normal rate of fire of 500 rounds per minute and was fed by a shallow drum that held 47 rounds. Later on, the drum was deepened to carry 97 rounds, and in this form, with the Hazleton muzzle attachment, it could be speeded up to about 750 rounds per minute. This weapon became the ideal gun for the observer, particularly after the Scarff mounting was produced. In its aerial form the Lewis gun weighed but 18 pounds.

On aircraft in which the gunner-observer sat in the front seat ahead of the pilot (as in the F.E.2b pusher) the Lewis gun was set on a socket-and-pillar mounting devised by Warrant Officer F. W. Scarff. The underside of the gun was fitted with a spike which could be slipped into any one of four different sockets arranged around the nacelle. This was replaced later by having the gun mounted on a pivoted metal rod that could be moved and placed into any of six prongs on a circular brace ring.

The British Vickers gun that became the standard fixed weapon of the Allied air services was a variation of the old Maxim gun, and was recoil-operated, in that the recoil was timed to work against a fusee spring that carried out the forward and backward movements of the mechanism. The original gun with its heavy bronze water jacket weighed some 74 pounds, but in the Vickers adaptation the general mechanism was actually reversed, every feature was lightened, and a gas muzzle cup improved the rate of fire considerably.

The original weapon was fed by a canvas belt that held 250 rounds, but this belt was affected by weather and atmospheric conditions and when damp or wet would tighten up, holding the cartridges in its grip so that the loading sequence would be seriously impaired and many stoppages experienced. Eventually the canvas belt was replaced by an aluminum link system in which the cartridge acted as a pin, and this feed system could be assembled to any length, any number of rounds, and was limited only by the size of the available ammunition box. Once the round was withdrawn from this link system the link itself was discarded along with the discharged cartridge case. Like the Lewis, the Vickers was a .303-caliber weapon.

The Hotchkiss gun was actually an automatic rifle, gas-fired, as was the Lewis, but fed by a series of metal clips, each carrying twenty-five rounds. It probably was as efficient as the Lewis, but its feed system was not suited to aerial action. On the ground it was usually handled by two men, one to aim and fire the weapon, the other to feed in the cartridge strips as they were expended. However, until the Lewis was simplified for air work, sometime in 1915, the Hotchkiss was used in many British and French Squadrons. It was the Hotchkiss gun that was first mounted successfully to fire between the whirling propeller blades of a Morane-Saulnier Parasol.

In the beginning the Germans put their choice on the Parabellum, their first air-cooled infantry weapon that had been introduced in 1913. This gun employed the short-recoil system of operation, a purely mechanical sequence in which the bolt, locked to the barrel for a short period of the recoil after firing, was unlocked and withdrawn from the breech for about three inches after the barrel had completed its recoil movement. It was chambered to take the German service cartridge of .311 and fed by a 100-round belt into the right-hand side of the feed block. This would seem to be an ungainly system, since this belt had to be carried on a good-sized (15 inches in diameter) metal drum and had to be bolted to the gun. Then, too, it still carried the infantry type of gun butt, whereas the British Lewis had a simple, very handy spade grip.

The Spandau gun, which became Germany's standard fixed weapon, was actually a German steal of Hiram Maxim's early infantry gun. As did the British, they too stripped it of nonessentials and adapted it for air-cooling, but fed it with a 500-round belt. A special factory was erected at Spandau to produce these converted Maxims, and shortly after the war began, they were known as Spandau guns. It is believed that the Spandau was somewhat more rugged than the Vickers, but the British weapon was more adaptable for speeding up, clearing of stoppages, and for automatic control with an interrupter firing gear.

When the Spandau was introduced in service squadrons, it required a rather intricate arrangement of levers to clear stoppages and to reload the gun. Like the controls of Allied weapons, the gun usually was fired from thumb pieces set in the center of the spade grip of the control stick. Baron von Richthofen, however, argued that it was more natural for a marksman to fire a gun with his trigger finger, rather than with his thumb; and since the Baron's every whim was law, production on all German fighters was held up for weeks while this new firing system was devised and installed.

In addition to these machine guns, various other types of guns of heavier caliber were used, either experimentally or as standard equipment. Noteworthy among these was the one-pound pom-pom, or cow gun, used by night-flying F.E.2b's in their attacks on troop concentrations and transport behind the German lines. A slightly heavier type of pom-pom was the Coventry Ordnance 1½-pound quick-firer, an automatic gun designed to fire a maximum of five rounds at one loading. This formidable weapon had a bore of 37 millimeters, and a muzzle velocity of 1,950 feet per second, but its excessive weight of 200 pounds restricted its use to flying boats or an occasional and specially strengthened D.H.4 of the Royal Naval Air Service.

The French employed a 37-millimeter "air cannon" early in the war that was mounted aboard the ancient Voisin biplane, but of how often it was used, or with what success, there is little to report. A refined version of this weapon was incorporated later into a specially designed Hispano-Suiza engine, one with a hollow crankshaft, against which the gun was mounted. In this arrangement the weapon was set between the pilot's feet in the cockpit of a Spad, and it is said that Captain Georges Guynemer, who flew one of these planes, had considerable success with it. However, much of the exhaust gas from the breech was blown back into the cockpit, causing serious nausea to the pilot, and the Spad cannon had to be abandoned.

AMMUNITION AND INCENDIARIES FOR THE BALLOON BOYS

Along with the developments of these new weapons were the requirements for various targets, and until the autumn of 1915 ordinary rifle ammunition was considered good enough. Tracer bullets had been devised and fired to improve the gunner's marksmanship, but these early bullets were something of a disappointment because they did not "trace" long enough to be of any value; they burned unevenly and thus spun off their intended direction, and were difficult to produce with assembly-line methods.

A new formula was evolved in 1916—one part magnesium to eight parts barium peroxide—that gave better results. This slug, known officially as the S.P.K. Mark VII-T, but more generally as the Sparklet, was finally approved for the R.F.C. in July of that year, and thereafter was used almost invariably in proportion of one tracer to three ordinary bullets in every Lewis drum and Vickers belt. I would add from my own experience that the tracer round was a waste of equipment. It did not maintain its form for any distance and went sparkling all over the sky shortly after it was fired. I noted, too, that some gunners began to rely on the tracer as an aim guide, a habit that was most unhealthy, for where the tracer was going had little to do with where the three regular rounds were headed. I did my best to discourage new gunners and observers from "firing on tracer," since I was certain it was a waste of good ammunition.

Three other rounds, all intended primarily for antiairship or balloon targets, were the Buckingham, Brock, and Pomeroy bullets. The invention of J. F. Buckingham used phosphorus as the basis of its incendiary composition and was first used by the R.N.A.S. in December, 1915, and by the R.F.C. the following April. In June, 1916, Mr. Buckingham further improved his bullet, which in its Mark-VII form, and later with a flattened nose, was employed for the rest of the war. The flat-nosed bullet was the result of experiments made in France, where it had been learned that the sharp-nosed round made only a small perforation in the balloon fabric and did not allow enough gas to escape and ensure ignition. The flat-nosed bullet did punch in a larger hole, but the shape of the missile affected its accuracy and in turn so weakened the sheath that the bullet collapsed before leaving the barrel of the gun. Additional improvements were made from time to time and were still in progress when the Armistice was signed. Nevertheless, the Buckingham round was used widely by all Allied air services, and some 26,000,000 rounds were produced and delivered.

Because of the "dumdum" effect of this bullet, the Germans made formal complaints concerning its use—after they had employed poison gas, flame throwers, and saw-toothed bayonets—arguing that the Buckingham round was an affront to all humane laws of the Hague Convention. As a result, in the Royal Flying Corps at least, whenever a pilot went out on a specified balloon mission carrying Buckingham ammunition, he was given a blue card that made it clear that he had been assigned to balloon targets only and would not fire his guns at ground personnel. Thus if he were shot down and taken prisoner, he would have suitable evidence of the objective of his mission, accounting for any Buckingham ammunition found in his aircraft.

The Brock bullet was created originally when it was believed that the exhaust gases from Zeppelin engines were led between the outer and inner fabrics of the envelopes to produce a layer of inert gas as a protection against incendiary ammunition. With this misapprehension, Commander F. A. Brock, a noted fireworks manufacturer and at the time a member of the Intelligence Department of the Admiralty, produced this special bullet designed to explode between the first and second fabric in such a manner that the hydrogen would come into contact with the outside air and facilitate ignition. Half a million of these Brock bullets were ordered and delivered, and though their use was suspended by 1917, they remained available throughout the war to the R.N.A.S. in their anti-Zeppelin missions over the North Sea.

The Pomeroy, or P.S.A. round, was still another form of the explosive bullet, first produced in quantity in May, 1916. It had qualities similar to those of the Brock and was so sensitive that it would explode simply on striking fabric. But even this was not always enough to set a Zeppelin on fire, and after much experiment the Pomeroy was so improved that it would pierce the outer cover of an airship without exploding, then burst on the surface of the inner bag. Its use was confined almost exclusively to home-defense units of the R.F.C., whose guns, when on antiairship patrol duty, were usually loaded with a mixture of the three types of bullets.

The last and most special round introduced into the war squadrons was the R.T.S., a combined incendiary and explosive bullet of great sensitivity. It was produced in November, 1917, and was so much in demand thereafter that by June, 1918, a weekly delivery of 200,000 of these bullets was being made. For some time this round was used only in England against raiding aircraft, but it proved so effective that its use overseas was sanctioned in September, 1918,

although in fact it was never used to any great extent on the
Western Front.

THE ACES EMERGE,
ALL DISPLAYING THE SAME CHARACTERISTICS

During those early weeks of 1914 a young lieutenant of the First
Uhlan Regiment was riding at the head of his troop six miles from
the German-Russian front. On the morning of August 3 they entered
a Russian village near Kielce, and Lieutenant Manfred von Richthofen went to the front door of a low wooden building and banged
imperiously on the portal with the butt of his riding crop. A tall
man in black robes responded to his knock.

The young officer clicked his heels and said, "Father, I inform
you that war has been declared between Germany and your country. Your village is now occupied and surrounded by my men. At
the first sign of any hostility from your villagers, you will be ex-
ecuted and I shall take such other measures as are necessary for the
protection of the men under my command and the proper pacifica-
tion of the inhabitants."

Five day later Von Richthofen's force was trapped and ambushed
by a patrol of Cossacks. He was in bed asleep when his orderly
aroused him, and on looking out the window, the young Uhlan saw
at least thirty Russians. He darted quickly out a rear doorway and
raced to a near-by field where two of his men had horses waiting.
Two days later his little party crept into a German garrison town
and erased their names from a list of German soldiers "wiped out by
the Cossacks." His squadron was mentioned in the German official
communique, then withdrawn from the Russian front and sent to
France.

In three years' time this young soldier became Germany's greatest
war hero. His photograph was on the bureau of nearly every young
girl in his country; he had won every decoration and award his
superiors could bestow on him; but he was to die before the guns
of a rank amateur airman, another young man who at the time did

not know whom he was fighting, or how the great success was accomplished.

A young, second-rate motorcar racer who had been a test driver for a number of American automobile manufacturers was in Britain conferring with officials of the Sunbeam Motor Company, with the idea of representing them on American race tracks. Edward Vernon Rickenbacker had never won a major race, but he had done very well in the famed Vanderbilt Cup classic held at Sheepshead Bay, and he had high hopes that the British firm would subsidize his plan to put a Sunbeam speedster in the next Vanderbilt Cup event. Unfortunately, the Sunbeam firm had been caught up in the European war and its shops and skilled workmen were now devoting their efforts to building engines suitable for aircraft, not racing cars.

Eddie Rickenbacker accepted this with good grace and spent some time at the well-known Brooklands track, where he watched not the testing of racing cars but the training of young men for the Royal Flying Corps. This experience never left him, and later, when America entered the war, Eddie conceived the idea of forming a special flying squadron of American racing drivers. But his plan was ridiculed in Washington, and he was induced to become General John J. Pershing's personal chauffeur instead.

A wan, puny young man of twenty named Georges Guynemer was holding down a light-duty sweeping-up job on a French training field outside Paris. The ravages of tuberculosis were already gnawing, but he was determined to serve his country in the war against her dread enemy. His parents had some influence with the military authorities, but Guynemer's persistent demands to be allowed to work on military planes, then to be given a flight test, eventually put him in the select circle of pilot trainees. He became France's most beloved ace and afforded a legend that school children still repeat and revere. His actual end is a mystery, but in France the artless belief still holds that Guynemer flew so high that he could never come back to France, and so far as they know, he is still circling above them, keeping watch on all loyal French airmen.

Ernst Udet was a young Prussian dispatch rider for a reserve Württemberg division, a reckless, irresponsible cyclist who had more tumbles and broke up more motorcycles than any courier in the German service. His superiors gladly permitted him to transfer to the German Air Service.

An Oberleutnant, Hermann Goering, who was an officer of doubtful ability in a scouting cyclist regiment, was in and out of hospitals with painful rheumatism. He too was an impulsive character with wild schemes concerning battle tactics, and during one of his hospital spells he met another German officer, Bruno Loerzer, who persuaded him to transfer to the Air Service. These two became famous as military flyers, but Goering tarnished his reputation in his later association with Adolf Hitler.

In Canada a young lieutenant of cavalry, a subaltern in a militia regiment known as the Mississauga Horse of Toronto, had no concept of his aerial destiny. His unit, which became part of the Second Canadian Division, did not reach Britain until 1915, and during the wait to cross the Channel to France, when Lieutenant William Avery Bishop came to the realization that cavalry could not play an important role in the ground war, he transferred to Britain's Royal Flying Corps. He spent four months in France as an observer aboard a rickety two-seater until his plane was shot down and he suffered a painful knee injury. Once he recovered, the young Canadian was allowed to take pilot training, thus beginning his fantastic fighting career.

James T. B. McCudden was an air mechanic, acting as a gunner aboard a two-seater Morane-Parasol of Number 3 R.F.C., then located at Annequin. The son of a sergeant in the Royal Engineers, Jimmy McCudden was born in a military barracks, and although his mother was of French descent, he probably was the most British airman of the R.F.C. group and became a fifty-eight-plane ace and was honored with the Victoria Cross before a ridiculous accident removed his name from the roll of Britain's fighting heroes.

A French hussar officer, Alfred Heurtaux, transferred to l'Aviation

Militaire, in which service he was wounded twelve times but scored twenty-one official victories before his twenty-fifth birthday.

Willy Coppens, a young Belgian, transferred from the Second Regiment of Grenadiers to train in England—at his own expense—at the Ruffy-Baumann Flying School, Hendon. He later became an ace, a crack balloon-buster, and was credited with thirty-six victories.

Another arrogant, self-assured ex-cavalryman, Max Immelmann, cracked up an old L.V.G. belonging to Flying Section Number 10 at Vizry and spent many more weeks learning to fly, but he too, by his own daring, proved to be one of Germany's great air heroes and another of the breed who died in a mysterious fashion.

Two American civilians, Norman Prince and Elliott Cowdin, arrived in Paris with the intention of volunteering to fly with the French. They were joined later by William Thaw and James Mc-Connell. Other Americans who had not heard of fighting in the air, such as Kiffin Rockwell, James Bach, and Edmond Genet, joined up to fight as infantrymen in the Foreign Legion. Before America entered the war, this nucleus of patriots started the thrilling history of the famed Lafayette Escadrille.

Andrew McKeever, who became the world's leading two-seater ace, was in the front line with the First Canadian Division. Albert Ball, a subaltern with the Sherwood Foresters, was buying flying lessons and receiving his training—before breakfast—at a field sixty miles away from his battalion training area. Another wild English youth, Reggie Warneford, was flipping about the French and Belgian coasts looking for Zeppelins. He finally caught up with one over Ghent and sent it down in flames. From that minute on, the future of the lighter-than-air dirigible as a war weapon was doomed.

A German schoolteacher named Oswald Boelcke, who was a nondescript Fokker pilot, had just transferred to Number 62 Section at Dessau, where he was to be assigned as an equipment inspector. Very little was expected of this man, but his luck and time brackets were right, and he co-ordinated his pedantic training with the fact that he was the first German to be given a Fokker-type fixed-gun airplane. Oswald Boelcke created the Flying Circus concept and unquestionably contributed more to Germany's military aviation strength than any other man in that service.

The author of this volume was working his way across the Atlantic on a cattle boat to volunteer with the British forces. Probably aboard the same creaky vessel was Paul Pavelka, who was to go on to glory with the Lafayette Escadrille. I wasted some servitude with the Northamptonshire Yeomanry before transferring to the Royal Flying Corps; but in 1914 I had never seen a military airplane. The term "ace" had not been coined; war in the air was the figment of a few imaginations; and a great many more believed the war would be fought and won by mounted men bearing swords or lances. The airplane was simply an adjunct to cavalry scouting—or so they believed.

CHAPTER 3

Antics and Action

Decisive action in this war was not of necessity confined to the outcome of any single air combat. Decisions often came with the association of two men, their opinions, misfortunes, or their co-operation during any critical situation. Georges Madon and Armand Pinsard together taught Allied airmen that prison camps and compounds need not restrain them. We also learn that the sole possession of a first-class aircraft does not assure victory, but the decision of a handful of American volunteers who were to serve with the French Aviation was to play an important role in the eventual development of an American air arm, two years later.

LUCK PLAYED A VITAL ROLE IN THE LIVES OF THE EARLY WARTIME AIRMEN

LIEUTENANT GEORGES F. MADON was possibly the luckiest airman to live through World War I. He survived a midair collision in combat—the direct hit of an antiaircraft shell—more than fifty aerial battles, and even made a successful escape from captivity, after which he was court-martialed. He ended his war with forty-one accredited victories.

Georges Madon was born in Bizerte, Tunisia, and in his youth was sent to Paris to complete his education but, instead, joined l'Aviation Militaire early in 1911 and went through the Étampes flying school and earned his brevet on a Blériot-39.

When war started, Corporal Pilot Madon was assigned to Escadrille 30, then located at Soissons. He was still flying Blériots, and in December of that year he was patrolling over enemy territory when a shell buried its nose in his plane's fuselage, but fortunately did not explode. The over-all shock, however, fractured much of the body framework, and on landing the whole tail assembly collapsed.

While flying with Farman Squadron 44, Madon ran into more trouble, becoming hopelessly lost during a long reconnaissance. He cruised around amid enemy shellfire until he ran out of fuel and finally sat down near Porrentruy, Switzerland, where he and his observer, a Sergeant Chattelain, were immediately interned. The two Frenchmen made half a dozen attempts to escape and on one occasion got as far as the Italian border, where they were caught. Nine months later they were contacted by a French agent, and new plans for freedom were devised. Late one night the agent chloroformed the Swiss guard and led the two airmen to a waiting automobile, and they were rushed to safety; but on their arrival in France both Madon and Chattelain were court-martialed for violation of Swiss neutral territory and the loss of their aircraft. Madon received sixty days' solitary confinement, but his observer got off with two months of ordinary imprisonment. By May, 1916, Madon was back in his superiors' good graces; he joined a Morane-Saulnier squadron and from there went on to unending fame.

Armand Pinsard was another Frenchman who seemed to have a charmed life. He had been a cavalryman as early as 1905 and had won the Moroccan Medal in North Africa. He transferred to the aviation service in 1912, and soon won the Médaille Militaire for his daring flights, particularly for his displays at the Picardy Military Trials of 1913.

Three days after the outbreak of the war Pinsard was assigned to a Morane squadron and soon was awarded eight citations for exceptional courage and devotion to duty. On one occasion he managed to get home from a point forty miles inside the enemy lines with a badly shattered wing. In October he was forced to land inside the German lines when the spark plugs of his aircraft engine fouled. He and his observer, a Captain Chaulin, spent the next two hours calmly removing and cleaning the plugs and working on the engine. Then swinging their own propeller, they just managed to zoom away as a troop of Death's Head hussars came charging through a hedge. Pinsard was awarded the Croix de Guerre for that escapade.

In February of 1915 Pinsard was shot down by rifle fire from the ground. He crash-landed in German territory, suffering two shattered ribs and a severe concussion. His captors figured that this ancient's war was over. He bided his time as he lay in a hospital for five weeks, and when he was removed to a prisoner-of-war camp he made two bold attempts to escape, but was recaptured each time and placed in solitary confinement. Twelve more tries for freedom were attempted, and once he got to within two miles of the Dutch border. This time, late in 1915, he was sentenced to the "escape-proof" Prinz Karl Fortress at Ingolstadt.

On March 26, 1916, Pinsard and a Captain Ménard dug their way through a wall twelve feet thick and had a six-hour start before the alarm was raised. These two Frenchmen spent the next three weeks completing their getaway, an epic adventure that was the classic escape of that day. Sometime in April two half-starved airmen presented themselves at the French mission in Switzerland—and asked to be assigned to active service.

The air war and its equipment had progressed tremendously, and Pinsard had to take a lengthy refresher pilot course; but by the middle of 1916 he was back aboard single-seater fighters, eventually headed the famous Storks Squadron, and was credited with twenty-seven victories.

THE LUCK OF BRUNO LOERZER

Bruno Loerzer was a fantastic figure in the German Air Service, in that he became an airman through a game of cards, so to speak. He had started life as a farmer, turned to the military, and in 1913

gained his commission with an infantry regiment garrisoned at Mülhausen. Once he accepted a trial flight with the chief test pilot of
the Aviatik factory, but found no particular interest in the experience. A short time later, while engrossed in a card game, his adjutant asked if he would register for training as an airplane pilot.
More interested in his cards than the inquiry, Loerzer just nodded
and his name was added to the list. To his amazement, he was accepted later, and transferred to the flying service.

The ex-infantry officer proved to be a better-than-average pilot,
but when the war broke out his former regiment went straight
to the front, whereas Loerzer was moved in the opposite direction,
since his airfield was within range of French artillery.

A short time later, after a period of routine patrols, he heard
that an old friend, Hermann Goering, was in a near-by hospital with
a touch of rheumatism.

"You've got to get out of here," grumbled Loerzer on visiting him.
"I need you."

"Me? What for?"

"I'm flying two-seater Aviatiks and I need an observer."

"But I've never been in the air," Goering explained.

"It will do that rheumatism good . . . good fresh air. I'll teach you
all you need to know."

That was enough for Hermann; he applied for a transfer from the
cyclist corps, but his commanding officer, who was short of energetic
lieutenants, refused to agree to the arrangement. So, ignoring all
military authority and tradition, Goering simply packed his gear and
moved in with Loerzer. Helpless in the face of such brash behavior,
his C.O. did his best to forget the incident, and within two months
Hermann had won the Iron Cross, 1st Class, and with Loerzer had
managed to find and barge into every aerial foray going on anywhere. By the spring of 1916 Goering was selected for pilot training,
and both he and Loerzer made great names for themselves, for they
were bold, valiant airmen in that war.

THE SAGA OF THE QUIRK

The beginning of aerial activity in the war was enlivened to some extent by the antics of the world's worst military airplane, the Quirk. This appellation was tagged on the infamous B.E.2c biplane. In one mood she could be the aerial-clown act of the front, and in another would fatten the scores of dozens of German aces. But strangely enough, three of the nineteen Victoria Crosses given to British airmen were awarded to pilots of this notorious biplane. She was ungainly, grotesque, treacherous, and unfit to occupy space on any respectable airfield. Powered with a government-built engine that, according to legend, blew off its cylinders in the order of firing, she was among the first to be sent into action. Yet when that more than four-year-long conflict was over, there still were 1,308 Quirks in service with the R.A.F. She was hurled against the enemy in France, Belgium, Palestine, Salonika, and East Africa. As a military type this airplane carried no regular armament during the early months of the war, and its built-in lack of maneuverability deprived it of all evasive action.

But it is the men who win wars, not the weapons, and the history of this most unworthy product of the Royal Aircraft Factory will bear out this statement.

Despite her Goldbergian design, her coffee-grinder power plant, and her inclination to fly backward in a high wind, this comic biplane managed to swagger about in the glory spotlight. She would perform the most unbelievable evolutions for no apparent reason. If you left her to her own devices and decided to take a snooze on the way home, she more than likely would seek out her own strip of turf and make a perfect landing—unassisted! An enemy gunner might shoot her to rags and raffia, but if the B.E.2c took it into her head, she would arrow home like a Spad. If there were two or three enemy planes some six miles away deliberately ignoring her, like as not, she would shed her wings, without a shot being fired, and auger into the nearest shell hole. There is one unauthenticated report that a Quirk that had been set on fire by antiaircraft allowed her crew to take bleacher seats on the leading edges of the wing, then under her own guidance actually flew into an enemy balloon, setting it on fire, crossed into her own lines, and made a perfect landing on top of an empty artillery truck that was heading for the back area. Everyone concerned arrived home safely.

Nevertheless, and in spite of this dreadful buzzard, the pilots and observers of the R.F.C. were doing extremely well on their reconnaissance patrols. On August 22, 1914, the British commander, Sir John French, held a conference at Le Cateau with General Charles L. M. Lanrezac, commander of the French Fifth Army. The Germans were thundering toward Paris and the Allied generals decided to fight a defensive action, hoping to hold on for at least twenty-four hours.

Royal Flying Corps reports had given some reliable hints that the German General von Bülow was massing troops across the Sambre River and that an enveloping movement was expected from Grammont. The next day the famous Battle of Mons was fought along a twenty-five-mile front. Allied artillery was on hand, all beautifully lined up, but there were no shells to fire, so all available planes of the R.F.C. patrolled unceasingly, marking the enemy's movements and spotting enemy batteries. That night the retreat began, and for the next nine days the pilots and observers of the R.F.C. were in the air almost constantly. Their reports told a gallant chapter in the history of the movement that was to save Paris and the French Army.

THE FIRST VICTORIA CROSS

The outstanding hero of this "Eyes of the Army" service was Second Lieutenant William B. Rhodes-Moorhouse of Number 2 Squadron, the first of the nineteen British airmen to win the Victoria Cross. Prior to the outbreak of hostilities Rhodes-Moorhouse was somewhat the playboy type, having been born in the early motoring age. He was a devil-may-care lad whose driver's license carried many red-ink citations illuminating a general disregard for his neck on the public highways. Since blue-coated officialdom frowned on such antics, this slim character with the toothbrush mustache naturally gravitated to civilian flying thrills at Brooklands. Being the inquisitive sort, he often speculated on what would happen if one zoomed an airplane steeply, then shut off the engine.

He tried the experiment and the plane slid back on its tail, an act that drove dozens of onlookers to the race track's repair pits. But William B. recovered in time, and another stunt, the tail slide, was added to the book of primitive aerobatics.

Rhodes-Moorhouse flew for about two years before he bothered to apply for an official certificate, his theory being that if you exposed yourself to officialdom you were likely to come under its ridiculous jurisdiction. He wanted simply to fly, not unravel red tape! However, he was finally induced to apply for his pilot's ticket in October, 1911, by which time he was a first-class cross-country flyer. In 1912 he finished third in Britain's Aerial Derby, and later established a record by carrying *two* passengers across the English Channel in an ancient Breguet. When war was declared he enlisted in the Royal Flying Corps and was posted to Farnborough, where he fretted and stewed until March, 1915. In all probability the R.F.C. instructors were trying to teach him to fly.

Lieutenant Rhodes-Moorhouse was eventually sent overseas and posted to Number 2 Squadron at Merville, where he began his active service career aboard B.E.2c Quirks. During the second battle of Ypres on April 26, a few days after the first German poison-gas attack, a message was received from Air Headquarters that the Courtrai railroad junction and station were to be bombed at all costs; German reinforcements were believed to be pouring through the town. With a hole two miles wide in front of Ypres where the Allies had been driven back by chlorine gas, the situation was most precarious.

Four aircraft were assigned to the mission but only Rhodes-Moorhouse succeeded in reaching the target. In place of an observer he carried a 100-pound bomb that was slung between the wheels of his aircraft in some prehistoric bomb rack, and before take-off he was told to use his own discretion as to how low he would fly before delivering his load. He went in at three hundred feet, released his bomb, and scored a direct hit on the signal box that was attached to the main building. He could have zoomed into the low clouds and smoke to escape and make his way back, but instead he circled the area picking up all the information he could. What he saw convinced him that the Allied troops around Ypres were in for a rough time.*

During the minutes that Lieutenant Rhodes-Moorhouse was over Courtrai he was bombarded with rifle and machine-gun fire, but he continued to study the ground movement. Then a bullet shattered the fingers of his left hand, so he decided to head home. Flying low over the city, he roared past the tower of a Courtrai church, where the Germans had set up a machine gun in the belfry. As the young Englishman buzzed past a long burst caught him cold; one slug smashed his thigh; another tore through his stomach. His base was thirty miles away, but below were many areas where he could have landed and requested medical assistance, even though he was well inside enemy territory. However, he thought only of the hordes of Germans moving toward the Courtrai station that could make the difference between hanging on or losing the war at Ypres. He sensed that the General Staff should know of this concentration—and the fact that he had destroyed the signal box.

One can only guess what Rhodes-Moorhouse suffered over those thirty miles. Once he was inside his own lines he could have landed immediately, but he hung on and flew to the rear area and dropped down near the British Headquarters, where he huddled in his blood-drenched cockpit and dictated his report to an infantry officer, then added before he fainted, "I didn't want them to get my old B.E. It's not too badly bashed about, is it?"

He died in a hospital twenty-four hours later, not knowing he had been recommended for the Victoria Cross. In his citation someone had written: "The bomb he dropped perhaps did more definite

---

* It is a historical fact that Germany's failure to get reserves into the gassed area in time completely nullified what initial surprise the poison-gas attack had created.

service on a great scale than any bomb released during the war, but his last act set a standard of courage which others may hope to equal but can never excel."

One young flying man ... one rickety old Quirk biplane ...

AMERICANS PAY DEBT TO LAFAYETTE

On a raw November day in 1914 a small group of American volunteers serving with the French Foreign Legion looked up from their mud-lined trench and watched a French biplane exchange a few bursts of fire with a German Rumpler. As an air battle it was of little importance, but it triggered a certain mass decision that was to have grave international implications and great significance. In that group were Bill Thaw, Bert Hall, and James J. Bach. Thaw and Hall were to become known internationally as outstanding members of the Lafayette Escadrille, but Bach remained an unknown, except for the fact that he became the first American airman credited with destroying a German plane in World War I.

After witnessing this early aerial engagement, Bill Thaw, who had been an amateur airman while a student at Yale, renewed an earlier request for an assignment to some French air squadron. To do this, Bill hiked about thirty-two kilometers to interview an old friend, a Lieutenant Brocard who had charge of a French squadron, and as a result Thaw, Hall, and Bach were transferred from the Foreign Legion by mid-December and had reported to the French Air Service headquarters.

THE STORY OF JIMMY BACH

All three men went through the routine and red tape of the day, but Bach's history, because of his immediate experiences, is most pertinent at this point in our narration. Jimmy Bach had been born in Paris of American parents, and had spent a great deal of his early life in European cities and earned his living as a mechanical engineer. He spoke French and English fluently, and although he had been registered with the American consul in Paris to assure his national status, Jimmy had a natural affection for the land of his

birth. On the outbreak of the war he enlisted in the French Foreign
Legion along with Bill Thaw, James Stewart Carstairs, Edgar John
Bouligny, Kiffin Yates Rockwell, Paul Ayres Rockwell, Charles
Sweeny, Dennis Dowd, Robert Soubiran, and Charles Trinkard. The
French poilu's pay was one sou, approximately one cent a day, and
payday came around every ten days.

Jimmy Bach was given a short course in map reading, engine
mechanics, and some general instruction in aircraft rigging, but
it was March 10 before he got to a flying school at Pau, a primary
field where students were permitted to taxi up and down the area
aboard what were known as Penguin aircraft—ancient Blériot monoplanes with clipped wings. These trainers would not get off the
ground, but since they were motivated by aircraft engines and
propellers, they did give the pupils some idea of the initial touch,
the feel of rudder and aileron controls, and the trick of operating
a rotary or radial engine. By July 4, 1915, Jimmy had been passed
on to the early Caudron and gained his pilot's brevet. He was then
promoted to corporal and assigned to Escadrille M.S.38 to fly
Morane-Saulniers. He reached the front line on August 29.

The Morane-Saulnier was a two-seater monoplane that had its
wing mounted high above the body "for visibility purposes," and
was soon dubbed the Parasol by British airmen. Originally it had
been designed as a reconnaissance machine to carry a pilot and a
trained observer, but in the course of events a few models were
fitted with two machine guns each, one mounted on the wing to
fire forward past the arc of the propeller; the second, intended for
the use of the passenger, was bolted to a primitive mounting, and,
in fact, could be fired through a fairly wide arc at enemy machines
attacking from the rear or broadside.

Until the early summer of 1915 air duels by aircraft with any
form of the fixed front gun were rare, for the value of this type
of air combat was not as yet appreciated fully, but here and there
such encounters did take place. It was the destiny of Jimmy Bach
to strike such a blow for the small American contingent, and to
get himself involved in a difficult international legal tangle.

Jimmy had been on a long-distance reconnaissance that had taken him into the vicinity of Mézières, and on the way back he met a German Aviatik homeward bound from a similar mission. Jimmy had a Lieutenant Giroux as his observer, although the American was only a corporal. In those early days in the French and German air services, piloting was not considered to be the premier duty; it was more important that intelligent and accurate information be gathered, and such data could be entrusted only to a commissioned officer—the pilot was just a chauffeur.

The observer aboard the German plane fired a long-range burst at the dainty Parasol, an impudence that enraged Jimmy. A second burst was more accurate, as slugs ripped through the linen fabric, battered at the engine cowling, and one sizzling through the cockpit, nipped at Jimmy's coveralls and made him lunge against his seat belt.

"What are you waiting for?" he yelled at Lieutenant Giroux. The monoplane peeled off into a tight bank and the 80-horsepower Le Rhône engine screamed under full throttle.

The Aviatik nosed down to get away, but the Parasol was some-what faster, and as both continued the dive Jimmy's Lewis gun chattered in short bursts. The chase went on until the French officer became concerned, fearing his pilot would follow the enemy plane all the way back to Berlin if necessary, but Jimmy ignored his observer's entreaties and poured burst after burst into the fleeing Aviatik.

When he had flown to within seventy-five yards of his target, Jimmy's gun jammed. He struggled in his seat to reach up and either replace the drum or haul back on the cocking handle to clear the stoppage. As he flew with the stick between his knees, he noticed that the German plane was acting erratically. He looked again and saw that the observer had been hit and was draped over his gun. Lieutenant Giroux tapped Bach on the shoulder and pointed at his own weapon. "I'll finish him for you!" he yelled.

"Well, thanks," Jimmy replied and took a long chance with the frail Morane, drawing the last few revs from the clanking Le Rhône and nosing down to gain even more speed. He went under the Aviatik, zoomed, and curled around to give Giroux a broadside shot as every wire strained, the wing creaked, and the struts showed some distortion.

Two short but accurate bursts slammed into the enemy aircraft and the propeller on the Mercedes proceeded to splinter and break up. The hub ran wild.

"Don't let him get away!" Jimmy yelled.

Lieutenant Giroux took another careful shot and the Aviatik staggered under the fusillade; pieces of wood, strips of linen, and spatters of dried paint flew off. Another burst and the wings collapsed as if struck by a massive hammer. She rolled and the body ripped itself clear of the tangle and tore through like a berserk dart. Once free, the fuselage began to spin and the runaway engine wailed its mournful story as it dragged a long, greasy plume of smoke behind it.

By now Jimmy was praying that his own fuselage would stay with his one wing, and he worked to ease down the engine and bring the Morane to a safe pull-out. The Parasol had not been designed for this type of activity, but fortunately he was able to keep her together and turn back toward his own lines.

When he opened the throttle again the rotary engine sniffed, choked, and coughed. He probably had fouled the plugs as he eased out of the wild dive, as happened so many times to other pilots. Also, the chase had taken them deep into the German lines, and as matters stood now, with the prevailing wind against them, Jimmy realized that he had a real dead-stick glide ahead of him if he hoped to land in friendly territory.

"You chased him too far," Lieutenant Giroux complained.

"I had to. He would have gotten away."

"I admit you got him. I just finished him off, but now they'll get us. Prisoner-of-war compound."

"Don't give up so easily," Bach taunted. "We're still flying."

The jagged pattern of trenches and sapheads that made up the front line seemed miles away, and the wind blew the telltale ground smoke toward the enemy back areas. Risking everything, even a deadly spin that could follow a stall, Jimmy stretched his glide over mile after mile. The French lines were visible now, plainly marked by the dull browns and whites of various excavations where thousands of infantrymen huddled and watched this little airplane as it dipped and fluttered on in its effort to reach safety.

With their share of luck they made it as the Morane's wheels crossed the friendly line with only a few feet to spare. There was no flat, cleared area and they stumbled through tangles of old barbed wire, thudding and bouncing, then floundered into a number of water-filled shell holes that finished their undercarriage; what was left slithered along on its belly and finally came to a halt.

Lieutenant Giroux, who had been standing up advising Jimmy how to handle this situation, was tossed out and received a broken arm, but Jimmy being well belted in, suffered not a scratch. On their return to the squadron, and after full details had been written out and assayed by their commander, credit for the victory was awarded to Corporal Bach, the pilot who had first given chase, delivered the first blow, and who had "courageously stayed in action until his observer could finish the enemy."

This was the beginning, and it was unfortunate that Jimmy Bach could not have continued to add to this reputation. But such was not to be, for shortly after, he was taken out of the play and almost lost his life in trying to save a comrade in dire distress.

THE GREAT SACRIFICE

At dawn on September 23, 1915, accompanied by a Sergeant Pilot Mangeot, Jimmy assumed one of the unpleasant duties assigned to some two-seater squadrons of those days. This was the delivery of intelligence agents into the enemy lines. These were important missions, thrilling and dangerous, and in many cases ended disastrously. Their task was to carry in their observers' seats two soldiers who were to be dropped near Mézières to destroy a length of railroad line between Mézières and Hirson. All went well until the two Morane planes turned around for their getaway. Jimmy wasted no time, for he knew that if he were caught he could be brought up on charges of aiding saboteurs or spies. The soldiers were wearing civilian clothes, and the Germans looked on this kind of activity with a jaundiced eye. Events proved how right Bach was.

The American made a clean take-off but his partner, Sergeant Mangeot, had the misfortune to clip a portion of hedge and his monoplane turned over. Bach throttled back immediately, curved around again, and moved into the wind to pick up the sergeant pilot. His second landing was perfect and Mangeot soon scrambled aboard, gratitude gleaming in his eyes. But then Jimmy's luck ran out, for in taxiing to get into position for the second take-off he ran into a difficult area and failed to select a clear runway. The Morane was almost air-borne when a wingtip brushed against the branch of a tree, and the monoplane spun and crashed. Neither airman was injured, but both realized what a serious position they were in and decided to lie low in a hedge until they were certain the two soldier agents were clear of the area. As they huddled in the scrub and thickets they heard some German troops examining the wrecked planes.

"I hope those agents got away," Jimmy whispered.

"If they didn't, and they find all four of us in the same area, *kaput!*" Mangeot added.

They then crept deeper into a forest section, climbed a small tree, and rested there until night fell, when they dropped down and walked until they found a plowed field, the furrows of which led them to the high wall of a farmyard. Both men were weary and thirsty and decided to risk entering, in the hope of finding a friendly French family. Instead, they walked into a group of German soldiers huddled around a small campfire.

Both men were caught, and since Bach was an American, a national of a so-called neutral country, but wearing a French uniform under his coveralls, he was branded as a *franc-tireur*—a mercenary. From the German point of view the penalty for conviction of a *franc-tireur* was the firing squad!

In their initial interrogations both men admitted that the wrecked Moranes were theirs, but they made no mention of their passengers or the object of their mission. Naturally, the Germans wondered why two two-seaters were in the same area, wrecked in much the same manner, but with no evidence that regulation observers had been carried.

Between September 24, when they were captured, and October 20, when a first trial was held, both airmen were kept under heavy guard. By the night of September 23 their two passengers had eluded capture and had carried out their job of destroying an important section of railroad track. It was easy to assume that the sabotage had been done by French agents flown into the area by airplane, and Bach and Mangeot could do nothing but maintain a strict silence.

A preliminary trial, in which Jimmy was allowed to plead his own case, was fairly routine. The court agreed that the evidence presented against the two men was not strong enough for conviction, so both were remanded for a second trial on October 30.

Bach realized that the Germans intended to concentrate on him as an American *franc-tireur*, but he managed to gain access to some of his French funds, which he used to employ a well-known Berlin lawyer to defend him. While willing to take the American's cash, this barrister admitted frankly that he could do very little in his behalf. In the next ten days both Bach and Mangeot could hope only that their passengers had escaped capture.

Their luck held in this matter, and by the time the German court convened for the second trial, the agents apparently were still at large. This left the field fairly clear for the Berlin lawyer, and to his credit, his impassioned plea won the day. Both Bach and Mangeot were found "not guilty," but were held and confined as honorable prisoners of war. Both airmen were locked up in a Laon prison after the trial, where they made many plans to escape, but their every move was thwarted. Finally Bach was moved to another military prison in Bavaria. Here he made several ambitious tries to get free, but he was always caught. He never gained his freedom until the Armistice was signed, three years after his capture.

In February, 1959, J. James Buck died in the Latter-day Saints

Hospital in Salt Lake City, Utah. He was seventy-four years of age. Mr. Buck had been teaching French at the University of Utah for more than fifteen years. In his obituary it was disclosed that Professor Buck had been a pilot with the French Air Service. He was of Danish descent, and at the outset of World War II had changed his name from Bach to the less Germanic Buck. The French Government had awarded him the Legion of Honor, the Médaille Militaire, and the Croix de Guerre.

ITALY PRODUCES SOME SPLENDID AIRMEN

When Italy decided to cast her lot with the Allies in May, 1915, a young gentleman farmer who had yearned for a military career was in Paris on a military mission—actually test flying a number of French aircraft, including the Nieuport, the Voisin, and the Morane. He had had the foresight to realize that his country would join the Allies eventually, and had seized every opportunity to keep up with the progress of military aviation.

Lieutenant Francesco Baracca's family had hoped that Francesco would follow a less violent career, but after he finished his university training, he enrolled at the Italian Military Academy at Modena in 1907. He specialized in cavalry work and on completion of his course was assigned to the 2d Cavalry Regiment, with which he served until 1912, when he volunteered for aviation. He received his training in France and won his brevet on a Hanriot two-seater.

During Italy's period of neutrality, Baracca, along with the rest of his country's airmen, made the most of every opportunity to fly whatever military planes could be made available. When Italy revoked the Triple Alliance, she first declared war on Austria; and when Francesco returned to his own country he was given a Nieuport two-seater and posted with a detached flight to cover the frontier in the Udine region.

Lieutenant Baracca did not encounter an enemy plane until September 7, 1915, but on that date while flying at 4,000 feet he investigated antiaircraft bursts over Palmanova. He discovered an Austrian plane and, climbing rapidly, engaged it, making a number of passes, but his machine gun betrayed him with repeated stop-pages, and the Austrian escaped. This combat, however, convinced Baracca that air fighting was exhilarating, and from that day on he became a relentless sky stalker.

Over the next few weeks encounter after encounter had to be broken off because of faulty guns, but toward the end of 1915 Italy managed to buy a few 13-meter Nieuport Baby scouts, and Baracca was honored with the first to be delivered. In a short time he was made a patrol leader of the Italian 70th Squadron and soon regis-tered his first victory over a two-seater Aviatik which he disabled and forced down in Italian territory. Before the war ended Major Baracca had run up a total of thirty-four victories. He was killed in action on June 19, 1918, when he was flying a Spad of Number 91 Squadron during a ground attack near Montello. As in so many instances, there is no reliable account of how the Italian ace met his end, but it is agreed generally that he was killed by a gunner aboard an Austrian two-seater. On the other hand, his squadron companions were convinced that Baracca was shot down by gunfire from the ground.

Silvio Scaroni, Italy's second leading ace, was a hard-working artilleryman at the outbreak of war, but shortly after, he requested a transfer to the flying service and quickly won his brevet and be-came a pilot member of the 4th Observation Squadron, and was flying on the Austrian front by August, 1915.

Air fighting was not such an everyday occurrence in this area as it was becoming on the Western Front. Many of the patrols were flown high above the grim white peaks of the Alps; combats were comparatively few; and in many instances the victims were shot down into mountain crevasses and lost forever. Others who had bad luck with engines had few areas on which to force-land, and were also lost with little trace.

Scaroni had a frightening experience shortly after going to the front. While he was flying over the Austrian reserve sector near Trieste, an antiaircraft battery registered a direct hit on his Caudron's engine. The power plant started to break up and then, shaking itself free of the bearers, fell 8,000 feet to the ground below. Silvio was left with nothing more than an engineless airframe, but although the enemy shot at him with all sorts of antiaircraft ammunition, he brought the wreck back and made a miraculous landing. Neither he nor his observer was scratched.

A short time later Scaroni's observer was killed; ten bullets went through Silvio's jacket; again his machine was shot to ribbons, but he brought it home and put it down on the runway.

Silvio Scaroni flew bombers and observation machines for nearly two years, returning from dozens of hair-raising patrols unscathed until at last he was rewarded with a transfer to a single-seater squadron. This honor came just as the Italians were suffering their most serious reverse, the Caporetto defeat that forced the Italian flyers back, and their airfields were taken over by six crack *Jagdstaffeln* from the Western Front and six experienced observation squadrons.

Silvio Scaroni flew his first fighter patrol on November 15, 1917, and was attacked instantly by two Albatros two-seaters. The gunners sprayed Scaroni's Nieuport, but one of the Albatros pilots crossed the Italian's path and was shot down in flames with one sure, telling burst. This was Silvio's decisive battle, for after that date enemy planes fell thick and fast; by December, Scaroni had shot down nine enemy planes. In an attack on an Austrian bomber squadron that was raiding the Istrana airdrome, where the famed British ace, Major W. G. Barker, had brought a squadron of Camels to support the Italian effort, Scaroni single-handed shot down three Austrian aircraft.

On July 12, 1918, Scaroni fought his last air battle while covering a number of artillery observation planes. He attacked a large enemy patrol that had moved in to drive away the "spotters," and performed heroically but was having a bad time of it until three more Italian scouts joined in, closely followed by a flight of British Camels.

Scaroni fought on until an enemy burst found him at last and knocked him senseless. His plane, a Hanriot fighter, went down in an uncontrolled spin for five thousand feet. Finally the pilot's mind cleared and he saw that he was falling into the Austrian lines. Instinct more than pilotage enabled him to guide the airplane toward no man's land, where by a miraculous stroke of luck the Hanriot ground-looped and tossed him into deep shell hole, where he lay until a patrol of infantry could crawl out and drag him to safety.

With twenty-six aircraft to his credit, Scaroni spent the next five months in a hospital, so that by the time his serious wounds had healed, the war was over. A few years later he was made commandant of a scout wing, then was appointed Italian Air Attache to Washington, where he remained until the outbreak of World War II, when he was made a general.

LIEUTENANT STRANGE'S WILD ADVENTURE

Nothing outstanding was accomplished through the early months of 1915 toward adapting the machine gun as a regulation feature of the military plane, and perhaps Lieutenant Louis A. Strange deserves an accolade for his attempt to arm the airplane.

A quiet, reserved man of Dorset parentage, he had been schooled at Oxford and in his undergraduate years had joined the Dorsetshire Yeomanry, a Territorial mounted-infantry regiment. In peacetime the yeomanry organizations were headed by country gentlemen who served as officers, provided their own horses, and commanded a force of urban types. These characters groomed all the nags, wore bandoleers, breeches, and spurs that clanked, and cluttered all the country pubs. Prior to 1914 it was harmless fun, but when Kitchener sent out the call that summer, the yeomanry proved to be a deadfall for those who had hoped to fight—a fact to which the author can subscribe. On my arrival in Britain in 1914 I was enamored of the yeomanry, but when I realized that their ranks were no place for a "would-be" fighting man, I spent months trying to get out of that service and became a gunner on an old pusher biplane. Anything but the yeomanry!

Louis Strange had probably come across H. G. Wells and the "battleplane" editorials of Charles G. Grey, editor of Britain's famous

aeronautical journal, *The Aeroplane.* At any rate, he was soon arguing with the old cavalry concept, and during their bosky-dell ex-
ercises would openly denounce the ridiculous antics his week-end
troopers were asked to perform.

"These are Boer War maneuvers," he would rage. "What the
devil good is all this? If ever we get into a to-do with the Germans,
cavalry will be about as useful as a platoon of Girl Guides!"

In a short time Lieutenant Strange had talked himself out of the
yeomanry and was buying flying lessons at so much an hour at
Hendon. After a few more issues of *The Aeroplane* he had talked
himself into the Royal Flying Corps and was sent to the Central
Flying School. By the time the Germans were halfway through
Belgium, Strange was one of the small number of daredevils who
were risking their necks flying Quirks across the Channel. His outfit
was stationed at Amiens.

Well, Lieutenant Louis Strange *was* flying, but on careful analysis
he realized that he had been foxed. He was doing all the same old
yeomanry bits, not on a horse, but aboard an airplane. The war-in-
the-air theory was just that. No one did any *fighting* in the air;
all were just looking.

Lieutenant Strange flew a two-seater Farman, and his observer,
Lieutenant Penn Gaskell, was another belligerent character. As they
floated about in this pusher with a nacelle (cockpit) wired between
the upper and lower wings, both of them put in time contemplating
the possibility of enlivening the everyday proceedings.

"You know," Penn Gaskell said one morning, "if we had a machine
gun . . ."

"Took the words right out of my mouth," Strange responded.

"Well, I mean to say, there are such things."

"Absolutely! Let's potter about a bit."

There were some old boxes in the squadron stores, and believe
it or not, some of them held Lewis guns that had never been
unpacked.

"Do you know anything about these things?" Strange inquired.

"I saw one fired once. As I remember, all you do is stick one of those tray things full of bullets on that peg there, and if you can get it loaded, you just press the trigger."

"Sounds easy," Strange agreed, and they wrapped one of the guns in burlap to smuggle it past the Orderly Room. When no one was looking, the weapon was stowed in Penn Gaskell's cockpit.

Although this may read as a somewhat amplified account, the full details have been part of the R.F.C.'s official history for years. It all took place on August 22, 1914, and on that date the records have it that a German Rumpler obliged by appearing over Maubeuge just as Strange and his observer had climbed to about 3,000 feet with their unauthorized Belgian Rattlesnake in the rear office.

The added load restricted their activities somewhat and they had difficulty in getting the Farman any higher than 3,500 feet, while the Rumpler crew, unaware of the fate planned for them, buzzed about at 5,000 feet, enjoying the scenery.

When it was realized that they had small chance of reaching the invading Rumpler, Penn Gaskell decided to "have a go," nevertheless, and see how the artillery worked. But he failed to advise the pilot of his plan and when the Lewis gun went off, the roar and vibration so startled Strange he yanked the gasping Farman into a steep zoom, almost flipping Penn Gaskell and his Big Bertha out of the nacelle. With that, and breathing a prayer of relief that all was still intact, they returned to earth.

"You never heard such a row," Strange admitted later. "The thing went off like a Jack Johnson!"

When their commanding officer learned of the experiment he ordered Penn Gaskell to return the weapon to stores. "If you two must stir up strife in the air, please use a rifle; machine guns are for the infantry, not airplanes!" he grumbled.

It has not been possible to trace much of Penn Gaskell's career after that, but Lieutenant Strange finished the war with a double row of decorations and a lieutenant-colonelcy.

While flying a Martinsyde scout with Number 6 Squadron the following May, Strange gave the front-line audience an unscheduled performance. He was cruising around at 8,500 feet when he spotted an Aviatik from a German squadron located outside Lille. As usual, the German outclimbed him while the enemy observer peppered Strange with his Parabellum. The Englishman hoicked his nose up and retaliated with the Lewis gun mounted above his top plane, but although he sprayed the sky with a full drum, nothing eventful happened.

The next problem was to replace the empty ammunition pan, and to do this Strange had to loosen his seat belt, try to hold the control stick between his knees, and reach up to get his fingers on the drum's release latch. In the middle of all this the Martinsyde suddenly went up into a stall, and before Strange could drop back into his seat, the plane went over on her back, and Strange went out of the cockpit.

"You know," he explained on his return, "I felt like an utter fool. I had been swearing because I couldn't get the damn' drum off, and now I was praying it would stay on."

The scout was on its back, Strange was dangling free of his cockpit and clinging to the machine gun's ammunition pan to keep from falling to the earth. Its sharp edge gnawed into his fingers as he tried to wriggle into a position where he could grab a rear center-section strut. All this time the Martinsyde was in a flat upside-down spin and circling over the German trenches. Exactly where the airplane was in relation to him was something of a puzzle; his chin was practically resting against the ammo drum and his legs were flopping about somewhere outside.

"I finally grabbed a center-section strut and felt more comfortable. Below, I could see the town of Menin twirling around and naturally wondered where I would crash, but I kept kicking upward until at last I got one foot hooked inside the cockpit. I took a second or two to get my breath, and finally got the other foot anchored."

Once he got most of his body inside, he worked the joystick over; that depressed one aileron, and finally the machine rolled itself into a normal position. When everything was in its right place, Strange dropped in with a plop and went straight through the wicker bucket seat and found himself sitting practically on the floor of the aircraft. While he had been dangling outside the plane, he had lost his seat cushion and everything else not nailed down. The engine, which had stopped when the Martinsyde was on its back, suddenly picked up again and the airplane dived toward Menin Wood, threatening to rip its wings off.

When Lieutenant Strange tried to pull the stick back to level off, he discovered that part of the broken seat frame had jammed it, and he spent a few more anxious moments clearing out the debris. Just in time, he zoomed above the treetops, and when he had leveled off to take over, he discovered that he had kicked out most of the instruments in his panel. But he was so delighted to discover himself alive that he did not bother with the niceties of flight, and found his field at Abeele with little trouble.

Some years later after the war while on a friendly tour of Germany, Strange became acquainted with the aforementioned *Staffel* leader, Hauptmann Bruno Loerzer, who remembered the astounding incident.

"We reported that fight, but no one would believe us when we explained that the pilot had gone down hanging from his wing gun while the plane was flying on its back." Loerzer said, and laughed.

"Same with me. I don't think I ever really convinced my C.O. how I had kicked out my instruments," Strange remarked ruefully.

CHAPTER 4

Wings for the Weapon

The development of the fixed, front-firing machine gun rev-olutionized aerial warfare, and Roland Garros scored the first series of decisive victories in the sky. Legend and persistent misconceptions imply that this combined weapon was designed by Anthony Fokker and that his invention almost wiped out the Allied air services. Such was not the case, for various forms and models of the front-firing machine were in the hands of Allied pilots from early 1915. However, victories scored by the early Fokker monoplane were conclusive, since they were staged over German-held territory. Thus Allied pilots, if only wounded, were lost to the cause if their planes were disabled and they were forced to land in enemy country.

WE WERE NOT "FOKKER FODDER"

In this chapter we shall attempt to clear up a list of inaccuracies and what have seemed to be determined misconceptions concerning the original adaptation of the machine gun to the fighter airplane. Some historians have stated persistently that the first aircraft to mount and fight with a fixed machine gun was Anthony Fokker's E-1 monoplane; to which they have added the repetitious chapter proclaiming that throughout 1915–16 Allied airmen were simply "Fokker fodder." A certain coterie of Hollywood and pulp-magazine writers first conceived, then universalized, this fabrication. It should

75

be noted that the phrase is never found in reports, histories, or accounts written by recognized authorities *during* the war.

Whenever the Germans appeared to have some definite advantage over Allied airmen, this superiority did not arise necessarily from any particular aircraft or weapon, but from the incontestable fact that they consistently refused to do battle anywhere but well inside their own lines. And why should they, since they had occupied a great portion of France and Belgium and had only to fight a defensive campaign and allow the Allies to bankrupt themselves, physically and financially, attempting to break through the five-hundred-mile submerged fortress that was trench warfare?

The selection of the battlefield was Germany's greatest weapon, for with it they had the advantage of the prevailing wind. If they suffered combat damage, they could land in their own territory, and their opponents had no choice but to put down in a German-controlled area. Thus they enjoyed the satisfaction of having their victims clearly accounted for, whereas Allied fighters had to be content with filing a claim for victory, hoping that two other members of their flight or squadron could confirm the claim. How many German pilots were seriously wounded, yet managed to get down safely, will never be known, since there was no way for their Allied opponents to determine whether their enemy had been hit.

NO CHOICE OF BATTLEFIELD

On the other hand, the Allies lost many men and machines that had not encountered an enemy fighter. Bombers penetrating great distances into enemy territory, or fighters escorting such formations, might never be engaged by the opposition, but faulty engines or the exhaustion of fuel on many occasions caused these misfortunes. The routine report would read: *Six of our machines failed to return,* but this in no way indicated German fighter superiority; more often it was the luck of the draw. From my own experience, I remember that we lost as many men and machines through engine failure deep in enemy territory as we did in aerial combat. By the same token, I again remind the reader that it was always most difficult for us to be accredited with victories unless one of our squadron mates actually saw our victims go down in flames or completely out of control.

GILBERT AND GARROS
ENVISION SINGLE-SEATER FIGHTER

On the morning of April 1, 1915, the crew of an Albatros two-seater was making a reconnaissance patrol near Epernay. French antiaircraft guns began to bark and spatter the sky with telltale blobs of white smoke, whereupon a French pilot in a Morane monoplane went to inspect the scene.

The two Germans watched him with only casual interest and continued their snooping. When the Morane curled into a position behind their tail the German pilot assumed that the Frenchman was out on an observation mission, too, and since the Allied machine carried no observer who might have a rifle or revolver to cause any trouble, the Albatros pilot saw no particular need for concern. Just as long as the Frenchman did not start crabbing up alongside from where he himself might trigger off a few rounds from a carbine, this could be only another observation mission.

The Morane concerned was a midwing monoplane, not the Parasol. It was neat, sleek, and powered by a Le Rhône engine. Thus, if he made any careful observation at all, the German pilot probably looked to see if this machine had one of those ungainly bipod structures bearing a Lewis gun mounted high to fire over the wingtips. There was no such tangle of superstructure or weaponry, so what was there to worry about?

A few seconds later a burst of fifteen rounds of Hotchkiss machine-gun fire tore through the German pilot's shoulder blades. The burst had come *straight* from the Morane monoplane directly behind him. Only the observer, Fritz Dietrichs, realized that the slugs apparently were coming through the sheen of the propeller, and then saw that a gun *was* mounted smack on top of the engine cowling—not on an elevated bracket. This weapon was actually firing through the whirling blades of the propeller. How could that be accomplished?

Dietrichs never lived to find out. He knew nothing about piloting an Albatros and he went to his end, utterly helpless to aid himself. In his final breath he must have screamed his disbelief that a French monoplane could shoot at him with a gun set behind the whirling blades of a wooden propeller. The Albatros plunged down with a dead pilot hunched over the control stick. A new weapon and a new breed of man had been created. The military force had been given a most lethal piece of armament. It made the airplane as important a war machine as the naval dreadnought. It turned a collection of rickety flying machines into an air service, and overnight the airplane became the platform for sky-high gunnery, not just an airy-fairy vehicle of observation. It had won the most decisive battle in air history.

Anthony Fokker, the Dutch airplane designer, had had nothing to do with any of this. He had never heard of a front-firing gun, or for that matter conceived such an idea. He was too busy trying to sell the German government a sports type of monoplane, powered by an engine that had been copied from the French Le Rhône rotary. Roland Garros, the French flyer, gave us the fixed-gun fighter.

The man who flew this fragile aircraft on this memorable patrol had started out to be a concert pianist. He had been born at Saint-Denis on the island of Réunion in the Indian Ocean in October, 1888. His father was a well-known lawyer who had been able to provide a luxurious home and a classical education for his son. Roland Garros was adept at almost everything. He had clever hands and could draw, paint, and play musical instruments, as well as manipulate most mechanical devices of that day. His parents decided early that Roland should be a professional musician, and before he became of age, he was sent to Paris to develop his piano technique.

But the City of Light had other attractions. It was in Paris that he saw his first airplane and became entranced with aeronautics.

He arranged an interview with the famous Alberto Santos-Dumont, who in 1909 was better known than either of the Wright brothers. This Brazilian coffee millionaire had thrilled Parisians with airship displays as early as 1898, and by 1906 was flitting about Europe in an airplane. He once produced a hybrid dirigible-airplane, using the gasbag to get the contrivance in the air, then skimmed over the chimney pots of Paris under power of the airplane portion of the invention.

"So you want to be an aeronaut?" the dapper Santos-Dumont queried. "And who doesn't, these days?"

"But I can afford to pay for my lessons," Garros explained, intending to convert the funds for his musical education into more exciting channels.

"Money is not important. Let me see your hands."

Garros held out his long, delicate fingers, and Santos-Dumont took them, turned them over and studied them carefully. They were almost replicas of his own.

"You are lucky. I take it you are a musician. With such hands you will make a splendid airman. I will take you."

Santos-Dumont had little idea how right he was. Within a year the quiet, unassuming music student had become one of the most skilled airmen in the world. It was fantastic what this delicate-fingered man could do with those early contraptions of bamboo, linen, piano wire, and bicycle wheels. In October, 1910, Garros went to America with a French aviation team and competed in the memorable Statue of Liberty race. It was won, after considerable controversy, by Count Jacques de Lesseps, who flew a Blériot monoplane. Garros was aboard a Paulhan biplane that was not maneuverable enough to make a tight turn around the harbor goddess and he had to be content with third place, but in 1911 he won the $100,000 Paris-to-Rome race, was first in the Paris-to-Madrid feature, and led the field in the Grand Prix d'Anjou event that same year.

In the summer of 1914 Garros was in Germany giving exhibitions with an early Morane monoplane—quite possibly the Morane Bullet—and held large audiences spellbound with acrobatic displays. At night he was the honored guest at banquets where he enthusiastically heralded the military value of the heavier-than-air machine. Every word was digested, and the German newspapers gave columns of space to his fascinating theories.

Although Garros' name was on every German tongue and he was most popular, he was a modest hero. Not only could he give an amazing exhibition of flying but on returning to the ground he would delight music-salon groups with his skill at the piano. He had never enjoyed such dual acclaim before, and his amazement and despair can be imagined when late one afternoon he slowly interpreted the newspaper headlines and the screeching of newsboys at the street corners. The Kaiser's troops had invaded his beloved France!

War? War *had been* declared!

He was agitated and somewhat bewildered. He had been all over Germany pointing out the value of the airplane in military operations and even had showed how it could be used for observation and bombardment. He was shocked that all these people who had posed as his friends had decided to make war on his country. According to the international rules of war, he could be held as a prisoner for the duration of hostilities. Even worse, the Germans might confiscate his exhibition machine, and might even fly it against his own people.

Determined not to be trapped by such legalities, Garros went back to his hotel, packed his bags, and, leaving by a rear exit, hurried through the city to the exhibition grounds. Fortunately, in the general excitement most of the guards had gathered in the nearest *Gasthaus* to toast the Kaiser and drink to Germany's victory. Garros dragged his monoplane from its shed, checked the Le Rhône engine and fuel supply, stowed his bags in the nacelle, swung his own propeller, and climbed aboard.

At that time few men had flown at night, but Roland Garros took off boldly, made for the nearest border, and landed safely in Switzerland. Several days later he continued on to Paris. A great furor went up in Berlin, and Garros' name was again in the headlines, but now he was being called everything from a habitual thief to the scurviest of international spies. What trickery! Exhibition flights, indeed! That scoundrel Garros must have photographed every fortress in Germany.

Roland volunteered immediately for military service and, along with Armand Pinsard, mentioned before, went to Saint-Cyr, where he was put into uniform and taught parade-ground drill and what constituted aviation tactics at the time. Then both Garros and Pinsard were sent on simple cross-country flights to prove that they were military flyers, after which they went to Paris for reassignment.

Morane-Saulnier Escadrille Number 25 was being formed at Buc, and Garros and Pinsard were ordered to report there. To their great delight they were soon joined by several other exhibition pilots, including Adolphe Pégoud, Jules Védrines, Eugène Gilbert, and Marc Pourpé. With Pourpé was a Wallingford, Connecticut, man, Raoul Lufbery, who had worked for Pourpé for nearly four years as his mechanic during exhibition flights that had taken them all over the world. At the time the war had broken out Pourpé and Lufbery were in Paris to buy a new machine, but now they felt that there were more important duties with the French Air Service.

Over the next few weeks all these exhibition headliners were actively engaged in trying to stem Germany's rush toward Paris, and were doing more than their share in turning the enemy advance along the Marne into a crushing defeat.

In October, military intelligence learned that the German High Command had established headquarters at Thielt, and remembering his earlier theories of using the airplane as a weapon of offense, Garros suggested that the German nerve center be raided—with bombs!

"It is wasteful," he argued, "to put our aircraft into the air for simple observation reports. Captive balloons can do that, and probably do it better. They can be sent up at night; they work in silence and can scarcely be detected. It is my honest opinion that most of the reports our observers bring back are not worth the essence they consume."

Armand Pinsard agreed with him. Eugène Gilbert, another theorist, was quietly working on a more practical idea, one that would transform the airplane into a true war bird. During one of the efforts to bomb Thielt, Pinsard had engine trouble, as explained previously, and was taken prisoner. His loss desolated Garros, for they had formed a warm friendship, and at one time Roland conceived the hare-brained idea of a rescue flight to spirit Pinsard from the enemy compound.

It was while contemplating this wild possibility that Garros concluded that he could do nothing with an unarmed airplane—he might as well cross over in a country-fair balloon. Flying deep into the German area was one thing, but to land there, rescue his pal, and fight his way out through a swarm of enemy aircraft that would be sent up to intercept him was something else.

HOW MACHINE GUN WAS
SYNCHRONIZED TO PROPELLER

Eugène Gilbert must have been reading Garros' mind, for he too was pondering some method of putting fangs and claws into the reconnaissance plane, and quite possibly had heard vague reports of some Englishman or German who actually had taken a machine gun into the air. Gilbert realized that to make an airplane really earn its essence, it had to be flown fast, handled with maneuverability and skill, and be able to strike—or thrust—like a master swordsman.

Once he arrived at that simple conclusion, the seed of military aviation had been sown. In the first place, the airplane had to be able to fire in the direction in which it was flying. It had to be small and fast, probably a single-seater. It should be designed for maneuverability, and handled like a rapier in the hands of a duelist. Ah, but that meant that the gun had to be mounted so that it would fire directly forward. If it were set outside the propeller arc anywhere on the wings or mounted on the undercarriage, it would be

of limited use. Simple stoppages could not be rectified and the
ammunition pans or belts could not be changed. No, the gun had
to be available to the pilot at all times. Any gun, to be conveniently
mounted, had to be set somewhere behind the arc of the wooden
propeller.

It must be assumed that Eugène Gilbert said: "Let's face it. We
have to mount any gun behind the propeller. A percentage of the
bullets *would* hit the whirling blades and pierce them. It would take
only a few to sever them, and ... *boom*—no prop!"

From this point on, legend, hearsay, and rumor muddle the
story. Some armament experts have stated that Gilbert wrapped
the butt ends of the propeller with lengths of steel tape; others report that he affixed a curved block of metal at the point where
bullets might strike the airscrew. In all probability a form of metal
wrapping was used.

Gilbert's first experiment was made at Luxeuil as early as December, 1914, when he mounted a Hotchkiss gun on the engine
cowling of a Morane Bullet. Some reports have it that in January,
1915, Gilbert shot down an Aviatik with this armament arrangement, but if so, the questions naturally arise: "Then why was the
device not used more widely, as crude as the arrangement was?
Why didn't Garros or some other pilot of M-S 23 know of it and
show more interest?"

History is imperfect at times, and often is nothing more than
the crystallization of popular beliefs. The real story possibly is
something like this: following the legendary success against the
Aviatik, Gilbert decided to improve his deflector device, and fabri-
cated two V-shaped wedges of armor plate that were bolted to the
back of each blade, on the assumption that the propeller could be
balanced better in that manner.

During gun-butt tests he asked a number of fellow officers to
help him raise the Morane into flying position, steady the wingtips,
and hold the plane relatively secure while he ran the engine and
fired a test burst at a wall of sandbags. Apparently the deflector
blocks were shaped incorrectly, and two officers were killed by

ricocheting bullets. Eugène Gilbert was so distressed by the accident that he ended his experiments and from all accounts never mentioned or considered the project again.

By coincidence, Roland Garros conceived the same plan for protecting the butt ends of the propeller blades, and spent long hours in the armorer's shed figuring weights, recoil, loading procedures, and rate of fire. Once he touched on this last point, he felt that he was on the right track. He checked the 300 rounds per minute of the Hotchkiss gun against the varied speeds of the propeller, and concluded that less than 7 per cent of the rounds fired would strike the propeller, or the deflector. From that point on, it was a simple matter to go into the air, aim his nose at an enemy plane, pull the trigger, and shoot it down.

The squadron's armorer sergeant was mildly impressed, but brought up the fact that Eugène Gilbert had tried the same thing with most tragic results. Garros was convinced that Gilbert had used a deflector that was curved at an incorrect angle, and he induced a Parisian machinist to turn out a collar of armor plate that could be bolted around the base of the propeller blade. This was designed with a sharp angle so that any bullet deflected would continue on in a narrow vee off the line of the undeflected rounds. He sacrificed some propeller efficiency, but he wanted, above all, to avoid further accidents.

When the collars were finished and delivered, Garros bolted them to the butt ends of the propeller blades of a discarded Morane, then had the armorer bolt a Hotchkiss gun along the engine and cockpit cowling. They devised a trigger cable that ran down to the joystick so that the gun could be fired with the same hand that held the control lever. In that position the gun could be loaded easily and stoppages quickly cleared.

Here again legend and hearsay combine to confuse the tale. In one account an unidentified pilot mounted a Hotchkiss gun outside his cockpit and went into the air with no protection for the propeller, and promptly shot himself down. Another states that

some young enthusiast stole Garros' plane and went over the line
to engage the enemy, and hammered the propeller clean off the
shaft and spun in out of control. Neither of these tales can be
substantiated.

At any rate, Garros left no stone unturned to make certain his
device would work perfectly. Clip after clip of Hotchkiss ammunition was fired into the buttress with the engine running at various
speeds; what few shots struck the propeller were deflected off harm-
lessly. With all this testing, Garros did not try his device against
the enemy until April 1, 1915, when he scored his first victory
against an Albatros. On April 11 he stalked two more unsuspecting
Aviatik two-seaters, and using the same strategy sent the first down
under a torrent of Hotchkiss fire. The observer of the second stood
and fought with a revolver, but Garros eventually sent this Aviatik
down in flames.

The following afternoon while returning from a visit to another
escadrille, Garros encountered an L.V.G., also a two-seater, and battered it into the ground near Dunkirk. Once more the German air
crew was deceived by the Morane Bullet's nose-on approach. Two
days later one of the newer Aviatiks armed with a Parabellum
mounted in the observer's rear seat was spotted flying toward the
French lines. The German pilot hurriedly dropped his bombs to
gain some maneuverability, and the observer's first burst caught the
Morane Bullet's wing root and punctured the reserve fuel tank.
Trailing a long cloud of gasoline vapor, Garros disregarded the possibility of fire in the air and closed in. The German observer died
with five bullets in his chest, the next five of the same clip tore
through the pilot's head, slammed through the instrument panel,
and ignited the fuel line. The Aviatik went down and burned to a
cinder in a marsh.

On the morning of April 16 Garros was attacked by four Albatros
two-seaters as they were returning from a bombing raid. A number
of rifle bullets penetrated his machine; one of them hit the engine
cowling and fell back into his lap. The moment the Frenchman's
fixed gun began to sparkle behind the sheen of the propeller,

all four two-seater pilots remembered important engagements else-
where. One appeared to be slower than the others, however, and
gradually lagged behind. Garros darted in to get within range,
and the others, noting their companions' danger, turned about and
tried to head off the determined Frenchman; but Garros was "on"
and his bullets tore away the left wing of the laggard Albatros. The
ill-fated crew went down in a fuselage that threw away the other
wing before it spun in.

AIR "ACE" APPELLATIVE IS COINED

Five victories in sixteen days! That was the initial harvest of
Roland Garros' front-firing gun. He was cited for the Legion of
Honor, and nearly every newspaper in France and Great Britain
carried the astounding news of his aerial accomplishment. The gay
boulevardiers screamed their cheers and toasted the newest war
hero in champagne. "Oh, that Garros," they cried. "Roland Garros,
our aerial savior! Five enemy flying machines he has destroyed.
Garros is an ace!"

The word *ace* was a popular catchword of the day in Paris, particularly in relation to athletes, and was applied to anyone who
had performed anything unusual. The latest Grand Prix winner was
an ace; the newest cycling hero was an ace; popular jockeys were included in this newest category of headliners. It was natural that
the word should be applied to Roland Garros.

This continued reference was caught by an American newspaperman in Paris who interpreted it to mean any pilot who had downed
five enemy planes and, in his next dispatch to New York, applied
the reference to Roland Garros without bothering to explain how
the Frenchman had run up his score or with what new weapon. It
thus became the journalistic standard by which a French fighter
pilot was rated.

Later the Germans doubled the requirements, and any airman
who scored ten victories was referred to as a *Kanone*—a cannon or
weapon. The British ignored all references to individual fighting
scores and still do not accept the "ace" designation. Not until late

in 1915 did they compile authentic records of enemy planes shot down, and they did not publish the names of their stars or the day-by-day scores of their outstanding airmen. It was only on the publication of decorations and awards that the victory scores of their heroes were mentioned. When I was awarded the Military Medal, the announcement coincided with what I considered my seventh victory in the air, but the citation simply mentioned my "devotion to duty, for courage in action and determination in the face of the enemy." No mention of any specific accomplishment. I believe this was typical of most citations for awards.

But the term "ace" and its requirements have lasted until this day. Roland Garros became the world's first ace and the man who, to a great extent, revolutionized aerial warfare. He was invited to appear before the Directorate of Military Aeronautics to present his views on this new phase of aerial combat. The date was set for April 25, but unfortunately Garros could not keep the appointment. Dame Fortune suddenly withdrew her patronage.

On the afternoon of April 19, 1915, Garros took off to bomb the railroad sidings at Courtrai. Why he was given such a mission with a flimsy single-seater designed expressly for fighting has long been debated. Although he was the war's premier air fighter, apparently he still carried out routine bombing raids; the importance of man-to-man combat was not yet fully appreciated.

That day the pilots of M-S 23 probably expected Roland to return with another credit to his account, but that was not to be. He flew all the way to Courtrai without encountering enemy aircraft of any kind; he assumed he would be more fortunate on the way back. Once over his target he cut his Le Rhône engine, went into the glide attack, swept over the freight yards, and dropped his contribution.

He had no idea what he hit, or whether he had missed the target completely; he was too much concerned with getting the impact-fuse bombs overboard without blowing himself to bits. When he switched on the rotary engine again, the Le Rhône refused to pick up. Nothing happened! The propeller just windmilled in the slip stream. He knew immediately what had occurred and probably swore at his imbecility. In the long approach glide for the Courtrai freight yard he had allowed the spark plugs to oil up, and had forgotten to "burn" them off with intermittent blipping of the ignition switch. So he had no alternative but to stretch his glide until he found a suitable spot to land.

He came down near Ingelmünster about forty miles from the Dutch frontier. His first concern was to destroy his plane and the details of the propeller's protective collar—the secret of his front-firing gun. He did his best to set fire to the Morane, even going to the extent of stuffing the cockpit with loose hay, but everything was damp and refused to burn. How ironical! Had an enemy bullet flicked a spark off a metal fitting near a punctured gas tank, the whole machine would have gone up like a pan of gunpowder. On the ground, with no slip-stream draft, nothing he tried would set up so much as a smoke smudge.

A squad of German soldiers soon arrived and Garros made one last desperate bid for liberty by running across the field and sliding into a ditch for cover where the depression was full of muddy water, weeds, and half-frozen sedge. He stayed there until dark, then crawled out and headed for the Dutch border, but as luck would have it he wandered straight into a group of soldiers who were out foraging for firewood. The game was up.

In the meantime, German aviation men had examined the undamaged Morane and naturally were interested in the unusual steel wedges bolted around the propeller blades. Blued bullet marks next disclosed the purpose of the plates, and with that, the secret of the gun that could fire bullets through the whirling blades of the propeller was revealed.

The Germans moved fast. The French *cocardes* were daubed out, and the Bullet was flown to Schwerin where a young Dutch engineer, Anthony Fokker, was called in to examine it.

Anthony Fokker's role in the development of early aircraft armament is fairly well known, although it sometimes has been distorted or wildly exaggerated. He has been given full credit by some people for the interrupter gear that controlled the flow of bullets *between* the whirling blades, but the fact remains that Eugène Gilbert first conceived the idea, and Roland Garros put the plan into operation. We also have evidence that an interrupter gear, designed for controlling a Lewis gun, was being experimented with by a Sergeant Mechanic Alkan of the French Air Service, a device that was tried out on several R.F.C. aircraft. It gave promising results and might have been accepted fully, except for the fact that other experiments were showing that the lighter mechanism of the Vickers gun was proving to be more suitable for such controlled fire. At least three British interrupter gears were in the process of development by the time Anthony Fokker was given the secret of Garros' weapon. One, the Arsiad, was designed in the field by Major A. V. Bettington, who commanded the Repair Section of the Number 1 Aircraft Depot. As a matter of fact, the Arsiad gear was fitted to a number of machines in France. Another, the Scarff-Dibovsky gear, was the joint invention of Lieutenant Commander V. V. Dibovsky of the Imperial Russian Navy and Mr. F. W. Scarff of the Admiralty Air Department, and was being used by several aircraft designers in developing new fighters. Another British interrupter gear was one designed by Vickers Ltd. and built expressly for their own weapon.

But it must be admitted that none of these devices was in extensive use on the Western Front. At the time the British were providing a number of substitutes in the form of pusher planes, particularly the D.H.2, a single-seater that was flitting about like a gadfly with a Lewis gun mounted to fire straight ahead, a weapon that required no synchronization because the engine and propeller were mounted aft. Two-seaters such as the Vickers Gun-bus and the F.E.2b, had this engine-propeller arrangement and needed no interrupter gear for their weapons.

The first extensive use of British synchronization gearing came during the Battle of the Somme in the early summer of 1916, and aircraft so equipped contributed considerably to the superiority the R.F.C. established during that Homeric struggle. For instance, A and B Flights of Number 70 Squadron, flying Sopwith 1½-strutters (two-seaters) used the Scarff-Dibovsky gear *and* the new Scarff ring mounting for the observer. Number 19 and 21 Squadrons, flying Nieuport two-seaters, were using the Scarff-Dibovsky gear—which was replaced soon after by the Sopwith-Kauper gear, a device that was so well designed that it was employed until well into 1917.

But back to Anthony Fokker. He was a self-taught engineer who had designed a few aircraft and won some renown during the early Military Trials and air races. His specialty had been sports planes for racing. He had set up a factory in 1912 at Johannistal and another at Schwerin in 1913—which indicates that he had considerable investment in German industry. However, on the outbreak of the war, when in all probability German authorities threatened to commandeer his plants and equipment, Fokker offered his designs and services to France, Great Britain, and Italy; at least he has said that he did, but we have no official confirmation of the fact. None of these Allied countries gave him much attention. France had plenty of planes and many first-class aircraft designers. Britain had little faith in the monoplane and even less in neutral Dutchmen who came offering gifts. Understandably, when a representative of the German Naval Air Arm made an offer for a number of his E.1 (Eindekker) monoplanes and spread real money before him, Fokker accepted, for he was in debt to his father and a few close friends and this tie-in with the Germans solved his immediate financial problems.

Some historians have derided the Allies for turning down Anthony Fokker, who proved to be an imaginative designer and a hard worker. This is second guessing, for in 1914 Fokker was an unknown compared with the leading designers available to the Allies. Also, he was a Hollander, a neutral, and the Allies trusted no neutrals, no matter what their announced leanings. If the Germans wished to gamble on this young man, that was their business; and in unprejudiced retrospect, it is clear that at the time Fokker had little to offer except youthful zest for experiment and an open-minded approach to any new problem. As a matter of truth, his

E.1 monoplane was a questionable performer, and had it not been
that it became the test bed for Fokker's interrupter gear, it might
never have been heard of.

ANTHONY FOKKER FACES A NEW PROBLEM

In all fairness to Fokker, he honestly believed that his future was
in the development of light sports types, and since he was positive
that the war would not last past the first Christmas, he retained his
Dutch citizenship and devoted his efforts to building twenty-four
Fokkers a day, as he had contracted to do.

Because of his independence and willingness to tackle any problem, Garros' Morane was turned over to him, and its fixed-gun
deflector device explained. At the time Fokker had never held a
machine gun in his hands, and had never fired one, but his quick
mind soon caught the value of the armament arrangement.

"We want you to duplicate this deflector-collar idea and incorporate it into a few of your Eindekkers," the German aviation
officials explained. They gave Fokker a Parabellum gun and a belt
of ammunition, and within an hour he had decided that the deflector
plate was not the answer. He was convinced that eventually either
one bullet would strike with such force that the propeller would
shatter from the impact, or a deflected bullet would ricochet into a
vital section of the aircraft engine.

He placed the gun on the engine cowling, and in some visionary
fashion conceived the idea of pressing the trigger only when there
was no blade in front of the gun barrel. In this vague manner he
evolved the basic idea for his interrupter gear, but as pointed out,
he was not alone in this thought. He knew the rate of fire of the
gun had to be interrupted whenever there was a propeller blade
in line with the gun barrel.

The rest was easy. Fokker simply fitted a light cam ring at the
back of the propeller boss. The cam depressed a lever which, operating through a series of cranks and rods either pressed or released the trigger at the proper instant. In theory the idea worked
beautifully. In practice a few bugs had to be ironed out to make

up for the irregularity of fire—caused by faulty ammunition or friction lags in the gun mechanism. At any rate, he mounted his device on an E.1 monoplane and within five days had German aviation officials on hand to see it work. As had Gilbert and Garros, he set up his machine opposite a test butt, started the engine, and fired three 10-round test bursts. When the officials inspected the propeller and found no damage, they thought Fokker had played some trick, so the Dutchman obliged again—with a 100-round burst. Again the officials went into a lengthy huddle, after which their spokesman made further demands. "We are satisfied with your device, Herr Fokker, but would it work in the air? Would you be willing to give such an exhibition?"

Although seething with indignation, Anthony Fokker finally agreed and ordered some of his men to take a couple of discarded monoplane wings and lay them out on the airfield as a target. He then went up into the air as the wary aviation officials crowded in close to the center of the exhibit. Fokker tilted over from 900 feet and nosed down at the ground, pouring a long burst of 100 rounds at the target. Earth was kicked up all around the wings and some of the slugs ricocheted in all directions. The Prussian military officials also scattered.

After Fokker had landed, they crept out of their shelter and inspected the bullet-riddled wings and also examined the E.1's propeller. All well and good, but the Dutchman had not convinced them yet.

"Excellent! Excellent!" they said, then asked: "But would you mind, Herr Fokker, making one final test for us?"

Anthony Fokker was bewildered, but said, "Not at all. What do you have in mind?"

"We realize your device works under these ... er ... factory conditions, but we feel that before awarding recognition, and a contract for its manufacture and application to your airplane, it should be demonstrated under active service conditions."

"You mean you expect me to go up to the front and shoot down a French or British airman?"

The committee bowed in full agreement.

"But I am a Dutch subject. I am neutral in this war."

"You also have several German contracts. You may have a very remarkable invention here, Herr Fokker. You wouldn't want to lose the financial reward, would you?"

Fokker felt trapped. There was no way out, and in a few days he and his little monoplane were sent to the front, where he was introduced to members of General Josias von Heeringen's liaison headquarters staff. The gun and its interrupter gear were demonstrated again before the German Crown Prince, who was delighted with the whole idea, but apparently confused as to who Herr Fokker was.

"I take it your father devised this gun and its interrupter gear," said the Crown Prince, beaming.

Young Anthony explained that his father was still in Holland and that it was he who had invented the gear.

But although the Crown Prince was delighted with the Fokker device, the top brass never gave up the idea of having Anthony try it out against the enemy. They even supplied him with a German Aviation Service uniform, a couple of war ribbons, and an identification card that presented him as Leutnant Anthony Hermann Gerard Fokker of the German Air Force.

Young Fokker went aloft for two days seeking out French or British aircraft, but there seemed to be very little activity in that area. Then moving up to the Douai front, he finally caught up with a French Farman two-seater that was tooling along some two thousand feet below.

Whether Fokker actually went down to attack the Farman will never be known. Years later when he wrote his memoirs for an American publisher he claimed that he decided then and there to abandon the whole idea. He could not find the determination to attack another plane, even though success would bring him large financial rewards. He claimed that instead of shooting at the Farman, he returned to the flying field at Douai.

"I am sorry, sir," he explained, "but I cannot in all conscience take such a part in this war. I am ready to cancel my contracts and return to Amsterdam."

From all accounts, his decision was accepted; he was relieved of the requirement, and his Eindekker was turned over to the German airman, Leutnant Oswald Boelcke, who, after several days of instruction aboard the machine, took it over and tested out the gun against the enemy. Anthony Fokker turned in his uniform and returned to Schwerin.

OSWALD BOELCKE TAKES OVER

To get the record straight, it should be explained that on June 30, 1915, Leutnant Boelcke took Fokker's machine on what might be considered an escort patrol, covering a number of two-seaters assigned to a special mission. A French plane, type not designated, attacked one of the German two-seaters, and realizing that here was an excellent opportunity to find out what the gun would do, Boelcke nosed down to intercept. He soon discovered that the dragonfly Fokker was more sensitive on the controls than anything he had flown before, and he did not put on a very good show. Also, the realization that his gun was actually firing a stream of bullets through his propeller may have aroused some concern. At any rate, he lost sight of his foe, after firing one burst in his general direction, and never found him again and could therefore not claim a victory.

A week later, July 6, 1915, Boelcke finally scored—but not with the front-firing gun. He was flying a two-seater Albatros and was attacked by a French Morane. Neither of these aircraft was equipped with front-firing guns, but in the ensuing scramble Boelcke's observer put a burst into the French pilot, and the Morane went down and crashed in German territory. This victory, scored by the gunner, was credited, *of course*, to Boelcke.

In the meantime a few of these Fokker gears had been assembled, and E.1's so equipped were sent to Boelcke's squadron at

Douai; one of these machines was given to Max Immelmann, and it was this German ace-to-be who first scored with this fixed weapon.

On the evening of August 10, Boelcke's Section 62 gave a party to celebrate certain honors that had come to the unit. As considerable beer and wine were drunk—and Boelcke had consumed his share —most of the pilots overslept the next morning. It was on this particular day that a squadron of British B.E.2c Quirks, disguised as bombers, appeared over the Douai drome and dropped fifty-pounders all over the landscape. Boelcke was aroused finally and, clad only in his nightshirt and without breeches or boots, took off. But Immelmann had taken off before him, and by the time Boelcke reached the enemy formation he saw one roll over, nose down, and plunge on to force-land near by. Boelcke raced to catch up and finally brought his Fokker to the tail of one of the British planes. Taking a clean sight he pressed the trigger, fully expecting to see the B.E. go up in flames; but nothing happened. The Parabellum gun jammed before a shot was fired, and in trying to clear the stoppage, Boelcke yanked too hard on the cocking handle and split the cartridge case so that the breech was fully jammed and fouled completely.

Immelmann, meanwhile, had gone to inspect his victim and discovered that the Quirk carried only a pilot; the gunner's place had been taken up by the bomb load. That explained why he had had no trouble in getting on the tail of the Britisher. The pilot was wounded in one arm, but more than forty bullets had passed through the instrument panel and battered the R.A.F. engine to junk.

Thus it was Max Immelmann, the Eagle of Lille, who first proved the value of Fokker's gun gear. The date was August 11, 1915, but because so few of them were available, it was not brought immediately to the attention of the French or British authorities. The unfortunates who had been shot down were either killed or captured and could not make a report on this new form of German attack. But a very young, impetuous German pilot, flying a new Fokker monoplane with the fixed gun, became lost in a fog and, running out of fuel, landed in French territory and unwillingly gave the Allies an undamaged Fokker-gun monoplane. He had ignored the rule that any pilot flying the new Fokker was not to risk crossing the front line, and in this infraction we see poetic justice for the undamaged Morane that Roland Garros had presented to the Germans.

This revelation started frenzied fixed-gun activities on both sides of the line, and armament engineers were put to work on all forms of interrupter-gear projects. Some of this has been explained previously, but a few readers may wonder why Garros' deflector collar was not adopted, at least as a temporary measure. The only answer to this is that when Roland Garros failed to return that day, his superiors came to the conclusion that what they had long feared had happened: the device had betrayed him. It might, they concluded, have deflected a round in such a manner that the engine was damaged or the pilot himself killed. It was some weeks before they learned that Garros was still alive and well, and more time was consumed in finding out what had really happened.

Although a few fixed-gun Fokkers were available to Boelcke's section and some victories were being scored with this weapon, the Allies were not exactly idle. The Nieuport was firing a fixed gun from a bracket on its top plane. The British D.H.2 required no interrupter gear of any kind, and Major Lanoe G. Hawker of Number 24 Squadron was running up an impressive score with this mount. In fact, records disclose that the D.H.2 was more than a match for the Eindekker, in that the gun was mounted flexibly and could be tilted or turned in a small arc to make up for any difficulty in getting a direct nose-on attack. Then too, the British F.E.2b, the Vickers F.B.5 and F.B.9, all good two-seater pusher types, were quite capable of taking care of themselves in addition to performing varied tactical missions. While Fokker's early gun gear was an improvement over Garros' deflector collar, it in no way afforded aerial superiority or justified the careless alliteration "Fokker fodder."

THE IMMELMANN FABLE

Max Immelmann, who immediately zoomed to fame—in German newspapers, at least—began his career with little promise. He had joined the Dresden Cadet Corps when he was fourteen and rose to an ensign's rank in an engineer battalion. He was a smart mathematician, but a not particularly good soldier, and when promotion lagged, he denounced the Army and resigned his commission in 1912.

Within a few days of the outbreak of the war he was ordered to report to his old regiment, but applied instead for a transfer to the Air Service, and was delighted when he was sent to the Aldershof Flying School on November 12, 1914. Surviving a number of training crashes, he was sent on April 12, 1915, to Flying Section 10 at Vizry, where on his first flight he smashed up an L.V.G. Two days later, while ferrying a brand-new aircraft, he crashed that one too. Within a week Section 10 shipped Max to Section 62 located at Doberitz, and here he seemed to improve. Oswald Boelcke was also a member of Number 62 and these two, although Oswald was a commissioned officer and Max a noncom, formed an immediate friendship.

Max Immelmann won his first Iron Cross—for being shot down! On June 3, while flying a photography patrol, a Farman caught up to him; its gunner put a burst in Max's engine and he had to make a wild scramble to get down safely. He must have brought back some worth-while film, because he was given the decoration.

When Anthony Fokker delivered his fixed-gun monoplane to Section 62, Boelcke allowed Immelmann to fly a couple of check-out flights aboard the machine, and when a second E.1 was received it was turned over to Max. His first victory with this weapon on August 11 has been related; it was not until September 9 that he scored again—another Quirk—and a third B.E. was shot down on September 21. Then in the middle of all the honors and awards, Immelmann was shot down himself by, of all things, a Farman two-seater. Apparently the observer caught Max napping and put nine holes in his gas tank, then proceeded to shoot away the undercarriage. Immelmann was exceedingly lucky to wobble down for a safe landing.

By December 15 Immelmann had scored seven victories; that hardly confirms the Fokker-fodder appellation, since it had taken him more than four months to run up this score. He was given his commission and enjoyed much acclaim. His accomplishments were standard features in German newspapers. He had several interesting engagements through the early days of 1916, but failed to add to his score until January 12, when a force of British machines crossed the lines on a bombing attack. Immelmann, Boelcke, and a pilot named Von Osteroth took off to intercept. Both Boelcke and Immelmann scored victories. Boelcke downed an R.E.5, an early form of the R.E.8 reconnaissance plane. A party was held that night, during which it was announced that the Kaiser had "been graciously pleased to confer his highest war order, the Pour le Mérite, on the two victors of aerial warfare—Boelcke and Immelmann."

The party was a great success, but Immelmann did very little flying over the next few weeks. However, he picked up where he had left off when on March 13 he destroyed two aircraft and sent down another inside its own lines. That same evening he attacked four planes over Arras and shot one down in flames. In his report Max stated that he had shot down a Bristol, a type which was not yet in service, but by now the Eagle of Lille could do or speak no wrong.

When his score had been raised to thirteen, he began experimenting with armament and had his mechanic bolt three machine guns behind his propeller. The interrupter gear could not accommodate all this mechanism, and when Max tried it out in the air he shot his propeller to matchsticks and was lucky to get the plane down, since the shock tore the engine from its bearers and almost ripped the machine to pieces. Later on, he compromised and settled for a two-gun arrangement, but once more the guns ran amok, and shot his airscrew to pieces, one chunk of which flew back and gave him a severe clout across the head. All these experiments and misfortunes played a part in Germany's explanation of Immelmann's eventual death.

On June 18 he took off with a Sergeant Prehn and a Corporal Heinemann, and they encountered two F.E.2*b*'s of Number 25 Squadron, R.F.C. The aircraft met over Annay and an F.E. carrying Lieutenants Robinson and Savage went down under the concentrated fire of all three Fokkers. Lieutenant G. R. McCubbin and Corporal J. H. Waller in the other British pusher put up stiff resistance. Lieutenant McCubbin fired several bursts and was then wounded in the arm. The aerial gunner, Corporal Waller, held on and shot Immelmann down and made the Fokker crash. Max was killed, but rather than admit that their *Adler von Lille* had fallen before the guns of an old two-seater, the Germans persisted in reporting that Immelmann's plane had broken up in midair when his guns ran wild and caused structural breakdown. It is quite evident from reliable British sources, however, that Corporal Waller was entitled to the victory.

Thus the war in the air progressed. The gun had been given wings and a new breed of airman was entering the lists to stage glorious battles in the sky with aircraft designed, built, and equipped for aerial fighting. Fantastic history was to be written day after day. Every combat was new, every result vital to the eventual outcome. Nothing like what was to come had been recorded, or even imagined.

CHAPTER 5

The Zeppelin Hunters

Dozens of decisive battles were fought to beat back Germany's first aerial attack on Britain. Little of this anti-Zeppelin history has ever been told, but its pages gleam with the gallant exploits of Reggie Warneford, W. Leefe-Robinson, A. de B. Brandon, Frederick Sowrey, W. J. Tempest, and the legendary Frenchman who was supposed to have flown his Morane straight through a Zeppelin in order to destroy it. This chapter also tells how a Police Constable Smith, singlehanded, captured the crew of L.33 after the dirigible had been shot down over Little Wigborough and the ensuing conversation— none of which would have been believed by the most gullible producer in Hollywood. But it really happened!

THE FIRST BATTLE OF BRITAIN

DURING the year 1911 Prussianism was beginning to flex its muscles, and as the German Imperial Navy grew, German truculence was manifest. In one instance, in a lecture delivered at Kiel, Captain Von Pustau stated: "Let us imagine our being at war with England, this England, which from time immemorial has had an unwarlike population. . . . If we could only succeed in throwing some bombs on their docks, they would speak to us in quite different terms. With airships we have, in certain circumstances, the means of carrying the war into the British country, and in England one imagines with terror that one can already hear the beating of the screws of the Zeppelin cruisers."

This warlike sentiment was uttered after the aforementioned Hague Convention declaration against tossing bombs from aerial vehicles.

But Great Britain knew the German mind all too well, and preparations were being made for the very eventuality the captain had in mind. The then First Lord of the Admiralty, Winston Churchill, already had assigned flights of aircraft to co-operate with the Royal Navy, and by September 5, 1914, before any German bombs had fallen on British soil, had advised the Admiralty that "there can be no question of defending London by artillery against aerial attack. It is quite impossible to cover so vast an area; and if London, why not every other city? Defense against aircraft by guns is limited absolutely to points of military value. The Admiralty and the War Office, with the group of public buildings in the neighborhood, and the Houses of Parliament, constitute a military area, and are sufficiently guarded by the three guns mounted there. The effect of these guns will be to compel the airship either to expose itself to dangerous fire or to fly so high that accurate bomb-dropping would be impossible. Searchlights should, however, be provided without delay. But after all, the great defense against aerial menace is to attack the enemy's aircraft as near as possible to their point of departure."

CHURCHILL PREPARES LONDON FOR RAIDS

Mr. Churchill then outlined plans to have a strong overseas force of airplanes to deny the French and Belgian coasts to the enemy's aircraft and to attack all Zeppelin bases in reach. He set up other plans for telegraphic and telephonic communication, but more important, he conceived the idea of having a squadron of airplanes based at Hendon to attack enemy aircraft molesting London. Landing grounds were to be prepared in all public parks; all airmen assigned to this duty were to be trained to fly at night, and their machines fitted with suitable lights and instruments.

At this point it is interesting to note how the aircraft were equipped to destroy the German dirigibles. In the first steps taken, the field at Hounslow was to accommodate two B.E.'s that were furnished with grapnels, or bomb boxes. At Joyce Green there were two Henri Farmans that carried rifles, grenades, flaring bullets, and Martini carbines; a few hand grenades with rope tails were also to be taken along whenever possible. It must be assumed that the grapnels were to be lowered from the planes and hooked into the airships, after which the airplanes would turn away and tear the gas cells to ribbons. The bomb boxes, of course, were to carry whatever bombs were taken along. The rope tails on the hand grenades are mystifying, unless they were fixed to be slung great distances, or dangled below so that enemy aircraft would collide with the missile. At any rate, Mr. Churchill seems to have left no stone unturned to protect London from enemy air raids.

As expected, the enemy finally struck, but he did not draw first blood; on October 8, 1914, the Z.9 was destroyed in her shed when the Düsseldorf field was bombed. Next, another dirigible was damaged seriously in a raid on the Friedrichshafen factory. When Cuxhaven was attacked, although no Zeppelins were destroyed, the German officials decided they had better send their gasbags to war before the British destroyed them all.

The first Zeppelin raid on Britain was made on the night of January 19–20, 1915, when two airships struck at Snettisham, King's Lynn, and Yarmouth, and four civilians were killed and sixteen injured. In the next few months six unimportant raids were carried out that took a toll of six British casualties. The raid tempo was stepped up in the summer of that year and the enemy dirigibles at last reached London. On the night of May 31 the famous commander, Lieutenant Heinrich Mathy, and Lieutenant Karl Linnarz led special attacks that hit London, killing five civilians and wounding fourteen, and forty-one fires were started. Lieutenant Linnarz, while returning from this particular attack, dropped a note of defiance near Dunkirk to show his contempt for British air defenses, an act that was to have a grave consequence.

LINNARZ LEAVES HIS CALLING CARD

On this particular evening, May 31, Lieutenant Linnarz took off from his airship base located at Evere just north of Brussels. He gained operating height over Belgium, then allowed a friendly breeze to carry him in silence over the British Isles. He eventually reached London, where the inadequate defenses went into action. Searchlights cut the night sky into segments, but could not pick up the raider. The ineffective guns grunted and spat but succeeded only in showering the suburbs with shrapnel. The Home Defense pilots took off to do battle, but no enemy airships could be found. A few bombs were dropped, a few fires started, and the civilian casualty list mounted.

On a secluded airstrip across the Channel in Belgium, Number 1 R.N.A.S. (Naval) Squadron had been set up to intercept returning airships, but so far little had been accomplished. On this night, however, Lieutenant Linnarz' dirigible passed over a tiny high-wing monoplane bearing the new British cockades, in the cockpit of which sat Lieutenant R. H. Mulock, who was vainly trying to reach the altitude path of the big gasbag. Whenever he could get his nose up he would tilt a loosely mounted gun and fire a few shots at the Maybach engine exhausts.

"Gunfire!" screamed a lookout from one of the nacelle watch posts of the gasbag "Gunfire from below!"

The commander rushed to his control panel and bellowed for emergency measures, for he knew that if one slug from any gun flicked off a spark, the hydrogen in his ballonets would go up like the fiery belch of a volcano. His command brought a quick response; ballast was dropped and LZ.38 lifted to safety. When he had flown out of range of the puny weapon below, he became the strutting Prussian once more, and taking an engraved card from his wallet, he scrawled:

You English! We have come, and we will come again soon to kill or cure!

LINNARZ

He snatched a weighted message streamer from a flag locker and inserted his card and its message in the stitched pocket. "See that this is dropped as near the Dunkirk aerodrome as possible," he ordered. "We will fly over it on crossing the coast line."

NOW WHO WAS REGGIE WARNEFORD?

Lieutenant Linnarz could not know it at the time, but with that card he had signed the death warrant of another Zeppelin commander, and a young Britisher, Reginald Alexander John Warneford, became the executioner. The victim was a Lieutenant von de Haegen.

Reggie Warneford was a gay composite of the British Empire. His parents were jovial Yorkshire folk who shuttled about the world on various missions and pretexts, and young Warneford had been born in India, educated at the English College in Simla, and later at the Stratford-on-Avon Grammar School. The family then moved to Canada, where Reggie continued his studies. His formal education was slanted toward the arts and classics, but he showed the usual schoolboy enthusiasm for motorcycling, mountain climbing, and hazardous chemical experiments.

When news of the war reached the Warneford family, Reggie broke out of school and bought a ticket for England with his pocket money. He first joined the much publicized Sportsmen's Battalion, an infantry unit made up of well-known sporting and athletic figures. However, since most headlined athletes are attuned psychologically for sport only, not war, the Sportsmen's Battalion was slack in unfurling its battle flag. Fearing the conflict would end before the delicate athletes could be whipped into combat condition, Warneford applied for an immediate transfer to the Royal Naval Air Service. By June, 1915, he was a flight lieutenant with Number 1 Squadron at Dunkirk, and his mount, a Morane Parasol, was armed with six incendiary bombs, a few darts, and little else.

Lieutenant Mulock was hardly a fit companion for polite society when he reported back to Number 1 Squadron. In wrathful tones, he complained to his C.O., Commander Spenser Grey: "There's no use trying to swat one wasp with a wisp of straw. A wise man would pour a kettle of hot water down the hole and scuttle the lot. What we've got to do is blast them out of their bloody sheds!"

And from that time on, Number 1 Squadron planned a new strategy, and its animosity was intensified when a Navy artificer beachcombing along the Dunkirk dunes found Lieutenant Linnarz' taunting message. Commander Grey accepted the challenge and sent a three-plane flight, under Lieutenant J. P. Wilson, to Furnes, just across the French-Belgian border; the rest remained at Dunkirk. This was done to disperse the squadron, because the Dunkirk field had become such an obvious target.

On the afternoon of June 6 Wilson's flight was ordered to report to Dunkirk, where Spenser Grey was holding a conference. Lieutenant Linnarz' calling card was displayed once more, and Grey explained, "The man who dropped this played merry hell over London about a week ago. Mulock did his best, but this Hun Linnarz returned to his shed at Evere unscathed."

"How do you know he's located at Evere?" Wilson demanded.

"Good boy!" Grey smiled. "I assure you he's holed up there. Keep thinking along those lines."

It was fairly obvious what Wilson was thinking. "One good night attack might be enough."

On their return to Furnes, Reggie Warneford, who was in Wilson's flight, confided that he had never been off the ground at night, to which Wilson retorted, "Well, there's no time like the present. We're taking off as soon after midnight as possible."

And that's how it started. Warneford was flagged off first, and before he realized what he had volunteered for, the Morane was well up in the air. He stared wide-eyed, then squinted as he tried to find the small grouping of instruments. A length of scarlet worsted, knotted to a center-section strut, flicked insistently at his nose, and he realized this very primitive indicator was warning of a dangerous sideslip. Gradually his eyes became accustomed to the yellow-gray nothingness beyond his Triplex windscreen, so he transferred his gaze to the altimeter. He was already at 3,000 feet!

Reggie looked around for Wilson and Sub-Lieutenant Mills, but there was nothing except the exaggerated roar of the Le Rhône and the silent drip, drip, drip of condensation off the center section that abrased his cheeks like the blade of a fret saw. A poisonous-looking glow he had never seen before hissed below; it was the blue-yellow flame of his exhaust. His indistinct compass float, dancing in a small window set in the bulge of the center section, showed something that looked like the letter W. Encouraged by this, he risked a turn, hoping to pick up his flight mates.

Although he circled for some minutes, he could find no sign of Wilson or Mills; but meanwhile he was adjusting slowly to the strange experience, and as the area remained fairly clear he wondered whether, regardless of his failure to contact his flying companions, he might still make himself useful. He was recalling that the Berchem-Saint-Agathe airship shed was just west of Brussels when something a few miles to the north caught his eye. He squinted and looked again. It was emitting the same blue-yellow flame as his Le Rhône. If that was Wilson or Mills, what the devil were they doing up there toward Ostend? And what in heaven's name was that long, black mass floating above them?

Wilson and Mills had made immediate contact with each other and, clearing the fog around Furnes, had headed for Brussels, seventy-five miles away. Then finding clear skies, Wilson decided to fly direct to Evere on the north side of the old Flemish city. Both of them hit their objective spot-on, and circling the shed area once, Wilson went in first, mainly to start a fire and give Mills a pathfinder target. He released three of his bombs from the primitive rack, but only created a great smoke pall. By that time the German defense gunners were aroused, and they plastered the sky with high-angle gun explosive. Then Wilson discovered that his last three bombs had become hung up in the rack and he was out of the play. With his Parasol wing fluttering, Mills finally went in, despite the ground fire, and pulled his bomb plug. All six of his 20-pounders slid clear and he was rewarded with a gigantic ex-

plosion that illuminated the sky for miles around. But Wilson, who
had conceived and planned the raid, had to return with little to
show for his effort.

Two weeks later British intelligence agents, working out of Antwerp, reported that Lieutenant Linnarz' LZ.38—the same airship
that had bombed London—had gone up in flames during the raid on
Evere. And in that manner, the R.N.A.S. took its revenge for the
impudent calling card.

LZ.37 GOES DOWN IN FLAMES

That same night the LZ.37, commanded by Lieutenant von de
Haegen, had been ordered to make a routine patrol between Ghent
and Le Havre. There was nothing particularly important or offensive
about this trip. It had been arranged mainly to give a number of
airship designers, specialists, and technicians from the Zeppelin
factory firsthand knowledge of the various problems experienced by
the crews on active service.

The LZ.37 was 521 feet long, and her eighteen main gas ballonets
carried 953,000 cubic feet of hydrogen. She was powered by four
new 210-horsepower Maybach engines and manned by a select crew
of twenty-eight skilled airshipmen. For defense her designers had
provided four machine-gun posts that were built into the outboard-
engine gondolas. These positions gave good visibility, a fairly wide
arc of fire, and efficient defense along both sides of the airship.

After flying north for a few minutes, Reggie Warneford stared
in amazement. He had encountered a Zeppelin that seemed half a
mile long! He had to twist his head from west to east to take in its
leviathan proportions. From its underside hung several glistening
observation cars, and the gleam of the fantail exhausts indicated
that the rubberized covering was daubed a yellow ocher. Warneford
wondered what the devil kept anything that big in the air. But this
was no time for cogitation. The Zeppelin's machine guns suddenly
opened up and slugs clattered through the frail wing of Morane
Parasol Number 3252. Warneford wisely heeled over and cleared
out of range.

He glanced around and saw that the fog was clearing up below. The Ostend–Bruges Canal was plainly evident. He decided that the big gasbag was heading for Ghent, when suddenly the huge snub-nosed dirigible shifted course and came roaring toward him. Two more streams of tracer-flickering machine-gun fire snarled from the forward gondolas and converged only a few yards from the Parasol. Reggie gave the Le Rhône all she could gulp and tried to climb, but the crisscrossing tracers penciled in a definite warning, and he had to peel off and dive. As he studied the situation he wondered what his carbine would do if he could hit something particularly touchy. After all, hydrogen . . .

He flailed the little Morane back and took the carbine from its prongs. Then maneuvering to a point below the mighty elevator and rudder framework, he gripped his control stick between his knees and, sublimely confident that he had not been seen, triggered a few .303 shells at the massive target. The first clip of cartridges was soon spent, and nothing encouraging had happened.

He stalked the LZ.37 a few more minutes, popping at it with his carbine, but it was like aiming at a cyclone-propelled haystack with an air rifle. Whenever he came within range or view, the German gunners sprayed the sky about him with generous bursts of Parabellum fire, and the persistent young Englishman was driven off time after time.

Von de Haegen then dumped some water ballast over Assebrok and left Warneford still potting away impotently from about 7,000 feet. From there the Zeppelin commander raised his speed and roared for Ghent. Warneford realized what had happened, but refused to admit defeat, and settled back to keep the Zeppelin in view and gain some much-needed altitude.

For the LZ.37 it was a race for safety, and while Von de Haegen maintained his height, Warneford was helpless, but the German commander knew that this was not an ordinary patrol. He worried about his V.I.P. passengers when he should have concentrated on maintaining a safe tactical procedure.

At 2:25 A.M. the Morane pilot, still stalking and trying to get above the Zeppelin, was delighted to see the big airship suddenly nose down and apparently head for a break in the 7,000-foot cloud layer that spread toward Ghent. Warneford had browbeaten the Morane up to 11,000 feet, hoping to get into a position where he could use his fire bombs, since his carbine ammunition was expended. Now the LZ.37 was actually below him, and for the first time he saw that its upper cover was painted what seemed to be a dark green and there was nothing resembling a gun turret on the top. The other guns were in the underside gondolas, and he was shielded from them by the bulging sides of the main framework.

She looked so big as he moved into position for his run-in that he felt he could make a landing on her topside. The ground smear that was Ghent lay below and slightly to the east when the gnat-like Morane nosed down for the 500-foot top panel of the LZ.37. He must have chuckled to himself as his wheels passed over the high elevator and rudder structure.

One ... two ... three! he counted as the Morane jerked with the release of each bomb. He reported later that he had expected the Zeppelin to explode immediately after his first bomb pierced the envelope.

Four ... five! he continued to count ... then a blinding explosion ripped up through the upper panel covering, baring the vague tracery of the framework.

Whong!

Spellbound, Reggie continued his run-in until the little Morane was swept up on a savage belch of flaming concussion, and whipped over with a violence that would have hurled Warneford out of his cockpit, had it not been for his safety belt. He gasped in astonishment, rammed the stick forward and tried to force her into a dive. Chunks of burning framework hurtled by as he floundered out of that aerial convulsion and streaked down through a curling pall of choking smoke. Over the next few minutes he was absorbed in skimming clear of the debris, getting back on an even keel, and frantically adjusting his air and gas mixture to dampen out a series of warning pops from the Le Rhône engine.

A few minutes later the doomed airship fell on the Convent of St. Elizabeth in the Mont-Saint-Amand suburb of Ghent. One nun was killed and several badly burned, but the helmsman of the Zeppelin had a miraculous escape. According to eyewitnesses, he jumped clear of the tumbling wreckage at about 200 feet, landed on the roof of the convent, crashed on through as if it had been made of matchwood, and landed in an unoccupied bed, suffering only minor injuries. He was the only passenger aboard the ill-fated LZ.37 to survive.

SAVED BY A CIGARETTE HOLDER

At 7,000 feet above the widespread carnage, Warneford waited for the wing of his Morane to part company with the fuselage. The Le Rhône snorted its wrath . . . and stopped cold! The gleaming wooden prop wigwagged to a halt just when Warneford figured he was at least thirty-five miles inside the German lines. Not a chance to stretch a glide and sneak home. There was nothing to do but accept the inevitable and hope for a safe landing.

Despite the darkness, the unaccustomed landscape, and the lack of ground flares, Reggie landed the beat-up plane safely in an open field—a turfed stretch that was shielded on one side by a long strip of woods. There was a darkened farmhouse near by, but no one emerged to question his unscheduled arrival. His first impulse was to destroy the Morane, but a quick investigation showed that there was a reasonable amount of gasoline in the tank—certainly enough to get him back across the line to Dunkirk or Furnes. His mechanical mind co-operated with his determination to escape, particularly when further investigation disclosed a broken fuel line, probably brought on by his violent aerobatics. A quick search through his pockets produced a cigarette holder. The wide outer end was exactly what he needed, so he broke it off, fitted it to form a journal at the original break, and bound the joint secure with strips of a linen handkerchief. An experimental tug on the prop assured him that the line was working again and sufficient fuel was reaching the carburetor, and he decided to try to start the engine himself. Fortunately, the Le Rhône was still warm, and after running through the starting sequence twice to draw vapor into the cylinders, he cut in the switch and snapped her over. The engine caught immediately; it was something of a scramble to get into the cockpit, but he succeeded, taxied to a take-off spot, and roared away.

As he approached the coast again he encountered fog, so he cruised up and down until he found a hole and dropped through. At 3:30 A.M. he checked in at Cap Gris-Nez, ten miles below Calais, where he picked up more fuel and called his squadron headquarters at Dunkirk. He was advised to sit out the bad weather and return to Furnes the next morning.

By that time the jubilant news was known, and within hours Reg Warneford's name was ringing from one end of the Empire to the other. All that week his photograph was flashed on hundreds of theater screens, to the delight of cheering audiences. That afternoon, in keeping with the traditions of the Silent Service, Commanding Officer Spenser Grey of Number 1 (Naval) Squadron posted a notice which read:

Though weather has been extremely unsettled, our pilots have been active and busy.

The next day King George V recognized Warneford's victory by awarding him the Victoria Cross, and the French government responded with their Cross of the Legion of Honor. And from that day on, the British people took a brighter view of the Zeppelin menace. More raiders would come to wreak more devastation, but there was always assurance that some young Britisher would mount the sky and take them on.

Flight Lieutenant R. A. J. Warneford lived only ten more days to enjoy the laurels of victory. He went to Paris on June 17 to receive his Legion of Honor, and after the ceremony was ordered to pick up a new Farman biplane at Buc. The machine was so new that most of its standard equipment had not been fitted, and more important, and most tragic, there were no safety belts in either seat.

An enthusiastic American newspaperman named Needham had asked to go along to Furnes, where he planned to write a story about Warneford and his Zeppelin victory. Reg agreed cheerfully, and they climbed into the biplane and took off. Almost immediately, for an unknown reason, the Farman pitched and bucked. Rolling over out of control, it turned on its back and Warneford and Needham were thrown out and killed, ending the brief but illustrious record of the first airman to destroy a German Zeppelin in the air.

ROUTINE ZEPPELIN PATROLS

Following Warneford's triumph, there were many baseless reports of other Zeppelin conquests. One of the most fantastic that persisted for weeks was that a French airman had tried to down a Zeppelin over Paris with a machine gun, and when that attack failed, boldly rammed the raider in midair by flying his Morane Bullet straight through the massive framework and, crashing out the other side, left a jagged outline of his machine. After that, the story went, the Zeppelin folded in the middle and dropped in a French cornfield. There was nothing to the report, of course, but faked photographs of this astounding adventure were on sale all over France for weeks.

Back in England the Home Defense squadrons flew seventy-nine sorties in 1915, but found no Zeppelins. Eight of the airplanes crashed on landing in the dark and three pilots were killed. The ground guns were no more successful. Expert artillerymen who could handle antiaircraft guns were at a premium and many of them had to be brought back from France to reorganize the ground defenses. The aircraft situation was even more tragic, for few pilots had had night-flying training. There was little in the way of ground control, and flared-path lighting was practically unknown. Some experiments were made with fuel cans stuffed with oily rags that were set out along the landing strip and ignited when planes were heard returning. There was no radio communication, and once off the ground, the pilots were completely out of touch with their superiors. Aircraft instruments were unlighted, and in concentrating on their location, pilots often found themselves spinning out of a stall. Blind flying was an aviation technique of the future.

The available, or devised, weapons were employed on a misconception of the vulnerability of airships. It was thought that the main gas cells were surrounded by an envelope filled with an inert gas, and that any bullets that penetrated would simply mix the inert gas with the hydrogen and no fire could result. To overcome this imaginary difficulty, Home Defense pilots were armed with bombs and explosive darts that, it was hoped, would burst inside the gas cells. Thus, attacking airmen were expected to gain positions immediately above the Zeppelins—positions that not only were difficult to attain but obscured the airships from the pilots' views. Several months passed before this fallacy was remedied, but while it was in vogue, airplane pilots were practically helpless.

In 1915 aircraft production was improving, and as more planes were made available, the R.F.C. took an increasing interest in Home Defense. In May of that year new stations were set up at South Farnborough, Brooklands, Hounslow, Joyce Green, Dover, and Shoreham. At each of these fields one machine was held at "alert" at all times—usually a Martinsyde S.1 scout. Each aircraft was supposed to be armed with six Carcass bombs (hollow pyrotechnic missiles), twelve Hale Naval grenades, 150 incendiary darts, and five powder (explosive) bombs. It had been decided by now that rifles were of little use, although R.N.A.S. pilot Warneford had carried one.

With all this preparation, planning, and gallantry of British pilots, no more Zeppelins were destroyed until the night of September 2–3, 1916—fifteen months after LZ.37 had gone down. This time it was a Quirk of Number 39 Squadron, R.F.C., that provided the weapon; on this occasion the victory was scored within sight of a million pair of British eyes, and the wreckage was piled up near the picture-postcard village of Cuffley in Middlesex.

The hero of this trumph, Lieutenant W. Leefe-Robinson, also had been born in India of British parents, and when his family had returned to Britain, he was put in school at St. Bee's in Cumberland, a small academy that produced three Victoria Cross winners. As a youth he traveled considerably in France and Russia, but by August, 1914, he had entered Sandhurst Military College. He was gazetted to the Worcester Regiment, but became disgusted with infantry training and in March, 1915, transferred to the R.F.C., where he first served as an observer. On May 9 of that year he received an arm wound while on patrol over Lille, and on recovery was given pilot training at Farnborough, receiving his ticket the following September. After various postings he eventually joined Number 39 Squadron, a Home Defense unit located at Sutton's Farm. Sutton's Farm became the famed Hornchurch fighter base from which many R.A.F. heroes of the Battle of Britain flew off in 1940 to defend their homeland once more. It may be of interest to note that it was from Hornchurch that such stalwarts as Paddy Finucane, Douglas Bader, Sailor Malan, Harry Broadhurst, Piet Hugo, and Brian Kingcombe flew to stop Goering's attempt to wipe out the Royal Air Force.

The Zeppelins were once more raiding Britain almost nightly and the civilian casualty roll was mounting. As in World War II, these raids, spectacular and damaging, did not seriously hinder Great Britain's war efforts, but the population was undergoing many sleepless nights. At the time the Zeppelin menace was probably overdrawn, as British newspapers made the most of every raid, but when we check the records we learn that over the four and one-half years of conflict, in both airplane and airship attack, 8,766 bombs were dropped, killing 1,316 and wounding 3,000—mostly civilians. Today automobiles kill more than 5,000 persons a year in England and Wales alone!

LEEFE-ROBINSON GOES TO GLORY

On the night in question Lieutenant Leefe-Robinson was sent off to patrol the area between Joyce Green and Sutton's Farm shortly after eleven o'clock. A warning had come through that Maybach engines had been heard approaching the British countryside. It was a beautifully clear night with a few puffball clouds, and the

stars twinkled in time to the throaty song of the B.E.2c's engines as
they rose to the challenge. Leefe-Robinson climbed to 10,000 feet.
Most Zeppelins of that day could cruise in comparative comfort at
12,000 feet and, if necessary, dump ballast and rise quickly to
higher levels.

Leefe-Robinson studied the landscape, then, at about 1:10 A.M.,
saw that searchlights had picked up a Zeppelin southeast of Woolwich. Some clouds had collected in this area, however, and the
searchlights had difficulty keeping the gasbag in their beams.

The Quirk pilot climbed to 12,000 feet, then flew in the general
direction of Woolwich, where he next saw the Zeppelin being fired
on by antiaircraft guns. Hoping to cut it off from an eastward direction, he moved gradually into an area that put him 800 feet above
the dirigible. As he maneuvered, the Zeppelin nosed into clouds and
disappeared, and although the young Englishman searched over the
next fifteen minutes, the raider completely eluded him. There was
nothing to do but return to his patrol area.

At about 1:50 he again noticed evidence of the dirigible—a red
glow northeast of London—and fifteen minutes later searchlights
picked it up and concentrated on holding it for the ground guns.
Leefe-Robinson saw shells bursting all around the raider and moved
cautiously until he reached 12,900 feet. Then, risking the ground fire
that was bursting high above the gasbag or well to its stern, he
bore in as some tracer shots passed dangerously close to him. When
he had the dirigible in line below him, he nosed down and flew
along *under* the craft and fired one Lewis drum of alternate Brock
and Pomeroy ammunition. This seemed to have no effect at first, so
he came out from below and tried a broadside burst, but this too
was worthless. In final desperation, Leefe-Robinson moved to a
position below and behind and from a distance of about 500 feet
poured another full drum of ammunition into its rear. He was now
at 11,500 feet.

Before the third drum had been expended the Zeppelin started
to glow and in a few seconds the whole rear section was blazing.
He scarcely had a chance to veer clear when SL.11 (Schutte-Lanz

type) exploded and threw wreckage in all directions. It fell a burning hulk, with its crew and commander, Lieutenant William Schrann, perishing in the blazing structure.

When Leefe-Robinson returned to Sutton's Farm, he discovered that he had been badly shot up by the Zeppelin gunners. There were bullet holes in one main spar; several had pierced his center section; and a gun guy wire had been severed.

Lieutenant Leefe-Robinson was honored with the Victoria Cross, but did not enjoy his award for very long. On April 5, 1917, he was a captain heading a six-plane flight of Number 48 Squadron's Bristol Fighters when his group was attacked by a Fokker circus. Instead of breaking up and flying as fighter scouts, Captain Leefe-Robinson first ordered his pilots to hold formation, then to try the Fee circle (all flying nose to tail). His element was badly shot up— it was the first and last time the Bristol Fighter was so mishandled —and Leefe-Robinson had to land in enemy territory with a damaged engine. He was taken prisoner and held in German compounds, including the infamous Holzminden fortress, where he was kept in solitary confinement for a time. His health was finally undermined, and shortly after he was exchanged with a few other physically unfit captives, he fell victim to one of the influenza epidemics and died January 31, 1918.

Leefe-Robinson's Zeppelin victory disclosed a device that permitted blind bombing through thick cloud cover. This was the invention of a German businessman named Hagen, who suggested that an observer in a small streamlined car be lowered on a long cable to locate the target while the airship remained unseen above in the clouds. This device was uncovered after SL.11 crashed in flames, and LZ.90, which had been in the air at the same time, had hurriedly jettisoned one of these observation cars in her frenzy to escape SL.11's fate. The car fell at Mistly in Essex and still may be seen at the Science Museum in Kensington, London. Whether the observer was still aboard and cruelly sacrificed—as indicated in Hollywood movies of the 1920's—has not been disclosed. The cable was quarter-inch steel about 3,000 feet long, and contained a brass core insulated for telephone connection. The car was lowered and raised on a winch, powered by one of the main engines, and in later developments contained a comfortable chair, chart table, electric lamp, compass, and bombsight. One of these observation cars was used on one occasion against Le Havre when that city was hit by well-aimed bombs at night from an apparently empty sky, as searchlights failed to detect the tiny observation car.

TROUBLE WITH PRISONERS OF WAR

Leefe-Robinson's destruction of SL.11 seemed to inspire the Home Defense pilots, and when eleven airships, including three of the new super-Zeppelins of 2,000,000 cubic feet, sailed toward England on December 23, 1916, Lieutenant A. de B. Brandon, also of Number 39 Squadron, sent down another.

This enemy formation headed for the Essex coast and by midnight L.33, commanded by Lieutenant Bocker, had moved into position over East London and dropped twenty bombs. As she turned away, an engine was hit by a chunk of antiaircraft shell, a propeller was damaged, and pieces of shell splinter punctured the bag. When a second shell caused more damage, Lieutenant Bocker decided to turn for home. Near Chelmsford, Lieutenant Brandon appeared aboard his B.E.2c and engaged in a running fight for nearly half an hour. Drum after drum was expended, but the airship refused to catch fire; and L.33 was so severely damaged by now that her commander decided to put her down in a field near Little Wigborough in Essex. From this time on, a comedy was played out to the very limit.

The Zeppelin flopped down on her crushed belly only a short distance from two small cottages, and although Lieutenant Bocker intended to set his ship afire, he was gentleman enough first to warn the cottagers. When he could arouse no one after knocking on the doors of both homes, he went back to his wreck and carried out his plan, but as it happened the whole dirigible burned without damaging either of the two little cottages. It was revealed later that one home held a stone-deaf woman who slept through the whole affair, while in the other a woman had been so frightened that she had hid under her bed and refused to answer Lieutenant Bocker's knock.

Having fulfilled his duty, the Zeppelin commander next formed his crew into some military order and started to march them to the nearest military post, but was stopped by a village policeman on a bicycle. When he explained his situation and asked to be guided to the nearest military depot, Constable Charles Smith wanted no part of a German's requests and promptly herded the crew into the Meldon Police Station cells.

Then Lieutenant Bocker's second-in-command asked Constable Smith to advise his sister that he was down and safe.

"Now 'ow would I do that?" Constable Smith gasped. "We're completely out of touch with Germany, you know."

"But it will be easy. My sister lives near by, here in Essex," the German dirigible officer explained.

It seemed that the lady in question was the wife of a well-known local landowner and had failed to explain her birthplace; she was advised of Clause 18b of the Defence of the Realm Act and interned for the rest of the war.

On the evening that saw the end of L.33, Lieutenant Mathy was aboard L.31, and with L.32, with Lieutenant Peterson in command, was probing over Dungeness. Lieutenant Mathy seemed to bear a charmed life. He and his crew must have been bullet-proof and L.31 indestructible. Nothing daunted him, and after carrying out bombing raids and free of his loads, he would move about the British Isles on important reconnaissance ventures. He and his L.31 might appear first over London, and a short time later be photographing the Portsmouth dockyards or inspecting the activities of the industrial Midlands.

This particular evening Mathy and Peterson had intended to strike at London, but while L.31 was guided direct in a bold stroke, Peterson appears to have hesitated and for a time floundered about over Tunbridge Wells. Finally, at 12:10 A.M. he turned north and headed for the Thames. Mathy was well hidden in cloud cover over the southern section of the river, but Peterson's L.32 ran into a clear area and was picked out immediately by searchlights. Gunfire bracketed him, so he dumped his bombs wildly, some of which fell on or near Sutton's Farm.

Lieutenant Frederick Sowrey of Number 39, who had taken off a short time before, crossed directly over the path of the retreating dirigible and, when he was at 13,000 feet, saw L.32. When he was within range he emptied three drums of Brock, Pomeroy, and tracer into the gasbag; upon which the outer envelope first caught fire, and the airship finally fell on Snails Farm, Great Bursted, near Billericay in Essex.

Lieutenants Sowrey and Brandon were awarded the D.S.O.

Lieutenant Mathy escaped by darting into heavy mist in the Lea Valley, but before he left he dropped bombs along a long line across the south of London that killed twenty-two people and injured seventy-four. This was Mathy's fifth successful raid.

MATHY'S FINAL RAID

It was his sixth that saw his finish, and again it was a pilot of Number 39 Squadron who proved to be his nemesis. Lieutenant Mathy's final flight was made on October 1, 1916, and for the first time he seemed to waver from the threat of gunfire. He did not get to London, but hesitated as he approached the northern limits of the city and jettisoned his bombs on Cheshunt. Five 600-pound bombs fell on a sports field, inflicting little damage, but others battered 304 private homes and flattened 6½ acres of greenhouses. There were no casualties.

Second Lieutenant W. J. Tempest, who had taken off from North Weald, was patrolling toward Joyce Green when he first sighted L.31 and set out after her. When he was at 14,600 feet over southeast London he noticed a small cigar-shaped object resting on a pylon of searchlight blades. He knew it must be at least fifteen miles away, since he was on one side of London and it was on the other, and to get to his quarry he had to fly through a hell storm of exploding rounds, blinding searchlight glare, and falling chunks of antiaircraft shells. It was a veritable inferno.

"Suddenly I realized," Lieutenant Tempest reported later, "that either the Zep sighted me or something had caused the commander to turn around. He unloaded his cargo of bombs all in one lump, tilted his nose up, and proceeded to race away northwards. At the time he dropped his bombs I judged him to be at about 11,500 feet. I made after him at the 15,000-foot level and was gratified to realize I was overtaking the dirigible. Again the antiaircraft fire was intense, and when I was about five miles behind the raider I suffered a very uncomfortable time."

Then, with all his problems, the mechanical fuel pump that was used to maintain pressure in his gas tank broke down and he had to resort to a hand pump, an exercise that was most exhausting at that altitude. Pilots of that time had no oxygen system to draw on, and the effort must have taken great determination.

As he closed in on L.31 he was relieved to note that the ground fire had quieted down, but the Zeppelin had reached 15,000 feet and was moving at greater speed. Tempest realized that he had but a slim chance to hold on, so he risked all in one dive as the dirigible started to "climb like a rocket." Pumping like mad to keep his engine supplied, he went down and fired one long burst dead into the bag. Continuing on and passing under it he triggered another burst and spat tracers in all directions. He maintained a position close under the rudders and elevators, where he was safe from the enemy guns. He fired part of another drum, then saw the whole envelope glow like an enormous Japanese lantern. A long, licking flame flickered toward the nose and Tempest knew she was on fire. L.31 climbed furiously for about 200 feet, and as the Quirk pilot continued on, she nosed down as if trying to collide with him.

Tempest put his nose down and dived for his life, and the doomed dirigible continued after him. "I expected every minute to be engulfed in its framework and flames. Finally I forced my bus into a spin and just managed to corkscrew out of the way as L.31 passed me, roaring like a giant blowtorch."

He righted the airplane, continued on down, and watched the dirigible hit the ground amid a great upsurge of sparks. To relieve his feelings Lieutenant Tempest sat and fired off a number of Very light cartridges, after which he said he felt sick and giddy and so exhausted that he had difficulty in finding his field. On landing in a low fog he turned over and cut his head on the machine gun.

With the gallant Mathy gone and four more of the original nine Zeppelin commanders dead or captured by the end of 1916, all pride and ambition were gone from the German Airship Service. The last Zeppelin had bombed London and as the defenses improved and spread, alternate targets, safe enough for airships, were more difficult to find. The roar of German bombs on Britain was practically stilled.

Now the enemy had to resort to heavier-than-air bombers, a decision that produced the famed Gotha, a name that became a household word in England through 1917 and 1918. The machine, a twin-engined biplane, bore many of the characteristics of Britain's Handley Page 0/400, one of which had been delivered intact into German hands through a navigational error on February 2, 1917. It is of interest to note that although the Gotha was in blueprint form as early as the autumn of 1916, no service types were available for actual raids until June 5, 1917, and other than the biplane tail of the Handley Page, both machines were startlingly similar. Both had nose-gun positions and "tunnel" or trap-door mountings to fire down and under the tail.

CHAPTER 6

The Advent of the Aces

With the continued development of the front-firing gun, imaginative and persistent airmen fought hundreds of individual battles, all decisive in their results and scope. These combats proved or disproved new theories. They raised unknown pilots to acedom and world-wide renown. They put the stamp of acceptance on aircraft or engines. They dominated the war news and hundreds of young men all over the world yearned to emulate the extraordinary exploits of the airmen of that era—a yearning and interest that continues to this day. No facet of war has ever approached the romantic appeal of these days of knightly combat in the sky. Everything conspired to make it so: the period of time, the equipment, the relationship of the machine gun to the maneuverability of the aircraft, and the fact that men had never before engaged in such thrilling combat.

HOW WERE VICTORIES CONFIRMED?

FOR many years the author has enjoyed discussions with aviation enthusiasts and has carried on pleasant correspondence with readers of his articles and stories concerning the reliability of victory claims, or the records compiled by certain high-scoring aces. The viewpoints spread from honest skepticism to complacent belief. There are those who are certain that many aces were denied "kills" because of arbitrary rulings, while many subscribe to the theory that certain aces were deprived of successes because most of their fighting took place too far over the enemy lines. Some grumble that certain "pot hunters" must have had friends in the kite-balloon squadrons who would confirm any claim made, and others point out that there were many of the idealistic type who never bothered to make any claims at all.

In the light of my own experience I am puzzled how victory records could be kept with any degree of accuracy. True, there are impressive-looking lists bearing the type of plane shot down, the date and in what sector the fight occurred, but I have seen many air combats involving various types of aircraft on both sides of the line, and in most cases I would hesitate to state who shot down whom.

Werner Voss's finish affords an interesting example. The famed German airman, one of the few to risk action on the Allied side of the line, had been trapped by a flight of Number 56 Squadron's S.E.5's led by Captain Jimmy McCudden. It was a wild foray with Voss smack in the middle and trying desperately to fight his way out. Every pilot in the flight must have fired at least one long burst at him. At the same time a flight of our Bristol Fighters of Number 22 Squadron came up and circled the fringe of action and several of our gunners shot at the unfortunate; but when it was all over and Werner Voss had gone down, the victory was credited to Lieutenant Erwin R. Rhys-Davids.

Why? Who decided whose burst had finished the Krefeld Dragoon? True, Rhys-Davids had followed Voss down and had fired the last few rounds at him, but by that time the German ace could have been dead; certainly he was out of control. Was the "kill" credited to Rhys-Davids because he was a popular—and most headstrong—youngster, or, as was done so many times, were cards cut to see who should be given the victory and any particular decoration that may have been awarded for the engagement?

As pointed out in the Introduction, how can anyone tell how many planes he shot down in a dogfight? In most instances there isn't time to make sure your enemy has caught fire or that a wing has finally pulled away, and there simply isn't the opportunity for other members of your flight to gaze on your handiwork and confirm your reports. Some airmen claimed every machine they fired at, while others were equally reticent. At best, the system must constitute some sort of a gentleman's agreement by which any reputable member of the flight has his claims substantiated fully by those who were in the air at the same time.

But what about the "lone wolf" operator, the pilot who preferred to prowl about the upper regions alone? There were many such, and most of them were credited with high scores; but who confirmed their claims? Certainly the kite-balloon observers could not check the outcome of every engagement, especially if it was fought at a high altitude. However, the air-war histories are filled with the tales of these heroes, and their scores are presented as gospel.

I recall one hectic afternoon early in 1917 when I was certain I had shot down three Albatros two-seaters. At the immediate time my pilot agreed that he had seen all three go down completely out of control. We were about twelve miles inside the German lines, and during the tag end of this engagement one of our planes had to land with engine trouble, and our flight commander was making a game, but senseless, quest to pick up the crew. Seeing this, my pilot joined in the attempt, which was unsuccessful. When all this wild activity was concluded and we had made our way back to our own lines, no one—not even my own pilot—remembered seeing my three planes go down, and I had difficulty convincing my flight commander that I had scored. I was credited finally with one, and was commended for going down to help out in the unsuccessful rescue of two popular members of our squadron—an act in which I had no choice!

Laurence La Tourette Driggs, a reputable historian who began writing air-war books before that conflict ended, has pointed out that many victories were never confirmed, and those that were often were erroneous. Many pilots never appeared on any ace list because their records were carelessly kept or their squadrons were destroyed in the many bombings of Allied and German airfields. This is a feature that few modern historians take into consideration. We of Number 22 Squadron lost much of our history when our recording office was damaged early in 1918, with the result that several pilots who were entitled to be aces have never appeared on any such list. My flight commander, Captain Carleton Clement, was one of this unlucky company. To my knowledge Clement downed at least a dozen enemy aircraft. When present-day historians search through the records they probably discover that there are no records to examine.

WERE ACES WORTH THEIR PAY?

The lists of aces in later chapters of this book are as reliable and authentic as can be offered under these circumstances, but at best are simply lists of men who fought with such courage and skill that they racked up a number of accepted victories. But an airman credited with fifty or more successes is no greater, no more courageous, than the man who scored ten. Is a Spad or Camel fighter who may have flown for six or eight months, and perhaps scored five victories, any greater or more important than a Quirk pilot whose equal time was spent spotting enemy targets or photographing the enemy lines? We know that air fighting was ideal for certain temperaments, whereas the stoic duty demanded of pilots and observers of the various two-seater squadrons was something else entirely.

The successful single-seater pilot might have been a complete washout at Army co-operation work. The most successful fighter, regardless of his score, was one who carried out his mission obligations to the full, day after day. If he scored often, yet consistently lost pilots and planes of his own flight, his worth was negligible. The headstrong and unpredictable, like Ball, Luke, Guynemer, Rhys-Davids, Voss, Nungesser, Immelmann, and Navarre, to name but a few, furnished whirlwind copy for the war news, but in the light of the theories of Hugh Trenchard and Billy Mitchell they seldom carried their weight or earned their pay. This may seem a treasonable appraisal of a few well-known war heroes, but in the long view it bears considerable merit.

However, the author will be the first to agree that single-seater pilots were not always cruising around hoping to find a sitting duck. Generally speaking, the grandstanding lone eagle had a fairly cushy time. He could attack or ignore the opposition, depending on how bloodthirsty he felt on any given day. There was no one to question his mood or courage. Who knows whether on the day he did not score, he may have spent his time flipping in and out of handy clouds, taking pains to avoid enemy formations, but piling up logbook time?

But if a fighter pilot is a member of a flight or element detailed to do a specific job, there is no backing out. He stays in formation, plays his part on the team, and distributes his allotment of fragmentation bombs and machine-gun ammunition. These low-down sorties were fifty times more hazardous than man-to-man combat at 15,000 feet. First, you risked the ground fire of ack-ack and machine gun. You had to know how to fly a tight formation or you set up dangerous collision conditions. You found yourself in real trouble if you became entangled with a balloon cable or the prop wash from a machine directly ahead.

But as so many of my readers have pointed out: "Your war in the air was as simple and direct in its conduct as anything in the Arthurian period. We understand it and it is easy to picture ourselves playing a part. When World War II opened up with its multi-cannon fighters, its super-speed, high-altitude bombers, and the complex radio-radar communications, there was no involvement. Pilots and aircrews were no longer individuals. They were just skilled operators of very intricate equipment. No; World War I saw the first and last of the true air fighter."

So with that pronouncement let us make a more careful study of the men who became the great aces.

BOELCKE, THE FIRST GREAT LEADER

Oswald Boelcke was the third son of a dedicated German school-teacher who spent many of his early years in Argentina, where he taught at the German Protestant School in Buenos Aires, before he returned home to accept the post of an assistant master at the high school in Halle. Later he was a full professor at the Antoinette School in Dessau. Oswald's brothers, Wilhelm and Friedrich, were born in South America, but he first saw the light of day at Giebichen-stein, near Halle.

It was decided early that Oswald would become a teacher, for he was croupy, studious, and liked books. Left to himself, he took to floating about in his grammar-school swimming pool, and when no one was looking practiced his stroke and kick. In a year or so he had gained some vitality, so much so in fact that he yearned for a uniform, the military life, and the strenuous side of adventure.

Unlike his brothers, who also hoped for military glory, Oswald did something about his dream. After deep reflection, he bypassed all regular channels and wrote a letter to Kaiser Wilhelm, in which he explained that his father could not afford to send him to a military academy, but that he had heard of some simple method of a palace appointment. At the time he was thirteen years of age.

One day a very impressive envelope was slipped under the door of Oswald's home, and his family was stunned to learn that Kaiser Wilhelm, evidently touched by the boy's sincerity, had enclosed an appointment to a near-by cadet school. "You will, of course, complete your grammar school subjects," the Kaiser had written in a friendly tone, "before you report to Lieutenant General von Schartzkoppen at Coblenz."

Oswald's brothers, Wilhelm and Friedrich, let out a bellow that could be heard all the way to Berlin. How could the sniveling little bookworm expect to get into the Army—and probably gain a commission too! Oswald just dug deeper into his books and eventually reported at Coblenz, where he served as color guard in a cadet telegraphic battalion. Later he moved on to Darmstadt, where he first noticed evidence of the fledgling Aviation Service, and devoted much time to his telegraphic duties, hoping to be selected for aerial observation work. Instead, because of his enthusiasm and his science background, he was sent to a school at Halberstadt, where he needed but seven weeks to qualify as an N.C.O. pilot.

By coincidence, his brother Wilhelm, who had enlisted previously in the Aviation Service, became an N.C.O. observer, and when the war broke out the two brothers were sent to the Champagne front. This set up an unusual situation, for Wilhelm immediately assumed the role of the elder brother and bullied and bossed Oswald until Oswald would agree to have him as his observer. This incident detracted from Oswald's standing with the other pilots, for they had little respect for a man who allowed himself to be ordered around by a brother who was a "mere" observer.

Throughout that first September, the Boelcke brothers carried out a number of routine observation patrols together, but later, when bad weather set in, they were grounded a great deal of the time. One day an officer observer requested Oswald to fly him on a special mission, and when they returned Wilhelm was on the Tarmac fuming because his brother had taken an officer as his observer. As a result, a marked coolness developed between them. Then on October 12 Oswald was awarded the Iron Cross for his devotion to duty, and a week later Wilhelm was granted the same decoration for having flown more miles on observation than any other German observer on the front.

Early in 1915 Oswald's bronchial trouble returned and he was sent to a hospital in Rethel for a rest, and on his recovery was posted to the German Aviation Service's inspectorate division, where he served for two weeks on routine assignments. Later, on being commissioned, he turned up at Douai, where we first met him along with Anthony Fokker and the synchronized-gun plane.

Although the Fokker fighter had promised the Germans air superiority, and obviously was a superior mount compared to most British extemporaneous devices and pusher-type aircraft, the Eindekker was woefully exploited, and its surprise factor was ignored.

Had the Germans first organized a complete squadron of these machines and trained a special corps of destroyer pilots to introduce the weapon, the effect would have been devastating. However, the Allies knew about it within a few days after Oswald Boelcke first flew the plane.

Few German airmen actually liked the Fokker E.1, despite its new armament and the prestige of flying it. Later on most of them preferred the new Halberstadt or the Albatros D.1, and when Boelcke indicated his personal preference for the Halberstadt, the days of the Eindekker were numbered.

THE RACE TO DEVELOP FIGHTER AIRCRAFT

The early part of 1916 saw a race for aircraft production as well as the first probing efforts toward fighter-squadron development. Throughout 1915 British factories had produced 2,656 war planes, of which 2,003 were two-seaters, 391 single-seaters, and 262 seaplanes or flying boats. In addition, 1,721 aero engines had been delivered in France and 371 held in reserve as spares. General Hugh "Boom" Trenchard also had taken over command of the Royal Flying Corps, and his firm hand is noted in the following order issued on January 14, 1916:

Until the R.F.C. is in possession of a machine as good as, or better than the German Fokker, it seems that a change in policy and tactics has become necessary. In order to ensure that reconnaissance and photography patrols are allowed a fair chance of success, all fighter aircraft will raid prominent enemy aerodromes and attack any hostile machine that offers combat.

Regardless of the considered superiority of German fighters, there was no question but that the British were expected to continue the initiative. As a result, Allied aircraft had to intrude on enemy territory throughout the war, whereas the Germans continued their economic policy of fighting only over their own areas.

To obtain the full value of available firepower, infantry machine gunners were being enticed from the trenches with the offer of flight pay—six shillings a day (about $1.50 in those days). History records that these young men, with no previous in-air training and still wearing their infantry uniforms and in many cases Highland kilts, did more than their share to stop the Fokker menace.

THE GERMAN AERIAL SET-UP

To clarify the German aviation situation it should be explained that by the early months of 1915 military flying was in the hands of a *Chef des Feldflugwesens* (Chief of Field Aviation) who was represented at the Army level by a *Stabsoffizier der Flieger* (Staff Officer for Air) who acted in a liaison role. In the spring of that year Class C aircraft—two-seater airplanes with a machine gun in the hands of the observer—were being introduced gradually. These planes carried out what the Army demanded in balloon defense, artillery co-operation, observation-photography, and when small bombs and anti-personnel missiles were produced, the Class C aircraft risked ground-attack missions against the enemy front-line earthworks.

It was not until British and French pusher types with their front-firing weapons, made this Class C program dangerous that German Staff minds appreciated an all-out fighter plane. Heavy losses of two-seaters were suffered in the Verdun fray, and even greater ones during the Battle of the Somme in 1916, despite the so-called superiority of the Fokker front-firing gun gear. As Oswald Boelcke was to point out, German two-seat aircraft were being ineffectively deployed so far as their having air-borne protection during critical missions was concerned. In the beginning, therefore, what fighters were to be developed with the Fokker gun gear were intended for defense, not for offense. It must also be understood that what a handful of Boelcke fighters were accomplishing on the Douai sector was but a small fraction of what was occurring over the whole 350-mile swath of the Western Front.

After the Verdun carnage, Hauptmann Haehnelt, Staff Officer for Air with the German Fifth Army, formed, on his own initiative, a group of small fighter units to combat the heavy losses the Class C

airplanes were suffering, and not until then did the true basis of
Circus formations become established. Later on, General Erich F.
W. Ludendorff, who earlier had favored a separate Air Force,
created—with the Kaiser's approval—the Deutsche Luftstreitkräfte
(German Air Force) and placed General Ernst von Hoeppner in
command. This officer made several important decisions and selected his staff wisely, and must be given much credit for the
development of the German service. At the same time a Major
Stempel, who was operating on the Bavarian Front, had formed
three units of fighter aircraft, each of which bore the title *Kampfeinsitzerkommando* (Fighting single-seater command) and it was
from Kampfeinsitzerkommando Number 2 that such stars-to-be as
Immelmann, Boelcke, and Max von Mulzer were recruited to join
the famed Section 62.

So it was late summer of 1916 before plans were formed to group
all fighting aircraft at the front into units composed solely of fighter
machines, and Boelcke was recalled from an inspection tour of the
Eastern Front to head and build up what we accept now as the
German Flying Circus.

GERMANY'S FIRST AIR HERO

If one realizes that the Circus concept grew out of critical necessity, not through the farsightedness of any one German airman,
Boelcke's career can be reviewed with clearer understanding. It must
be agreed, however, that it was his personality, drive, and ability to
transmit his ideas and his day-by-day example in the air that developed the circus into a fighting force.

Not that he had an immediate glory road; far from it. A study
of the early days of his air fighting gives a clear picture of the
tenacity and determination of the British volunteer gunners. The
Dessau expert scored forty official victories between July 6, 1915,
and October 26, 1916, thirty-one of which were French or British
two-seaters. Only four were Sopwith two-seaters, and most of his
proficiency was gained against old Farmans, Voisins, Quirks, and
R.E.8's. This is no reflection on his courage or skill, but it does show

how the fixed gun prevailed against slower, poorly armed machines.

In January, 1916, Oswald started well by destroying four British machines, a B.E., an R.E.8, a Morane Parasol, and a Vickers Gunbus. This last mount gave him an unforgettable fright. He had not encountered such a pusher before and possibly expected to make short work of it, but the British bus flipped around so fast and the gunner was so alert and skilled that Boelcke had to clear out and study this new situation. Going back, he tried to outmaneuver the Vickers but found this pusher to be a veritable gadfly. They jousted for twenty-five minutes and the gunner was giving Oswald a bad time. Gradually both ships lost much height and were practically down over the Douai airfield. At this point the Britisher made a foolish move. Boelcke took advantage of it and a short burst killed the pilot, and the Gunbus piled up on the edge of the aerodrome.

Oswald Boelcke was visibly shaken by this experience, but an official engagement with the Kaiser, who had decided to reward him with the Pour le Mérite, possibly erased the scare and helped him to forget the experience.

The month of March added little to his logbook, for he was transferred to the French front to take part in a proposed aerial offensive over Verdun. No sacrifices were to be too great. The cream of land and air forces were moved into the area, and every airman was expected to take part in the over-all program of aerial reconnaissance and rear-area bombing. Air fighting, as such, was to be ignored.

But Boelcke had no use for such a theory, and on March 13 he spotted a formation of creaky old Voisins returning from a raid over German territory. Since he was alone, he moved cautiously until he spotted a laggard that seemed to be having engine trouble, and when all factors were in his favor, he moved in like a shrike. Drenched with the impact of the first burst, the Voisin floundered upward in agony, fell off in a stall, and began to spin. Oswald had noted such moves before and suspected trickery, so he followed the big biplane down carefully. Both aircraft nosed through a layer of overcast, and when Boelcke came out in the clear he saw the Voisin in a wide, helpless circuit with the French gunner clambering along the spar of the lower wing trying to provide weight leverage to right the machine. Boelcke flew in so close that he could see the gunner's face, his fear-stricken eyes flashing his appeal for a few minutes of grace.

A short wave of mercy held Boelcke's trigger until several anti-aircraft bursts snapped him back to reality, and he felt it was folly to be humane when he himself might be shot down in hostile territory.

He sensed that his first burst had probably damaged the cable controls and that the gunner had tried to provide some artificial equilibrium in order to get down and perhaps save two lives. It was a gallant gesture and deserved its reward. But Boelcke never fired another burst. While he was considering the quality of mercy, fate solved his dilemma. The left wing of the Voisin dropped toward the earth and the plane rolled like a great bird in an agony of torment. There was a flash scene of a helpless man being hurled from his frail security and flung into the dreadful nothingness of the sky. With an ache in his heart Boelcke turned back to his own lines.

In successive days this German flyer shot down three more Farmans and now had thirteen planes to his credit. He became the idol of his Fatherland, and only Max Immelmann came anywhere near him in the *Kanone* lists. Max was a more spectacular showman and possessed the personal magnetism that attracts the affection of the masses. He gained more headlines and columns of news, but Oswald was entertained more often by the German nobility.

Since he was now burdened with the command of a *Staffel*, Boelcke was expected to assume reams of paper work, administrative responsibility, and the development of squadron training. It was at this time that his new evaluation of the Flying Circus was hatched.

After a routine inspection of the complete German Air Service he returned to Douai to learn that his war birds were no longer having things all their own way. The British were staging a gallant stand with their D.H.2 and their two-seater pushers. Boelcke possibly remembered his close call with the Vickers Gunbus. He also realized that the Aviation Staff was handling German two-seaters with little understanding of their full capability. They had been useless during the siege of Verdun, and German observation planes had been sent into the air with little or no escort protection. There was no teamwork or cockpit co-operation between the pilots and gunners, and as a fighting element, the aircraft were not worth the fuel they were consuming. Unfortunately, since Boelcke was instinctively a fighter pilot, he could not devise or suggest any improved two-seater strategy. The fixed-gun had set up a mental block where two-seater action was concerned.

THE PACE BEGINS TO TELL

Boelcke also experienced another psychological disturbance. The loss of Immelmann left a mark on him, and regardless of the varied explanations of Max's death, Oswald realized now that war in the air was no longer a romantic sport. It was fast becoming a deadly gamble in which very many factors played vital roles. These combined concerns needled the nerve-wracked hero into making childish denunciations and braggart threats against the British, and the German High Command took full advantage of these tirades to offhandedly encourage him to devise new tactics and to assume a more disciplined leadership.

These new fighting maneuvers were most efficient, and in a short time Boelcke's Staffel Number 2 became an outstanding squadron for its initiative, dash, and boastful confidence. All this was grist to the German news mill, and as the focal figure Boelcke found himself in an unenviable position. Unless he shot down a Britisher every day he was considered something of a slacker.

It must be said to his credit that he put up a great display. During the month of September, while showing his fledglings how it should be done, he destroyed eleven British machines. His bag included three D.H.2's, two Vickers Gunbus two-seaters, and two Sopwith 1½-strutters. Between patrols or during bad weather he made hurried visits to Berlin to push his fighter-squadron ideas, hoping to inject up-to-date viewpoints into the minds of the General Staff, which still thought in terms of kite balloons and long-range artillery with which to fight the stalemated war.

During one of these visits he became acquainted with a rookie airman, Manfred von Richthofen, the Prussian nobleman who had become a pilot. Boelcke was holding conferences at Koven when he heard of this headstrong young baron who, although a member of an Albatros two-seater *Staffel*, wished to become a fighter pilot. Boelcke needed all the dynamic types he could lay his hands on, for unquestionably the British held the initiative, an advantage they had gained since the Battle of the Somme.

Three days later Von Richthofen was heading for Jagdstaffel 2 and was a member of Boelcke's formation when Oswald scored his next three victories. Then on September 17, under the guidance of Boelcke, the young Prussian from Schweidnitz gained his first success, and before his light was extinguished Baron von Richthofen claimed seventy-nine more.

Oswald Boelcke's visits to Berlin resulted in another service improvement. He insisted that his fighters be equipped with the new Albatros D.1, a tough, sleek-flanked biplane that carried two fixed guns. He had seen enough of Tony Fokker's frail monoplane with its sports-plane structure, its tangle of guy wires, and unsatisfactory Oberursel engine. The D.1 was powered with a 160-horsepower Mercedes engine and had a top speed of 110 miles per hour. The fuselage had a wooden *monocoque* structure made up of light wooden formers covered with three-ply. The wings, tail surfaces, and control areas were fabric-covered. It was fast, maneuverable, and when employed in massed formations, it regained some of the lost superiority. It was not until the cheery little Sopwith Pup with its single fixed gun appeared on the scene, December 24, 1916, that this Albatros armada was challenged in any way.

Boelcke's Circus formations, while leaving great areas uncovered, did raise hob with any smaller elements encountered. As the days slipped by, Oswald brought his score up to forty. What the rest of the German Air Service was doing was another story but over the Somme area the Flying Circus was having something of a field day. At the same time, in the last four months of 1916, Manfred von Richthofen ran his score up to fifteen.

It will be seen that Oswald Boelcke was the inspiration and brains of the German Air Force. He no longer cared about his own score, for his schoolmaster destiny had caught up with him. He spent untold hours drilling newcomers, lecturing his flight leaders, devising new fighting tactics, and attracting ambitious candidates to his banner. He wrote out his views, sketched technical drawings, and toured his whole area giving talks and spreading his experience. He set up skeletal formations that were to become new *Jagdstaffeln,* and to make sure his pupils recognized him in the air he had his plane painted all black, a feature his understudy, Manfred, was to adopt—and take full credit for later.

BOELCKE'S TRAGIC FINISH

Another promising airman was Erwin Böhme, a youngster whom Boelcke considered a pilot superior to Von Richthofen, and had not tragic events cropped up to shatter Böhme's spirit, Boelcke's opinion might have been vindicated.

On October 28 Boelcke led a six-ship element on a formation drill. Von Richthofen and Böhme flew close behind their leader's wingtips. They were to observe his technique. Near Pozières, then inside the German lines, two D.H.2's of Number 24 Squadron, R.F.C., flown by Lieutenants A. G. Knight and A. E. McKay, were out on an offensive patrol.

Boelcke raised his right hand, his fingers clenched down, to signal the attack. Moving in from behind, he led his formation up and under the blind spots of the British pushers. Then came tragedy. In trying to maintain his wing position Böhme accidentally slithered into Boelcke's plane. To the pilots in the rear it seemed that the two machines scarcely touched, but the Albatros in which Boelcke had so much confidence was damaged seriously. Böhme's wingtip had knifed through the slim interplane struts, and the wing of the black airplane collapsed. As the bay folded back slowly, the leader's

Albatros turned with the drag of the wreckage. The stick went
dead in Boelcke's hand, and there was little height in which to attempt a recovery. The heavy Mercedes engine hauled the crippled
Albatros to its doom and plowed into the blood-drenched territory
of the Somme, the area that had seen so many of Oswald Boelcke's
victories.

Understandably, the German flyers had a hard time with Erwin
Böhme when he landed. He begged for a minute alone with a
service Luger, but wiser heads talked him out of that and com-
forted him in his grief. To his credit, Böhme returned to his duty
and eventually commanded the Boelcke Jagdstaffel, but his fate too
was explicit, for in November, 1917, Erwin Böhme was killed, the
day before he was to be decorated with the Pour le Mérite.

THE LAFAYETTE ESCADRILLE BECOMES A REALITY

On April 20, 1916, an organization of American volunteers was
accepted into the French Air Service and for want of a better name
was called l'Escadrille Américaine. On French rosters it was known
as N. 124 Squadron. The volunteers were William Thaw, Elliott
Cowdin, Kiffin Rockwell, Norman Prince, Charles C. Johnson, Clyde
Balsley, Victor Chapman, Laurence Rumsey, and James R. Mc-
Connell. All had taken and passed French Air Service training and
by now were fairly proficient Nieuport Scout pilots.

The airplane they were to fly in action was the Nieuport 17C.1,
one of the first of the Allied single-seaters designed to fire a fixed
gun along its line of flight. The arrangement provided two V
brackets mounted on the spars of the center section, on which
a Lewis gun was bolted so that its bullets passed just over the tips
of the whirling propeller. It carried the infantry-type ammunition
pan holding only forty-seven rounds, but later the air type carrying
ninety-seven rounds was furnished.

In the early mountings it was impossible to tilt the weapon in
order to replace an empty drum, and the fighter pilot with this
primary equipment went into action with only forty-seven rounds
of ammunition. Later the bracket was improved and the Cooper-

Foster rail allowed the pilot to draw back the gun, then tilt it to replace the drum. In this arrangement the weapon was secure at all times, and some Nieuport pilots, notably the famous Captains Albert Ball and Billy Bishop, used this device to fire up at enemy planes above them, thus utilizing the flexibility of the mounting.

These volunteer Americans, who were commanded by a seasoned French airman, Captain Georges Thénault, did not saunter into an aerial picnic. The opposition did most of its fighting well on its own side of the line. It had better equipment, and at the time its planes were better-armed. Also, French training, as far as air fighting was concerned, was not well organized. Formation flying and team tactics were not for the Gallic temperament, and their efforts were more often along individualistic lines rather than a general squadron effort.

Although they had a program of routine training comparable to that provided to any other in the French service, the original pilots of the Escadrille Américaine were handicapped to some extent by the language barrier. True, one or two spoke French fluently, but they did not think in French, and whatever theories or advice was available was given in French, then mentally translated into English.

Ready or not, the Escadrille Américaine, located at Luxeuil-les-Bains on the Vosges front, was soon taken on its first sortie. Captain Thénault decided that they should do an early-morning patrol, and ordered everyone out on the line by 6 A.M. This foray proved to be something of a scramble, for no plans had been made for maintaining a regular formation. This May 14, 1916, morning was misty, with small groups of cloud here and there, but over Belfort they identified the French trenches; and after drawing his stragglers together, Captain Thénault decided to take his fledglings over. The cloud bank was left behind, and ahead ranged the Alsace plain stretching toward the Rhine. Flying at 13,000 feet, they could recognize Dannemarie and the gaunt trench systems of the enemy.

This pleasant routine was soon shattered, however, when two large blobs of black smoke blossomed ahead, followed by two

crashing explosions. The Americans crouched in their cockpits as
more antiaircraft shells erupted all around them. The smoke spat
jets of scarlet flame, then gave off the telltale stain, white, yellow,
or green, indicating what type of ammunition was being fired.

After crossing the line Captain Thénault turned north. The town
of Mulhouse spread itself below; the twin lakes of Gérardmer
sparkled in the early light, and as the morning lengthened the
pilots noted ground activity and heavy guns pounding in the Hart-
mannsweilerkopf region. It was bitterly cold at this level, and most
of the American pilots noticed for the first time the effect of rarefied
air and soon learned to take long, deep breaths to feel comfortable.
The patrol, interesting and instructive to these neophytes, attracted
no enemy aircraft and they were not molested in any way.

Four days later Kiffin Yates Rockwell scored the first aerial victory for the Escadrille when he downed an enemy two-seater over
the old town of Thann with the expenditure of only four bullets.

Kiffin Rockwell was the epitome of the idealistic volunteer and
was probably the first American to volunteer his services to France.
He not only offered himself, but included his brother, Paul Ayres
Rockwell, when on August 3, 1914, he made a formal application
for enlistment with the French consul at New Orleans.

Unable to wait for the unwinding of consular red tape, these
two brothers sailed from New York on August 7, 1914, and on their
arrival in Paris enlisted in the Foreign Legion, along with twenty-
nine other enthusiastic Americans. Kiffin was quickly sent to the
front and by May 9, 1915, had been wounded in a bayonet charge,
an engagement that wiped out nearly half of his regiment. Although
not critically wounded, he had to drag himself across an open field,
clawing and hauling at tufts of grass or the roots of low brush.
He spent some time in a hospital and chafed with impatience when
he learned that his Third Regiment had once more gone into action
—and had again been cut to pieces.

The leg wound gnawed and pained, and although French officials
must have realized that he was no longer capable of long marches,
he was sent back to the trenches. About this time the first vague re-

ports of the possible formation of an American air squadron were heard, and Rockwell was among those who put in for a transfer, a release that did not come until September 2; but with Thaw and the others, Kiffin weathered the training, won his brevet on an old Maurice Farman, and became one of the original members of N.124 the following April.

AMERICA'S FIRST SCORE

The honor of scoring the Escadrille's first victory came to Kiffin on May 18, a "kill" scored under typical conditions of that day. He had decided to do a lone-wolf show on his own, and shortly after crossing the enemy lines his engine started to splutter, and he turned back, hoping to make some carburetor adjustment and continue his quest. Before any remedy could be made he spotted a German aircraft about 2,000 feet below tooling up and down just inside the French lines. He cut back on his engine and nosed down, by which time he realized that he had taken on a two-seater, and the buzz of hornets indicated that the enemy gunner was taking no chances on him.

The first burst caught Rockwell's Nieuport clean and the machine rattled with the fusillade. Kiffin did not turn away but kept straight on until he was about seventy-five feet from the biplane. He tugged on the trigger cord and his gun fired only four rounds. He had then to swerve sharply to avoid a collision, and as he passed the enemy plane he saw that the gunner had fallen away from his weapon, and the gun hung with its barrel pointing straight up into the air. The pilot also was draped over the coaming of his cockpit. The two-seater fell off helplessly and turned for its own lines. Smoke poured from under the engine cowling as the plane nosed down into a sharp dive. As Sergeant Rockwell circled to make certain of the location, the doomed airplane struggled toward its own area again and finally piled up amid the wire, shell holes, and debris of the enemy line, where it burned, assuring Kiffin of a clean confirmation.

It was Rockwell's first combat, the first time he had seen an enemy plane, and the first time he had fired his machine gun. An observation post telephoned the news of his victory to the squadron before his return, and his comrades provided a roaring welcome. The squadron armorer verified the story later, for only four rounds had been fired from the drum still attached to Kiffin's Lewis gun.

It was the Escadrille Américaine's first victory, and, although not particularly important in the over-all picture, it was most decisive and inspired the handful of Americans to even greater efforts.

BERT HALL, THE LEGEND

Whether or not they were ready for real action, the Americans next were ordered to the Verdun front. The machines were flown to the new field and all other equipment went by truck or tractor. The volunteer personnel now included Bill Thaw, who was a lieutenant, Adjutants Norman Prince, Bert Hall, Raoul Lufbery, and Didier Masson. Kiffin Rockwell, Dudley Hill, Paul Pavelka, Charles Chouteau Johnson, and Laurence Rumsey were sergeants.

This Bar-le-Duc sector was a hive of aviation activity, for there were many flying fields in the Verdun area, and the Escadrille Américaine was placed on schedule with other front-line units and given specified flying hours and missions. Their Nieuport aircraft were still the same early model, and all hands worked to keep them in action so that they could fill the many new duties. They had hardly settled down at Bar-le-Duc when Bert Hall shot down a German aircraft, the second credited to the Americans.

This Hall, not to be confused with James Norman Hall, was the "character" of the Escadrille, a mystery man, a typical soldier of fortune. He was a braggart, careless of his speech, one who would make a statement one day and contradict it the next. In one mood he would state that he had been born in Kentucky around 1880; on other occasions he roundly claimed Higginsville, Missouri, as his birthplace. He was at his entertaining best when he was telling amazing stories of how he had fought—on one side or the other— as an airman, of course, during the Turkish-Bulgarian war of 1912.

In the next breath he would relate that he had been in Kitchener's Army and had saved England at the Battle of Mons. Before his listeners could clarify these dates, Bert was fighting with the French Foreign Legion and taking credit for active service between August and December, 1914! He even wrote a book about his sacrifices with the British Tommies.

But with it all there were times when Bert was a lovable rogue, and no one would have questioned him had he insisted that he had guided Dr. Cook to the North Pole. It was useless to argue with him, for he probably would prove his point by producing a fur cap, a can of whale oil, and perhaps even a polar bear. He had medals, the like of which would bewilder the International Society of Numismatics.

Like Thaw and a few others, Bert sought his way out of the trenches and applied for transfer to the French Aviation, where, despite his long list of glorious air battles for the Turks—or Bulgarians—he displayed no evidence of having encountered an airplane before. Nevertheless, he went through the training courses at Pau, Avord, and Buc until he was brevetted on August 19, 1915. Through that early summer and the following autumn he was a member of MS.38, a Morane-Saulnier squadron, carrying out routine observation missions, and apparently doing his part, for he was accepted for the new Escadrille Américaine by April, 1916.

Once back in the company of his own countrymen, Bert came under suspicion of espionage. It seemed that while he was in training at Avord he was under continual surveillance by French Secret Service officials. At one time two Army Intelligence men, posing as student pilots, were assigned beds on either side of Bert's. He was seldom out of their sight, but from all accounts, he never proved to be other than a happy-go-lucky, garrulous, ne'er-do-well adventurer. His manners were not always courtly, and it must be recorded that his American companions found him difficult when playing cards, rolling dice, or signing mess chits. Although he had downed three enemy airplanes and been awarded the Médaille Militaire and the Croix de Guerre, he was "invited" to leave the squadron.

In reply, Bert, with majestic dignity, requested a transfer, and for a short time was posted to N.103, a French Nieuport chasse squadron with which he served for about a month and received another special citation that declared him to be a "clever, energetic, and courageous pilot, full of spirit, daily attacking enemy planes at short range."

Why he left N.103 Squadron has never been clearly explained, but in January, 1917, he was granted permission to accompany a French Aviation Mission to Rumania—although some reports have it that Bert went to Russia. Shortly after this assignment, Bert requested and was granted permission to return to the United States, ostensibly to join the United States Aviation Corps. He failed to turn up at any American enlistment bureau, and to this day he is still listed as a deserter in French military records.

Along with all these meanderings, Bert Hall found time to become a writer, and in a short time the bookshelves of wartime literature were agleam with his *One Man's War*, and *En l'Air*, two volumes that added little to military history, but mystified their readers as they attempted to prove how one man could be in several places at the same time.

As may have been expected, he came to an unfortunate end when he was killed in a tragic automobile accident. Few Boswells of the Lafayette Escadrille have awarded Bert much space in their journals—and that is unfortunate, for he must have been a fascinating character.

HAWKER, BRITAIN'S FIRST ACE

A British airman, now almost forgotten, had a tremendous influence on air fighting tactics in the Royal Flying Corps. He was Major George Lanoe Hawker, an ace credited with only nine victories, but his spirit, leadership, and quiet determination set the seed for the illustrious traditions and inspiration that carried so many other young Britons on to glory. There are some survivors of those rousing days who declare that Major Hawker must have downed at least thirty German aircraft, and explain that in his serv-

ice such successes were rarely set into the official records, and thus
he was denied his rightful place in the list of British air heroes.

Major Hawker fought on the Western Front from October, 1914,
to November, 1916, and in that time was honored with the Victoria
Cross and the Distinguished Service Order, and considering the
mounts and armament available at that time, his influence on combat flying in the R.F.C. cannot be overemphasized.

He was of medium build and height, a quiet, shy man with clear
eyes and a smile that hid an iron will and the heart of a lion. He
possessed an affectionate nature and on the ground was most
generous with his friendship. In his photographs, he reminds me
of my Captain Bush.

George L. Hawker had been born in December, 1890, and thus
was somewhat older than the average R.F.C. playboy type. He
began his teen-age education at the Royal Naval College but transferred later to the Royal Military Academy. He secured a commission in the Royal Engineers and was one of the first small group
of officers selected for pilot training in what was to become the
Royal Flying Corps. He was an ideal pupil and by March 4, 1913,
was awarded Aero Certificate Number 453 after making his gradu-
ation flight aboard a Deperdussin monoplane.

After the outbreak of the war Hawker flew an R.E.5 of Number
6 Squadron across the Channel and arrived in the war zone in time
to see the fall of Antwerp in October.

On April 18, 1915, flying a B.E.2c, Hawker headed for the Zeppelin hangars at Gontrode. He carried three melinite bombs and
a haversack of hand grenades. Arriving over the target, he was
greeted by a storm of ground fire, but he continued on and noticed
a kite balloon that had been set up for the purpose of signaling the
approach of attacking aircraft. He decided to tackle the balloon
first, and flew over it while the observer banged away at him with
a Parabellum machine gun. The first two melinite bombs missed
by a mile; he went in much lower and tossed over half a dozen
hand grenades, but had no better luck with these, and was being
harassed by the gunner. Hawker then decided to find the gunner's

blind spot and try again. Two more hand grenades were thrown, and when these blasted out a great chunk of the bag, the balloon gradually folded up and fluttered to the ground. Using this bulbous mass as a shield, Hawker next attacked the Zep hangar, and with his last melinite bomb scored a direct hit: a brand-new Zeppelin shed went up in flames.

This mission took about three hours, and on returning to his field at Abeele, he counted more than thirty-eight bullet holes in his Quirk. He was given the D.S.O. for his one-man raid, and shortly after, Gontrode was abandoned as a Zeppelin base and redesigned as a Gotha field.

In June, Hawker rigged a top-wing mounting on a Bristol Scout that held a Lewis gun in much the same manner as the Nieuport contrivance, and after testing it, he established an intelligence warning system by posting in the front line a number of mechanics who were instructed to telephone him whenever a German machine moved up near Allied territory. He also used a number of Quirks as decoys, and if an L.V.G., or an Aviatik, pounced on these unarmed biplanes, Hawker would swoop out of the skies with his wing-gun Bristol.

According to surviving members of his squadron, he soon had the Abeele front littered with the skeletons of German aircraft. At any rate, he became the idol of admiring British infantrymen, and his name was the first ever to be associated with this type of aerial warfare.

Over the next few months Hawker was a one-man scourge. He was in the air continually, not only as a fighter but also assuming his share of bombing and reconnaissance tasks. During the poison-gas attack near Ypres he flew low for hours on end, trying to hold back the German advance, and finally was wounded in one foot. This did not ground him, however, and he was soon back in action. On July 25 one of his reporters told him of an Aviatik prowling about near the British lines. Hawker's initial attack was so sudden and fierce that the German pilot nosed down until he had crashed inside his own lines. Later that afternoon Hawker caught another

Aviatik that was flying a photography patrol near Houthulst Forêt. One burst from Hawker's gun piled up the enemy plane in the British lines. Then returning to his own area, he encountered a Rumpler, and although the enemy observer sprayed the Bristol with Parabellum fire, Hawker nosed down, came up under the two-seater's tail, and sent it down in flames with thirty rounds of ammunition.

He was awarded the Victoria Cross for this day's work. He was next promoted to major and put in command of a new Number 24 Squadron which was being formed in England and equipped with DH.2 pusher fighters. Hawker put the outfit through five months of intense training, building up confidence, formation flying, and keen gunnery. When they went to France in February of 1916, the effort paid off, for Number 24 immediately ran up an impressive record. In the absence of a mechanical interrupter gear, the DH.2 became Britain's answer to the Fokker fighter. It had an unobstructed field of fire, was most maneuverable, and had a top speed of 105 miles per hour, compared with the 95 miles per hour of the Eindekker and the Albatros D.1's 110 miles per hour. Number 24 Squadron did so well with this mount that by the end of 1916, 222 DH.2's were in service in France, and these gnatlike fighters were to give Britain her great aerial edge during the Battle of the Somme.

By the middle of 1916, Number 24 Squadron was probably the best known on the Allied side of the line, and under Hawker's able leadership registered victory after victory. During the month of June the squadron had seventeen confirmed scores. In July, twenty-three more enemy planes went down. Over August, September, and October the pilots of Number 24 destroyed forty German aircraft.

Then the grim law of averages took its toll. Major Hawker was killed November 23, 1916, by young Manfred von Richthofen. This epic fight took place between Bapaume and Albert and was recorded as one of the most famous air battles of World War I. Certainly it was decisive for Von Richthofen, for he was just getting into his stride and this victory, his eleventh, over Britain's outstanding airman must have given him a great boost in confidence.

Details of the action are sparse, but it appears that Major
Hawker was flying alone when five Albatros fighters hove into view.
He attacked immediately, without hesitation, selecting the leader
as his foe. In the ensuing duel, which lasted for thirty-five minutes,
both airplanes kept at the wild merry-go-round, firing whenever
either could get a portion of his enemy's plane in his sights. Von
Richthofen, of course, had two guns, Hawker only one, and as they
circled, the fight moved deeper and deeper into enemy territory.
Then, as the Englishman realized his fuel supply was running low,
he made a move to break off and get back to his own lines. In the
flash of a few seconds Von Richthofen saw his chance and fired
a long double burst. It was the last of the 900 rounds his plane
carried, and one of these creased Hawker's skull, knocking him unconscious. Unable to help himself, he went down and crashed
inside the German lines.

That night Von Richthofen wrote to his mother:

Congratulations on your birthday. I trust this will be your last
in wartime. My eleventh Britisher was Major Hawker, twenty-six
years old and the commander of an English squadron. According
to prisoners' accounts, he was the English Boelcke.

He gave me the hardest fight I have experienced so far, until I
finally succeeded in getting him down ... Unhappily, we lost our
commander three days ago, and eight days ago a plane of our
squadron was brought down.

Von Richthofen's mechanics brought him the fabric serial numbers from Hawker's plane and several other souvenirs, among them
the Lewis machine gun, which for years could be seen over
the doorway of Manfred's old bedroom in his mother's home in
Schweidnitz.

NUNGESSER THE INDOMITABLE

An ex-cavalryman, Lieutenant Charles Nungesser, who had already won the Médaille Militaire for capturing singlehanded a
German Staff car bearing a party of high-ranking field officers,

joined Escadrille N.65, a Nieuport scout squadron, on May 23, 1916. The next morning he went out and destroyed an observation balloon, and his superiors were at a loss to understand how he had found his way about on this unfamiliar front. The truth leaked out shortly after, when it was learned that during a month's leave when he was supposed to be convalescing from a wound received in a previous bombing raid, he had been flying with the Escadrille Américaine—simply to keep his hand in.

Nungesser had transferred to aviation in November, 1914, and obtained his brevet flying bombers. He soon became known for his daring and determination and won a "mention" after completing fifty-five successful raids. It was after being wounded on one of these forays that his persistent request for a transfer to a fighter squadron was finally considered. Prior to this he had scored regularly with a Voisin's flexible gun, had broken every rule of discipline and flying regulations, and had in fact become something of a problem wherever he was posted.

The wound he received as a bomber pilot was the result of an antiaircraft shell that snapped him into a spin from which he couldn't recover. His plane crashed and he broke both legs, and the control stick dislocated his jaw and perforated his palate. This seemed to spell the close of Nungesser's aerial career; but as soon as he could move about on crutches he headed for Le Bourget, where he "borrowed" a Nieuport. Climbing aboard, crutches and all, he proved to himself that he could still fly, and induced his superiors to reassign him to a fighter squadron. It was following this that he had a few days with the American volunteers and scored another victory, which may not have been credited to him, since he was supposed to be convalescing at a rest hostel at the time.

Once he settled down with N.65 his career, which was to close with forty-five victories, was renewed. June 14 was a red letter day for he attacked four L.V.G. two-seaters, shot one down in flames, and put the rest to flight. Two days later he attacked and destroyed another balloon, and on the 19th he staged a battle with five Fokkers and almost lost his life. He destroyed one, but the others riddled him from every angle; he was wounded again, and lucky to get down safely.

Ignoring the bloodletting once more, Nungesser continued to stalk the skies, but it was July 22 before he bagged his tenth, an L.V.G., over Forges Wood. Within a week he was back in the hospital with a bullet in his shoulder. It should be pointed out that most of his troubles stemmed from the fact that he usually used what was known as the "whipstall" maneuver to initiate his attack. In this the pilot dives, then whips up in a terrific zoom for the underside of his target. If the gunnery aim is true, and if there are no stoppages, all well and good; but if the enemy escapes, the attacker is in a tight corner. With no real flying speed left, Nungesser's machine would flutter down and the German above would have a simple target. Time and time again the French ace was peppered, but some lucky star usually saved him.

Charles returned to the squadron late in August and made up for lost time. His eleventh success came on August 25, followed by two L.V.G.'s and a Fokker. By the end of September he had run his score to seventeen with a wild afternoon's work that nearly finished him. His first victim was a kite balloon that fell in flames near Le Transloy. Next he got into a running fight with two Fokkers and an L.V.G. He attacked the two-seater four times, but on every occasion the D.3's—*Doppeldekker*—biplanes poured burst after burst into his Nieuport. Finally the Frenchman was forced to hide in a cloud bank, but still continued to stalk the trio. Darting out from his cover over Rocquigny, he selected one of the scouts and started a fire with a burst from point-blank range. The Fokker reared up, folded back its wings, and went down.

Later that evening he attacked two L.V.G.'s over Neuville, shot down one in flames, and was lucky to make a forced landing when the other riddled his gas tank and shot the drum off his Lewis gun.

Before 1916 had closed out, four more enemy machines fell to Nungesser, and the last of them, his twenty-first, provided a new twist to the aerial victory story. He went into the air for a test flight with a Nieuport that had just had a complete overhaul, and over Chaulnes Wood spotted an L.V.G. two-seater. He immediately dived for its tail, but the German observer saw him and sprayed the sky with lead. The Frenchman went into his whipstall and suddenly realized that he had omitted the matter of a machine gun, having forgotten that it had been removed during the overhaul.

It was a desperate situation and demanded desperate measures. Knowing that the enemy gunner would riddle him the instant he tried to pull out of the fight, Nungesser decided to try to scare off the L.V.G. with the pretense of a deliberate ramming. The ruse worked better than he deserved. Believing that this crazy Frenchman was determined to crash into him, the German pilot pushed forward his joystick, dived for a clearing inside the French lines, and set fire to the machine the instant it rolled to a stop.

A few days later Nungesser was wounded again, and the French government offered him an honorable discharge; but he ignored the mercy gesture, and by April, 1917, with a free-lance, roving commission, was back in action where the fighting was thickest. He continued to be the determined fighter even when his numerous wounds had reduced him to a cripple. This broad, blond young man was always hobbling around on some airfield, supported by walking sticks, or climbing laboriously into his Nieuport for another take-off.

May, 1917, was marked by the arrival of several crack German fighter squadrons along the French front, and it was at their expense that Nungesser increased his score, destroying six machines in three weeks. But his wounds and injuries continued to torment him and he was not able to make any further gains until late that month. By the time 1917 had closed, he could claim only three more victories.

On May 20, 1918, he had thirty-six official victories to his credit, and was made an officer of the Legion of Honor. During the next two months he was wounded three times. He attacked two Pfalz scouts on June 7 and sent both down in flames, only to have his own plane set on fire a few minutes later when he was surprised by a flight of Fokker D.7's. In this instance Nungesser owed his life to the fact that he was flying a Hanriot Scout fitted with a Lanser fireproof gasoline tank, in which the flames, unable to gain a hold, died down after burning most of the fabric from around the container. He was able to make a landing with nothing worse than a scorched foot and a slight burn on one hand.

On August 3 he dived on a Halberstadt two-seater and shot off its wings before the gunner had time to fire more than one burst. His last fling at glory came on August 14, when he crossed the lines to joust with five enemy kite balloons. Two went down in as many minutes, and the ground fire forced Nungesser to draw away. Once out of range, he flew low, and from a height of but fifty feet attacked balloon number three. There was a sudden blast of yellow flame; then he turned his guns on the fourth. The observer jumped, but not soon enough, and the burning gasbag fell over his parachute like a grim shroud. Four balloons on one patrol!

Less than a week later Charles Nungesser was back in the hospital after five Fokkers had caught him under a cloud and inflicted his seventeenth wound. He refused to die, but the war was over before he could fly again.

CHAPTER 7

Heroes and Epics

Forced into more decisive action against the build-up of Allied air power and the growth of Allied armies, the German Air Force decided on further development of the Flying Circus, and Baron von Richthofen was appointed to head this organization. The Circus system had its advantages in the area where it operated but it failed to provide tactical aviation support for German ground forces. In the meantime new heroes volunteered from the trenches and flamed across the war skies on all fronts, but none as yet had matched the wild, madcap career of Captain Albert Ball of Great Britain, who set a pattern few were ever to match. It was the record of this Nottingham boy that brought to England the realization that the Royal Flying Corps was fighting a glorious campaign.

THE GROWTH OF THE CIRCUS

FOLLOWING the death of Oswald Boelcke, Jagdstaffel 63 was renamed Jasta Boelcke and remained the elite fighter organization of the German Air Force. Lieutenant Stephen Kirmaier was rewarded with Boelcke's command, but after leading the unit for nearly a month, during which time twenty-four more Allied aircraft were destroyed, Kirmaier was shot down and killed. Captain F. Walz then assumed leadership. Over the following winter months comparatively little was accomplished, but in April good weather permitted a renewal of activity and their Circus tactics had some success.

Twenty-one victories were scored in April, 1917, most of them resulting from the guns of Lieutenants Fritz Bernert and Werner Voss. As a matter of record, Bernert claimed five aircraft on April 24, a feat never before registered. Jasta Boelcke might have gone on to unprecedented glory, had not an official decree against too much first-class talent in one organization broken it up to form new Circus squadrons.

Voss, Bernert, and Tutschek were sent to other squadrons, and Captain Walz left for the Palestine front. In January, 1917, Von Richthofen had been ordered to form a squadron of his own, known as Jasta 11. When Jasta Boelcke was re-formed it was headed by Erwin Böhme, the pilot who had collided with Boelcke the previous October, and was sent to the Flanders front, where it about held its own, but the scores were nothing like the earlier days. Only thirty-five Allied planes were destroyed in the months of September, October, and November of 1917, and Böhme himself was shot down and killed over Zonnebeke on November 29. Such noted stars as Walter von Bülow and Max Mueller took over, only to die; then Carl Bolle finally brought the *Jasta* back to some semblance of its former glory. When the war ended and Jasta Boelcke had to turn over all its aircraft to the British, it claimed 336 victories for the loss of four commanders and twenty-six pilots.

Oswald Boelcke's organization had been built on sound planning in which flying skill, precision formation, accurate gunnery, and fighting tactics that had been worked out in action formed the complete program. Von Richthofen's Jasta 11 appears to have worked on the Flying Circus pattern in which the leader took a swarm of fighter aircraft into a critical area and completely overwhelmed any opposition. There was no real pattern of attack, and as some disgruntled German airmen have pointed out, most of the victories scored were credited to the leader. This was quite possible, for whenever a "victim" was trapped by these great odds, practically every pilot in the formation had at least one shot at him; and if the harried plane went down, the leader usually followed, covered by his pack, to claim the eventual reward.

Boelcke and Von Richthofen were in no way alike. Oswald was a sensitive, learned, dedicated leader who could devise, plan, and teach. He was not an aristocrat, nor did he display any militaristic braggadocio. Basically he was a tactical-aviation man, never particularly interested in compiling a great score for himself. Von Richthofen, on the other hand, was a Prussian aristocrat whose family had been a product of the military regime for years. He had never been a ranker, and he is always remembered for his cold, impersonal discipline. Neither kindness, understanding, nor affection for any member of his team was in him. He compiled an unbelievable score of eighty victories, but he lost far too many members of his squadron to justify the position he holds in the opinion of many aviation enthusiasts. He had a dynamic personality, and once the German press publicized him, he soon won the admiration and imagination of the public. Honors and awards came in great numbers, and eventually the German Staff had to create new decorations and ranks to keep up with his meteoric career.

In referring to the Von Richthofen Circus, it must not be assumed that the Red Knight, as he was called later by writers in the popular press, always went out with a thunderous pack of single-seaters behind him. There were occasions when he took a small flight of six or eight machines into the air on routine patrols, chiefly to search out and practice on laggard raiders or Allied machines that had suffered engine trouble on the way home from bombing missions. But generally speaking, he preferred to cover his territory with as large a formation as he could, patrolling up and down well inside his own lines harrying any six-plane flight that might be encountered.

Shortly after his victory over Major Hawker, his appointment to the command of Jasta 11, and his award of the Pour le Mérite, Von Richthofen was almost killed when the upper wing of his Albatros D.3 buckled in the air. He was most fortunate to get down without personal injury. In fact, he lost three machines that same day, possibly because of this obvious structural weakness.

All through so-called Bloody April of 1917 Manfred enjoyed unprecedented success, and must have been at the top of his form. This was the period when the British had decided to hold back the introduction of the S.E.5, the Bristol Fighter, and the Sopwith Camel, with the idea of producing whole squadrons of these first-class mounts in the summer of 1917. Second-guessing makes one wonder why. But these new German successes demanded immediate measures, and once these fine fighters were turned loose, new plans had to be devised by the opposition.

Jasta 11 had now become so famous that it was flaunting circus-type decorations, markings, and color patterns on its planes. This appears to be standard reaction in all highly publicized flying organizations in any war. It must be the tribal instinct. At any rate, although Jasta 11 started out with a fleet of Albatros fighters painted red, the high-ranking performers had to identify themselves further. Von Richthofen retained a bright-red mount, while his wingman, Lieutenant Schaefer, daubed his tail and part of the fuselage black. Karl Allmenroeder preferred a white tail. Kurt Wolff and Lothar von Richthofen, the baron's brother, had green and yellow markings, respectively.

The so-called Richthofen Circus resulted from the new offensives of the Royal Flying Corps. Once the Bristol two-seater fighter and the S.E.5. ranged the skies, the German Staffel leaders realized that new measures would have to be taken, and Von Richthofen elected himself "ringmaster" and arranged for other *Jasta* units to be settled in his Courtrai area, permitting mass-formation defense flights to be set up. Among these were Jasta 4, Jasta 6, and Jasta 10, which, with his own Jasta 11, became, in the popular phrase the Richthofen Circus.

VON RICHTHOFEN'S LEGENDARY FINISH

The history of Baron von Richthofen, written with varying degrees of partiality by so many authors, is still vague and uncertain.

That he ended his career with eighty victories—all British aircraft—has been told over and over. That twenty-one of these scores could not be verified in official Berlin records after the war has been admitted, but the record is still carried in practically all histories. His end is the basis for a dozen arguments, especially by writers who were not there, or had not even been born in 1918. We do know that he was shot down and killed on April 21, 1918, while flying a red Fokker triplane, and that he fell inside the British lines near the Bray–Corbie road. At the time the baron was chasing Lieutenant Wilford R. "Wop" May, a young Canadian Camel pilot, and Von Richthofen was being chased in turn by Lieutenant Roy Brown, another Canadian also flying a Camel.

One school of decision has credited Brown with the victory over the Red Knight, although Brown *actually* never claimed to have shot him down. He simply reported that he had fired at him and that other pilots of his squadron had seen the triplane go down.

In an article published in the early 1930's I wrote that a number of Australian artillerymen acting as antiaircraft gunners were protecting an area being held by a Royal Garrison Artillery battery not far from the Bray–Corbie road. Among them were a Gunner Brue, George M. Travers, Donald L. Frazer, and a Sergeant Popkins. Bombardier R. H. Barron had a Lewis-gun post, while the R.G.A. battery was armed with two 13/18-pound field guns. All these had once been part of the retreat from Cambrai with the ill-fated Fifth Army, but now were attached to the Fourth Army and were in support of Australian troops holding the line less than a mile away.

Bombardier Barron remembered seeing a Camel come over the German lines, flying very low. Another followed immediately, and behind these two roared a red German triplane that was firing at both in turn. This is Barron's version, remember. He opened fire immediately with his Lewis gun, and the Australian artillerymen near by opened with another. After a few bursts, the triplane pulled into a sharp right-hand turn, went down in a steep dive, and crashed behind the ridge. Barron and several others ran over to the scene and found the pilot—Von Richthofen—dead.

Two of the Australian gunners were awarded the Distinguished

Conduct Medal for their part in the action. Lieutenant Brown, the Camel pilot who was supposed to have shot down the Red Knight, was not rewarded in any way.

This was the most decisive battle in Von Richthofen's history, but who defeated him will never be known. Popular accounts prefer to give credit to the Canadian who was "protecting his squadron mate," and who, in this victory, proved that the Camel was superior to the Fokker triplane. It *was*, in this instance, but not when it was above 12,000 feet!

As in the history of so many other stars, we shall never know how the baron died.

TWO BOLD AMERICANS GO DOWN

A native New Yorker, Victor Chapman, was studying architecture at l'Ecole des Beaux-Arts in Paris in the spring of 1914, and at the outbreak of the war was touring England with his family. He returned to France and enlisted in the Foreign Legion and was assigned to the Third Marching Regiment. He received his early training at the Reuilly Caserne, Paris. He mastered the machine gun and was in nearly every exciting engagement his regiment encountered.

After spending three months in the trenches, Victor learned of Norman Prince's attempt to form an American group of flyers, and after some consideration put in for a transfer to French Aviation. He had to wait until August 1, 1915, before leaving his Foreign Legion comrades, and instead of receiving pilot training, he was sent immediately to a front-line bomber squadron—V.B. 108—as a machine gunner. He put in about a month of exciting day and night raiding with this Voisin outfit, during which time he acquitted himself so well that he was released for pilot training.

On his arrival at Avord he became acquainted with Kiffin Rockwell, and these two men became firm friends. Flight-training time was scarce and school equipment even scarcer, and Chapman could not garner enough time to qualify for his wings until January 9, 1916. When he was graduated there were no openings in any of the service squadrons at the front.

To keep their hands in, both Chapman and Rockwell volunteered to fly with the Paris Air Guard, a temporary organization assembled to defend the city from enemy air raids.

On the face of it the duty promised medals and glory for any-one fortunate enough to destroy a Gotha or a Zeppelin, but to carry out this important duty the pilots were given ancient Voisins, a front-seat gunner, and *one* machine gun! It was dreary and tiresome work, since few Germans risked flights that far. The Eiffel Tower was probably their greatest menace, and what thrills there were came during night operations when flying these slovenly pusher biplanes without proper night-flying equipment or ground facilities.

By the time the Escadrille Américaine became a reality, both Chapman and Rockwell were relieved of their nocturnal patrols and were sent to join the new organization. Here everyone was anxious to get into the real cocking main, and as soon as their Nieuports had been fitted with guns and a few primary instruments they took to the sky. Chapman and Rockwell were especially keen to prove their worth, and they never gave up until enemy gunfire ended their sterling careers.

Victor flew incessantly. He would take off and fly a two-hour patrol, return, and as soon as his plane was refueled and checked, he would go out on any pretext and scout the enemy lines for two more hours. This program was continued hour after hour, day after day. He was the first off the ground in the morning and the last one to land at night. He munched his meals as he walked up and down the Tarmac awaiting maintenance. What citations and deco-rations came his way were ignored, dismissed as unimportant. He just assigned such credits to his squadron and seldom wore the rib-bons or mentioned that such awards had come to him.

On May 24 he was cited for the Croix de Guerre with Palm for a courageous attack on three enemy aircraft. He soon discovered in this combat that he had taken on more than he could handle con-veniently, but he stuck to his task, throwing the frail Nieuport about the sky amid a hail of enemy fire, hoping to come out in a position from which he could draw a bead on one of the enemy.

The opposition was too much, however; a number of bullets clipped or pierced his coverall and one drew a hot, searing brand along his forearm, making him wince. It was soon evident that this was not his day, and at the first opportunity he pulled out, nosed down, and escaped into a muffin of cloud.

Matters continued in this way over the next three weeks, and his companions realized that this six-foot American with the thick black hair was without emotion in all his activities. He had nothing but contempt for the enemy, attacked against impossible odds, and fought like a man charged with some idealistic quest. On the ground he was the consummate gentleman. His artistic temperament rejected the blood and tragedy then, and took in only the beauty of the day, the scene, the environment, and the quiet glory of his love, France. The shell-torn landscape, the crumbled villages, the stark ruin of the battle-seared forests blended into classic pictures, for his nature saw the beauty and erased the unpleasant. He accepted his many companions on the same optimistic terms.

Victor had a narrow escape from death on June 17 when, as usual, he was flying alone and met a formation of five enemy planes. Two Aviatiks were heading across the French lines to take photographs and were being escorted by three Fokkers, probably D.3's. French antiaircraft bursts had pointed them out to Victor and he flew headlong into the fray. When he saw the three-ship escort above, he eased off and circled to find an opening. Secure in their numbers, the intruders ignored him, for none of them expected a lone Nieuport to interfere.

When the Aviatiks split up to cover their assigned area, Victor saw a faint chance to make a strike and swooped down like a hawk. His Lewis gun chattered, and a photography pilot, intent on holding his course, was startled to feel his aircraft being stitched with short, snarling bursts. He immediately changed course and darted for a position below his Fokker escort. Victor was determined not to let the two-seater escape, and kept after him, pounding the full drum of bullets into the broad-tailed biplane. Every burst went home clean. The Aviatik whirled, then staggered; the pilot fell forward on the stick with half a dozen slugs in his back, and the enemy gunner was killed before he could crawl away from his camera, which was mounted on the floor. The Aviatik fell off and plunged to earth in long, flame-streaked sweeps.

With revenge in their hearts, the Fokker pilots bore down on this impudent Nieuport pilot. Spandau fire made Victor turn, and from that position he sensed that he was being hounded by a group of Oswald Boelcke's *Jasta*. They poured down on him from three tight angles, and once more the American must have realized his rashness. All his skill, daring, and chance-taking had to be employed. He darted, twisted, and zoomed hoping to retain some altitude. He next saw that he had used all the ammunition in the drum, and had to replace it before he could really defend himself. He had no alternative but to grip the stick between his knees, haul down the gun from its impractical mounting, get a new pan affixed and the loading sequence run through once more.

The Fokker pilots used him as a training target during this frantic activity, as they saw his brave effort to replace the drum and knew how handicapped he was. There never would be a better chance to get in some foolproof target practice. Bullets screamed all around Victor's head; slug after slug crashed into the machine, and several pierced his instrument panel, as other bullets hissed and ripped away long sections of wing fabric, tearing streamers of material that dragged back from the trailing edges.

Finally, a telling shot was scored as one bullet caught the metal aileron bracket protruding from the upper wing. The bracket was severed and the slug ricocheted and tore through Victor's helmet, hacking a gash four inches long across his scalp. With practically no aileron control, the plane started to spin. Chapman, partly blinded with the blood that streamed over his forehead, tried vainly to remedy the aileron situation, and somehow, despite his many difficulties, pressed the broken halves of the bracket together and held them with his gloved hand. This at least provided neutral aileron effect and he was able to revert to his wriggling and darting, hoping to evade his tormentors. Once, he allowed the Nieuport to fall off, giving the impression that he finally had been sent down, but when he was clear, he eased the Nieuport out and, still clutching the jagged ends of the aileron bracket, landed on a French field located at Froids.

He was given emergency medical care, refreshment, and a meal. Mechanics repaired the aileron control, and later that afternoon he flew back to his own squadron. On his arrival with his head swathed in bandages, he laughed off the situation and refused to go to a near-by hospital for full medical attention.

"I'm quite all right," he insisted. "You know how scalp wounds are; they bleed a lot, but unless you suffer some concussion or skull damage, there is no real danger. I am fine, I tell you."

Bill Thaw, who was C.O., suggested that Victor take a few days off and go to Paris.

"I don't think this is the time for a furlough," Victor countered.

"Well, you're not flying for a few days. You must have a large-sized headache."

"It's no bother," Victor insisted. "I feel fine!"

"Well, please try to get some sleep," Thaw begged.

CHAPMAN'S MERCY FLIGHT

The next day, June 18, Clyde Balsley, a native of San Antonio, Texas, was shot down near Verdun and had to be moved to Vadelaincourt Hospital, where his condition seemed critical. As soon as he heard this, Victor Chapman went over to see him. Balsley was the Escadrille's first serious casualty.

With his own head in bandages, Chapman tried to rouse Balsley, and said, "Hello, old man. I just brought your toilet kit. How goes it?"

Clyde was seriously wounded and feeling most despondent. "Victor! I'm so glad to see you. I'm not too bad, am I? It's just that I'm so thirsty all the time, and all I'm allowed is that old wet rag to suck on."

Victor did not tell Clyde how serious he was, but cheered him with, "Think nothing of it. I'll be back again with some oranges. They'll let you suck on an orange."

"Oh, that'll be wonderful. How's everything?"

"Everything's fine. Take it easy. I'll be back tomorrow."

Chapman fully intended to return, but the next day he made some concession to his head wound by sleeping late. Then a new Nieuport was flown in and he busied himself adjusting the compass and machine gun. As the weather was not good, he was content with flying the new aircraft around the field to work out some control bugs. Some Germans were reported over the French lines, and Victor joined the rest in the search, but the report proved to be a false alarm.

Although he was warned and appealed to, Victor refused to ease up or take a short leave. He flew without a helmet because his head was so swathed in bandages that none would fit. The morning of June 23 was fine and Chapman insisted on flying a regular patrol, taking his turn with the others. Fortunately, there were no enemy planes in the air and the patrol was uneventful. After lunch, Victor procured a basket of oranges, which he intended to take to Clyde Balsley, but when he went out to the hangars he discovered that Captain Thénault, Norman Prince, and Raoul Lufbery were warming up their planes to go on a flight.

"Look," Chapman explained, "I'll put the basket behind my seat. I'll go up to the lines with you, and if there is nothing important going on, I'll just break off and drop down to see Clyde."

"Go deliver your oranges," Thénault ordered. "You've flown enough today."

"Take it easy, Victor," Lufbery pleaded.

Their engines were turning over, and on a signal from Thénault all three rumbled away for the take-off. Annoyed, Victor called a mechanic, had his prop swung, and headed after them. Captain Thénault's group quickly found two enemy planes on which they dived, and while they were engaged with these two, three more dropped out of the clouds above, and the Escadrille pilots wisely withdrew. They made a routine patrol up and down the lines without encountering Chapman, and on their way back to their field assumed that he had gone to the hospital to see Balsley.

Still believing that Victor had gone on his errand of mercy, the Americans felt no concern until late that afternoon when a pilot of a Farman plane that had been in the same area reported that he had seen three Nieuports in combat with five German aircraft, and that in the middle of the engagement he had noticed a fourth Nieuport diving in with all speed to join the combat. The Farman pilot was positive that this plane, for no apparent reason, had gone down with its engine full on.

There is another version of this story. The German planes concerned were two L.V.G. observation machines, and as soon as Captain Thénault signaled for an attack, he found the two-seaters were being covered by three Fokker fighters; realizing they were too far over to engage such a force, he decided to pull out and get back to his own lines. In the meantime Chapman, who had followed them, nosed down to give what aid he could. Apparently no one in the Nieuport formation saw him, and he was left to fight his way out of the tangle. It is not known whether any of the Germans attacked him; but it is thought that after his first attack, seeing that he was all alone, he started a number of wild maneuvers to get away. Harried and outnumbered, he may have overdone the violence of his tactics and pulled off his wings. A German report has it that Victor was shot through the head, and this may be what happened. The French Farman pilot insisted, however, that Chapman simply went into a full-power dive from which he never recovered, and must have been killed instantly.

Thus was lost one of the finest characters of the Escadrille Américaine—a man who may have been the victim of his own strong determination. He was typical of most of the men who had volunteered to fight for France and the freedom of all men.

BIG AND LITTLE BARACCA

A man named Flavio Torello Baracchini, a member of the Italian 76th Squadron, was becoming well known on the Italian-Austrian front. He had flown many times with Major Baracca, and their names, being somewhat similar, linked them in the public mind as Baracca and Little Baracca.

Baracchini was little heard of until 1917, when he began to run up an amazing score, for he was possessed of a deadly precision of aim and a playboy's courage in an attack that put the Italian high scorers in the shade.

For instance, while patrolling with Baracca along the crest of Mont Nero some eight miles inside the Austrian line, they came upon an Albatros heading toward Isonzo near the Italian trenches. This was the period of the August offensive and the Austrians were keeping a vigilant watch on the sky. Heavy antiaircraft fire barked up at the two Spads, which made them zigzag to avoid the bracketing bursts.

The Albatros ignored the two Italians and continued on a straight course, even when the Spads nosed down on it. The gunner, with rare confidence, sprayed the attackers until the single-seaters had to break away and try new tactics. Baracca went in direct, head on from the front, while Baracchini snapped down from above and behind. Thus Little Baracca's intense and accurate fire broke the back of the Albatros, and the tangled wreckage tumbled to the ground.

Then, ignoring the heavy antiaircraft barrage, Baracca and Baracchini returned to the scene and photographed the scattered wreckage for evidence of their victory. This was a typical Baracca-Baracchini attack, and within a few months Little Baracca had run up a score of twenty-one "kills" before he was killed in 1918.

Another Baracca companion who must have learned much from the Italian master was Fulco Ruffo di Calabria, a descendant of a noble family that included Cardinal Ruffo, soldier-cleric of the eighteenth century. Captain di Calabria was a member of Number 70 Squadron during the summer of 1916, when, flying a Nieuport with Baracca and Luigi Olivari, he encountered an Austrian reconnaissance two-seater that was photographing the Italian lines near Tolmino. The three Italians attacked at once, but the Austrian pilot continued his work. When he decided that the opposition was too much, it was too late. Ruffo was on his tail, and stayed there in spite of the venom of the rear gunner. He poured burst after burst into the snooper until it fell in flames somewhere near the ruins of Biglia. Baracca was fascinated by Ruffo's determination, his accurate gunnery, and his behavior in a tight formation. He could anticipate every move of his enemy, as well as the intent of his companions— a quality invaluable in this type of aerial warfare.

On another occasion it was Ruffo's smart summing up of a situation that resulted in victory. Again he was flying with Baracca —then a captain—and Lieutenant Olivari. They were patrolling the Plezzo sector when they noticed a machine that was approaching from the direction of the frontier. It turned immediately, as if the pilot had spotted the Nieuports, but Captain Ruffo was on it like a shrike. It was an Austrian Löhner two-seater, and the Italian's first burst killed the pilot. The plane started to spin, but the observer managed to take over what went for a dual control, and somehow smoothed it out and regained some command before it struck the ground. The Löhner was wrecked, and after their return to their own field, the three Italian pilots borrowed a squadron car and worked their way out to Monte Stol, where they found and rescued the wounded observer.

In January, 1917, while flying alone, Ruffo attacked an Austrian two-seater near Duino and shot it down beyond the front lines. While making certain that the observer had been killed and would not be able to salvage this disabled plane, Ruffo was joined by Major Baracca and together they attacked a reconnaissance Albatros, which Baracca shot down.

A Number 91 Squadron was formed from a nucleus of Number 70 Squadron and Baracca was placed in command, with Ruffo a member of Baracca's flight. This squadron was equipped with Spads and ran up many victories with the new mounts. Ruffo was on patrol over Carso on June 7, 1917, when he encountered a five-ship formation of Austrian two-seaters, of which he shot down one and scattered the rest. Returning with Baracca to that scene later the same day, they searched the area until they found the wreck. The dead pilot's body was still in the cockpit, but no observer was to be found. Whether he had managed some sort of a dual-controlled landing and then scurried off for cover and escaped was never discovered.

By the end of that September, Ruffo was second to Baracca, with thirteen victories to Baracca's nineteen. When 91 Squadron destroyed six enemy aircraft on October 25, Ruffo had sent two of them crashing in flames inside the Italian lines. By the time the war ended he was promoted to captain and credited with twenty victories.

THE EPIC OF CAPTAIN ALBERT BALL

To the author's way of thinking, Captain Albert Ball, a young, curly-haired airman who dominated British aviation between the summer of 1916 and the spring of 1917, was the most fabulous character of World War I. Strangely enough, he has never intrigued American interest, despite the fact that he downed forty-four enemy aircraft, and who, for wild, uncontrolled pugnacity, had no equal on any front—in any war. Frank Luke, the Arizona Balloon Buster, was an introverted choirboy in comparison.

A true maverick, a devil-may-care type who had no regard for his own safety, rules or discipline... There was a time when he was a confirmed Hun hater. He was the world's leading air fighter before he was twenty-one years old—in fact, the first high-scoring pilot produced by the Royal Flying Corps. Yet during the many years that the author has been writing aviation adventures and histories of wartime aces, no American magazine publisher has been interested in presenting the career of Albert Ball.

He had the tenacity of a bulldog and the views of a poet. He liked music, books, and paintings and could write with the skill of an essayist. Aflame with honest patriotism, and buoyed up by what he considered his bounden duty, his career may seem like that of a fiction hero in these days of national service, draft acts, military conscription, and the cold dread of total war.

I knew Albert Ball for a few short weeks in 1917 when he was a star performer with Number 56 Squadron. He tended a small hutch of rabbits with adolescent concern, and since he was a commissioned officer and I a mere first-class air mechanic, our intercourse could be held only at this barnyard level. As I remember, we talked about what rabbits prefer to eat. I suggested dandelions, but Ball thought that cabbage leaves or lettuce would be their choice. We both agreed that in picture books rabbits always nibbled on carrots. That was the last I saw him, and I have always wondered what became of his mangy pets.

Albert Ball went to middle-class schools, joined the Boy Scouts, pursued all the usual hobbies, and had a knack for engineering. His father was at one time mayor of Nottingham, Albert's home town. He was devoted to his mother, and adored his sister Lois, but his brother Cyril was someone to be endured. This mutual disregard seemed to last for a long time. In a recent interview, quoted in the *Cross and Cockade Journal,* Cyril had been asked if he had any idea how Albert met his death, to which he had replied, "After all these years, who knows or even cares?"

When he was seventeen Albert set himself up in business which he called the Universal Engineering Works, and his business cards were impressive, to say the least. They proclaimed that the firm was "On Admirality and War Office Lists," giving the impression that the young man was manufacturing battleships and 16-inch guns for the government. The war put an end to that project, and on the very day hostilities began he enlisted in his county regiment, the 7th Battalion of the Sherwood Foresters, the Nottingham company of which was called the Robin Hood Rifles. Within a month he had won his sergeant's stripes, but in his desire to get into action against the common enemy, he was plagued by the ill fortune of all idealists. He had joined up to fight, but was promoted from sergeant to commissioned rank and kept in Britain to train other men; many who had joined up with him at the outbreak of war had long before gone to Flanders where the poppies grew—he read about them every day in the casualty lists.

He also read about W. B. Rhodes-Moorhouse one evening in

May, 1915. The next morning he rose at 3 A.M., threw his leg over a motorcyle, and roared over the sixty miles from Luton, his base, to a private flying school at Hendon. The long summer daylight in the British latitudes was his first fortunate break in his so far dull military life.

Making a quick deal, Ball paid out ten pounds from his own pocket for a few flying lessons, and before he left that morning he experienced a few minutes of dual control on an old French Caudron. He then whizzed back to Luton in time to make his early-morning parade. He arrived dusty, begrimed, and road-streaked, and his colonel had him on the carpet for appearing in an oil-stained uniform. The penalty brought extra duties, most of them decidedly unpleasant, but Albert had caught the whiff of Castrol, and he continued to buy flying lessons. He simply rose half an hour earlier each day so that he could get back in time to change his attire.

He eventually earned his "ticket," although he had two amusing crashes which he somehow deleted from the records—and from the knowledge of his mother. By October, 1915, he had sufficient training to warrant a transfer to the Royal Flying Corps, and during the following Christmas holidays he was granted special leave; not until then did he tell his mother of all the "wonderful things that were happening."

"Now don't worry," he explained. "It's not a bit dangerous. In fact, if you didn't wear long skirts I'd take you up in a minute."

"Well, you can take me," his sister, Lois, exclaimed. "Mine aren't that long." Albert just kissed her, and promised, then hurried back to his R.F.C. training camp.

Early in the new year, Ball was offered the opportunity to go out to France—but not as a pilot. The R.F.C. was short of observers and aerial gunners, but Albert felt that since he had bought his wings he was entitled to fly as a pilot. By February, 1915, however, his luck changed and he was posted to Number 13 Squadron in France, where they were flying old Quirks. He soon learned that Caudron, Farman, and Avro flying in England compared in no way with what was going on over the Western Front, and he wisely concentrated on learning the ropes instead of following his natural headstrong thrust. The old B.E.2c was no "battleplane," but for a time it was too much for him. There was a period when his C.O., a Major Marsh, considered sending him back for further training, but Ball put on such a scene that Marsh relented and allowed him to stay.

WOULD VOLUNTEER FOR ANYTHING

In order to gain added experience, Ball volunteered for a number of secret missions, flights in which he boldly flew British intelligence agents over the line and deposited them in enemy territory. He did an excellent job of getting them in safely, but on several occasions he had to use his limited authority to get them to disembark.

These agents were usually Frenchmen or Belgians who had knowledge of the German language. They were well paid and most of them enjoyed the work while it was connected with comfortable quarters and pleasant instruction; but often it was difficult to induce them to put what they had learned into practice.

Twice, Ball took off from Izel-le-Hammeau with one of these reluctant agents, and twice he had to turn around and fly him back. It was a spirit of behavior the British youth could not understand. If a man agreed to do a job, he should do it. He finally settled the issue by unceremoniously booting one of these passengers out of his cockpit, pointing to a near-by hedge, and taking off again. He never had any trouble with intelligence men after that.

Besides these agent missions, the everyday program was full of hazard. There were artillery shoots to carry out. The weather was dreadful. Machine after machine failed to return, and Albert Ball began to view the "intrepid airman" appellation in a new light. Nevertheless, he went headlong into everything he did, and accepted extra work and additional patrols with no question or complaint.

When bad weather gave him days off, he would wander about the back areas and look on the wreckage and strife. This side of the war affected him more than the daily combats with enemy aircraft.

"It's enough to make your blood boil with rage," he wrote home. "The shattered houses, the beds and furniture tossed about in the streets, the ruins of churches angers and saddens me."

As the weeks passed, Ball became a reasonably good Quirk pilot. He was never spectacular, and what stunting he tried was not smooth or precise. At best he was just another journeyman pilot, but he was capable of judging relative values. In many instances he found it difficult to work in harmony with other airmen, particularly in Army co-operation work. He was ever the individualist, continually thinking in terms of air fighting when his observer wished to carry out the required mission; and it gradually dawned on Ball that if he hoped to be happy in this war, he would have to transfer to a single-seater squadron.

It was the practice in those days for some two-seater squadrons to have assigned to them one or two single-seaters that could be flown in support of the co-operation machines. At Number 13 they had two Bristol Scout single-seaters for such sorties, and Ball began to spend more time on these aircraft than he did on the Quirk. He became reasonably adept with them, too.

On one occasion he was over the line with a faulty gun-control gear and on firing at an enemy Albatros practically shot off his own propeller. He sensed what had happened, however, and, running his engine at half speed, got back safely to his field. A few days later Major Marsh, probably hoping to get rid of this young firebrand, sent Ball across the field with a note to the C.O. of Number 11 Squadron that stated, "This young man can be entrusted with the best single-seater on the front. Please give him something to do."

Number 11 had a few decaying Nieuport scouts on its equipment list, and Ball took one up and gave the personnel of both squadrons a rare exhibition, with the result that Major W. H. Hubbard of Number 11 was delighted to take the young man off Marsh's hands. He arranged for Ball to fly Nieuports and protect the tails of his Quirks. As a matter of fact, Albert Ball carried out these lone-wolf flights for both squadrons all through the early summer of 1916, flying the Bristol Scout or the Nieuport. No one seemed to have any regular duties for him, so he "stayed out of the way" by going over the line in one single-seater or another. The resulting exploits were exciting but did not result in confirmed victories. He would engage whole formations of Fokkers, split them up, and chase them down to the ground, but he never returned with any evidence of an actual "kill."

It may have been fun, but at the same time it was nerve-wracking, and after many weeks of this double-duty service, Ball was entitled to some leave. Unfortunately the Battle of the Somme—July, 1916— was in the offing and all leave was canceled. He did not accept this decision with the best of grace, and his letters to his mother indicated his honest dreads and fears.

When his disappointment was at its peak, he would take a slice of plum cake his mother had sent him, climb into the Nieuport, and roar off across the line, nibbling at the food-parcel goody until he was in enemy territory. These pointless patrols went on and on, but young Ball was becoming a daring and relentless scout pilot, despite his inner feelings.

But his fortune changed, and late in June he was granted ten days' leave. He returned just in time to take part in the Blood Bath of the Somme.

BALL'S FIRST DECORATION

When he arrived at his squadron he discovered that his favorite Nieuport had been crashed, and the pilot who had been flying it killed. The squadron had taken a severe beating; many pilots were wounded or completely exhausted; and only four were available to fly the missions required. Young Ball rolled up his sleeves and went to work.

The Battle of the Somme provided trench strafing, kite-balloon attacks, battles with enemy aircraft, and low-altitude co-operation with the advancing troops. Number 11 was in the thick of it. Ball put in ungodly hours, but registered his first victory, an enemy kite balloon, one of the six brought down that day. It was the only balloon he ever destroyed, and it brought him the Military Cross.

He next went aloft with a group of F.E.2*b* pushers, and these two-seaters, led by Ball, barged into six Roland two-seaters. The "Fees" destroyed one and Ball got another, the first aircraft of his spectacular career. That night he wrote to his mother:

DEAREST MOTHER,

I received your very sweet letter yesterday and I am very pleased for I am very poo-poo just now.

Yesterday I was up at 5 A.M. and during the day made twelve flights, and at last Nature is asking to have its own way. However, I am not done yet. Dad says, "Let the devils have it." Yes, I always let them have it all I can, but really I don't think them devils. I only scrap because it is my duty, but I do not think anything about the Hun. He is just a good chap with very little guts, trying to do his best. Nothing makes me feel more rotten than to see them go down.

These were the words of a young man who had set out to do his duty. That summer in France was beautiful. The skies were wide patches of postcard blue embroidered with gossamer clouds. The fields were green and the trees gave off their seasonal scents. Up the line a thousand shells an hour tore the vitals from hundreds of men huddling in the trenches or skulking along the communication roads. Those who flew saw the great canvas of it all—and went on with the killing at hand.

Ball continued to fly with both Number 11 and Number 13 squadrons, and his logbook indicates that he made a few routine reconnaissance flights aboard the old Quirk, and carried out half a dozen types of patrols. By the middle of August he was living with Number 11 and had planted a small garden behind A Flight's hangar. He also downed his second Hun after attacking five enemy machines singlehanded.

After this success he was made acting flight commander (captain) and transferred with a number of Nieuport pilots from Number 11 Squadron to make up the famous Number 60 Squadron, which was to produce Major Billy Bishop, the outstanding Canadian ace. Before Ball left Number 11 he destroyed another Roland after a wild melee with five others of the same type.

When Albert Ball arrived at Number 60 he discovered that an unfortunate advance notice concerning his behavior had been spread about in which he was listed as a lone wolf, one who would desert a formation to go off fighting on his own. The report may have been true in some respects, since he dreaded tight formations and refused to take part in sham (practice) air flights. He felt that they were unnecessarily dangerous—and he was right!

But a few sage minds of the R.F.C. command realized that Albert Ball was a fighter totally unlike any other in their service. He was at the threshold of his career, and they sensed that his arrival would create an *esprit de corps* worth a dozen fully equipped squadrons in the field. His fame eventually was so great that his material success became a legend and at times perhaps was exaggerated. But history must view his value from its true angle, which is not that of the number of enemy aircraft destroyed.

Major Smith-Barry, C.O. of Number 60, soon learned that Ball was not amenable to restraint, and after a short break-in period, he was allowed to fly alone. There can be no doubt that he must have destroyed many machines for which he cannot be credited. It was obvious also that to have engaged in so many duels, he had to win many to stay alive.

THE SCORE PILES UP

Bad weather hampered Ball's first few days with his new squadron but on August 28 he came upon two Roland two-seaters of a new type. He saw that both were well armed, for the pilots and observers had two guns each. He moved cautiously, then suddenly slipped beneath them and, using his upper-wing Lewis as a semi-flexible weapon, poured about twenty rounds into the lead Roland. The first two-seater slipped off, went into a spin, then landed in a cornfield. The observer of the second Roland blasted Ball, who had to move fast to escape.

On the way out of that fracas he met another Roland, but the pilot saw the young Britisher in time and nosed down at speed for safety. Later that day Ball engaged in fight after fight, using five drums of ammunition without any result; but he persisted, and as night began to fall, he found an old L.V.G. two-seater flying low, and quickly shot it down.

This was a typical day in the air-war career of Captain Albert Ball. Nothing came easy, since he was not a good pilot and must have been a poor shot. But he never gave up trying. Most of his flying at this time was over the Bapaume–Cambrai road; those who were there will remember the blurred, smoky trench lines, the battered village of Flers, and the unholy wreckage of factories and farmhouses. I particularly recall the eye-like crater of a chalk pit. If you went along farther you flew over the old sugar factory at Fremicourt, and beyond that lay the scars of Beugny, Vaulx-Vracourt, and the Fontane-Notre-Dame. Over the hill lay the dark smear of Burlon Wood and Cambrai.

While flying alone one day at 11,000 feet, Ball spotted a formation of twelve Rolands, bashed in, opened fire, and broke up the group. Darting sideways, he closed to within fifteen yards of the nearest two-seater and poured fifty rounds into the pilot's cockpit. The enemy plane went down completely out of control and piled up east of Bapaume.

By now three German formations of Rolands, Albatroses, and L.V.G.'s tried to concentrate on this daring midge. Turning in a tight circle, Captain Ball sprayed the air and sent down another to spin into a wood. His Lewis gun was out of ammunition, and as he fumbled to replace the drum his engine quit cold. It had been hit by a long-range shot from one of the Jerry observers.

He had enough height to glide into his own lines if unhindered, but the Germans sensed that he was in trouble and they all piled in. Fortunately, at that moment Providence riding with a swarm of British fighters roared in, and Ball just managed to reach a clear space near Colincamp. On landing he discovered that most of his ignition system had been shot away.

Over the following weeks Ball perfected his "getting under"

maneuver to such an extent that one day he followed his own squadron commander all the way home from the line without that worthy knowing that Ball was anywhere in the vicinity. When anyone else tried it he usually fell off into a spin, after tangling with the upper man's slip stream.

Thus, while running up his remarkable score, Ball was employing a method totally at variance with what was being taught in the fighting schools. "Get on top—and stay there!" was the motto of the day. Ball was years ahead of Churchill's World War II phrase "Strike them in the soft underbelly!"

Early in September, 1916, he again went home on leave, and the *London Gazette* proclaimed that Captain Ball had been awarded the Distinguished Service Order. Before he returned to France it was announced that a Bar had been added to his decoration, meaning that he had won it twice. A second Bar was won a short time later.

Back at the front by September 11, he was commanding A Flight. On the other side of the line the older German planes were being replaced by Halberstadt and new Albatros two-seater fighters. The German circus formations were cruising up and down the British front. Nevertheless, British scout pilots, equipped with all types of front-firing guns, were attacking with new fury, and the Red Knight of Germany wrote, "Since mid-September, of twelve pilots in Boelcke's *Staffel,* six are dead, one wounded and two have suffered complete nervous breakdowns—all in six weeks!"

Boelcke's Staffel had been assigned the Cambrai-Bapaume road, where a young scourge, flying a Nieuport scout that flaunted a scarlet nose spinner—a present from his admiring mechanics—was on the rampage. Not all of his targets went down in flames or out of control; most of them were driven out of the play by the fury of his blazing attack, and their wounds were deeper than any inflicted by .303 Kynochs ammunition.

Ball seemed to have a particular hate for enemy two-seaters, and his unorthodox methods of attack were noted by German designers. They were to incorporate "tunnel guns," firing through open ports cut in the fuselage floors of their Junkers J.1, the Gotha G.5 bomber, and the Friedrichshafen G.3 bomber, in the hope that they could halt this original method of attack.

A MATTER OF SERVICE PUBLICITY

On October 3 Ball was suddenly relieved of active duty and posted to Home Establishment. He had scored thirty-one victories by this time, but these figures were not made available to the British press. At the same time Germany was flooding the world with bold reports of her leading aces, and American newspapers in particular were giving these stories wide promotion. The French, who had unwittingly originated the "ace" character, found that to counter German propaganda, they would have to keep a more detailed account of their own fighting airmen.

Captain Ball tried to keep the facts of his record from the press, but Fleet Street declared:

If we expect young men to volunteer to fly with the R.F.C., we must offer them the chance to become heroes—like Captain Ball. Here in Britain we are playing down our airmen and are having to go into the trenches to beg young infantrymen to volunteer for flying. What a chance! They see war in the air every day—in all its grisly action. But over in Canada and America every young kid who can read, wants to learn how to fly. Why? Because all they know of war flying comes from the stories of French and German aces and how they are winning all the medals!

All this was true, for the people of France knew more about Captain Albert Ball than did the good folk of Nottingham. In Canada, Ball was a national hero; in Britain he was simply a young man who for some reason or other had won the Military Cross and the Distinguished Service Order, and . . . oh, yes, some mysterious medal awarded by the Russians. What he had done to earn all these honors was offered as "most conspicuous and consistent bravery," but none of the details was obtainable.

Once he was safe in England, officialdom decided to send him on a lecture tour of the flying schools, but Captain Ball had no idea what he was expected to say. He was even ordered to take a new aerial gunnery course at a fighter school. "Of all the fools' games," he wailed. "I shall pass away if I don't get a different job soon. Why must they be such fools?"

While on leave he dabbled in the automobile business and wanted to open a salesroom in London. Then he persuaded the Austin Company to build a single-seater fighter of his own design. It was boxy, chunky, looked something like a Spad and performed even worse, but luckily never went into production.

Late in February, 1917, Ball was permitted to return to France, where he joined the crack Number 56 Squadron. He was both pleased and disappointed. He was delighted to get out of England and back on the front, but he was dissatisfied on learning that he would be flying the S.E.5. This would seem to point up the fact that there was something wrong with young Captain Ball, for the S.E.5 was a tougher bus than the Nieuport, had a greater working ceiling, higher speed, and, although it would not stunt like the French mount, was a far more worthy warplane.

It was at Estrée Blanche that Ball had his hutch of rabbits, and also performed his full repertoire of violin solos—as excruciating a set of discords as one might hear in any beginners' school. He also learned that there were a number of up-and-coming young pilots at Number 56 who were making names for themselves, including Major Jimmy McCudden, Lieutenant A. P. F. Rhys-Davids, Captain Meintjes, Major G. J. C. Maxwell, Captain A. Mayberry, and Lieutenant Knaggs. The war news was including the deeds of Billy Bishop and William Barker, and the handful of Americans in the Lafayette Escadrille were lighting a glory trail across the French front. Within a few weeks the United States would be in the war, and many more new names would be added to the gallant tradition.

After his long period in England, all this was new to Captain Ball, and for a time he was unable to comprehend what had happened to his war. He discovered he was "an ace" and was expected to act the role, but he had no idea how an ace was supposed to perform. More important, he was homesick, for he had fallen in love with a girl who was serving in one of Britain's women's services, and he spent every spare minute writing letters to her.

It will be seen that Captain Albert Ball was a disturbed young man.

He resumed his war flying, but was so dissatisfied with the S.E.5 that he was given a Nieuport whenever he wished, but he was required to fly his routine patrols with the Hisso-powered British machine. Finally, he settled down to his old prowling ways, and once more the red-nosed Nieuport was a-wing over the Bapaume–Cambrai road.

Between April 22 and May 7 he shot down and destroyed eleven enemy aircraft. With the thirty-one credited to him previously, he had forty-two victories and led the Allied field. But he was a different fighter now; there was an air of maturity about his behavior and he gradually forsook the little Nieuport for the S.E.5. He realized that one had to progress. The British biplane was better equipped to engage the new German fighters, and he finally accepted the new mount with no reservations of any kind.

THE GUN IN THE CHURCH TOWER

Captain Albert Ball reached the end of his short but flaming career in the early evening of May 7, 1917, and his passing has been the subject of more arguments than that of any other in the history of the air. You can get one opinion in any British town, and half a dozen others in the lobby of the Tempelhof Hotel in Berlin, where the ghosts of German aces stalk nightly.

No one knows actually how Ball died.

This is how the mystery story begins.

Officials of the 9th Wing, R.F.C., decided that a formation of Spads, Camels, and S.E.5's was to patrol over the Douai-Cambrai sector throughout that day. Another Battle of Arras was in progress and the British were concentrating on the village of Bullecourt. At 5:30 P.M. a three-element formation from Number 56 Squadron, headed by Captains Ball, Crowe, and Meintjes, set out for the area.

All pilots rendezvoused as arranged, formed up in three tiers, and crossed into enemy territory through heavy clouds and rain. Ball and Knaggs broke away from their group during these unpleasant conditions and prowled about together at 7,000 feet, while Meintjes and Crowe took their little packs up through the clouds to 9,000- and 10,000-foot levels. Over Burlon Wood just west of Cambrai they ran into even worse conditions and were widely dispersed. Meintjes' flight came upon a German Albatros and one of them shot it down.

Gradually, the whole S.E.5 formation collected itself and came roaring out of some clouds nose on to a circus of red-and-white Albatroses. Everyone went into action with no particular order. Meintjes had to spin out when two Huns got on his tail. Cecil Lewis, who became famous later for his remarkable book, *Sagittarius Rising*, was Meintjes' wingman and got into the same trouble. Ball and Knaggs had to go to their rescue. Meintjes then returned to the fray and shot down a red fighter that fell east of Gouy-sous-Bellone. Hoidge, another 56 Squadron pilot, knocked an Albatros smack into the streets of Cambrai.

When the melee became too broken up to be managed, the British fighters turned and re-formed over Arras, and more intensive fighting took place as fast as formations could be collected, and continued in this manner until the S.E.5's ran out of ammunition or fuel. Finally, Ball, Crowe, Hoidge, and Knaggs were widely separated, but Crowe reported later that he had seen Ball fire two red lights, indicating that he had spotted more enemy aircraft. Crowe peered around but could not see anything to shoot at, so he followed Ball, who was heading for Lens.

Ball suddenly went into a dive and Crowe saw him firing at an Albatros single-seater below. Crowe joined in the fight until Ball took full command and followed the German eastward into a heavy cloud. That was the last Crowe saw of Captain Ball.

What seems to have happened was reconstructed later by military and civilian officials in the area.

Ball went on to finish what is now credited as his forty-fourth victim. Then, finding himself out of ammunition—he had been in the air more than two hours—he dropped through the clouds and came out into the clear just east of the village of Annoeulin. He recognized the hamlet and, following an old habit, decided to check on the time. Although he wore a wrist watch and had a small clock set into his instrument panel, Albert, the Sunday-school boy, trusted implicitly in church clocks. Whenever he was in that area, and on his way home, he usually sped past the Annoeulin church and checked with the time-encrusted hands of the tower clock.

The villagers knew it, and the Germans occupying the area eventually learned of this habit. They all recognized the British scout with the red nose spinner, since Ball had had his lucky trademark switched from the Nieuport to the S.E.5. His habit was an invitation, and early in May the Germans put a machine gun in the church tower—and waited.

On the evening of May 7, 1917, Captain Albert Ball sped past to glance at the church clock. A few seconds later he crashed just outside the village of Annoeulin. A spray of bullets from that sanctuary had accomplished what the whole German Air Force had failed to do. At the end of that month—more than three weeks later —German newspapers were proclaiming the death of Captain Albert Ball. The reports said that he had been shot down by Lothar von Richthofen, brother of Manfred von Richthofen.

But the villagers of Annoeulin knew better. The British knew better, since Lothar von Richthofen stated in his combat report, or at least a combat report credited to him, that he had been victorious over Captain Ball, and had shot down his *Sopwith triplane* near Annoeulin. Somehow he had produced the motor number of Ball's S.E.5, but he couldn't give the aircraft number! When he was charged later with the mistake of calling Ball's S.E.5 a triplane, he stated blandly that in the heat of an action he *often* mistook biplanes for triplanes!

But Lothar von Richthofen could never explain this "victory" over Annoeulin on May 7, 1917, because on that date *Lothar von Richthofen was in Berlin on sick leave!*

As was to be expected, the German propaganda machine credited this "kill" to one of the Von Richthofens. Details mattered not. Facts could be woven and twisted into any required pattern. All that was needed was a glory tale to bolster the sagging morale of the German Air Force.

The Germans have never denied the fact that Ball's identification disc was on view in a German hospital where it was shown to several wounded British airmen with the proud explanation: "Well, there's the end of your great Captain Ball. He was shot down the other night by a lowly infantryman who was hiding in a church tower. He knew that the Britisher always passed that way . . . and, well, it was as easy as that."

But the years have added bewilderment to the story. It has been hashed and rehashed. Those who are always starry-eyed about the Flying Circus credit the victory to one or the other of the Von Richthofens, ignoring the fact that Manfred was on leave in Berlin, having been given a long period of retirement after shooting down his fifty-second victim. He had left the front on May 1 and did not return until June 14. Other reports claim that Lothar, who had been wounded early in May, was in a hospital in a state of shock, and was facing a long period of convalescence.

Cyril Ball, Albert's brother, who also served in the R.F.C., seemed to have no definite opinion as to how Captain Ball was killed, but stated that some people had accepted the story that Lothar von Richthofen had shot him down. Cyril had once talked to a peasant woman in Annoeulin who had told him that she had pulled Albert out of the crash. He was still alive at the time, but had a serious head wound and died shortly after while she held him in her arms. Some years later his father bought the field in which his son's plane had fallen, and had the spot concreted over to mark where he fell. Ball was buried in a nearby German cemetery.

On June 3, 1917, less than one month after his final flight, Captain Albert Ball was honored with the Victoria Cross. It was the tenth V.C. to be awarded after nearly three years of air fighting. Of those gallant ten, six had died in winning it.

CHAPTER 8

Knights of the Black Cross

The Allied airmen had no monopoly on courage or person-ality. The crack German cavalry regiments, put in the discard by trench warfare, contributed hundreds of heroic flyers to their cause, although many, like Boelcke and Gontermann, came to tragic ends. With the enemy running up high scores in fights inside their own lines, the British next concentrated on new, fast aircraft designed especially for particular tactical situations, co-operating with ground forces and tank battalions. But there were still thrilling combats being fought along the coast line by naval flyers bent on carrying out their nautical missions. A new parachute was devised and accepted by the Germans, and on two occasions the famed Ernst Udet's life was saved.

KNIGHTS OF THE BLACK CROSS

THE German Air Force, like its opposing organizations across the line, seemed to attract the most intriguing characters. All prejudices and personalities aside, it must be admitted that many of them were as high-minded, noble, patriotic, and as fabulous as could be found anywhere. Few of us who encountered these gentlemen daily ever considered them in the same class as the detested Prussian militarists, or counted them among the savage, unbridled exponents of barbarism found in the ranks of the German land and sea serv-ices. They fought boldly and died valiantly. They usually treated

182

their captives with sympathetic courtesy, and it was not until airmen prisoners were turned over to German Army officials that cruelty and inhumane treatment were suffered.

Most German airmen lived up to a great tradition, fighting to the end. They were the last to give up the conflict when famine, disorganization, and revolution had ended all ground and sea resistance.

It is interesting to reflect that the cavalry staff that had put up so many hindrances to the full development of the aviation force should provide so many of its fighting stars. This was noticeable on both sides of the line. Hundreds of ex-cavalrymen became aerial aces, and whether this phenomenon can be credited to the fact that men who had managed horses with the skill of their hands and sensitivity of their seats were better suited for the "feel" of the joystick so necessary in the aircraft of that day, or whether cavalrymen could be spared more easily than skilled infantry or artillerymen, will be debated. The fact remains, however, that a large percentage of German airmen previously had been members of crack mounted regiments.

Max von Mulzer, a pupil of Max Immelmann, was an N.C.O. in a cavalry regiment when war broke out. The son of a Bavarian doctor, he had been born in Kimratshofen near Kempten on July 9, 1893. On December 13, 1914, he was awarded his commission after winning the Iron Cross for a courageous cavalry action the previous September. Because of his cavalry training he was quick to realize that scouting could be carried out better from the cockpit of an airplane than from the saddle of a horse. He applied for and received a transfer to the Aviation Service and was a pilot with Section 4 by the end of 1915. He moved through the various assignments and eventually wound up with Section 62, where he came under the influence of both Boelcke and Immelmann.

Max von Mulzer was a handsome young man, smart, well groomed, and meticulous in everything. He was a long time in getting started on his fighting career, but once he had made his initial score he soon ran up six more, and was the fourth German airman to receive the coveted Pour le Mérite, which came to him on July 9, 1916. He also was given the responsibility of heading a newly formed Jasta 32, and a short time later, Max, who now was being called the Second Eagle of Lille, was honored with the Bavarian Max-Joseph Order, which in turn made him Ritter—or Sir Max—von Mulzer.

But all this glory was followed by a tragic end. In September of that year Max was ordered to Valenciennes and asked to test the new Albatros D.1. Intending to put the aircraft through every known military maneuver, he became the first victim of the D.1's faulty structure. The wing collapsed after a short flight and the aircraft augered into the ground. Von Mulzer had prophetically predicted his end. "I shall go next. Immelmann is dead; Parschau" (Otto Parschau, an eight-victory airman) "is dead; Kurt Wintgens is dead. I am next in line."

Another ex-cavalryman with the Parisian name of Oliver von Beaulieu-Marconnay was the son of a Prussian Army captain. Oliver joined the Fourth Dragoon Regiment in 1915 and saw service on the Eastern Front through 1916; but during the summer of 1917 he applied for a transfer, and by the autumn of that year was a member of Jasta 15 under Josef Valtjens.

Beaulieu-Marconnay was popular with everyone, and he put his training to good use by destroying his first enemy on May 28, 1918. He was flying a Siemens D.3 at the time, an aircraft that was slow in ordinary maneuvers, but could outclimb anything on the front. Later versions of this aircraft, modified to cut down its climb capability, improved the general flying characteristics, but it never was as popular as the Fokker D.7.

On September 2, 1918, Beaulieu-Marconnay was promoted to leader of Jasta 19, by which time he had been credited with twenty-five victories. A month later, while downing his twenty-sixth, he was wounded seriously and died in a hospital ten days later, the day on which he was awarded the Pour le Mérite.

Georg von Hantelmann was a lieutenant in the 17th Hussars Regiment, and transferred to the aviation service, becoming a pilot with Jasta 15 by February, 1918. Georg did not record a victory until June of that year, but from that time on his scores came in quick succession. Twenty-six fell before his guns, and many of them were Americans assigned to the Montdidier sector. Georg von Hantelmann was recommended for the Pour le Mérite, but never received it. The revolution that marked the close of Germany's resistance disposed of all such rewards and honors.

GONTERMANN DIES IN CRASH

Heinrich Gontermann, who had been born in Siegen, Westphalia, was a member of the 6th Uhlan Regiment, and at the outbreak of the war made a valiant attempt to get into the aviation service, but it was late in 1915 before his request was granted. By that time he had been made a lieutenant in the 80th Fusilier Regiment, but after some training at Doberitz and Johannisthal he finally gained his pilot's certificate. He then had a severe crash, and following that was given a refresher course on Ago and Albatros C.3's. When he was aboard one of the latter he tried to take on three Nieuports and was severely shot up. While flying a Roland C.2 he became something of a character on the front when he established a new type of plane decoration, a daubing of greens, browns, and in fact nearly every color of the spectrum. His activity and determination to fight in the air won him a transfer to a fighting school at Cologne, then to Jasta 5, where in less than a week he scored his first victory. He was awarded the Iron Cross, First Class, and, following an air crash, was made commander of Jasta 5. This crash came during a melee with a British formation when Lieutenant H. Berr, a ten-plane ace, crashed into a plane piloted by a Sergeant Hoppe. Both were diving on the same Englishman when they came together. Berr was killed, and Gontermann was given his command.

With the coming of fair weather in March, 1917, Heinrich tried some of the theories he had worked out during the winter, when adverse weather had limited air operations. He had made a study of Allied aircraft, concentrating on their critical points of construction and the blind spots of the pilots, and believed that he had discovered how to destroy the opposition with the least expenditure of ammunition. From his subsequent activities it was apparent that he had some reward for his investigations.

He ran his score up to five within three weeks, destroying a Fee over Bapaume on March 5, another went down on the 11th, a Sopwith Pup was shot down on the 14th, and five days later a Sopwith 1½-strutter became his victim. On the 24th, however, retribution set in when he took on a Spad of Number 16 Squadron, R.F.C., and the pilot shot him to rags and raffia. Gontermann had to land his Albatros minus much of its fabric and part of the top wing, and with a riddled undercarriage. He himself was unharmed, but he nurtured a determination to get revenge, and the next day went into the air and found two Sopwith 1½-strutters. He fired the gas tank of one of them with one short burst, and the resulting explosion enveloped the second, sending both British aircraft to earth in smoke and flames.

The following "Bloody April," when many German airmen fattened their scores, Gontermann added twelve victories to his logbook. This was the period when the R.F.C. Staff decided to hold back the appearance on the Western Front of the Bristol Fighter, the Sopwith Camel, and the S.E.5, presumably to produce them in squadron strengths during some future unannounced push. This decision left the war in the hands of the D.H.2's, Sop Pups, Fees, a sprinkling of Martinsydes, and what few Nieuports could be borrowed from the French. To expect these machines to go deep into enemy territory and take on great formations of Albatros, Halberstadt D.2's, Fokker D.3's, and the new Pfalz was criminal. The toll of Bloody April quickly reversed the decision, and the Jerry uprising was quenched.

It was during the height of this German success that Gontermann began his new forays against Allied kite balloons. He roared down on one of these observation bags near Armentières, sent it down in flames, and within three minutes caught another. He destroyed a third the following afternoon. After these successes Gontermann was ordered to command Jasta 15, replacing Lieutenant Reinhold, who had been shot down by a French Spad pilot. Although Gontermann was an able leader, he made few friends, and those who flew under him declared that he was overbearing and distrustful of any opinion other than his own.

Nevertheless, he continued to score victories and on May 5 shot the wings off a Nieuport, and downed another on May 11. With the registering of his twelfth success, Heinrich Gontermann was awarded the Pour le Mérite, given a month's leave, and as part of his rest and recreation he joined several other leading airmen in a recruiting campaign for the German Air Service. This flying furlough was brought to a hurried conclusion when it was learned that during Gontermann's absence his *Jasta* had been almost wiped out. He returned on June 19, went into the air, and found a Spad, which he shot down. Four more balloons fell before his guns during the next three weeks, but by now the rest of his squadron had been so battered by Allied airmen that it had to be withdrawn from the front and given a rest until August 12.

While new machines were being furnished, and new pilots drawn from other *Jasta* units or training schools, Gontermann returned to the front on his own, and on August 9 attacked a French balloon near Verdun. This bag went down with his first pass, but a second gave him considerable trouble. As he flew past at basket level, the observer opened up with a Hotchkiss gun and poured a full clip into Heinrich's Albatros and almost shot one of the Spandaus out of its mounting. Heinrich turned back in a wild rage, and used his remaining weapon to shoot down the Frenchman and his kite balloon in flames.

Three days after this narrow squeak, he went back to the same sector and set fire to another gasbag, but as he turned away in triumph three Spads darted down on him, and it needed all Gontermann's skill to escape their first charge. Once he had evaded these three, he whipped up, pulled a fast half roll, and went down on one of the Spads and sent it down. On August 18 he bagged two more balloons, and on the 20th, his greatest day, destroyed three kites during a single patrol. This feat was staged near Soissons, and it is believed that the balloons were British. The first one was fired before the two observers in the basket had any idea they were under attack. The burning balloon fell on the basket before either one could climb out and use his parachute. A short distance on, Gontermann fired two more, sending them down in the strange greenish-red glare that marks the end of these helpless bags. Since he still had plenty of ammunition and considerable fuel, he remained in the area and was taken on by a young Spad pilot who probably had noticed the burning gasbags. The German ace sat calmly and waited for the Spad to approach. The instant the Frenchman came into range, the German pressed his triggers, sending twelve bullets through the Frenchman's body. Three kites and a Spad in one offensive patrol!

Two more victories, a balloon and a Nieuport scout, went crashing down under Gontermann's fire before the month of August closed, but Heinrich was beginning to show the strain and after his thirty-sixth victory was ordered home for another month's rest. When he returned to Jasta 15 it was evident the leave had done him little good. On his very first flight after his return he made one of his infrequent bad landings, seriously damaging the machine. On September 29 he tangled with a Sopwith Camel. The British pilot flew rings around him and chased the German ace home with twenty-seven bullets in his plane's fuselage.

In October some of his old skill and daring came back when during a so-called dogfight, deep in German territory, between seven Albatros scouts and five Camels, he shot the wings off one Sopwith and sent another down in flames. How many of his own force was destroyed German records do not explain.

On October 3 Gontermann destroyed his thirty-ninth and last victim. On October 22 a new Fokker Dr.1, Anthony Fokker's three-winger that had been copied from the popular Sopwith triplane, was flown to Jasta 15's base for a test program. When Heinrich was on leave in Berlin he had expressed a wish to try one of these Fokker fighters, and when one was available, it was turned over to him for his expert opinion.

Adverse weather prevented a test until October 29, but at 4:15 P.M. that day the new plane was wheeled out and prepared for flight test. The Dr.1 was having a freakish history. First presented in August, 1917, and powered with the 110-horsepower Oberursel engine that few German airmen liked, it produced some amazing performances. Its three main planes permitted a short wing span which in turn gave it tremendous maneuverability and climb. At the hands of Werner Voss, twenty-two British aircraft were shot down on the Ypres sector within twenty-one days. This brought the plane to the attention of Baron von Richthofen, who adopted it with some success. It should be explained that since the British had been flying the Sopwith triplane for some time, the Fokker three-decker was often mistaken for the British mount, an error that was fatal in many instances.

The Dr.1 proved to be a very smart "dogfighter," and compared favorably with the Camel in tight maneuvers. But it was a comparative dud where level speed was concerned, although some German records insist that at sea level the Fokker triplane could fly at 121 miles per hour. On the other hand, it would climb to 10,000 feet in six minutes. It had the torque pull of the Oberursel, as did British machines powered with rotary engines, but it was the great amount of wing surface, augmented by a large airfoil type of fairing over the wheel axle, that gave the Dr.1 its tremendous lift for climbing. It had several tragic structural faults, however. In a long dive the fabric of the upper wing often would strip away, and in other instances the wing structure itself would collapse under any unusual stress. Baron von Richthofen was so pleased with the mount that he continued to fly it after the German air staff decided to condemn it, and was given a special, improved model for his own use. It was while flying in this plane that the baron met his end.

Gontermann possibly hoped that the triplane would give him a new zest for flying, and seemed particularly pleased with his new mount that day. The take-off was normal, and he appeared to have no trouble handling the rotary engine. Then at about 1,500 feet he started a series of simple school maneuvers, tried a loop and then a "falling leaf." Suddenly the Dr.1 dived toward the ground, and the spectators below thought Gontermann was making a simulated dive attack when, to everyone's horror, parts began to float away from the triplane. The top-wing center section buckled, and the aircraft crashed less than five yards from where it had left the ground.

Heinrich Gontermann was still alive when rescuers arrived, and although he was given every care, including an emergency operation, he died in the early hours of the following morning. There were some people who thought that Heinrich had fainted in the air, worn out by his weeks of determined activity. Others blamed the aircraft, and Germany buzzed for weeks with this controversy, but to this day the point has not been settled decisively.

And so passed a gallant airman, an ex-farm boy who served his country well and died untouched by Allied ammunition.

LOERZER, A FIGHTING GENTLEMAN

Captain Bruno Loerzer deserves more than passing mention, and should not be discarded from the ranks of the honored because of his lifelong association with Hermann Goering. The association was unfortunate, in that it continued on after the war, and during World War II Loerzer found himself playing the role of "pilot fish" to Goering, then Hitler's right-hand man and one of the most offensive Nazis of the period. It appeared that Loerzer could not discard this hated and, at times, ridiculous political clown.

Bruno Loerzer had wished always to be a farmer. Routine schooling bored him. He loved the outdoors and tasks that required manual effort. Although he reached the classrooms of the Königstadt High School in Berlin, he yearned for the freedom of the fields. Instead of continuing his education, he left school and took a train for Spessart, where another Loerzer worked on a farm. That is to say, he did for one full summer, but by that time he realized that farming was not all green fields, rosy-cheeked milkmaids, and wholesome meals. It required long hours of hard toil in rough farm garb in daylight that seemed unending.

That autumn he returned to Berlin, his body filled out, his muscles hardened, and, more important, with a clearer view of life. He finished high school but continued to work as a farmer during the summers, and when he had received his certificate, the German Army claimed him. After a term as color bearer to the 112th Infantry Regiment in Baden, his association with the regimental standard and the glory of marching at the head of the battalion stirred new ambition in him. He knew now that only a soldier's life would satisfy. He was also wise enough to realize that a private had no social standing, and at the first opportunity he entered the military training school at Potsdam. Displaying more zeal than he had shown in high school, Bruno applied himself to the new studies and by January, 1913, at the age of twenty-two he reported to the garrison at Mülhausen in Alsace, a fullfledged lieutenant. In the same regiment was another young officer named Hermann Goering.

It has been related in a previous chapter how Loerzer's concentration on a hand of cards led to his transfer to the aviation service, and how Goering followed him and became his observer. Loerzer must have realized that Goering seemed to dog his footsteps, but he could not refrain from inviting him to join in every move or adventure. It was when Goering was in a hospital with an attack of arthritis and seemed to have come to the end of his military career that Loerzer thought of the idea of getting Hermann out of the infantry and into aviation, at least as an observer. He could not possibly have known what effect that kind gesture would have on world history years later.

It is interesting to note that Loerzer's commanding officer wanted no part of Goering, although Hermann had crawled out of the hospital and deserted his infantry command to become an airman. Number 23 Staffel had more than enough observers, but was short on pilots. Again, Loerzer pleaded for Hermann, and he was allowed to stay on. This strange duo worked together like clockwork, and shortly after they were posted as a team they shot down a French plane over Verdun.

But Hermann was not satisfied with flying as an observer for long, and soon managed some pilot training to fly two-seaters. By the middle of 1916 Loerzer was commanding Jasta 26, and when Goering contrived to join that squadron he performed so well that within a short time he was made C.O. of Jasta 27, sharing the same field with Loerzer.

An interesting incident cropped up in Loerzer's career. When on leave in Berlin he learned that there were many new planes and much unusual equipment on display at Aldershof, an airfield on the outskirts of Berlin. Bruno hurried out there and arrived in time to watch a bumpety-bump landing of a weird civilian aircraft, after a wild display of crazy aerobatics that had threatened every spectator on the field. When its wheels finally touched down, the machine came to a halt and a gray-haired man, wearing a broad, good-natured smile, stepped out of the cockpit.

He introduced himself as Jacob Wolff, forty-six years of age, who had bought a plane, learned to fly, and was here offering his services —and his plane—to the German Air Force.

The commander of the field let out a booming laugh. What sort of fool was this, forty-six years old and trying to get into the most rugged section of the military forces? He tried to shoo him off, but Mr. Wolff would not be rebuffed. He argued that he could fly and was entitled to fly for his government. He had many sound arguments, too.

The field commander turned to Loerzer in desperation. "Here, lieutenant! You are a front-line pilot. Please assure Herr Wolff that war flying is a profession only for young men."

Bruno Loerzer looked at the ancient one; then his eyes twinkled. "Herr Wolff is, I think, young enough, and he certainly flies better than I did when I first went to the front."

The field commander spluttered and tried to control himself while the portly Wolff thanked Loerzer with a beaming smile. Jacob Wolff would not be stopped, and in spite of opposition from many quarters, he eventually donned a flying-service uniform. Loerzer forgot the incident, and when his leave was up he returned to the front. On his next patrol, while flying over Cambrai, he mistook a French two-seater for a single-seater and moved up with the idea of getting on its tail.

A vagrant wind fingered under his goggles, almost blowing them away, and while he took time to adjust the elastic bands, the gunner aboard the French plane poured at him a sharp burst that inflicted a severe wound in his right leg, another in his shoulder, and a third bullet creased his temple.

Shocked and unable to fight back, Bruno put his plane into falling-leaf maneuvers and found himself at about five hundred feet above the Maas River. He had somehow glided about fifty miles, dizzy with pain and half blinded. He peered about and finally made some sense out of his situation and aimed his craft at a friendly airfield. The ship was riddled, and he had to put it down carefully. When the wheels stopped rumbling, Loerzer collapsed. As he came to, he saw that he was being helped out of the cockpit by Oswald Boelcke.

Bruno was in a hospital for weeks, and it was some time before he could think of flying again. While he lay there he heard that Boelcke had been killed, news that saddened him but at the same time spurred him to get back with his unit. However, when he returned, his old comrades noticed a great change in him. He was nervous, irritable, and no longer exuded the gay and carefree spirit that had marked his early days. Realizing that in this condition Loerzer was not fit for the opposition the British were setting up in this sector, he was ordered to take more rest. The "rest" took the form of joining an area-defense two-seater *Staffel* based at Metz that was assigned to protect the great munitions works in Lorraine.

Sensing the comedown in his tactical importance, Bruno went to Metz in a discouraged and disheartened frame of mind; but the minute he entered this new squadron he was greeted by Lieutenant Jacob Wolff. Wolff was delighted to see Loerzer and did his best to enliven him—so much so that these two became bosom pals and

Loerzer decided to fly as Wolff's observer. Old Wolff was such a wild man in the air that few gunners or observers would make more than one trip with him. When Loerzer announced his intention to back up Wolff, the rest of the *Staffel* decided that he had lost his mind, and predicted a quick end for the convalescent fighter pilot.

On December 10, 1916, Wolff and Loerzer took off together, with old Jacob at the controls. They flew toward Nancy, where they found action. Four Caudrons boxed them in, and it needed all the ammunition Wolff had for his front gun, and that provided for the observer, to get them out of this melee. The Caudron gunners riddled the Aviatik from prop to rudder, but eventually Jacob saw a hole, barged through it, and headed home. Luckily, they both returned without a scratch, but the two-seater was in the repair shed for some time.

This foray did wonders for Wolff and the *Staffel*. In the first place, Jacob felt vindicated, and the action had aroused a new spirit of enthusiasm in Bruno. Wolff no longer had trouble in getting observers, and Bruno performed so well with the defense squadron that he was eventually recalled to a more important front, and given command of Jasta 26.

THE CHESSBOARD PILOTS

As a *Jasta* leader Bruno realized that he would have to select and train a special group of young, ambitious pilots, and one of the first called for was Hermann Goering. The next one was Bruno's brother Fritz, who was known as the Flying Pastor. A third candidate was Walter Blume, who was to score twenty-eight victories, gain the Pour le Mérite, and finally command Jasta 9. These men, along with eight more young eagles, filled out a twelve-pilot organization that Loerzer trained in a sheltered valley near Colmar in Alsace. For two months they went through a stiff course consisting of gunnery, formation flying, aerobatics, and aircraft recognition. When Jasta 26 was ready, their twenty-three-year-old leader took them up to Arras, where the heaviest air fighting was in progress.

They did so well that Von Richthofen urged Loerzer to adopt a *Jasta* marking that would identify the unit, and mark them as airmen other squadrons could rely on.

The idea intrigued Bruno, and he called on his men for suggestions. Blume said, "You have trained us to fight with our heads and to fly always a thought or two ahead of our opponents. Like a chess player." Walter Blume beamed, and added, "That's it. Why not a chessboard for our insignia?"

The others were delighted, and from that day on, the Albatroses of Jasta 26 were painted with black-and-white chessboard designs, and their sleek fighters were recognized from one end of the sector to the other. It was while leading this marked squadron that Loerzer finally racked up his fourth victory. He doubled the score over the next two weeks, and the Order of the House of Hohenzollern was added to his Iron Cross decoration. The spirit of the Checkerboards ran high for a time and they increased their scores week by week, but with the coming of summer, 1917, the British Camels and Bristol Fighters were taking a new toll. It was clear that once more the Allies were forging ahead.

This demanded new alignments, and when Von Richthofen formed four *Jastas* into a *Geschwader*—a Flying Circus—the German High Command saw the light. Bruno Loerzer, who was to receive the Pour le Mérite, was named to head a new and broader command, Geschwader 3, a circus of his own. The four squadrons under his leadership were headed by Fritz Loerzer, Carl Bolle, Hermann Goering, and H. Bongartz. It was well, for by now the March push of 1918 was about to jump off, and Germany would need every pilot and plane available.

THE BRITISH REPLY WITH TACTICAL OPERATIONS

Staying with their new tactical concept, the British devoted patrol after patrol to rear-area bombing, the beating-up of German airfields, and low-down ground attacks against enemy trenches. The German task was to fight off anything that came over, and as was to be expected, her fighter forces ran up new scores—but did not stop the Allied drive that surged out of the March setback. Even Von Richthofen went down in April.

When the spring and summer campaigns erupted, German fighter airmen fought like eagles, and at one time Bruno Loerzer was given fourteen *Jastas* to fly together as his circus. Again, he insisted on a period of intense training and, during the fight for Kemmel Hill, was given the responsibility of holding the sky. He did the best he could, but the Allied strength was overpowering. Next he was sent to bolster the situation along the Chemin des Dames, and what was left of Von Richthofen's circus joined him when for the first time German fighters encountered the Nieuports and Spads of the American Air Service. Fritz Loerzer was shot down and captured, but in the Champagne area the two German circuses claimed to have shot down thirty-five Allied planes in a very short time.

But the counteroffensives of the British Army and the new Royal Air Force were too much. They swarmed over Cambrai, headed by a new fleet of Mark IV tanks, while tight formations of Bristol Fighters, Sopwith Dolphins, S.E.5's, and the ever-reliable Camel swept everything out of the skies; even the vaunted Fokker D.7 had no chance against this new breed of winged attackers.

Loerzer and his men hung on like leeches, but the cards were stacked against them: circus formations had been cut to the bone; there was little fuel; and the people back home were not maintaining the factory pace. Now the German circuses were having to fight formations that outnumbered them three to one, and the German flyers possibly realized what the French and the British had withstood in the past when they continued *their* tactical operations against such overwhelming odds.

Loerzer held his dwindling formation together as long as he could. He had scored forty-four successes with his own guns, but the gray-green armies of the Kaiser no longer could hold the line. The airfields were bombed out as fast as Loerzer's pilots selected bases from which to make the next stand. They were driven back, back, flying anything that would get off the ground—never surrendering, but never making a dent in the onrush. Captain Loerzer, who was one of Germany's greatest air heroes, lived through it all, only to be involved once more with Hermann Goering and the further degradation of his homeland.

THE FIGHTER OF ZEEBRUGGE

The story of a lesser-known German airman, Lieutenant Friedrich Christiansen, sometimes known as the Fighter of Zeebrugge, offers a change of pace, because he never flew a single-seater in action and, in contrast to the general war pilot, was thirty-seven years old at the height of his career—not as old as Jacob Wolff, who ended the war with ten victories, but certainly well beyond the average age of the men who fought in the skies.

Christiansen basically was a sailor, having been born into a naval family at Wyk on Föhr Island in Schleswig-Holstein December 12, 1879. After the routine of naval life, he gained a pilot's certificate and passed out on a Gotha-Hansa Taube in 1914. The next year he was attached to the aviation station at Zeebrugge, but as few efficient seaplanes were available there, Friedrich made the best of the situation and stayed out of trouble for about two years. Then in 1917 he was placed in command of the Zeebrugge flying station, and shortly after, several Hansa-Brandenburg seaplanes were delivered there. This low-wing monoplane floatplane was powered with a 260-horsepower Maybach engine and had a speed of 106 miles per hour. Equipped as a naval fighter, it carried two fixed Spandau guns for the pilot and a single Parabellum on a ring mounting for the observer. It was designed and developed for the German Navy in its attempt to gain control of the Belgian coast line and the North Sea. At one time the Zeebrugge station had thirty-five of these mounts and the Ostend depot fourteen.

Christiansen enjoyed his first success when he damaged the British submarine C.25 and, shortly after, on December 11, 1917, caught and destroyed the British coastal airship C.27 with its crew of five men. It went down in flames off the East Anglian coast. At

the end of the war he claimed twenty-one victories, including airplanes, flying boats, balloons, an airship, and a submarine.

The flying-boat incident was hardly a victory, since the British
F.2A—Felixstowe flying boat—had been forced down with a broken
feed line, and on being attacked by the Brandenburg, the pilot was
forced to taxi his machine to Holland, where he beached it and set
it on fire.

The submarine also was not actually destroyed. It was attacked
and damaged, but it returned to its base. His claim to the coastal
airship was not questioned, for it left Pulham, England, on the day
the German airman claimed it and was reported missing by night.
By coincidence its sister ship, the C.26, was lost the following day
when its engine failed and it drifted to Eesmess near the Zuider
Zee, where its crew was interned by the Dutch.

After the war Friedrich Christiansen took a position as captain of
a Hamburg-American steamer, and in later years gained further
fame when he piloted the Giant Dornier Do.X around the world.
With the rise of Hitler he became first chief of the Nazi Flying
Corps, a semi-military organization that was formed to promote
new interest in aviation. During the 1939–45 war he was head of
the military government set up in the Netherlands and was charged
later by the Allies with the cruelties perpetrated by the SS and German armed forces in his zone. He was sentenced to imprisonment,
but was pardoned eventually. He resides in West Germany today.

ERNST UDET, PLAYBOY ACE

One of Germany's most colorful airmen was a young Prussian
named Ernst Udet, the son of Adolf Udet. The name is pronounced
"Oo-det," although for years the British and Americans have said
"Yew-det." He was the youngest ace in the German Air Service, and
with his sixty-two victories was next to the Red Knight of Germany.

Udet was a true playboy, and his gaiety in the bars, night clubs,
and hotels of Berlin during his furloughs matched his four years of
fighting on the ground and in the air. His was a far more appealing
character than Von Richthofen, Voss, Immelmann, or Erich Loewen-

hardt, for he had a sense of humor. He fought on every front and aboard nearly every type of German aircraft. He also was the luckiest, for on two occasions he was shot down, but in both instances his life was saved by a Paulus parachute, a safety device then being given to German airmen. As a matter of fact, Udet, the "beer and baloney" airman, as so many called him, may have been the first wartime aviator to be saved by this pack-seat device.

Ernst showed little interest in books or routine study, but as a schoolboy was impressed by the aircraft of his time. There is a story to the effect that when he was thirteen he made the acquaintance of Otto Lilienthal and constructed a glider with him; but since Lilienthal was killed August 9, 1896, the year Ernst was born, this was impossible. But Udet's life story is crammed with such tales, including the one in which he jumped with an open umbrella from the balcony of a house and landed on the head of a passing policeman.

Bypassing these schoolboy legends, we learn that at the age of eighteen, still only a couple of inches taller than five feet, Ernst Udet tried to join the Army at the outbreak of the war, but was turned down in Bavaria; he went to Prussia, where he became a motorcycle dispatch rider. His most important job seemed to be the delivery of mail for the troops, a most popular role.

During the bitter fighting around Strasbourg he was severely injured in a motorcycle accident. A long period in the hospital and a term of convalescence followed, during which time he discovered a civilian flying field that was owned by an old friend, Gustave Otto. Here he bought a short course in flying and completed the requirements before the end of his sick leave. He applied for a transfer to the Aviation Service, but was turned down time and again until June, 1915, when he finally reached his goal. However, as there were hundreds of other candidates ahead of him he was listed as a private in the Third Company of the Third Flight Battalion. He endured the indignity of manual toil and parade-ground drill until the fact that he had a civilian flying ticket reached the

desk of his captain, and he was quickly transferred to a military flying school at Darmstadt.

His early training put him in advanced classes and he was soon
sent on his final cross-country, a hop covering about two hundred
miles. Inviting a friend, Lieutenant Gerlich, to furnish the necessary
confirmation, Udet took off across the Rhine and landed at Bonn
with no trouble at all. The two men went into the town to mark
this achievement, where they tested the beer and baloney. After
a lengthy session of such refreshment, they returned to the field,
where they discovered that one tire of the airplane was flat. Neither
airman was in any condition to make a suitable repair, so Ernst took
off both tires and flew the rest of the circuit with the steel rims.

After that effort, Udet was promoted to master pilot and sent
down to a fairly quiet front in southern Alsace. Although this area
was not too active, compared to the sectors farther north, the
Germans were hoping secretly that a route might be forced through
the mountains, and kept up a continual program of observation and
artillery spotting. His bow on this front was somewhat tragic, for
on his first take-off, trying to impress his flight commander, Ernst
made a climbing turn close to the ground, dug a wingtip in, and
completely wrecked the bus. He was placed in a hospital under
arrest and told that he would be tossed out of the Air Service when
he recovered; but during this time Ernst thought of a convincing
plea, and when his period of arrest was over, he was permitted to
return to duty.

His second war flight was somewhat more encouraging. He had
drawn a Lieutenant Justinus as his observer, and getting off smartly,
they soon were over the trench area. They encountered a French
Farman, but Justinus ignored it, going about his observation business, since both he and Udet knew that the Frenchman was armed
no better than they. After an hour of snooping, the observer told
Udet to buzz home.

The next approach to the enemy lines was almost Udet's last.
All the Aviatiks in the area had been ordered to make a bomb raid
on the town of Belfort, each plane carrying six light bombs and

two Mauser automatic rifles. The weather deteriorated and heavy clouds were encountered at 15,000 feet, and since their aircraft could fly no higher, the formation broke up. Udet, who was flying as the leader, signaled the other planes to wheel and try to get back to their own lines, but as Udet's Aviatik made its turn, something fouled a control and he could not haul the plane back to an even keel. It fell off in a series of jerky sideslips. After some moments of endeavor Udet was able to bring his craft to a fairly level position. He then noted a broken control cable that threatened to leave the elevator in a depressed position. He tried to yank it loose, or free, but it would not budge. He tried fanning the elevator with the propeller, but this only increased the angle of their dive.

At this point his observer, Lieutenant Justinus, suggested that they try to get down in Switzerland to avoid being taken prisoner by the French. When Udet hesitated, the observer left his seat and crawled out on the left wing, hoping the shift of weight would level the Aviatik. But nothing of the sort happened, so Justinus kicked out some fuselage panels and found another elevator cable, which he pulled and tugged until the nose of the plane came up slightly. By easing back on the throttle Udet was then able to maintain a fair amount of control, and finally landed the Aviatik inside the German lines. Justinus was awarded the Iron Cross, First Class, and Udet the Iron Cross, Second Class.

FIXED-GUN ENCOUNTERS

But a greater honor was to come to Udet. He was transferred to a new Aviatik *Staffel,* but given a new Fokker fixed-gun fighter with which he was expected to provide air protection for the observation planes. A short time later he had his first real air fight when he came upon a Voisin biplane and opened fire at about six hundred yards. The Voisin gunner replied in kind, both men banging away at this ridiculous distance until they had expended their ammunition.

A second encounter had a different ending when Udet met a Caudron and this time moved in close before opening fire. His gun jammed after but three bullets had been fired, and while he attempted to clear the stoppage, the French gunner peppered him with plenty of ammunition and forced Udet to dive and run for home.

Victory came at last one day when he was over Colmar and spotted twenty specks heading toward Mulhouse. Ernst climbed to escape their notice and waited above. He saw that they were were Caudrons and Farmans. When the French formation was directly below him, he nosed down and fired from fifty feet. A Farman burst into flames, and so fascinated him that he forgot about the others until he found himself in the middle of a fantastic melee with gunfire streaking across the sky from all directions. While basking in the glory of his first victory, Udet had not noticed that other German planes had joined the fray, thus setting up one of the near-dogfights of that time.

Ernst Udet was awarded the Iron Cross, First Class, for this performance.

A short time later, when returning from the lines, his engine stopped and he made the mistake of selecting a cornfield for his forced landing. The Fokker turned turtle and Udet was trapped inside for fifteen minues as he frantically tried to free himself before the hulk went up in flames.

Udet then took part in another German defense of the Oberndorf munitions works, a target the French and the British had been watching a long while. The first big attack came on March 18, 1916, and when the raiders appeared, every fighter plane in the area took to the air to head them off. Udet, who had become separated from his flight, spotted seven Allied aircraft heading toward the Rhine, and two Nieuport scouts flying above them. Then the seven dual-place planes became twenty-three, and Udet hesitated, wondering whether or not a lone Fokker could risk so many enemy guns. Below were well-known towns, houses, hotels, gardens, cafés, and the geometrical pattern of streets. There were a thousand round discs that represented upturned faces. Ernst realized that he was alone and had every right to await the arrival of some of his comrades. Years later he wrote that he had been torn between two great emotions—one based on the law of self-preservation, and the other on honor.

"I somehow realized that if I failed to open the battle immediately, I should never have the courage to do so afterwards. In that case I would land, go to my room, and then in the morning, Pfälzer [his roommate] would have the task of writing my father that there had been a fatal accident while I was cleaning my revolver."

He took the plunge and opened the most decisive battle of his flying career. He went down on a big Farman nestling in the center of the Allied formation. As he opened the throttle and dived with the engine full on, the bomber spread its wings and seemed to grow in size. For a few seconds he could distinguish every detail, as if examining the machine through a microscope. The observer turned around and he could see his round leather helmet, which became the bull's-eye for his machine gun. He opened fire from a distance of about ninety feet, and the Farman faltered almost immediately. A glaring blue flash stabbed from the exhaust, followed by a spume of white smoke, and Udet knew the fuel tank had been hit. A second or so later a spatter of enemy machine-gun bullets drew his attention from his victim. Turning sharply, he saw he was under the fire of two Caudron gunners.

But he passed this ordeal with no concern. He was perfectly calm, and carried out the rest of his maneuvers with the poise of an advanced aerobatics student. Diving once more, he caught up with the Farman that by now was roaring across the sky like a giant torch hurled in anger. A figure with outstretched arms and legs was catapulted from the wreckage.

"I never considered that either of the men was a human being. That never occurred to me. I was only conscious of one sensation—victory . . . triumph! The iron band about my chest snapped, and the blood coursed freely through my body. The tension was over. I had been blooded in action," he said some time later.

What happened then was typical of all such general engagements. Other German aircraft joined the battle, and other Allied planes were shot down and some German machines were lost. Ernst Udet did not get another, although he saw and caught up with a laggard Caudron. His gun jammed after he had fired a burst into one of its engines. He saw the propeller wigwag to a halt, but the Frenchman evidently limped home.

The year 1916 saw the life and death sparkle of many of Germany's early aces. Immelmann and Boelcke were the first to go, and others enjoying a brief hour of fame were snuffed out during that dreadful summer. Youngsters who showed any inclination for this mad cocking main were drawn from other squadrons and other areas to take up the fight against the British, who were having their hour of success.

Udet continued to forge ahead in Alsace, adding to his skill and score, chiefly against French opposition. By December, 1917, he was credited with twenty-one victories and was transferred to the Aisne sector, where he was posted to Jasta 15, commanded by Heinrich Gontermann. He flew a new Albatros, probably the D.3, better known as the Vee-Strutter. The opposition was stiffer, but Ernst reveled in it, performing remarkably well. For a time he tried to emulate Gontermann, who seemed to shoot down a balloon whenever the opportunity arose. But Udet had little luck. Every time he went down on one of the observation bags, a Spad bearing a Storks insignia would arrive to drive him off.

The Frenchmen in this area included Nungesser, Dorme, Heurteaux, Navarre, Lenoir, Chainat, and Deullin. They were encountered continually on this front, harrying the German airmen. Jasta 15 received the brunt of this, and in time Udet was placed in charge of Jasta 37 on the Flanders front to fight the British. On one occasion he picked on a straggling Bristol Fighter, but was given a wicked reception by the gunner. Amazed at this opposition, Ernst nosed down and found that he was being shot at by the British two-seater's pilot who had followed him. He thought his war was over for a minute, but suddenly, for no apparent reason, the Bristol Fighter exploded in midair. It may have been one of those million-to-one shots from an antiaircraft gun; but whatever, Ernst knew he had been spared once more.

The winter of 1917–18 saw little fighter action, but Udet was awarded the Pour le Mérite. Baron von Richthofen gave a decorations party and during it invited Udet to join his circus. Three days later he was flying tail guard to the baron, a day on which the circus destroyed twelve Allied aircraft. Udet's skill and wild daring were now recognized, and he was next given command of Jasta 11, then of Jasta 4. When Baron von Richthofen was unable to lead the *Jagdgeschwader*, Ernst was given full command of the circus in the air.

UDET TAKES TO THE SILK

In the last year of the war, during the German March push, Udet had another close call. After attacking a British B.E. observation ship, he became careless, believing he had disposed of the rear gunner. Before he knew what happened his own plane was shot apart. Going over the side with the seat-pack parachute that many German airmen carried, he was shocked to note that the device had opened too soon, and a portion of the canopy had fouled on the plane's rudder and fin. For a minute or so, while his triplane whirled in helpless circuits, Udet was slung about on the ends of his shroud lines and harness. The canopy was partly open, and for a time it looked as if the pilot would go down with the whirling wreckage.

Fortunately, the Quirk gunner had so damaged the rudder assembly that the weight of Udet swinging about eventually tore it apart. The parachute floated free at last and the German ace landed safely. No luckier escape had been recorded.

The great Von Richthofen went down in April, and the Allies were shooting down German fighter pilots like ducks in a shooting gallery. The bomber squadrons were being raided for pilot talent, and only a handful of capable leaders was left to hold the remains of the circus *Jasta* group together. On the other side of the line, where first-class aircraft were plentiful, hundreds of young, inexperienced but high-spirited youths were swarming to the lines, hoping to emulate Albert Ball, Guynemer, McCudden, Nungesser, or Billy Bishop. The result was what might have been expected. The experienced performers fattened their scores against the newcomers, or their improved mounts outperformed the equipment flown by the other side. It was in the summer and autumn months of 1918 that dozens of inspired young men either went down in flaming cockpits or fought their way to glory in the "ace" columns. It was unclassified murder, a period in which military aviation was criminally employed, when so many fine men were sacrificed needlessly to furnish "victory" headlines. Only a handful of wise men held to the rules and laws of tactical aviation, and a lesser number tried to promote strategic aviation—the soundest policy of aviation employment. But today, no matter how many months or years we have served, no matter how many observation patrols we have carried out, nor how many photo reconnaissance missions we have completed, we are seldom considered as having done our bit unless we can produce fantastic scores—victories in the air against other victims who were fighting their air war as they had been ordered, but not fully trained to do.

We know now that to place so much importance on the history of the aces is folly. Their lives were glamorous and thrilling from the standpoint of knightly action, but their influence was nothing more than a great illusion. We know now that Udet, Ball, Von Richthofen, Guynemer, and Mannock, although popular figures in air-war histories, contributed little to the ultimate conclusion. Had the two-seater fighter been developed to its fullest potential, the first war in the air might have been fought more efficiently, at less cost, and brought the conflict to an earlier finish. If, instead of concentrating on the pattern of single combat, the Allied Staff had developed a true program of tactical aviation to support the ground forces, then had built up gradually a strategic force to batter the German war production before it could be put into action, the war would have been won early in 1917, instead of some eighteen months later.

But the insanity went on and on. By the middle of April, 1918, a handful of American air squadrons appeared on the front and, after the routine of preliminary probes, began to take over small sectors and assume some of the responsibility. On July 12, 1918, the American 27th Squadron of the First Pursuit Group was on patrol south of Château-Thierry. Lieutenant Fred Norton was leading nine Nieuports flying at 16,000 feet, and they ran into a small Fokker formation of eleven planes. Lieutenant W. B. Wanamaker, now an Akron, Ohio, lawyer, was holding a "coffin corner" position at the rear. It was he who first spotted the opposition when a German plane nosed on Lieutenant Grant. The Ohio youth took up the defense and tried to drive off the German who was threatening Grant, and in doing so eased into a cone of fire triggered by another Jerry pilot. When a long burst peppered his wings and shattered his instrument panel, Wanamaker turned down and went into an evasive spin.

THE WANAMAKER INCIDENT

His adversary was Ernst Udet, bagging his thirty-ninth victory, and Wanamaker was lucky to live through the next few moments. Burst after burst banged into his Nieuport, but he got down alive. In recent years Wanamaker has stated that once he realized that he was being forced down in enemy territory, he did what was expected of him, and deliberately crashed his machine to prevent its falling into the hands of the Germans. Since hundreds of Nieuports in various stages of destruction had been picked up over the war months, it is difficult to understand what this valiant gesture accomplished, but he is to be commended for his spirit. When he came to, he found himself out of the cockpit on the ground and surrounded by a number of German soldiers.

Wanamaker tried his limited German on the group, but none would draw near him to give him any aid. He next remembers Udet striding through the circle and ordering the soldiers to lift him from the proximity of the wreckage. He introduced himself and offered Wanamaker a cigarette, then tucked the rest of the package into one of the injured man's pockets.

"Do you have any bullet wounds?" he asked him.

"No, I don't think so."

"Well, don't feel downhearted," Udet explained in English. "I had downed thirty-eight others before you."

It was not until the injured pilot was put on a stretcher that Udet realized he was wearing an American uniform. With that he ripped off a portion of the rudder fabric of Wanamaker's machine and requested him to autograph it.

It was discovered in the hospital that the American had suffered severe injuries to his spine, had a broken leg and ankle, and several painful cuts.

About a month after the Wanamaker episode, Udet, who seemed to get into scrapes and near-disasters that would have broken the nerve of a lesser man, was flying a low-level patrol with several other pilots of his *Jasta* when a lone Camel came down from above with both guns singing. Udet did a tight bank, went into an Immelmann turn, and finally worked his way to the tail of the Britisher. The Camel went into a dive and Udet followed.

At about 1,000 feet the R.A.F. pilot zoomed suddenly and twisted into a tight turn. Udet stuck to his original course, expecting his foe to swerve aside. Determined not to give the German a clear shot, the Britisher made a new move, and the Fokker and Sopwith collided. There was a terrific crash and the Camel's wings crumpled when hit by Udet's undercarriage. For an instant both planes clutched together, then gradually fell apart, with the Camel starting a tight spin. The Fokker hung together, and with rare luck Udet put her down in a near-by field. The British pilot finally pulled his damaged plane out of its spin, then pancaked the hulk on some plowed land. This was the German's forty-seventh victory—a very questionable credit, one in which the fortunes of war played the most important role. Had the encounter taken place over the British lines, the credit would have been reversed.

The war ground through its final stages with the Allies taking longer chances to get to the enemy's sources of supply. They forced their way in deeper and deeper, and what German fighter pilots were left continued to add to their scores, although by then they all knew that their war had been lost. Udet's sixty-second and final victory was scored over a British D.H.9 bomber that was heading for Metz. He had dispatched another of the same type a few minutes before. Thus ended the war career of the ranking living German ace, probably one of the most picturesque figures to wear the uniform of the German Air Service—certainly one who was respected on both sides of the line.

CHAPTER 9

The Lafayette Escadrille

This small band of American volunteers wove a tapestry of heroism which few war stories or action novels can match, and the plain, simple tale of this amazing group will long remain a classic. No chapter in the story of the professional soldier can be more stirring than the adventures of this handful of amateur Galahads. Fatigue, frustrations, and defeats were their daily lot, for previous to their enlistments they had had no conception of what trials modern warfare can produce. Above all they could smile in the face of adversity; humor, horseplay, and the courage to laugh at themselves enlivened and soothed their trials.

PAYMENT OF THE DEBT

THE Escadrille Américaine, that brave little band of volunteers determined to pay their country's debt to France, suffered many of the repulses and reverses of fortune that beset all men of high ideals and generous intent. Theirs was a rugged path to the stars, for it had taken Norman Prince nearly two years to see his original idea come to fruition; and although by 1916 there was a Nieuport squadron manned by a handful of his countrymen on the Western Front, he knew that they were being nursed along, given the best equipment available, and not burdened with too many hazardous missions.

There were reasons other than comradely concern for this solicitous handling of the volunteers. Although fully appreciative of the

210

original gesture, the French took the realistic viewpoint that an American squadron serving in its Air Service had important political implications. France wanted the whole world to know that her cause was right, that it had attracted the finest of America's young gallants; their every patrol and air combat was proclaimed to the limit. Whenever one of the volunteers was promoted or awarded a decoration, the news was cabled around the world, for it was realized that through these men and their activities American support and sympathies could be inflated to a valuable level.

This idea had begun to pay fair dividends to some extent. The members of the Escadrille Américaine were headliners and heroes; in fact, the pilots of N.124 were sometimes outraged by the ridiculous tales of their exploits that appeared in American newspapers and magazines. But not all of the United States was favorable to the Allies. There were groups of foreign-born which resented the contribution of these volunteers, and made some official moves to have them declared mercenaries, arguing that they had forfeited their rights as American citizens. In fact, whenever the volunteers were given furloughs home, they had to discard their uniforms and appear in civilian clothing.

GERMANY PROTESTS AMERICAN SQUADRON

The publicity surrounding the activities of the Escadrille aroused German diplomatic authorities, and they stormed to the White House and presented their formal remonstrances to President Wilson. They objected to the activities of the Americans, who as representatives of a neutral state were engaging and destroying German aircraft and thereby shattering all rules of international amity. The German officials were outraged that American citizens were flying French aircraft and challenging German airmen in the sky over German territory. It was further pointed out that their aircraft bore American flag insignia, and that their squadron designation actually included the name of America. What sort of neutrality was that? Germany's tearing up of the "scrap of paper" that assured Belgium's neutrality, her U-boat warfare against unarmed merchant shipping, and her use of weapons that had been strictly forbidden by the Hague Convention were, of course, ignored.

The Wilson government bowed to the German representatives for political expediency, and orders were issued through diplomatic channels that the American volunteers could no longer operate under the name Escadrille Américaine. This was a blow to the group, for most of them felt that they would lose an important feature of their identity. As members of Escadrille N.124 they were anonymous, unattached, and deprived of their birthright. They argued that they were Americans who had volunteered to fight for France, and could see no reason why they could not continue to do so under their own colors.

Dr. Edmund L. Gros, an American physician living in Paris who had provided a business office in his home for the volunteers, offered a solution to the difficult problem. After some heated discussion with French military officials, he suddenly remembered that the debt the Americans were attempting to honor was originally contracted with the Marquis de Lafayette during the Revolutionary War. It was therefore simple to submit "Lafayette Escadrille" to replace the objectionable Escadrille Américaine. This satisfied all concerned, for it indicated the objective of the American volunteers; it paid further honor to the young Frenchman who had volunteered to fight for the colonies; and it eliminated any actual reference to the United States.

Only thirty-eight Americans can claim that they were members of the Lafayette Escadrille—those who were actual members of N.124. Dozens of other American volunteers who could not be accommodated in that squadron, but who served in other French escadrilles, are listed today in what is known as the Lafayette Flying Corps. The two organizations should not be confused.

THE DOUGHTY RAOUL LUFBERY

The outstanding figure in the Lafayette Escadrille was Raoul Lufbery, who was not a native American. He was born in France March 14, 1885, and was somewhat older than the average World

War I airman. His mother had died one year after his birth, and
in 1890 his father remarried and shortly after took his new wife to
the United States. Young Raoul and two brothers were left with
their grandmother while their father sought his fortune in the New
World.

When he was in his early teens young Raoul had a job in a
chocolate factory and for nearly four years sent his father most
of his earnings, money that helped M. Lufbery to establish a comfortable home in Wallingford, Connecticut, and later on set up a
flourishing stamp business. At the age of nineteen Raoul decided to
see the world, and eventually arrived in the United States with the
intention of seeing his father. Lufbery Senior, however, had left
Connecticut on business, and on the very day his father sailed from
New York for Europe, Raoul arrived in that same port. As events
turned out, they never did meet again. Raoul stayed in Wallingford
for nearly two years, picking up a smattering of English; but he was
not geared to settle down, and he next moved to Cuba, swung back
to the United States, and, after various jobs, evaded the panic of
1907 by joining the U.S. Army. He was shipped immediately to
the Philippines, where his military service entitled him to claim
American citizenship some years later. He completed a two-year
hitch, gathered his savings, and headed for Japan and China.

In 1912 he was in Indo-China, where he became acquainted with
Marc Pourpe, a noted French aviator who was giving exhibition
flights with a Blériot monoplane. Lufbery assumed the task of boss-
ing a group of coolies who were erecting a canvas hangar for the
monoplane, a job that led to his agreeing to travel with Pourpe
to handle the heavy work and in time learn some of the skills of an
aviation mechanic. These two men barnstormed around Europe
and Africa for the next two years, and when Marc attempted a
flight from Cairo to Khartoum and return, it was Raoul who made
the flight possible. Without his superhuman efforts to keep his pilot
supplied with fuel, spares, and mechanical service, the epic flight
could not have been completed. Marc Pourpe became one of the
outstanding airmen of the period as the result of this effort.

In the early summer of 1914 they returned to France to buy a Morane Parasol with the intention of going back to the Far East for another exhibition tour, but war broke out and Pourpe offered his services to the French Aviation.

Contrary to popular belief, Raoul Lufbery did not enlist with his companion. He accepted the breaks of fate, bade Marc good-by, and was among the first American volunteers to gather at the Hôtel des Invalides in Paris, and joined up as an infantryman in the Foreign Legion on August 24. Whether Pourpe exerted any influence, or whether Lufbery's mechanical skill had anything to do with it, within a week he was transferred to Pourpe's squadron as an aviation mechanic. Three months later Marc Pourpe was killed in action.

Raoul remained in the squadron, servicing other airplanes, but perceptive French officers sensed the spirit of devotion that had existed between these two men. Pourpe had been an artist in every sense of the word, but Lufbery was a hard-bitten adventurer with no basic roots, family ties, and little formal education. He had been a heavy drinker, a man who took his fun where he found it. Nevertheless, there had been a strange affinity between Marc and Raoul, and when it was obvious that Lufbery was badly shaken by Pourpe's death, someone suggested that he take pilot training. Raoul accepted gratefully, with no dramatic resolutions or theatrical declarations of revenge. He was not capable of such histrionics. He simply picked up his gear, took one last look toward the east, and strode out of the camp.

Raoul received his early training at Chartres and earned his wings on a Farman. Later he had bombing instruction on a Voisin, and his first war flying was with VB.106, where he proved to be a workmanlike performer, carrying out his duties creditably. He made no outstanding contribution and won few citations. After a reasonable number of hours on bombardment duty, he applied for chasse training. His commander, who realized that experienced bomber pilots were at a premium, tried to dissuade him and, when that failed, used every means to keep this impassive but reliable airman. But Lufbery was rewarded eventually and went to Plessis-Belleville for training on the Nieuport. He displayed no particular skill or brilliance, for he was heavy-handed, and for a time his instructors feared he would have to be sent back to the bomber squadron. But Luf persisted until he had gained some proficiency, and eventually joined the Escadrille Américaine.

THE UNKNOWN HERO

When he arrived at Luxeuil he was a total unknown. In appearance he was small, chunky, not much over five feet tall, with broad shoulders, a scowl, crude speech, and apparently no emotions of any kind. He seldom laughed, but when he did it was a hearty tavern roar and his eyes would sparkle like polished brilliants. He made few friends, and seemed inscrutable to his companions. Even Ted Parsons, who lived, flew, slept, and shared leaves with Lufbery, admits that he never actually knew him. Raoul seldom spoke of his past, and his speech was a polyglot of every patois he had picked up. Certainly he did not speak like a New Englander. He had few outstanding personal qualities or social graces, but he was to gain these attributes through his association with the various men who were to build up the Escadrille. There can be no reflection on his skill or daring, for he had the makings of a great "ace"; and had Lufbery been more fortunate, had history been kinder, had he remained with the French after the United States entered the war, he might have become an outstanding airman, one in the same class as Mickey Mannock, who also came up from the dregs of poverty.

Few people today know who Raoul Lufbery was, or where he came from. No flying field has been named for him, although an ancient defensive maneuver known as the Lufbery circle bears his name—though it is debatable whether he originated it, any more than that Max Immelmann first performed the Immelmann turn. The trick of a number of planes latching on to one another's tails and flying in a tight circle as a defense against an enemy moving into that critical position was known on every front from the time aircraft worked in elements, and airmen on both sides of the line had adopted the protective maneuver long before Raoul Lufbery had flown solo.

This mystery man joined N.124 on May 24, 1916, but did not score a victory until July 30, when he downed singlehanded an enemy airplane east of Etain in the Verdun sector. This victory triggered his air-war career, for he registered his second in the same area that afternoon. From that time on, Raoul became a relentless stalker, prowling the sky hour after hour, never returning until his fuel was exhausted or his ammo containers were empty. He was not a skilled duelist at first, for he often landed with his Nieuport a veritable sieve of bullet holes and shrapnel tears.

Only those who have engaged in such battles can understand the physical strain and the spirit it drains from the combatants. There is the effort of searching and seeking out, the decision as to what type of plane has been spotted; and when at last an enemy has been brought into sight, some other influence takes over. You wonder about your guns, your fuel, and your actual position with regard to the front line. You can't remember whether the hydraulic interrupter gear has been set for action. If not, the weapon will fire "late" and shoot your propeller to matchwood. All these queries arise and in turn attract others. You wonder what your speed is but dare not take your eyes off your opponent. When, after some uncertain maneuvering, you think you have your enemy exactly where you want him, you suddenly realize that he may be "bait" and that at any minute someone else will pour a deadly stream of lead into your back.

While you make other plans to ward off the inevitable, you next remember that you began this brawl well inside the enemy lines. You have performed an untold number of crazy circuits by now and you wonder how far inside the area of danger these battle gymnastics have taken you. What was the wind like when you took off? How long has this circling been going on? If you risk a glance at the topography below, you might miss your great chance. Nine times out of ten you have no idea what the area below represents. You are positive you have never before seen this spread of

real estate—and where the devil are the five other pilots who started
out with you?

A CONTEST WITH BOELCKE

Possibly Lufbery's most decisive battle was on the day he encountered Oswald Boelcke, and paradoxically it ended with no
decision of any kind. But the fact that he lived through the contest and held off this master duelist must have given Raoul a
tremendous boost in confidence. From all accounts they met quite
near to the French–German lines, and Lufbery immediately recognized his opponent's plane by its scarlet *décor*, but he felt no
sense of inferiority and plunged into the attack. The German stayed
out of trouble, but attempted to draw his opponent well into the
German lines. Both pilots exchanged burst after burst, but both
were able to evade the opposition slugs. Both men took wild chances
with the structure of their aircraft, and whenever a wingtip came
into view long bursts were triggered.

These efforts eventually brought their aircraft down to a dangerous level, and their ammunition supplies were fast being depleted.
Lufbery's flying boots had taken two Boelcke bullets, and two more
flicked through his coverall. By the time they were jousting over the
treetops both knew that the battle was over, and they broke off by
mutual consent. Each airman had fired practically every round in
his belt or drum, but there was no especial damage on either side.
Of course, legend takes a hand in reporting that when Lufbery
floundered to his field, his plane was so riddled that it collapsed
around him. While there may have been some substance to the
story, these dramatic returns were in most cases concocted by wild
writers of the "yammering gun" school. After many months on the
Western Front, and when I had often anxiously awaited the return
of friends from some of these blistering experiences, I never saw
such a dramatic climax. Anything that would "completely collapse"
on landing could scarcely be expected to stay together in the air
under the strain of powered flight.

Raoul Lufbery kept up his good work all through August, putting in innumerable hours over the line. On August 8 he came upon an Aviatik near Fort Douaumont, and shot it down in flames. Another Aviatik fell before his guns on October 12 during a raid on the German Mauser works. This was Luf's fifth—which made him an ace.

By becoming the first ace in this all-American group, Lufbery naturally enjoyed popularity on both sides of the Atlantic. He was not the first American ace, however, for Fred Libby of Colorado, who had joined the R.F.C., had already been accepted in that gallant company. But Lufbery was widely accaimed and Libby was not, but at the time Lufbery was honest enough to know that much of his aerial success thus far had been pure luck. He was the toast of the boulevards, and other noted airmen, including Guynemer, Fonck, and Nungesser, accepted him as an equal. Since he could respond to their cheery greetings in fluent French, he was accepted universally and told how great he was.

But once the spirit of the cognac and backslapping died down, a new simplicity marked Raoul's behavior. He no longer made showoff displays on his return from a patrol, realizing that structural damage, unseen or unnoticed, could betray him. He usually came in well throttled back, easing into careful turns to make sure that no undue strain would be put on the bullet-pocked wings. He knew by now that too many exuberant airmen had ended their lives in these unnecessary displays of triumph. This was the Lufbery who was to become the fighting mainstay until America entered the war and reclaimed her flying sons and once more Raoul Lufbery was placed in his old situation of uncertainty, distrust, and dilemma.

THE RAID ON OBERNDORF

An Allied air attack on the German Mauser arms plant at Oberndorf gave the Lafayette Escadrille its first big chance to work on a combined offensive. The assignment meant much to the small force, for all were grateful for the feeling of acceptance. Till now they had felt like a group of unorganized rookies playing amid a pack of hardened professionals.

This raid, one of the first with a true strategic concept, had been in the planning phase for some time, and about eighty bombers of various types were selected for the mission. The main striking force was to be provided by the Royal Naval Air Service, flying Sopwith 1½-strutters. (This name indicated the splayed center-section struts that appeared to be composed of one and one half struts, the inner short and the outer long.) It is of interest to note that these two-seaters, possibly the first aircraft fitted with trailing-edge flaps, were flown solo in order to carry four 100-pound bombs. The French squadrons involved flew Bréguets and Farmans.

Fighting scouts of the period could stay in the air for only two hours and could not accompany the bombers all the way to the target, some 150 miles away. As was the general rule, they did the next best thing; they covered them as far as they could, turned back at the last possible moment, and refueled on an emergency strip at Corcieux in the Vosges. Then, timing their take-offs to pick up the returning bombers as soon as possible, they furnished escort over the rest of the journey home.

N.124 could contribute but four Nieuports and pilots, so the four most experienced airmen in the group were selected: Lieutenant de Laage de Meux, one of the French liaison pilots, Raoul Lufbery, Didier Masson, and Norman Prince.

Generally considered the originator of the Escadrille Américaine, although the idea had been nurtured by several Americans early in the war, Norman Prince had had a discouraging time as a war airman. Although he had worked hard to bring the organization into being, he seemed to have no luck in the air, and it was weeks before he could claim his first success. No matter how many patrols he flew, or how many engagements he joined, no enemy plane fell before his guns. He fought boldly and well, never giving an inch. He took on the enemy singly or in groups, but his only reward was patterns of bullet holes, damaged engines, and battered structures. Plane after plane that Norman flew was rendered unserviceable, although he never had anything worth while to show for his effort but the number of flying hours jotted in his logbook.

SURRENDER IN THE SKY

The day Norman broke the ice was a memorable one, for it also saw the death of Kiffin Rockwell. Prince took off in a spirit of revenge for Kiffin's death and when well over the enemy line encountered a two-seater Aviatik that was acting suspiciously like a "bait" plane. Norman wanted to roar in for an immediate attack, but decided to avoid being drawn into a trap. Once he was certain that there was no skulking formation of enemy single-seaters above, he pounced and struck.

His first burst took out the observer, and the German pilot was at the mercy of this Nieuport airman who flaunted a screaming Seminole's head on the side of his fuselage. Trying to outmaneuver that gnatlike fighter with a blundering Aviatik was hopeless. The two-seater pilot lost Norman for a few seconds, then saw that the Nieuport was standing on its tail somewhere below, sending up short bursts from close quarters. The German tried to make a diving getaway by tipping the Aviatik over on one wing, but Prince was after him like an enraged hornet.

Then came an incident such as had never been reported before. The frightened German pilot flipped his belt, stood up in his cockpit, and raised his gloved hands above his head in a gesture of surrender.

For a moment Prince was incredulous; then he realized that here was the opportunity of a lifetime. For weeks the Escadrille had been hoping to down a German plane in Allied territory, if only to see what it was made of, but chiefly to prove to cynics that an American actually had shot down an enemy aircraft. But this was even better—if the situation was genuine and not some midair phantasy. For a few seconds Prince realized that there was a possibility that this frantic pilot might be persuaded to fly his plane into Allied territory, landing it intact on the Escadrille's field. Why, the poor devil might be induced to relate his side of the "fight" from start to finish. Lady Luck was smiling at last.

Then Prince remembered Kiffin Rockwell, and a cold, deep re-

venge billowed up in a crimson surge. Why should this man be
allowed to surrender? What right had he to life when his gunner
had died in his defense? Norman considered finishing his opponent
then and there, but he suddenly realized that the fighting action had
taken them to within ten kilometers of the front line. Amazing!
There was a chance, after all, of accomplishing this unbelievable
coup.

Norman leaned out of his cockpit and pointed toward the French
lines. The German pilot nodded his helmeted head and slid back
into his seat. With a quick glance above and behind, Prince moved
to a position aft of the "captured" Aviatik and herded it home.
Each time the enemy pilot appeared to be easing off course Norman
drilled a burst of sparkling tracers past his wingtips. This put the
German back into the proper mood, and eventually both arrived
safely over the Luxeuil field. The airplane was landed with no
damage, the pilot taken prisoner, and the Allies had a flyable Aviatik to inspect and check out.

NORMAN PRINCE'S FATAL CRASH

The victory brought promotion too, and Prince was made an adjutant, the final step up the military ladder before he would be
commissioned. In the face of this, Norman was named to represent
the Escadrille on the Oberndorf raid, which as a mission was more
successful than had been hoped. The Germans were caught completely unaware, and considerable damage was inflicted on the arms
plant. No real opposition was encountered in the air on the way
out, and all the fighters returned to the refueling strips. The
bombers found their various targets with no trouble, and a good
pattern was delivered.

In order to evade the enemy planes that were sent up to intercept them, the bombers flew a circuitous route home and were a
long time making contact with the escort planes. It seemed hours
before the Nieuport pilots could find the bomber formation, and
they arrived just in time to face a covey of determined Fokkers,
bent on beating down the raiders. The light was fading fast and

it was difficult to distinguish friend from foe, but in one of the melees, Norman Prince shot down a Fokker.

Once the bombers were brought in and escorted safely across their own lines, the four N.124 pilots broke off and made for the same emergency field that had furnished the extra fuel and ammunition.

Prince must have become confused with the unfamiliar surroundings in that uncertain light, and as he spiraled down and S-turned to approach his glide-in position from over a small patch of woods, he failed to see a high-tension cable looped just over the treetops. The wheels of his landing gear caught this trip wire and the Nieuport was snubbed so hard that it nosed down suddenly and crashed. The safety belt that might have saved Norman broke as the plane hit and he was somersaulted from the cockpit. The double shock multiplied his injuries. Both legs were broken and he had serious internal wounds; but despite his condition and pain, Norman made a brave effort to make certain that no one else tangled with the same obstruction. When ground crewmen rushed to help him, Norman waved them away, gasping, "Light some gasoline and make some sort of a warning flare. We don't want anyone else to hit that cable."

Lufbery, who had landed a few minutes before, ran up to console his friend. "Don't worry, Norman," he said cheerfully. "You're going to be all right. We'll get you to a hospital fast. A good night's rest . . ."

All the way to the near-by town of Gerardmer, Luf did his best to keep up Norman's spirits by croaking wartime ditties, telling jokes in his amusing accent, and whistling the popular tunes that had churned from the squadron phonograph. He had no idea how severely Prince was injured, but when he went to visit him the next day, his friend had sunk into a coma. Every effort was made to revive and encourage Prince. The best available skills and care were provided, and a Captain Happe, accompanied by a number of the Escadrille officers, formally promoted Prince to second lieutenant as he lay on what was to be his deathbed. He was awarded the Legion of Honor later, but he knew little of this, for he died on October 15, 1916. His body was returned to Luxeuil, where a very impressive burial was arranged. In May, 1937, the remains of Norman Prince were brought back to the United States and entombed in a memorial chapel in the National Cathedral of Washington, D.C.

Shortly after Norman's death, Frederick H. Prince, Jr., Norman's older brother, was posted to N.124. This member of the family proved to be a worthy successor to carry the laurel. He died late in 1962. Frederick enlisted directly into the French Aviation on January 29, 1916, and trained at Pau, Buc, and Cazaux until he was graduated on a Caudron on May 21, 1916. He arrived at Luxeuil to join the Escadrille a few days after Norman's death and served there with typical devotion until February 15, 1917, when he was returned to Pau as an instructor. Following that duty, he was ordered to join the French Military Mission in Washington and did not return to France until late in September, 1917.

After filling several such posts, Frederick was released. He attempted to join the U.S. Air Service, but despite his long experience in war flying, his ability as an instructor, and his varied administration tasks, he failed to pass the presumptuous standards devised by the experts in Washington. When he was even refused the chance to serve in some executive capacity, still determined to do his bit, Frederick accepted a lieutenant's commission in the Quartermaster Corps, where he probably finished his war signing indents for cavalry spurs, McClellan saddles, and dress swords for the top brass.

VOLUNTEERS SWARM IN

Shortly after the Oberndorf raid the Escadrille was transferred to the Somme front and based on a field beside Cachy Wood, where Willis B. Haviland of Chicago and Robert Soubiran of New York joined the organization. Haviland had been driving an ambulance for the American Field Service but transferred to the French Aviation early in 1916. After nearly a year with N.124 he was sent to Spad 102 for two months, then was transferred to the U.S. Naval Aviation and became the chief pilot at a U.S. Naval Air Station located at Dunkirk. For a time he was also attached to Number 13 Squadron of the Royal Naval Air Service, but eventually was sent to Italy, where he was commanding officer of the U.S. Naval Air Station at Porto Corsini, where he served until the Armistice.

Bob Soubiran was an intriguing character. He had been an expert mechanic and a racing-car driver and was among the first group of Americans who volunteered at the outbreak of the war. He was of French descent and spoke the language fluently. After some preliminary training he was assigned to the French Legion and fought as an infantryman for nearly two years. On October 19, 1915, he was wounded during the Champagne offensive, and later on when French soldiers were called on to harvest the crop of winter wheat, Bob ran a threshing machine. He was unlike any of the other airman volunteers. In the first place he had spent so much time with French infantrymen that he had absorbed many of their active-service characteristics and manners. With his fluent French he could have passed for a native Frenchman, and most of the villagers were astonished to learn that their favorite *estaminet* patron was an American.

But this New Yorker became a valued asset to the Escadrille, for he was one of the early camera "bugs," and might have become a professional had not the war intruded into his carefree life. Bob seemed to be on hand whenever the squadron moved. He turned up at every crash or amusing accident, and recorded every ceremonial in which his pals took any part. Had it not been for him, much of the pictorial history of the Lafayette Escadrille would not have been published. Today his many photographs are priceless.

Soubiran put in an unusual length of service, and his career encompasses a complete log of the Great War. He fought for about eighteen months as an infantryman, then flew almost daily with some unit of French Aviation over the next two years. When he transferred to the U.S. Aviation on January 26, 1918, he flew for nine months until the Armistice with the 103rd Pursuit Squadron, the first American unit built upon a cadre of Lafayette Escadrille pilots. In other words, Bob Soubiran was one of the first Americans to take an active part in the war and one of the last to lay down his arms.

Another colorful character who joined the Lafayette at Cachy was Paul Pavelka, a volunteer from Madison, Connecticut. Paul had been brought up on a New England farm and had served a long stretch as an infantryman before the men of the Escadrille had ever heard of him. Paul left home at the age of fourteen over some difference of opinion with his stepmother and through his teens worked as a cook in a sheep camp, as a cowboy, a male nurse in a San Francisco hospital, then was a seaman, voyaging to many ports of call all over the world. When the war started, Paul was living at a seaman's home in New York City and made several efforts to join one of the Allied armies. He finally accepted the offer of an English recruiter, who sent a number of British volunteers to Halifax, Nova Scotia, where they were callously abandoned with some vague explanation that if they nosed around the docks they might find a way to work their passage to England. In fact, ready to sail was a cattle boat which might require men to feed and water eight hundred horses intended for Kitchener's Army.

I can vouch for this arrangement, for I too "worked" my way over early in October of 1914—quite possibly on the same vessel, the R.M.S. *Etonian* of the Leyland Line. I enlisted in the British service and transferred eventually to the Royal Flying Corps. Paul Pavelka appears to have joined some mysterious organization called the Army of the South American Republic of Counani, a fictitious force devised to enable a number of these volunteers to cross over to France to enlist in the Foreign Legion. At any rate, Paul signed on at La Rochelle, France, on November 28, 1914, and served with some distinction until October 10, 1915, when he was wounded during an attack on German positions north of Arras. During his convalescence he applied for a transfer to the French Aviation and was accepted October 18, 1915, although he still limped from a bayonet wound. He won his wings on February 23, 1916, and was sent on to join N.124. Shortly after his arrival, Paul had an experience that would have completely dismayed many an airman. On this occasion his engine caught fire, and since he had no parachute, he had to solve the problem or sit it out. He kept his head and performed a number of falling-leaf sideslips to keep the flames from his cockpit, and although the next few minutes must have been terrifying, he managed to hold the Nieuport together and finally pancaked safely into a swamp.

"CAT'S EYES" PAVELKA'S NIGHT FLIGHT

On another occasion Paul took off in total darkness hoping to intercept two or three German bombers that had sneaked over to bombard the Cachy field. This was on the night of December 9, 1916, and Paul, who had developed "cat's eyes" and showed rare skill in night operations, went up into the night sky hoping to get one of the Jerries whose bombs had scored a direct hit on a hangar of the famous Storks squadron, then headed by Georges Guynemer.

The German aircraft continued to circle the field, making the most of the illumination from the burning hangar. Paul, whose machine had been rigged with navigation lights and extra instrument-board illumination, took off; but soon after he was air-borne these extra aides died out suddenly and he had no lights of any kind. His first instinct was to turn back and land, but considering the condition of the field, the excitement below, the uncertain glare from the burning hangar, and the fact that he had gone aloft to attempt something against the enemy attack, he decided to continue on, relying on his night sight.

Almost immediately the ground guns started firing at him as well as at the raiders. He had no contact with the men below, and to add to his troubles a couple of searchlights were broken out, which compounded his problems and the general confusion. Going into a steep climb, he evaded the first layer of explosive and shrapnel hoping to find the enemy bombers, but the flare of antiaircraft fire and the crisscrossing searchlight blades formed a garish pattern of theatrical lighting. Whenever he thought he saw the outline of a bomber, a scissors of searchlight clipped off the shadow, or a splintered splash of explosive eradicated the indistinct target.

Finding that he had taken on a hopeless quest, Paul decided to head for Amiens on the assumption that some of the enemy force might be attacking there. Unfortunately, as was to be expected, the defense authorities at Amiens decided that Paul was a member of the opposition, and all the lights in that area were immediately doused. The night was black enough, but when all artificial light was eliminated, there was nothing to identify any section. Paul was aloft with no night-flying instruments, no lights, and no way to explain that he was a "friendly" airman. His Nieuport carried fuel for about two hours of normal flight, and dawn was some time away.

As his night vision improved, Paul decided to ease down in the hope of finding an uninhabited area where he might risk a landing; but every time he dropped below two thousand feet "friendly" machine guns opened from all sides. There was nothing to do but to tour about trying to find space and conditions for an emergency landing. Here and there were vague patterns of open space, but he did not know whether they were plowed fields or meadows. There was no way of spotting shell holes or abandoned defenses of barbed wire.

Paul reset his air valve and manipulated the butterfly carburetor of the Le Rhône until it was just ticking over, and in this manner clung to the last few feet of altitude until dawn finally drew a fringe of gold across the eastern sky. Paul held his breath and waited, his prop still ticking over; then as some faint detail of the ground was visible, his engine conked out with the last drain of fuel. It was neck or nothing, and Paul risked the misty half light and made a dead-stick landing without bursting a tire or snapping a wire. He was within the British lines at a village called Martainville, nearly forty miles from Cachy. Ten minutes later a heavy fog closed in, but luckily he was found and taken in by officers of a

British regiment who were billeted at the time at an old chateau. He had to stay there for four days, but his companions at Cachy were delighted to learn that he was safe and well. Most of them had been betting that he was down somewhere in the German lines, either killed in a crash or taken prisoner.

A short while later a call was issued for volunteers to serve on the Salonika front, and Paul offered to go, as he had always been interested in exotic cities of the world. In February of 1917 he arrived in Salonika, where he enjoyed the new life. The picturesque background of the Near Eastern Front fascinated him, and he was pleased to learn that the polyglot enemy forces there were not as skilled or daring; in fact, their aerial gunnery was practically nonexistent.

Paul Pavelka proved to be a valuable man; his work was quickly recognized, and he was mentioned in Allied dispatches and was finally awarded the Croix de Guerre. He was given a Nieuport single-seater and an Italian A.R. Caudron-like two-seater, which was used for observation and artillery spotting. All went well on this Macedonian front until November 12, 1917, when he met an untimely, and tragic, death. On that day, while walking for exercise in the Salonika sector, Paul met a British cavalry officer whom he had known in the Foreign Legion. He was invited to visit the British regiment's quarters for a drink and a meal, and during his stay there, Paul, who was an excellent horseman, asked for permission to ride a remount that had just been sent to the regiment. This beast turned out to be a vicious devil and did its best to unseat Paul and, failing that, reared suddenly, rolled over on its back, and crushed its rider beneath it. Paul's neck was broken in the mishap and he died a few hours later.

DUDLEY HILL, MAN OF MODESTY

Possibly the most modest and self-effacing member of the Lafayette Escadrille was Dudley Lawrence Hill, a native of Peekskill, New York. Few World War I aviation buffs could identify the

name, for Dud managed to keep out of the "intrepid airman" lime-
light, although he racked up nearly twenty-eight months of active-
service flying with the French, and later on with five different
squadrons of the U.S. Air Service.

In addition to his modesty, Hill deserves credit in that he was
unfit physically for active service, since he had defective vision
in one eye; but like the famous Mickey Mannock, another one-eyed
wonder, Dudley had devised tricks to fool the medical examiners.

He joined the American Field Service in 1915 and made the
routine transfer to aviation by August 3 of that year, and somehow
managed his way through the usual complex of aviation schools
from September 25, 1915, until he took his brevet on an ancient
Caudron on March 17, 1916. During this time he hoodwinked half
a dozen medical experts who were certain that Dud was a semi-
invalid. Now and then Dr. Gros would examine him, rearrange his
findings, and decide that he was fit for service; but whenever Hill
arrived at the next training squadron other doctors would discover
alarming defects. He was proposed for a medical discharge on
several occasions, but apparently Dudley's eyesight was so poor that
he could not read the recommendation and ignored the kindly suggestions. Later on, his flight instructors agreed generally that this
decrepit American was unfit for acrobatic training and made out
reports to that end. However, French military organizations apparently moved as slowly as those of the other belligerents, and Dudley had taken up and passed his acrobatic course long before the
report stating that he could not had reached any important level.

Somewhat perplexed with these varied opinions and his own
reactions, Hill arrived at Luxeuil after N.124 had returned there
from their Somme tour. He served with modest distinction over the
next nineteen months, despite his inner dread that one day he
would be unmasked and relieved of duty. He never missed a
mission and volunteered for any risky assignment, but nothing spectacular ever happened to him. Dud was there, day after day, wearing
his old French uniform with no gaudy decorations, cords, braid, or

any particular insignia. Most of the time he looked somewhat like a light-duty poilu who swept out the place.

Whenever American correspondents arrived in quest of a new story, Dudley hied off to curl up in a corner behind a month-old newspaper. He admitted that he knew little about the war and furnished little copy for his interrogators. Something in the pattern went awry, however, for one day Adjutant Hill was honored with the Croix de Guerre with Star; but for the life of him he could not explain it, and it has not been possible to trace any photograph of him wearing the ribbon or the medal.

When the Lafayette was transferred to the U.S. Air Service, Hill was assigned to the 103rd Pursuit Squadron, with which he served until June 1, 1918, and was then transferred to the 139th, flying regularly for two months. He was made commanding officer of the 138th on August 1 and ended the war as C.O. of the Fifth Group, a command he held for exactly eleven days.

TED PARSONS, THE SEMI-INVALID

Another semi-invalid who conquered his infirmities to become one of the leading aces of the Lafayette Escadrille was Edwin Charles Parsons of Holyoke, Massachusetts. This gay cavalier, who was born on September 24, 1892, is still hale and hearty. Ted, as he is known, set a high standard as a fighting airman, despite his many early physical limitations, and finished his war with eight confirmed victories. He was a striking figure aloft or on the ground, for he flew in the dreariest pair of breeches, a ragged mackinaw jacket, and an outmoded crash helmet given him by some amused Britisher. Since this leather monstrosity was decorated with a Death's Head Hussar insignia, it gave Ted a particularly terrifying aspect, and he says there were times when he dreaded to look in his rear-view mirror for fear he would catch a glimpse of the man in his cockpit. On the ground he was a fashion plate, a veritable Scarlet Pimpernel, for he sported a smart kepi, an Ascot stock, a neat French tunic, breeches, and glossy field boots. When he dis-

played all his decorations, the Médaille Militaire, Croix de Guerre
—with eight Palms—the Belgian Croix de Guerre, and the Croix de
Leopold, topped off with a natty *fourragère*, he would have stopped
General Billy Mitchell in his tracks. Later, some years after the
war, the French remembered to add the Cross of the Legion of
Honor to his display.

Ted Parsons contributed more than his share to the American
volunteers' effort, not only fighting long and well but proving to
be a lively historian. His book, *The Great Adventure*, written in
1937, is one of the more engrossing volumes on the history of this
organization. It is out of print today, but deserves to be reissued
to take its rightful place on all World War I bookshelves.

Parsons, who is still a most delightful companion, admits to being
an amateur adventurer, and would be the last to profess to any
high ideals or belief in the French cause; but his actions and devotion are evidence enough of his unswerving loyalty. He never felt
the necessity of proclaiming any Gallic sentiment, nor has he ever
written of his own gallantry; quite the contrary, for he can tell jokes
on himself and laugh uproariously.

He received his early schooling at Phillips Exeter Academy, after
which he went to the University of Pennsylvania for two years. He
ran up no record as an athlete or a scholar, being continually tor-
mented with enlarged tonsils and one eyelid that tended to droop,
producing a piratical leer. He had lost most of one little finger as
the result of an infection caused by a signet ring of questionable
alloy. As a schoolboy he had smoked like a tar factory, and his
respiratory system bewildered or entranced examining medicos.
And to top all this, Ted had a touch of color blindness.

"If I had ever tried to get into U.S. Aviation in those days, I
would have been booted out on my ear," Ted explains. "I mean to
say, how could I expect to fly a Wright biplane with a couple of
joints missing from one pinky, two eyes that never could seem
to make up their mind, and a respiratory complication that would
have been diagnosed as the heaves by any second-year veterinarian?"

It should be added that during World War II Parsons offered his

trembling frame to the U.S. Navy and wound up a rear admiral!
So much for muscles, biceps, and brawn.

Ted left the U. of P. in 1912, responding to wanderlust. He went to
California, where he encountered a flying school at Dominguez
Field outside Los Angeles, and whatever he learned there enabled
him to take a captain's commission in the Mexican Aviation Corps;
and from various sources, mostly unreliable, it is learned that he
may have led an aerial armada against General Obregón's legions.
There is some evidence that he did take part in that campaign,
but Ted is not too communicative about any such activity.

Once this musical-comedy campaign came to a close, Ted returned to Massachusetts and learned that a much better war was
being fought in Europe. It was 1915 and it was obvious from reports
in the newspapers that this was a real dinger, with men flying
real airplanes, shooting machine guns, and a lot of people were
being killed or wounded. Although he was a physical wreck, he
was game and thought that with some luck he might be accepted
as an ambulance driver. He put the proposition to his father, hoping
he would shell out for a first-class ticket to Paris; but Dad Parsons
remembered the Boer and Spanish-American affairs, and couldn't
conceive of his semi-invalid offspring's being involved in anything
that was going on along the Marne or in Flanders. He flatly refused.

Drifting about, Ted learned finally of the cattle-boat deadfall
and signed on as a veterinary surgeon, proving that he was not
only generally incapacitated but suffering delusions of grandeur.
But his equine charges fortunately were fairly healthy and there
was no especial need for his services. Ted was so emboldened by
his ability to survive the cattle-boat regimen that he tossed all caution to the wind and offered his services to the French Aviation. He
was told that he would have first to serve with the Foreign Legion,
a stipulation that shook him back to his original infirmity. He tottered away to join the American Field Service, and so built up his
mouselike brawn that he was able to take charge of a complete
ambulance section at Mrs. Whitney Warren's hospital near Juilly
behind the Soissons front.

HOW TO PASS A MEDICAL EXAMINATION

By April 13, 1916, Ted did manage to get into French Aviation, but only after faking his way through an almost unbelievable medical examination routine. At its close he was congratulated on being such a perfect physical specimen, and the examining doctor said that as far as he was concerned, "you can go out and get yourself killed at any time, *pour la France.*"

"I fooled him though, and didn't get killed. Despite my tremendous handicaps, including the fact that my college education was of very brief duration, I served nearly three years with the French pursuit and got more than my share of victories. The physical examination was a farce and no mention was made of mental requirements. I couldn't even speak the language at the time," Ted wrote later.

How right he was. To the French it was a self-evident fact that a pilot candidate did not have to be a genius or a physical marvel to fly a war plane. Good health was an asset, but by no means an absolute requisite. Courage and marksmanship were more important qualities.

Georges Guynemer, who scored fifty-four official victories, was frail, consumptive, and weighed less than one hundred pounds. Nungesser was literally wired together with silver, but he downed forty-five enemy aircraft. Georges Madon crawled back from an enemy prison camp, after months of cruel incarceration, and scored forty-one successes. Mickey Mannock had but one eye and a limited education, but downed seventy-three Germans. Jimmy McCudden was born in a military barracks of lowly Scottish-French (not Irish) parentage, and had little formal schooling, but he more than earned his keep with fifty-eight victories. René Fonck, France's greatest ace, began life as a peasant boy with a sketchy education, but led France's ace pack with seventy-five confirmed planes.

To close this summation, it is interesting to note that more than 70 per cent of all flying men in French Aviation were noncommissioned officers, many with only primary-school educations, and the majority from peasant stock; yet their magnificent records speak for themselves.

There is not sufficient space here to present the backgrounds and careers of all members of the Lafayette Escadrille, or its offshoot, the Lafayette Flying Corps, but it might be well to trace the organization to its eventual conclusion. When the United States joined the Allies in April, 1917, steps were taken to induce these men to transfer to their own colors. However, once the Lafayette Escadrille had been taken over formally by the U.S. Aviation Service, much of the interest in these volunteers began to fade. There were still many American pilots scattered through other French squadrons, and it took all of the winter of 1917–18 and much of the spring of 1918 to complete the transfer of those who so desired. Some were to remain for weeks or months on detached service with their former units; others were sent as instructors to the American training schools at Tours or Issoudun. Those who had volunteered late in 1917 and who had completed their training in French schools were accepted by the United States service as soon as they were ready for active duty, but it was not until June 1, 1918, that the bulk of those who had applied for transfer had received their American commissions and were entitled to wear American uniforms.

Naturally, all this was of vital importance to the men concerned, but at the time their varied appeals received little attention. The over-all problem of creating an all-American air service left them a small, insignificant group whose former glory and service were gradually forgotten. Few Americans who were to follow them across the Atlantic had any idea that 267 volunteers had made the great gesture long before America had actively entered the war. Of this number, forty-three were released before completing their training because of illness, inaptitude, or injuries suffered in flying accidents. Those who had served at the front in French uniforms numbered 180, and of these, sixty-six had flown in pursuit squadrons, and twenty-seven had put in their time with observation or bombardment squadrons. Ninety-three of these trained pilots were transferred to the U.S. Air Service and twenty-six went to U.S. Naval Aviation. Five died of illnesses and six by accidents in the aviation schools; fifteen were taken prisoner—of whom three escaped to Switzerland; nineteen were wounded in combat, and fifty-one were killed in action.

The members of both the Lafayette Escadrille and the Lafayette Flying Corps shot down 199 enemy machines, all of which was confirmed officially.

CHAPTER 10

Storks and Other Birds

The history of French aviation is replete with stories of in-dividual gallantry, for their Gallic dispositions would not ac-cept routine patrols, tight formations, or standard programs of operation. Frenchmen were fighting for their own country above the ground occupied by the enemy, and they battled on, each man seemingly inspired by his own personal intent and association with the district concerned. Rank or regimental standing meant little, for they fought as air gunners while holding the rank of captain or they downed the enemy in single combat wearing only the chevrons of a corporal. Most important was that, private or general, all were eligible for the same decorations bestowed for gallantry.

GEORGES GUYNEMER, FRANCE'S GREATEST

THE MOST outstanding French fighter squadron by far was Spa.3, which contributed such noted airmen as Georges Guynemer, Jules Vedrines, Albert Deullin, René Dorme, Alfred Heurteaux, Mathieu de la Tour and Georges Raymond. The squadron was established early in the war as Escadrille M.S.3, flying the Morane Saulnier, and as the primitive equipment was replaced, M.S.3 became N.3 to designate its Nieuport mounts, and finally Spa.3 when it was fur-nished with Spads.

It was known originally as the Storks because it had devised a classic form of that bird as its insignia, but when France's Number

12 Group was organized with Spa.3, Spa.26, Spa.73, and Spa.103, they all carried some heraldic version of the stork insignia and eventually the Group became known as *Les Cigognes*—the Storks—but it should be understood that the original Stork Squadron was Spa.3.

A youth named Georges Marie Ludovic Jules Guynemer was the leading ace of Spa.3, although a more improbable character to assume that role scarcely can be imagined. The only son of an ex-Army officer who had relinquished the military life to be a historian, Georges was a sickly child, coddled by a loving mother and two affectionate sisters. He was not a good student, although he showed a keen and lively intelligence; but his schoolmates remembered him as a disorderly, quarrelsome, unreliable, careless, self-willed companion who was studying for the Polytechnic.

Looking more like a boy of fifteen than a young man of nineteen, Guynemer was turned down when he attempted to enlist at the outbreak of war. He tried again the following November 21 and was accepted as a pupil-mechanic at the Pau flying field, where he performed such menial tasks as sweeping out the hangars, washing spare parts, and dismantling aircraft crashes. His father still retained some service influence, however, and with that and Georges' continual pleading, Captain Bernard Thierry permitted him to train as a pilot. He began the course on March 10, 1915, and by July 28, 1916, young Guynemer had filled fifty logbook pages with flight reports, racked up 348 flying hours and destroyed eleven enemy aircraft.

When he began his flying career as a corporal pilot, Guynemer weighed approximately one hundred pounds and in his military gear looked even younger and more wistful than when he had entered the service. The truth of the matter was that he was suffering from tuberculosis, and although medical authorities did their best to build him up and restrain his activities in an attempt to cure his malady, the youth ignored all advice and orders. He seemed to be charged with some strange spiritual inspiration to keep on the go and to be in the air hour after hour.

As a fighter pilot he was assigned to M.S.3 on June 8, 1915. Captain Brocard then commanded M.S.3, the pilot list of which included many airmen who were to reach great heights as fighters, and Georges must have seemed a mere infant among these redoubtable performers. But within a month he had destroyed his first Hun and been awarded his first Croix de Guerre. On August 4 General Dubois added the Médaille Militaire for his daring, spirit, and willingness to carry out dangerous assignments. Guynemer received his first setback in September, when he was shot down in combat with a German formation; but with rare luck he crash-landed in no man's land, where he was rescued by French infantrymen. This was the first of seven such times that he was shot down.

Guynemer was awarded the Legion of Honor on his twenty-first birthday, December 24, 1915, and cited as a pilot of great gallantry, a model of devotion to duty and of courage. He downed his eighth victim on March 13, 1916, and two days later was wounded in an air fight over Verdun. His injury was not serious, and he returned to the Storks and was one of the first front-line airmen to fly the new Nieuport scout. Aboard this mount he soon proved he was in reputable company for such greats as Heurteaux, Dorme, and Deullin, and De la Tour. In fact, N.3 was cited for its work under Captain Brocard, having shown a drive and devotion to duty during the operations over Verdun and the Somme. From March 19 to August 19, 1916, it took part in 338 aerial combats, destroyed thirty-six aircraft and three balloons, and forced thirty-six other severely damaged airplanes to land. A week later Guynemer added to the Storks' glory by shooting down three German planes in one day, and was then shot down himself from the 10,000-foot level. His Nieuport was badly damaged but he was unhurt.

From this point on, Guynemer piled up a tremendous score. Between November 10, 1916, and January 23, 1917, he increased his victories from eighteen to thirty, and on March 16 racked up a triple, and downed four more on May 25. On June 5 he shot down his forty-fourth and forty-fifth victims.

But the pace was beginning to tell. Time and time again Georges was "requested" to take a rest from operational activity, but he always rejected these suggestions. On July 5, 1917, the Rosette of the Legion of Honor was presented to him in a special ceremony in Paris and his own airplane, dubbed *Le Vieux Charles* (Old Charlie), was put on display during the investiture.

NEW PLANES, NEW GUNS

By now young Guynemer could have practically anything he desired. He had for a long time thought that a 37-millimeter gun could be fitted to a Spad, and when a suitable Hispano-Suiza engine was designed, one which permitted the weapon to be mounted behind its hollow crankshaft to fire through the center of the prop boss, he was given the first model to test. This was designated as the Spad-12, using what was known as the *moteur canon*, but the arrangement, unfortunately, was not too efficient. For one thing, reloading was difficult; also exhaust gases from the breech collected in the cockpit and often nauseated the pilot. Both Guynemer and René Fonck claimed to have shot down a number of enemy aircraft with this weapon, but full details of these exploits are lacking.

The best that can be said for the Spad-12 is that the basic model, with the 200-horsepower and later 235-horsepower Hisso engines, evolved into the Spad-13, probably the best of this line and said by some to be comparable to the Sopwith Snipe and the Fokker D.7. This point is argued long and loud by devotees of the Sopwith line. For one thing, the D.7 did not appear on the Western Front until late in May, 1918, and not in impressive numbers until July. Thus it could not have played any important role in the more than four years of aerial warfare. From the American point of view, the Fokker D.7 was the last word in fighter aircraft, but it must be remembered that there were no American squadrons in action until late spring of 1918, and what enemy opposition they faced came chiefly from these new Fokker models; it is quite understandable that they should compare all enemy aircraft on the basis of the D.7.

Those of us who flew through 1916, 1917, and 1918 had had a more diversified experience, and since the D.7 was well countered by the S.E.5, Camel, Bristol Fighter, Sopwith Triplane, *and* the Spad-13, she never loomed as such a devastating mount. In the early fall of 1918, when the D.7 was replaced by several other German fighters, American newcomers understandably thought that that particular plane was the last word in enemy fighter aircraft design, and this impression has been presented widely ever since.

While tough, well designed, and capable of 138 miles per hour, with the 235-horsepower engine, the Spad-13 was not as maneuverable as the Camel or the Snipe, and certainly never ran up the score compiled by the LeRhone biplane. All too often American historians downgrade the Camel, insisting that it was difficult to fly. This, of course, is incorrect. It was a highly maneuverable machine and, because of its size and power, very sensitive on the controls; but once a pilot had mastered her in the first hour or so, no fighter aircraft was more delightful or satisfactory to fly. The Camel's reputation for trickiness was formed when a number of American students, direct from Curtiss Jenny training in the United States, with little or no experience with the torque developed by high-speed rotary engines, found these British fighters too sensitive for their ham-fisted operation. They immediately branded them "killers," ignoring the fact that just as many Texas-produced newcomers were having difficulty with French Nieuports and Spads while training at Issoudun.

GUYNEMER ENDS ON A LEGEND

When his score had reached fifty-three by August 20, Guynemer was urged again to retire from active-service flying, but refused once more, although it was obvious that he was seriously ill—certainly in no physical condition to withstand the continual strain of aerial warfare. But what sort of military discipline prevailed in the French Air Service at the time when a junior officer could continually disregard official commands and ignore all merciful requests to limit his activities? It must have been clear to his superiors what the effect would be on morale if he were killed or taken prisoner.

But even the great Guynemer could not continue forever on the strength of his indomitable patriotism or personal determination.

The end came on September 11, 1917, when with a Lieutenant Bozon-Verduraz he went on an early-morning patrol. Very little is known of what took place, but one report, penned by a member of the Lafayette Escadrille, has it that Captain Guynemer and his companion were flying at about 16,000 feet over Poelcapelle in Belgium when they met a German two-seater. Guynemer made a half-hearted attack while Bozon-Verduraz stayed above to protect his tail. As Guynemer maneuvered to evade the German gunner, eight single-seaters appeared above, and Bozon-Verduraz attacked boldly to hold them off while Guynemer took care of the two-seater. The escort pilot performed his duty so well that none of the German fighters got through to fire at Guynemer; but when they had dispersed, Bozon-Verduraz could not find his leader, and it was presumed later on that another aerial gunner had scored against a high-ranking pilot. The Germans had another story that stated that a Lieutenant Kurt Wissemann, a five-victory ace, had shot down Guynemer.

No trace was ever found of Guynemer or his aircraft, and the Germans explained later that the wrecked Spad had fallen into a battle area and both the pilot's grave and his machine had been obliterated by heavy British shelling.

FRANCE'S ACE OF ACES

France's leading ace of World War I was René Fonck, a native of the Vosges, who downed seventy-five enemy aircraft before the conflict ended. He had taken a keen interest in aviation as a young man and at the outbreak of war had high hopes of learning to fly with his country's air arm, but had no such luck. When mobilized in 1914 he was posted to the 11th Regiment of Engineers and over the next five months was engaged in trench digging, bridge building, and other humdrum duties. By February, 1915, he gained a transfer and went to Saint-Cyr for preliminary aviation training, and eventually graduated as a pilot on a 60-horsepower Caudron and was assigned to C.47 located at Corcieux, near his home grounds.

Most of his flying consisted of bombing or reconnaissance work, but he did live through several engagements with enemy two-seaters occupied with the same work—combats that were fought with automatic rifles. Fonck completed several important patrols and was soon cited for his efforts, but not much in the way of aerial combat could be noted in his logbook. He was still flying Caudrons by the summer of 1916, but the G.4 had now been fitted with a forward-firing machine gun, and while flying over Roye on August 6, he was attacked by two Fokkers. Fonck turned to counter, and one German was damaged seriously and had to break off while the other fled without firing a telling burst. A few minutes later Fonck and his observer, Lieutenant Thiberge, caught up with two Rumplers flying toward Montdidier, and as French antiaircraft fire burst all around them, Fonck attacked one of the Rumplers, which had gone into a dive. He followed it down, firing whenever an opportunity presented itself, and was amazed to see the German pilot put the undamaged Rumpler down in French territory and surrender. An action that compares somewhat to that experienced by Norman Prince.

In March, 1917, René's squadron moved to Fismes, where he still flew Caudrons; while operating from there he and another pilot, a Sergeant Raux, were attacked by five Albatros single-seaters and Raux was shot down. The German fighters followed him to make sure he was not faking his plight, upon which Fonck followed the Albatros machines and shot down one of them in flames. During all this, Raux recovered some control and landed inside his own lines, although he was seriously burned and his gunner dead.

This second confirmed victory in more than two years of two-seater flying brought Fonck a substantial reward. He was recommended for fighter-plane training, finally joined the Cigognes, and remained with them until the end of the war. By May, 1917, René had registered his first fighter victory, a score that never has been fully confirmed; and on May 5, along with three other Spads, he engaged five Fokkers and sent down one that crashed. A week later a Rumpler went down in flames, and before the month was out another two-seater fell before his guns.

While René was away on leave, the Cigognes lost the venerable René "Papa" Dorme, a twenty-seven-year-old pilot much beloved by the Storks. Dorme had scored twenty-three victories and had flown as a gunner, observer, two-seater pilot, and finally as a chasse pilot with the Storks. While flying with Albert Deullin on May 25, Dorme engaged in a combat during which he was shot down in flames.

When Fonck returned from his rest on June 12, he went aloft seeking revenge for Dorme, and soon found two Albatros single-seaters. Moving up into the sun, he dived to the attack and one Albatros went down immediately; the other turned to attack, but was also shot down near Fort de Brimont.

The Cigognes were sent to the Belgian front in July, 1917, and located at Dunkirk, where they were hounded by German night bombers. During the day they encountered great formations of German Flying Circus fighters, and soon learned the facts of life, as the British had been doing for months. The casualties here were Heurteaux, Deullin, Auger, Matton, and Guynemer, killed, captured, or wounded. It was soon apparent that the same circus-formation measures would have to be adopted. At first Fonck tried leading seven or eight other pilots; for the first time French fighter squadrons had to attempt tight formation flying, but for a while no great success was enjoyed. Then on August 9 Captain d'Harcourt took up the whole Spa. 103 and encountered a German group of thirty-two Fokkers that had been harassing a formation of French bombers over Dixmude. Fonck sent down one enemy plane to crash in flames, and another was driven down out of control. The Fokker formation turned away, and the French bombers continued on with their deliveries.

MAN OR MISSILE?

Shortly after Guynemer disappeared, Fonck sought revenge when Commandant Brocard said all hope had been abandoned. He went into the air and came on a German two-seater. His first burst so startled the enemy pilot that he pulled up into a fast loop that tossed his gunner into midair. Fonck had to flip away fast to miss colliding with the unfortunate man, but the enemy plane burst into flames, burning all the way down to the ground.

Late in September while flying at 12,000 feet René saw another two-seater carrying out a reconnaissance mission just inside the French lines. Diving down from the sun and coming up beneath his target, Fonck poured a long burst into the German aircraft. The pilot and the gunner were both killed and the aircraft rolled over sideways, breaking off a wing, then spun down, throwing out the bodies of the two crewmen as it descended. Papers found on one of the men indicated that the pilot was Kurt Wissemann, whom the Germans had credited with downing Georges Guynemer. Why a single-seater ace was flying a two-seater was never explained.

Fonck raised his victory score to twenty-one in mid-January, 1918, an occasion when he found himself leading a small four-plane element with which he tackled a large formation of Fokkers. Before the fight began, one of his companions had to spin out with engine failure, and Fonck was left with two novice pilots, but nevertheless continued the attack. Then noting a pack of Fokkers that was following his disabled companion, René went to his aid and shot down one of the Germans; the others escaped. Then spotting a French kite balloon going down in flames, he raced toward that area and found four Fokkers turning for home. Again he attacked and shot off the wings of one of the enemy ships and saw the fuselage bearing the dead pilot fall into the French lines as the wings fluttered away and splashed into the Meuse River.

A month later Fonck saw a new type of aircraft that was leading a formation of Albatroses, and he decided to get this newcomer, hoping to bring it down in French territory. He climbed to 20,000 feet and from a point well inside the German lines made his single-handed attack. He was so successful that the new aircraft went down in flames before the escorting Albatros fighters could head off the Storks' star; but Fonck did not learn the identity of the experimental aircraft, because it was destroyed completely before it reached the earth.

The Cigognes were moved back to the Champagne sector, and by this time rivalry was intense among many of the French aces. Madon, Deullin, and Fonck had the same score, with only Nungesser ahead of them. Fonck, who greatly admired Charles, felt that they were taking advantage of the man who was in and out of the hospital with his constant injuries, but he continued his raids on the enemy and scored his thirty-fifth success on April 12, 1918.

Captain Fonck had for some time nurtured the hope of downing five enemy planes in one day. Until May 9 no one had performed this feat, but on that day it was accomplished—with a dividend! The amazing feature was that Fonck did not start his flying until 4 P.M., for it had been foggy since early morning. The minute some clearing was evident, he took off with a Captain Battle and a Lieutenant Fontaine. They climbed to a fair height and came upon a reconnaissance two-seater being escorted by two two-seater fighters. Fonck took the first out of the play with one short burst which killed the pilot. Easing out of that dive, he turned back and downed one of the escort planes, while the third, believing he had escaped all this carnage, hurried toward home. Fonck stalked him, went down once more, and the two-seater fighter broke in midair with one burst. The wreckage of all three was found near Grivesnes.

On returning to his field, René was pleased to learn that his three-plane victory had already been confirmed by telephone. At 5:30 he was in the air again with a Sergeant Brugère and a Lieutenant Thouzelier, and by 6:20 he spotted another enemy two-seater over Montdidier. This time Fonck played it carefully; going into a small cloud, and timing his exit beautifully, he came out directly under the German biplace. One short burst was enough to finish it, and as the French Spad curled away from its fourth victory, four Fokkers and five Albatros fighters broke out of another cloud. They seemed to have missed the Frenchman entirely, and Fonck, timing his moves again, picked off a rear-rank Fokker, and then, apparently heartened by his five-plane success, threw all caution to the wind and continued on, to down the Fokker leader.

The six-plane victory had been confirmed by eight o'clock that evening and René Fonck was awarded the Cross of the Legion of Honor for that day's work.

This accomplishment set off a series of multiple victories, doubles, and trebles until August 1, when he downed a single to register his fifty-seventh victory. René was now ahead of the great Guynemer, and he put on a fabulous show on August 14 when he encountered a three-plane formation, attacked all three head on, and destroyed the lot in ten seconds. All three crashed inside a 100-yard circle near the town of Roye, bringing his score to sixty.

THEY WERE NOT ALL WILD MEN IN THE AIR

An outstanding feature of Fonck's fighting was his determination to take no unnecessary risks. He also believed in conserving his ammunition and seldom wasted any in long bursts. He became a student of air fighting and spent hours studying the tactics of his opponents, and worked out in detail successful plans for attack in all conceivable combinations of circumstances. He was a master of deflection shooting, and any victim he selected was usually doomed —five or six rounds being sufficient, for he was a deadly marksman.

On September 26 Fonck racked up another sextuple. Flying from a field north of Châlons, he first attacked five Fokkers, and shot down two immediately. French antiaircraft fire then pointed out a two-seater near Suippe, and he cut off the wings of that machine and killed the gunner. Aloft later in the day with three other pilots, Fonck was attacked by eight Fokkers; but luckily a Captain de Sevin of Spa.26 came on the scene with another Spad formation and a wild melee ensued for a few minutes, during which Captain de Sevin was forced out with a dead engine. A number of Albatros fighters joined the fight, but Fonck meanwhile had knocked down a Fokker that previously had hammered the tail off Adjutant Brugère's plane. Then another Fokker and an Albatros were sent crashing down, giving Fonck his second six-ship victory. At this point his guns had serious stoppages and he had to withdraw.

His last enemy plane, his seventy-fifth, was downed on November 1, 1918. It was a two-seater that had been dropping propaganda leaflets. His decorations included the Croix de Guerre with twenty-eight Palms, the British Military Cross and Bar, the Belgian Croix de Guerre, the British Military Medal, and the Cross of the Legion of Honor. He died in Paris on June 18, 1953.

BOYAU HATED BALLOONS

A French sportsman who excelled in soccer, Rugby football, boxing, cycle racing, and various track events was Maurice Boyau, who had been born in Algeria May 8, 1888—which made him older than the average wartime flyer. It took Boyau a long time, also, to get into aviation. He began as an Army truck driver and did not transfer into French Aviation until well into 1915. Then, because he proved to be such an excellent student, he was assigned as an instructor at Buc, much to his disgust. After some wire-pulling, Maurice was elevated to a corporal and posted to N.77, which was then being formed.

Boyau scored his first victory under rather tragic circumstances. He was assigned as one of a fighter escort for a Nieuport two-seater on a photographic mission, and when some French antiaircraft bursts pointed out a German plane, one of the fighter escort planes broke off to engage it. Boyau lost sight of this for a few minutes, and when he realized what had taken place, he saw his Nieuport companion being tailed by an Aviatik fighter. Before he could get into the action, the Aviatik had shot down the Nieuport pilot, and the best Boyau could do was to get revenge by downing the German. This back-handed victory was scored on March 16, 1917.

On one occasion, bored by the lack of enemy action, Boyau decided to liven things on his own. He gathered a number of incendiary bombs and flew deep into enemy territory, where he attacked a German airfield at Marimbois. This had remarkable success; three hangars exploded and went up in flames and the enemy had no time to take to the air and intercept.

Kite balloons also attracted Boyau's attention, but he had several fruitless excursions before he scored. He attacked a *Drachen* on June 3, 1917, and saw the observer escape by parachute before the balloon was set afire. A short time after, he downed another before the observer could escape. When he next went after a gasbag, Boyau had a scare when his engine cut out as he was maneuvering for the attack. Since he was well behind the enemy lines, he faced a forced landing and capture; but just as his wheels touched down on enemy ground, the engine picked up, for some unaccountable reason. As he scrambled for some altitude, Boyau was given a warm send-off as he floundered at 600 feet trying to escape to his own lines. For his safe return and courage Boyau was awarded the Médaille Militaire.

On June 24, Boyau, along with a Lieutenant d'Hautefeuille and a Sergeant Boillot, attacked a German balloon and drew a force of enemy single-seaters on their track. Five Fokkers went after Boillot, but Boyau turned smartly, roared back into action, and shot down one and scattered the rest. His sixth victory came when he trapped an enemy plane over Nancy, and he capped this with a low-level attack on a railroad station that destroyed several buildings occupied by German troops.

After his seventh victory and being awarded a commission, Lieutenant Boyau ran into a stretch of ill luck. When there were enemy aircraft to attack, his guns refused to fire; when his weapons were operational, there were no targets to shoot at. Not until January 3, 1918, did he break his luck, when he destroyed a balloon. Then, in company with Gilbert Sardier, he destroyed an Albatros D.5 that he had picked out of a formation of eight. The next day he found two Albatros fighters attacking a Bréguet, but before he could get to it the reconnaissance plane was shot down. Boyau then shot down one and chased the other Albatros until he finished that one. On the way home he destroyed another enemy kite balloon.

With twenty-six victories to his credit, Maurice Boyau was made an officer of the Legion of Honor on July 18—which he celebrated by downing three balloons and an enemy airplane near Fresnes. In mid-August, along with Corporal Letz-Mitchell, Maurice downed his thirtieth, and on their way back the corporal, acting as bait, lured down a German two-seater to attack him. Boyau moved in like a flash and sent the biplace down in flames, after which the two Spads flew back toward the French lines. Suddenly Letz-Mitchell's plane exploded at a height of 1,000 feet, burst apart, and fell in several pieces to the ground. Unable to account for this, Boyau quickly glanced around and saw that a second two-seater was intent on making the most of its moment of triumph. The Frenchman made a sharp climbing turn and came about fast and put a long burst into the German, sending it down completely out of control.

Lieutenant Boyau went on leave in September, and on his return went aloft early one evening and engaged six enemy fighters. The ensuing fight was a thriller in which Maurice disabled one of his opponents, but his own machine was shot to splinters, and he had to force-land near the front lines. What was left of his Spad was quickly dismantled by a number of American infantrymen—for souvenirs!

After Boyau's thirty-fourth victory, he went up for his last fight on September 16, 1918, when he was flying in company with Corporal Walk. Neither man returned. Walk wound up in a French hospital with an incendiary bullet in his back and explained that Boyau had attacked a kite balloon about six miles behind the German lines. It took three passes to set it afire and by that time seven two-seater fighters—possibly Rumpler C.5's—appeared from nowhere. Walk made one dive attack to help Maurice, then streaked for home with all seven two-seaters following. Boyau went to his aid but had to dive under the burning balloon and apparently into a cone of intense ground fire. His Spad was hit, started to spin, righted itself for an instant, then nosed straight into the ground.

VICTORIES AND DEFEATS

Another semi-invalid ace who came to a tragic end was Michel Coiffard, who in a very few years packed a complete military program into his life before making the great sacrifice. He was born in Nantes and enlisted in the artillery as early as 1910. He went through the Tunisia and Morocco campaigns of 1911, during which he was wounded three times. Shortly after the beginning of the war he was made a *maréchal de logis*—quartermaster sergeant—and returned to France, where he was awarded the Médaille Militaire for his courage in action. Dissatisfied with artillery work, he transferred to the infantry and was wounded again on August 19, 1915; that graded him as unfit for further service. He somehow managed to be selected for pilot training, however, and gained his brevet on April 19, 1917. After two more months he was capable enough to join an operational squadron.

From that point on, Coiffard's career must have been as wild as that of Guynemer, for between June, 1917, and October, 1918, he downed thirty-four enemy planes and was awarded nearly every decoration his country could bestow. His end came late in October, when, acting as fighter escort for a photographic patrol, he was wounded over Saint-Loup but managed to bring back his aircraft to the Allied lines. He died in an ambulance as he was being rushed to a hospital. His score of thirty-four victories included twenty-eight balloons.

Another native of Nantes was the famed Alfred Heurteaux, who destroyed twenty-one enemy aircraft and was one of the greatest squadron leaders in the French Aviation. Since he was a student at the Saint-Cyr Military Academy at the outbreak of war, Heurteaux was commissioned immediately with the 9th Hussars. His time with this unit is replete with gallant action and complimentary citations, and once, dismounting his troop to fight on foot, he saved a complete French battery. Later on, when cavalry troops had little to do in the static phase of trench warfare, Heurteaux applied for flight instruction and was posted to M.S.26 for training as an observer.

After a series of painful crashes with incompetent pilots, the ex-hussar eventually changed seats and became a pilot with M.S.38. Fortunately, this escadrille was re-equipped with Nieuport scouts, which were flown all through the Battle of Verdun. Lieutenant Heurteaux performed so well in that campaign that he was assigned next to N.3 of the Cigognes group and ran up his "ace" quota within a month. When Captain Alfred Auger was killed, Heurteaux was placed in command—just in time to lead this elite squadron into the Battle of the Somme.

By this time the old top-wing fixed gun had been replaced by the Vickers that was synchronized with the British Constantinesco gear. Next, two of the first Spads were made available, and Heurteaux and Guynemer had the honor of testing them in action. Thus N.3 became Spa.3, and in the following six months these veterans shot down more than two hundred enemy planes, a record unsurpassed by any squadron on any front in World War I.

Much of the credit for this must go to Captain Heurteaux, who was an exceptional leader and a skilled strategist and was charged with ruthless determination. During a short period in 1917 when he was out of action with an arm wound, several valuable pilots of Spa.3 were lost in action; in fact, forty-seven Cigognes pilots were killed or wounded in one month. Not long after, Captain Heurteaux received a wound that ended his war flying. While testing a new Spad with a 200-horsepower engine, he spotted a German two-seater and dived to the attack, only to find that his guns had jammed. Before he could withdraw to remedy the stoppages, the German observer's gun scored a hit and an incendiary bullet smashed through his thigh. The new Spad started to go down in flames and Heurteaux did not recover consciousness until he was dangerously low, but luckily had enough altitude to crash-land.

He was rescued by two British soldiers and taken to a hospital, where it was discovered that the incendiary bullet had worked a miracle. Although the femoral artery and the saphenous vein had been severed, the burning phosphorus had cauterized the wound, preventing his bleeding to death. He was never able to fly again, but between the two World Wars he served as Inspector of Fighter Aviation, and for a short time served in the Armée de l'Air in World War II. After France's capitulation, he joined the Resistance movement, taking part in many underground activities. He was arrested finally and deported to Germany, where he was imprisoned in the infamous Buchenwald concentration camp. He returned home at the end of the war and was promoted to the rank of general. When last heard of he was still living in Paris, where he holds the presidency of an association of surviving air aces.

Another refugee from the trenches who became a twenty-victory ace was Albert Deullin, a product of the Champagne region. He had been a brilliant scholar in primary schools and at the Lycée of Pau, and also spent a year studying in Germany before fulfilling his military service with the 31st Dragoons. Once this training was over, Deullin went to England for more university work; but the war broke out before this term could be completed, and the young Frenchman again put on a uniform and spent the winter of 1914–15 in the trenches during the Lorraine campaign.

One winter below ground was more than enough for Albert, and he made overtures for a transfer to French Aviation. He was luckier than most experienced ground fighters, for he was training on Farmans by April, 1915, and qualified for his brevet on June 14. His first active service unit was M.F.62—Maurice Farmans—where he put in his apprenticeship flying reconnaissance and artillery-spotting patrols. In February, 1916, he was relieved of this chore and transferred to fighters and joined the rolls of Escadrille N.3, where he found himself in most illustrious company.

Deullin proved his worth almost immediately, for his first victory came on March 31, along with a painful bullet wound in one arm. This grounded him for a time, but on May 17 he rejoined his unit at Cachy and discovered they were flying the Spad-7. This machine apparently was built expressly for Albert, for he soon ran up a score and was awarded the Legion of Honor. His eleventh victory came on February 10, 1917, after which he was selected to command Spa.73, another Cigognes escadrille.

From that time until the close of the war, Captain Albert Deullin continued to fly and command. He gave plenty of time to the newcomers, but also brought his own total up to twenty. His escadrille played a prominent part over the battles of Saint-Mihiel and Château-Thierry. In his last citation accompanying the Rosette to the Legion of Honor it was stated that he was "... a wonderful fighter pilot, an officer of the highest quality, a model of all military virtues, whose bravery, strength of character and skill have become proverbial in French aviation. Three times wounded in aerial combat, he has always returned to duty before being completely fit. He has most exceptional qualities of leadership allied to admirable fighting ability, and his ceaseless hard work has made the group which he created one of the elite units of the service."

A twenty-three-plane ace of the French service, Claude Marcel Haegelen, started his air career by being shot down three times in a row. After a period of service with the infantry and a bout of typhoid fever, he transferred to aviation in 1916, becoming a pilot with a Maurice Farman squadron. The artillery-spotting and photographic-reconnaissance work was hazardous, Haegelen went down three times before he won someone's sympathy and was transferred to a fighter squadron, Escadrille N.103. On his arrival he soon showed his worth by scoring two victories in his first two days. In the second set-to, however, he was severely wounded and had to crash-land just inside his own lines. He was in a hospital for several months, and his name did not appear again until July, 1918; but from that time on, despite the Fokker D.7's, Haegelen soon ran his score to twenty-three, which included twelve observation balloons. He was awarded the Médaille Militaire and the Legion of Honor, and survived the war to become chief test pilot for the Hanriot company and won his place in the list of acrobatic pilots. He died in 1950.

MILITANT MAN OF THE CLOTH

Jean-Pierre Léon Bourjade was studying for the priesthood when World War I started, but gave up the cloth temporarily to join an artillery regiment. After fighting through the first Battle of the Marne in 1914, he was made a quartermaster sergeant and so served until 1916. By that time aerial combat attracted this bearded aesthete, and after making several requests for a transfer, he was finally accepted, qualified as a pilot on October 20, 1917, and was posted to N.152 on the Vosges front. Nothing much happened to Bourjade until March 27, 1918, when he destroyed an enemy kite balloon. Inspired by this, he apparently concentrated on the gas-bags and on July 14, 1918, destroyed three more within five minutes. In the following eight days he accounted for six more, and before the war ended this priest-to-be had a score of twenty-eight, twenty-four of which were kite balloons. On July 17, 1918, he followed a balloon down to nearly one thousand feet and was severely wounded by a machine-gun bullet fired from the ground. After the war Bourjade returned to his religious calling and went to Waina in Oceania, where he died on October 22, 1924, while ministering to lepers.

Although most French aces were mature and seemingly several years older than their British contemporaries, Pierre Marinovitch was but twenty years old when the war ended. He had scored twenty-two victories and was by far the youngest of the French aces. He was born in Paris and enlisted in the 27th Dragoons in 1916, but when trench warfare denied him glory astride a charger, he transferred to aviation in June of that same year. He joined N.38 in March, 1917, and transferred later to Spa.94.

Marinovitch started slowly and did not score for two months, but by January, 1918, had shot down four planes, and continued at this easy pace until August 10, when he had downed thirteen. He was only nineteen when he was made an adjutant and had been awarded the Médaille Militaire and the Legion of Honor. Among his many victims were Karl Schlegel, also credited with twenty-two victories, and Prince von Bülow—Lieutenant Walter von Bülow—who is credited with twenty-eight victories. Pierre Marinovitch was killed in a flying accident in Belgium on October 2, 1919.

Another high-scoring ace who survived the war and lived to become a noted air-race pilot was Henri Joseph de Slade, who was born in 1893. A product of the Saint-Cyr Military Academy, he first served with cavalry units until late in 1916, when he transferred to aviation and spent wearying months in the dangerous reconnaissance, ground-support, and artillery-spotting work of the two-seater squadrons. When he was posted to a fighter squadron later, he scored his first victory with Spa.159 on May 20, 1917, downing a D.F.W. at 15,000 feet. Through the continued action along the Somme and the Aisne, De Slade was commissioned a captain. He devoted his efforts to kite balloons and enemy two-seaters, and became an ace on December 5, 1917, when he attacked a Rumpler two-seater at 18,000 feet. Another Rumpler went down in flames over Noyon three months later, and on May 18, 1918, he attacked a German two-seater that was being escorted by eight Fokkers, and shot it down despite the fury of the "protectors." He was awarded the Legion of Honor.

Then, while conducting a front-line trial of a new 300-horsepower Spad, De Slade destroyed five enemy machines in as many days, including a Fokker D.7. His final score was nineteen, which included two observation balloons.

Jacques Louis Ehrlich often partnered Michel Coiffard and learned the trick of working at low altitudes. He racked up nineteen victories before he was shot down and taken prisoner during the last few weeks of the war.

Ehrlich started his war career as a truck driver, but transferred to aviation in December, 1916, and decided he would become an ace. He evaded the usual trial-and-error period of two-seater squadrons, and his first assignment after completing his training was to Spa.154, where he was quickly spotted by Coiffard, who recognized the newcomer's determination.

These two men carried out many low-level attacks, but Ehrlich had little luck and did not get into the news until April 10, 1918, when he completed two especially dangerous low-level attacks in the Saint-Quentin area. On both occasions he brought back his plane riddled with bullets and shell splinters, and was lucky to walk away from two crash landings.

At another time he received two bullet wounds and was sent to the hospital, but on his release he went back to the same wild combat, returning time after time with only empty ammo boxes, bullet holes, and damaged engines. He was downed and reported missing on two occasions, but he showed up each time with more determination than ever to shoot down every balloon on the front.

But it was not until June 30, 1918, that Jacques finally downed a *Drachen*, and the thrill was so encouraging that he went out the next day and destroyed another. He was really in the groove now, and a third fell before his guns on July 5. For a time he showed that he was equally efficient against powered aircraft when, accompanied by Coiffard and Robert P. I. Waddington, a Frenchman of English descent, he defeated a German single-seater on July 12. Later that evening Ehrlich scored against another kite balloon.

Now a confirmed ace, Ehrlich went after his sixth victim, ranging far behind the enemy lincs, where he was set upon by five hostile fighters, and in the scramble may have shot down one. At any rate, he evaded them and returned to his favorite level and sent down another balloon in flames. On July 18 he destroyed two balloons in the space of one minute, and downed a third later that day. In other words, Jacques Ehrlich had leaped from a nonscoring unknown to a ten-plane ace in twenty-five days, but he was still rated a sergeant and could display only the Croix de Guerre. By September 18, 1918, he was credited with eighteen victories and promoted to adjutant, but on that day the law of averages caught up with him.

Ehrlich was flying with Adjutant Petit and an unnamed rookie pilot to show the novice how to attack enemy balloons. Once a gasbag was found, it took three attacks to set it afire, and as the three Frenchmen turned for their own lines, they were pounced on by eleven Fokker D.7's. Only the newcomer evaded the attack and got back to his own lines; it was learned a few days later that the two other pilots were prisoners of war. While spending the last few weeks of their internment in Germany before the Armistice, Ehrlich and Petit were given commissions, and Ehrlich recommended for the Legion of Honor. Jacques Ehrlich died in 1953.

THE TRAGIC JEAN NAVARRE

One of the more interesting but tragic figures in French aviation was Jean Navarre, who learned to fly before the war. He was born at Jouy-en-Morin in 1895. At the beginning of the war he flew with M.S.12, a two-seater squadron. He was an especially skilled pilot with the Morane-Saulnier, having been an exhibition flyer before the war drums rolled. Corporal Navarre had as observer for a time Lieutenant René Chambe, who later also became a single-seater pilot.

Reconnaissance was far more important in those early days, since no one had any idea how or where the war would be fought, and the work of the early reconnaissance teams has long been overlooked, considering how necessary tactical information was at the time. M.S.12 performed a heroic task in the French defeat of the Germans on the Marne and, later on, when Von Kluck's forces were driven back to the Aisne.

We are again reminded of the primitive equipment carried by the early flyers when a number of Zeppelins were reported over Paris on the night of March 21–22, 1915. Several machines of M.S.12 were ordered aloft to intercept—but with what? Some carried rifles or revolvers; some risked a sensitive-fused 90-kilogram artillery shell that was fitted with temporary fins and carried in the lap of the observer. Navarre reportedly carried a large kitchen knife with which he intended to attack any dirigible that came close enough. It would be interesting to offer a blow-by-blow account of any Navarre engagement, but it must be regretfully reported that all Zeppelins returned safely to their hangars.

A short time later, Navarre, with an observer named Lieutenant

Robert, met and attacked a German Aviatik two-seater over Fismes and, using Army rifles, fired only three rounds before the German pilot was wounded and crashed the aircraft in French territory. From all accounts this was the third enemy plane brought down by French airmen, and the victory was rewarded with a luncheon with General Franchet d'Esperey, better known as Frantic Frankie. That same night M.S.12 had another party for the designers and builders of the Morane-Saulnier, and at this affair Lieutenant Robert was nominated for the Legion of Honor, while Corporal Navarre was recommended for the Médaille Militaire.

Early the next morning, while the squadron was sleeping off the effects of the night before, Lieutenant Chambe, Navarre's observer, took off with Corporal Pelletier-Doisy, who was Lieutenant Robert's pilot. They intercepted an Albatros two-seater; again using a rifle, this time Chambe fired four shots, and once more a German pilot was forced to land in French territory. The age of aerial combat was thus introduced.

In a short time Navarre, who is still remembered for flying with a woman's silk stocking for a helmet, was promoted to sergeant and given a Morane N-type midwing monoplane. This mount was sometimes called the Bullet, and was the same type with which Roland Garros developed his front-firing gun. Navarre flew in this machine for a considerable time as an escort to the two-seater teams, and was then transferred to N.67, where he ran up a score of twelve enemy planes. He was severely wounded when he was shot down on June 17, 1916, while he was working over the Argonne sector. This injury, combined with the news of his brother's death, affected Jean's mental health, and it was more than two years before he could return to active duty. He made a brave attempt to adjust to the new equipment and fighting conditions, but the Armistice ended his hopes of adding to his score.

But Jean Navarre loved flying and refused to give up when the war ended. He worked for a time as a test pilot for the Morane-Saulnier Company, and while checking out a plane in which he intended to fly through the Arc de Triomphe in France's Victory Parade, he crashed and died July 10, 1919.

In summarizing France's great contribution to the winning of World War I in the air, it is interesting to note how many of her first-class flyers concentrated on kite balloons. One is prone to remember only Frank Luke's wild career as the Balloon Buster, but in glancing over the records it is apparent that several Frenchmen compiled astounding scores against the observation balloons. For instance, Coiffard is credited with twenty-eight, Boyau with twenty, Haegelen with fourteen (the same number as Luke). Armand Pinsard downed eight balloons and nineteen aircraft. Major Willy Coppens of Belgium is credited with twenty-six balloons, and Heinrich Gontermann of Germany destroyed eighteen.

The ace system that began when Roland Garros first downed a number of German aircraft with his fixed-gun idea became an important factor in the development of France's fighter escadrilles. Although frowned on by most British authorities, the ace system was responsible for the high standards registered by the five squadrons of the Cigognes group, for here were gathered all the aces who could be brought together to form this elite company. As pointed out before, many readers may consider only Escadrille 3 as the real Storks squadron, but the term applies to the whole Number 12 Group.

CHAPTER 11

A-Wing, Over There

America, propelled into the war by continued German U-boat attacks on American shipping, had little to offer but men and money. No one had taken any notice of the advance in military aviation along the Western Front and we had no up-to-date equipment to contribute to the cause. When pilots of the Lafayette Escadrille volunteered to serve under their own flag, they were ignored for months while the politicians back home and the armchair generals decided just what the A.E.F. would contribute to the war in the air. Finally, only out-and-out American courage and willingness to fight with second-class equipment brought honor and glory to our arms. When it was all over and the effort totaled up, our accomplishments amazed friend and foe alike.

THE YANKS ARE COMING

AMERICA's entry into World War I was not the glorious extravaganza the song writers and publicists would have us believe. It was almost two years after the sinking of the *Lusitania* that on April 6, 1917, Congress took up the cause, and from that date on, practically nothing of military importance occurred. We who were in France almost forgot that the United States was now a member of the Allies. As an illustration, it was not until October 23, 1917, more than six months after the declaration of war, that Battery C of the U.S. 6th Field Artillery moved a French 75-millimeter gun into an abandoned dugout east of the village of Bethelémont in the Meurthe-et-Moselle district and lobbed a shell into German territory. It was here too that the first three American soldiers killed in the war fell on November 3, 1917.

America's air effort moved just as sluggishly. When war was declared she had not yet begun to create a military air arm. Although her experts and military observers had watched the progress of aviation along the Western Front for nearly three years, practically nothing had been done to develop an air force, or to design one aircraft or aero engine. There were many predictions and proclamations, and the publicity writers of America's aircraft industry promised to deliver 22,000 aircraft during 1917, ignoring the fact that in March of that year there were but twelve small companies in the country capable of producing an airplane of any kind.

History shows also that by January, 1918, production had been stepped up to 700 engines and 800 aircraft, 700 of which were primary trainers of doubtful value; but not one first-class combat plane had been assembled. Still, no one seemed disturbed, and in the theaters and the vaudeville houses, and against the song screens of the motion-picture theaters the Irving Berlin—George M. Cohan vocalists assured the world that the Yanks were coming. A few did, here and there, but they brought nothing with them. They had nothing but their buoyant spirits and New World enthusiasm.

WE STARTED FROM SCRATCH

Eventually a cadre of an air service was organized, and in nineteen months the 1,200-man Aviation Service of the Signal Corps expanded more than one hundred and fifty times. Twenty-six flying schools were established in the United States and sixteen more in Europe. Of the 6,300 planes delivered to the American Air Service in France, only 1,200 D.H.4's came from the United States. About 4,500 aircraft were purchased from the French, and by November 11, 1918, the actual strength of U.S. Aviation in the Zone of Advance was 1,005 military planes, of which 325 were American-built

D.H.4's, and the rest such Allied products as Spads, Salmsons, Nieuports, Camels, and Bréguets.

This American Air Service came into being when U.S. Aviation was transferred from the Signal Corps to two agencies, the Bureau of Aircraft Production and the Division of Military Aeronautics under the Secretary of War. John D. Ryan, former head of Anaconda Copper, was named director of the Air Service and Second Assistant Secretary of War, an appointment that was not made until August 27, 1918.

In the meantime, Colonel William Mitchell, who had made his way to France from Portugal, almost singlehanded set up headquarters of an American Air Service. He hoped to build this service into two distinct forces—one to consist of a number of squadrons attached to the ground armies under the control of ground commanders, the second to be built up of large multi-engined aeronautical groups trained for strategic operations against the enemy and enemy matériel stored great distances from the front line. He suggested that the bombardment and escort-pursuit squadrons of this second force would have an independent mission, and would be used to carry the war deep into the enemy's country.

Major General Hugh M. Trenchard, former head of the Royal Flying Corps, was already operating his Independent Air Force in strategic operations against German industrial targets, and anxiously awaiting the development of the Handley Page four-engined bomber so that he could plan night operations against Berlin and other major German cities. Mitchell and Trenchard became firm friends in a short time, and Mitchell always gave Trenchard credit for his understanding and appreciation of strategic aviation.

CONFUSION IN PARIS

When General Pershing arrived in Paris, he appointed a board of officers that included Mitchell to recommend the composition and organization of the Air Service, A.E.F. This board suggested a strategic force of thirty bomber groups and thirty fighter groups, with a secondary force of a size based on the strength of the ground forces to which it would be attached. It can be seen that America's original air-power concept chiefly concerned a strategic air force.

General Pershing, unfortunately, did not accept the recommendation but, instead, insisted on units trained and equipped for Army co-operation missions. Although later programs included bombardment and pursuit squadrons, permission never was granted to establish an American strategic bombardment force.

All these good intentions were affected later by the types and numbers of aircraft available, rather than by any program or doctrine. American manufacturers were bewildered by the emphasis the British and French were placing on strategic bombing, whereas the popular concept in the United States was to put dozens of fighter squadrons and hundreds of fighter pilots on the front in order to show what could be accomplished by American airmen. They were warned also that the American ground forces would require supporting air units if they were to carry out their part on the Western Front. A third priority was for bombers and long-range fighters for a strategic air force, but by the time American production was in a position to turn out such equipment, the war had ended.

In the summer of 1917 Colonel Mitchell had an Air Service headquarters in Paris, but no aircraft. A field-artillery officer, Brigadier General William L. Kenly, was chief of Air Service, Major Raynal C. Bolling served as assistant chief in charge of supply, and Colonel Mitchell became Air Commander, Zone of Advance. While this force was attempting to cope with the situation, General Benjamin D. Foulois arrived in France with a ready-made headquarters staff of 112 officers and 300 enlisted men, an organization that had been formed in Washington without consultation with General Pershing.

General Foulois immediately replaced General Kenly, and the resulting complications created serious difficulties, and handicapped all efforts to build an organization. At this point General Pershing stepped in, in May, 1918, and appointed as Chief of Air Service his old classmate, Brigadier General Mason M. Patrick, and Mitchell was subordinate to Foulois, who had been placed in charge of aviation at the front. Colonel Mitchell ignored the arrangement and hacked through red tape wherever possible; General Foulois suggested finally that Colonel Mitchell be given the combat command, and requested that he be appointed assistant chief of Air Service under General Patrick.

From this point on, the Air Service expanded rapidly and additional combat commands were organized as new American armies came into the field. By October, 1918, Colonel Frank Lahm was made chief of Air Service, Second Army, and Mitchell, newly promoted to brigadier general, became chief of Air Service, Army Group. The establishment of Air Service, Third Army, just before the Armistice completed the air organization at the front up to November 11, 1918.

GERMANY PREPARES NEW OFFENSIVES

It is important to remember that the U.S. Air Service's air operations were subsidiary to the field army. No independent air operations were carried out by American aircraft comparable to the strategic missions of the British and French. The A.E.F. air arm was involved in three major campaigns: Château-Thierry, Saint-Mihiel and the Meuse–Argonne, in each of which American airmen saw considerable action. Château-Thierry was the last great *defensive* battle fought by the Allies in Europe and was the culmination of the frantic series of German offensives that opened on March 2, 1918.

In early summer it was evident that the enemy was preparing an operation planned to pierce the French lines on each side of Château-Thierry, a small town on the Marne River. The French, wearied and almost drained of manpower, were in a desperate situation, and General Pershing allowed an American Army corps to be employed as a reinforcement. Colonel Mitchell and seven willing but inexperienced squadrons of the American Air Service went along with the corps. They were comprised of the First Pursuit Group and the First Corps Observation Group, organized into what was to be known as the First Brigade.

On July 15 the Germans began their push, which was quickly stopped, and as a countermeasure the Allies opened a new thrust that shoved the Germans back to the Vesle River. Once consolidation work had been completed, General Foch turned his attention to the Saint-Mihiel sector.

This was the largest operation to be attempted by the American Army thus far, and the objective was to snip off a German salient the spearhead of which was at Saint-Mihiel. General Pershing planned well and Colonel Mitchell contributed a large air force to support the infantry, actually gathering in 101 squadrons and providing 1,476 planes, most of which were French, but also included support by General Trenchard's Independent Air Force.

All these squadrons, with the exception of the Independent Air Force, were under Mitchell's direct command. As General Pershing had previously refused to allow any American force to serve under any other Allied commander, we must assume that it all depends on which foot is wearing the shoe. The French contributed forty-two squadrons of pursuit and bombardment aircraft; and of the force of 1,476 aircraft only 609 were American; 1,346 of the total amount were under the direct command of Colonel Mitchell. It must be said that he handled them with rare skill and imagination.

General Pershing's next effort was to move north between the Meuse River and the Argonne Forest, where the objectives were to cut the chief communications of the German Army, which by then was beginning its final retreat out of northern France and Flanders. The air arm available to Mitchell was virtually the same, except that most of the French squadrons had been withdrawn; only the night-bombardment and a few corps observation squadrons remained under his command.

Britain's Independent Air Force could furnish only occasional aid, for they were too busy providing long-range support for their own front. Thus, there was a net reduction of the aircraft available to the First Army from 1,476 to 836 between September 12 and September 26.

This summary is to explain how the failure of American aircraft manufacturers to produce the necessary equipment hampered Colonel Mitchell's hopes and plans; and had it not been for the continued production of British, French, and even Italian factories, American pilots would have been grounded for long periods of time. As an illustration, in October, 1918, the newly arrived 155th Aero Squadron, the A.E.F.'s first night-bombardment squadron, had to be equipped with British F.E.2b's, a model that had been withdrawn from day-fighter operations early in 1917. They had been painted black and resurrected for night operations and were filling in with Trenchard's Independent Air Force while Handley Page bombers were being built.

American pursuit squadrons had to be equipped with obsolete Nieuports, including the atrocious Nieuport-28, Spads, British Camels, S.E.5's, and Sopwith Dolphins. Had the war continued into 1919, American Aviation would have experienced a very critical period, for although we had tremendous manpower potential, our aircraft manufacturers never fulfilled their wild promises.

U.S. AIR SERVICE IGNORES LAFAYETTE PILOTS

As pointed out before, for ten months after the United States declared war on Germany, its only active-service representative in Europe was the Lafayette Escadrille, and this picturesque organization had produced only a few pilots of any stature: Raoul Lufbery, Ted Parsons, Bill Thaw, and Paul Baer. The early publicity given these men had encouraged many other Americans to join the French service or the Royal Flying Corps, and all told, there was a wealth of fully trained and experienced pilots and observers available to America, but no one seemed to know what to do with them. For weeks and months there was much talk but little action. The volunteers were asked to apply for acceptance by the American Air Service, then were put through most arbitrary examinations by so-called aviation experts from Washington, most of whom had not heard a shot fired or seen a military plane in action.

As Ted Parsons wrote later:

Just when we were on the point of despairing of ever hearing from the American brass hats, the American Army in October sent out another delegation of top-rankers to examine the Lafayette Escadrille pilots.

After comprehensive physical examinations, which, much to the dismay of some of the boys, included urinalysis and blood tests, we were put through a long series of rather ridiculous physical contortions which weren't helped by frequent visits to the bar to bolster our courage.

Then the awful truth came out!

In solemn, owlish conclave, the board decided that not one of us, despite our hundreds of hours in the air, most of us aces, all thoroughly trained pilots, could ever be an aviator. Their tests definitely showed that physically, mentally and morally we were unfit to be pilots.

Dudley Hill had one blind eye. Bill Thaw's vision was hopeless and he had a crippled arm. Lufbery couldn't walk a crack backwards. Dolan's tonsils were past all redemption and Hank Jones had flat feet! All this was revealed in the light of pitiless publicity. We were simply a broken-down crew of crippled misfits. There was hardly a man on whom they wouldn't have to ask waivers.

However, we were still the only American outfit on active service, but of course we were not fit to wear the uniform of our own country. At the same time the Lafayette was again cited by the appreciative French, which allowed us, as members of a twice-cited organization, to wear the *fourragère* in the colors of the Croix de Guerre. It was the second escadrille in the French Army to be so honored, the only one preceding being Escadrille Spa.3 of the Storks.

This unpleasant situation has been glossed over in many U.S. World War I histories, and in looking back, it is difficult to judge whether most of the American volunteers actually wished to transfer to their own colors. As the war groaned along it was seen that much of the back-home boasting was just that, and many Americans serving with Allied squadrons gradually came to the conclusion that as long as they had to fight the war, they were better off with an organization that was armed, geared, and trained for fighting in the sky. While a few may have realized that such a transfer might bring a respite from the daily grind, they also sensed that once the American squadrons-to-be were properly organized, they would most likely go flat out to prove themselves—as was quite understandable from novices and newcomers full of beef and beans. But with a certain number of inexperienced airmen in every flight or squadron, no matter how experienced the ex-volunteers, the prospects were not too rosy. In fact, many of them turned down the chance to transfer to the new American Air Service.

Generally speaking, the pilots of the Lafayette Escadrille and others with various French squadrons were disgusted and indignant over the attitude of top officials of the American Air Service. Instead of being allowed to continue to fly as a unit, as Spa.124 had requested and hoped, it was broken up and only a few of the original members of the Lafayette remained together until the end of the war. Some were shunted to Paris where they languished for months, waiting to get back in the cockpit again.

LUFBERY'S DISMAL GROUND JOB

Raoul Lufbery's experience was particularly tragic. Possibly he never wanted the change. Ethnically he was more French than American, since he had spent but a short time in the United States as a young man, and could have absorbed little of the American spirit or been influenced by American customs.

At any rate, Lufbery was first assigned to the 94th Pursuit Squadron and given a major's commission. He was not the actual squadron commander, and from all accounts never was; but at this point it must not be assumed that there was such an organization for him to command. The 94th Pursuit was chiefly on paper, and to occupy his time Raoul was sent to the instruction center at Issoudun, where he was given an office, a swank desk, some paper and pencils, and was told to sit there and allow the nonflying specialists to organize the aviation service.

Lufbery knew nothing about paper work, even when there was any. He cared less about the forms, figures, and routine organization a squadron commander was supposed to handle. Even worse, it was insisted that he wear a complete American uniform that made him feel like a dressed-up tailor's dummy. All the old free-and-easy glamour of the front-line airman was stripped away; his friends were scattered; and his new associates were alien to him. It is easy to understand how unhappy he must have been.

Luf knew that he was not earning this new money, and that in his silent office he was of no use to anyone. He resented this kiwi status. Instinctively, he knew that his real worth was in acting as a combat leader, not an administrative officer, and he yearned to be back with a fighting organization.

Front-line flying men know the dangers of these periodic letdowns, particularly if the rests are too prolonged or, worse still, if they do not afford a complete change from the usual war routine. Short breaks from daily patrols that gave a complete change of program were ideal and most valuable. Periods of leave in old cities, pleasant country homes with good companions, chances to look on and enjoy contrasting scenes were Mother and Medicine to war-weary flying men.

The accepted picture is one in which wild-eyed heroes roared through the bars and hotels of the war capitals, presumably to forget what they had left behind; but more often it was one of unhurried rambles through country lanes, a change of clothing, quiet nights of pleasant companionship, and plenty of much-needed sleep. Airmen who pursued these furlough activities usually returned with new enthusiasm, interest, keenness, and in full possession of their faculties. The simple life was no assurance of longevity, but it at least kept hundreds of men from breaking down under the strain, and saved them for more important roles in the campaign.

Raoul Lufbery was allowed no such pleasures. He was withdrawn from the line, deprived of most of his companions, and placed in a position where he had little to do but sweat and fume. He was not considered an instructor, and any advice or suggestion he may have made was probably resented. When he received his own squadron and roster of pilots he could make use of his experience, but in the meantime "expert" instructors were teaching the students to fly.

Up at the front line, matters were far from satisfactory. The German push of March, 1918, had hurled the British and French back for many miles. The Channel ports were threatened again, and only the airmen were holding their own. Just when the experienced pilots were needed most, the men of the old Lafayette Escadrille were doomed to wander about inactive airfields that had no planes, mingle with men who had no idea what was going on, and sip the dregs of enforced idleness.

Finally, since there were no more reasons for him to idle away his time at Issoudun, Lufbery was sent to Villeneuve in the Champagne sector, where the United States 94th and 95th Pursuit Squadrons were being organized. He found some mild activity there, but no actual war patrols to lead. There were a few decrepit Nieuport-28's lined up in front of the hangars, but there were no machine guns for them, and few trained armorers to mount them, had any been available.

Lufbery took time to study his pupils and noted three in particular who showed considerable promise. One was a former automobile test driver named Eddie Rickenbacker, another with the Scottish name of Douglas Campbell, and the third was Reed Chambers, who was to become a seven-victory ace and a squadron commander. Rickenbacker and Campbell were selected to make their first war patrol with Luf, a foray that was dull and uneventful to the newcomers; but once they were back and making out their patrol reports, they were amazed to learn that four German Albatros fighters and a German two-seater had stalked them for most of the patrol. Initial air blindness had prevented their noticing these enemy planes, and they were shocked; but Lufbery assured them that they had done well to stay in formation as long as they had, and explained that it took some time to learn to "see" in the air.

As the days and weeks went by, they added to Lufbery's despair. He was getting more action fighting with the brass hats of his new service; his old spirit ebbed away and he seldom smiled. In all probability his flying skill was being dissipated too, for there was no friendly competition to keep his touch and accuracy honed.

But he worked with what he had and, after leading several five-ship patrols, decided that his boys had been eased in long enough, and he set up a three-ship formation, led by Captain David Peterson, with Rickenbacker and Chambers off Peterson's wingtips. This threesome took off early in the morning of April 18 with orders to patrol a line between Saint-Mihiel and Pont-à-Mousson. Captain Peterson was, of course, ex-Sergeant Peterson of the Lafayette Escadrille.

WINSLOW AND CAMPBELL SCORE

History was to be made in this first all-American patrol, for in a suffix to the order, Lieutenants Alan Winslow and Douglas Campbell were to stand by to be available, should Peterson's flight be chased back to the field.

Shortly after Captain Peterson's trio had taken off, a sudden fog crept in, and when the three Americans found no activity over the line they returned. Peterson and Rickenbacker landed safely, but Chambers became lost and wisely set down on a near-by friendly strip. By the time these three pilots had landed, a report came in that two enemy planes were poking about in the vicinity, and when the fog started to dissipate, Winslow and Campbell went into the air.

The first victory for the 94th was scored by Winslow, who shot down an Albatros D.5 a short distance from his own field. The townspeople of Toul saw the fight, and before that thrill had died away a second, a Pfalz D.3 fell to the fury of Campbell's guns, splashing within five hundred yards of the 94th's airdrome. Both German pilots were alive and explained that they had been sent up to intercept three Nieuports that were patrolling the line, but had lost them in the fog. They themselves were then uncertain where they were and, while trying to identify the field near the town of Toul, had been set upon by Winslow and Campbell. Since they were so low, they were sitting ducks for the two Americans.

Toul and the surrounding area celebrated. Old Moselle wine flowed freely; champagne and cognac foamed and gurgled. Colonel Billy Mitchell joined the festivities and sent back a most laudatory report to Washington. It was assumed immediately that American airmen were as good as any experienced German, but more important was the psychological effect of this two-plane success on other Americans who were volunteering for the new Aviation Service.

Major Lufbery was delighted of course with this initial victory and did his best to nurture the resulting enthusiasm. He held daily talks and answered every question put to him, and from all accounts his main concern in these sessions was his dread of fire in the air. There was little an airman could do if his craft caught fire. There were no parachutes available to Allied flyers, and the only move one might take was to put the machine into a sideslip in the hope of preventing the flames from burning the main spars and wings, and thus keep the framework together as long as possible.

LUFBERY JUMPS TO HIS DEATH

Raoul Lufbery's last flight is composed in great part of legend. One phase of the tale is that Luf was pitifully afraid of fire in the air and on more than one occasion had sworn that he would not sit it out and die in that manner, but would step out and take what he considered the easier way. Some men who remember Lufbery well deny this fear and claim that Raoul always insisted that everyone should at least try the sideslip measure, arguing that in many cases the fire would burn itself out within a short time, and related incident after incident to prove his point.

Legend also has another variation of Lufbery's final day. Some airmen who were on the 94th's field at the time declare that Raoul lost his life while attacking an Albatros two-seater, whereas others insist that it was a three-seater armored photography plane. Ted Parsons points out that it must have been an armored machine, since Luf shot several telling bursts into it with little effect.

At any rate, the tragedy took place on May 19, when a German photography airplane was moving back and forth within sight of the 94th's field. Everyone raced for a Nieuport, but Luf, whose regular mount was unserviceable, grabbed the first on the line, and a crew of mechanics had the prop ticking over in short order. With Raoul first in the air, it seemed obvious that no one else need take off. The major would soon dispose of this intruder.

What happened from then on is confused and uncertain. Luf was soon at the level of the photography plane, and those on the ground saw him use all his wiles to gain a commanding position. He moved in and out and then started his attack. He fired two long bursts with no apparent effect on the multi-seater. Another burst from an even closer range brought no reward, but the enemy gunner popped up from below and took charge. Some people believe that Luf had a gun stoppage, for he never fired again. He did go back and make one more pass at the enemy ship, but the German gunner stood his ground and poured a number of bursts at the American Nieuport.

Witnesses saw the plane stagger, wobble, and fall away. There was a gush of scarlet flame that fanned out from the joints of the engine cowling and threatened to wrap a blanket of fire over the cockpit, and Luf's friends wondered what he would do.

Raoul did try to get her into a sideslip as he pulled up into a stall to lose flying speed. The flames swirled as if coming from a fluted nozzle, and it seemed minutes before the Nieuport lost any forward speed. It was at this point that Lufbery was seen to jump, probably forced out by the searing heat as he was trying to lose forward momentum.

Another version of the legend is that, realizing he could stay no longer with the burning aircraft, Raoul climbed out and tried to control it from a position on the wing root. And a still further story is that he tried to work the Nieuport to a point over a small stream, hoping by some miraculous stroke of luck to break his fall by landing in the water. Perhaps he did, but it was not Luf's lucky day. He fell instead on a picket fence that surrounded the cottage garden of a shoemaker on the outskirts of the town of Maron. The cobbler's wife ran out of her kitchen and saw the broken body of Lufbery draped over the fence. She tried to pull the airman clear and discovered that a length of picket was impaled in Raoul's throat. She stood horrified for a few minutes and then, hoping to relieve the airman of some of his pain, pulled the length of picket away and wrapped it in a piece of clean paper. She was still standing there, holding the broken splinter in its wrapping and her sixteen-year-old daughter was covering Raoul's body with flowers, when members of the 94th Squadron arrived on the scene of Lufbery's tragedy.

Air-war heroes have many strange ways of dying, and it would be of interest to know how many top-scorers were brought down by some unnamed aerial gunner.

UNDER WAY AT LAST

The bulk of the Lafayette Escadrille was finally turned over to Colonel Mitchell and became the 103rd Aero Squadron. Since this was the first real American front-line organization it may puzzle the layman who will wonder where were the other 102 squadrons. This numerical ruse was intended to delude the enemy; whether it worked is debatable.

The 103rd was commanded by Bill Thaw, and it should be added that of the twelve pilots who transferred from Spa.124 and six other Americans who joined them shortly after, seven later were made flight commanders, seven squadron commanders, and two reached the grade of Pursuit Group commander.

The 94th and 95th Pursuit Squadrons, the first American outfits produced at the Issoudun center, had an unsteady time getting into action. The lack of machine guns hampered the 94th, and the 95th's pilots were sent to the front with no machine-gun training at all, and had to be sent back to the pursuit-training center for a quickie course in the Vickers gun and its interrupter gear.

When Alan Winslow and Reed Chambers scored the first all-American victories, the 94th received a welcome inspiration that started them on a sterling career. The 95th was not back into action again until May 4, when they joined the 94th to form the nucleus of the First Pursuit Group. By the end of May the 27th and 147th Pursuit Squadrons, commanded by Majors H. E. Hartney and G. H. Bonnell, both of whom had served with the Royal Flying Corps, joined the First Pursuit Group on a quiet front where only second-class German *Jagdstaffeln* were based.

This indoctrination period lasted until June 28, when the First Pursuit Group was sent north to Touquin for the expected German attack at Château-Thierry. From that time on, America knew that she was really in the war, and it must be said that the men of the American Air Service acquitted themselves remarkably well. On November 11, 1918, General Mitchell had forty-five combat squadrons under his command, in which were 767 pilots, 481 observers, and 23 aerial gunners. Two of these units, the British-trained Number 17 and Number 148 Pursuit Squadrons, had just rejoined the United States forces after serving with the R.A.F. on the British front since June, 1918. In Italy, Captain Fiorello H. La Guardia led a detachment of eighteen bomber pilots against the Austrians, and all in all some sixty-five American pilots, flying Caproni bombers, saw action on the Italian front.

American fighters had confirmed claims of 781 enemy machines and seventy-three balloons. Seventy-one airmen qualified as aces, and this select group destroyed 450 planes and fifty kite balloons. Two hundred and thirty-seven American airmen were killed in action, and many of these might have been saved, had aircraft parachutes been furnished.

The most poignant history of America's contribution in the air in World War I is to be found in the individual stories of her air heroes. Above all, they brought a new triumphant spirit to the war-weary who, although they had encountered some of the New World dash in members of the Lafayette Escadrille and those who served with the Royal Flying Corps, had not as yet been exposed to the mass effect of the Yankee enthusiasm that was unleashed once an American force began to operate on the Western Front.

It was resented at first and tabbed collegiate rowdyism, but these outpourings gradually congealed into a definite measure of service vigor. Charged with healthful confidence, ignited by the volatile publicity they read, and probably believed, they swarmed into the various war areas like triumphant athletes. They were alive with interest in the war, astonishingly ignorant of the facts and figures, but voracious for data and details whenever they could corner anyone who had served time over the line. Despite their sophomoric enthusiasm, they all seemed much older and more mature than the British, and compared to the French they were gigantic figures, and much more volatile than their new Gallic comrades.

They were flush with money, had expensive but most impractical uniforms, and were overly generous in their social contacts with any of their new Allies, regardless of rank or service. They had no idea of the breadth of the front, how long the war had been in progress, or the fuel range of a Spad or a Nieuport.

But these vociferous young gods were good for us who had been out there so long. They brought new life and a new language to the war. They revolutionized our furloughs and many of our regimental social codes. Most certainly they widened our taproom and men's bar behavior. We who had served through so many campaigns nurtured new hopes of military co-operation, for these were airmen who thought as we did. Tyros they were, but willing to listen, and they gave us a warm promise of a brighter future. I, for one, sensed that at last we had been joined by trustworthy comrades who would willingly share our war skies and co-operate generously in any aerial undertaking.

AMERICA PROVIDES MANY KINDS OF AIR HEROES

It always has been difficult to select the typical American airman of this era, for, as in the Canadian and Australian services, there was every type, character, personality, and ethnic representative of the New World. Eddie Rickenbacker was a mature, steadfast, calculating figure who realized the hazards of the profession and paced himself accordingly. As a result America's Ace of Aces—twenty-six victories—probably was the least conspicuous figure in the service. On the other hand, Frank Luke, the so-called Arizona Balloon Buster, was an untamed, unbridled reactionary who hated war, hated the idea of serving, and despised nearly everyone in his squadron. He was the outstanding figure on the American front, while he lasted, and although he was credited with twenty victories, there always has been some question whether he fulfilled his potential. One wonders why Luke could not have been brought under control to run up an even greater score, and live to see the Allied victory. His service record is a classic of wild adventure, but his passing was one of the tragic and useless sacrifices of the war. Possibly he would have wanted it that way, for he was a maverick from the outset, refusing to conform, and would not bow to military discipline. Like Baron von Richthofen, he ran up a remarkable score, but how many of these victories were offset by the losses suffered by a weakened air element?

We all have our favorites, and these opinions may be tempered by the fact that we once knew, or still know, many of those World War I performers. The author is especially proud to know George A. Vaughn, Jr., who downed thirteen enemy aircraft, for he is typical of the type of airman the author admires. He is quiet, unassuming, seeks no personal publicity, but enjoys the company of those who also served and like to exchange anecdotes. Vaughn is one of the best-loved representatives of the flying service.

Douglas Campbell was born on June 7, 1896, in San Francisco. His father was head of the Mount Wilson Observatory and Doug's early education began in the public schools of Mount Hamilton,

California, after which he entered Harvard. He left college shortly after America entered the war and received his entire aviation training in the United States; on arriving in France he was assigned to the 94th Pursuit. Along with Alan Winslow, he brought down the first planes credited to that squadron on April 14, 1918. Campbell's career came to a close less than two months later, when, while attacking a Rumpler, an incendiary bullet fired by the enemy observer struck just behind his head and a number of burning fragments became embedded in his back. He managed to reach his own line safely, however. Because of his initial victory, Campbell was sent back to the United States to recuperate and to add to the publicity needed by America's air service. When he returned to the 94th to take up the gauntlet once more, the Armistice was signed before he could reach the front line.

RICKENBACKER, AIRMAN OF DESTINY

Captain Edward Vernon Rickenbacker, top-ranking ace of the American Service, was born in Columbus, Ohio, on October 8, 1890. He was the son of William and Elizabeth Reichenbacher, and since there was little money in the family, Eddie had to leave school at age twelve to work in a glass factory. Later the automobile industry attracted him and he took a correspondence course in mechanical engineering which led to various positions. He became a test driver and went into the auto-racing world, and although he never had any important wins, he was a consistent performer and by 1917 is said to have earned $40,000 a year.

As stated before, he was induced to become General Pershing's chauffeur when America entered the war and went to France with him a few weeks later. One time during a trip up the lines, Rick helped another American driver get a disabled car moving. Colonel Billy Mitchell, who was in that automobile, was impressed with Rick's expert ministrations, and when he learned that General Pershing's chauffeur was a former race driver, he made an offhand suggestion that he would be more valuable in his country's Aviation Service.

Rick was more than pleased with this idea, but when he put the proposition to Pershing, the general said, "But, Eddie, you're too old for war flying. That's a job for crazy youngsters." Rickenbacker was nearly twenty-seven years old at the time; but he persisted and was given a transfer and received his flight training at the 2d Aviation Instruction Center at Tours, where his knowledge of engines overshadowed his skill in the cockpit. So he was made Chief Engineering Officer of the 3rd A.I.C. at Issoudun.

Rick accepted this for a time, but continued his flight and gunnery training and after several requests was finally permitted to join the newly formed 94th Pursuit Squadron. His first score was made on April 29, 1918, and by May 30 he had brought down his fifth, which placed him in the "ace" category.

Rick's maturity stood him in good stead, for he fought carefully with sound logic. He had great patience and would wait for the right opportunity to attack. His rare judgment soon made him a flight commander, but he began to suffer from an ear infection. He was placed in a hospital where after lengthy treatment an examination disclosed the need for a mastoid operation. He was out of action through July and August, but on his return resumed his old skill. During the last two weeks of September he downed six enemy aircraft, and in October destroyed fourteen more. He was appointed commander of the 94th Squadron on September 25, but was never commissioned a major.

After the war Rickenbacker entered various projects connected with automobiles, and in 1936 was made head of Eastern Airlines, and saw this organization rise to be one of the most important in the air transportation industry.

PECK'S BAD BOY OF THE AIR

Frank Luke, who was the complete antithesis of Rickenbacker, was also of German pioneer stock, but he grew up an undisciplined young man. He wanted no part of the war, but was persuaded to join up by his sister, who had become a nurse. Frank first enlisted as a private in the U.S. Signal Corps, but through suggestions of friends applied for training in the Aviation Section. To his own amazement he was accepted and received pilot training as a flight cadet in Texas and San Diego, California. He was commissioned a second lieutenant January 23, 1918, and after a short leave sailed from New York for France on March 4.

He had advanced flying at Issoudun and aerial gunnery at Cazaux in southern France, and for a time was a ferry pilot at Orly at the Aviation Acceptance Park. He acquired considerable experience in flying several service types, but this did not satisfy the belligerent Luke, and he demanded a posting to a front-line squadron. He was finally sent to the 27th Pursuit Squadron, then commanded by Harold Hartney, a Canadian who had served for some time with the Royal Flying Corps. How Harold Hartney got into the U.S. Air Service is not clear, for he did not become an American citizen until 1923.

The 27th was located at Saintes at the time, and Luke was in trouble from the day he arrived. He displayed the combination of a braggart and the self-consciousness of a newcomer. He resented any advice, military discipline, or regulations. He started out with an unfortunate incident when, after deserting his formation to go prowling about on his own, he claimed to have shot down an Albatros. Since he could not describe the aircraft, where the combat had taken place, or exactly when, his claim was denied, and his squadron mates lost respect for him. From that point on, Luke deserted his formation on any pretext; Major Hartney knew he had a maverick on his hands and let him have his head for a time to see what happened.

Another outcast in this squadron was Joseph Fritz Wehner, who came as near understanding Frank Luke as anyone. Wehner, who had been born in Boston of parents of German descent, was under U.S. Secret Service surveillance when it was learned that after attending Everett High School and Phillips Exeter Academy, he had served with a Y.M.C.A. unit in German prison camps until the United States entered the war. Although he was accepted for the Air Service and took his training in Illinois and Texas, he was harried continually by Secret Service men and actually arrested before he embarked from New York for England.

It was understandable that with this background, Wehner was shy and felt friendless until Luke appeared on the scene. These kindred spirits teamed together and for a time were one of the most devastating duos on the front.

For some unknown reason Luke had a dislike for enemy kite balloons. There have been several explanations for this enmity, but the most acceptable is that he overheard a French officer explain that a *Drachen* was more difficult to destroy and was more important to the enemy than an airplane. Some fantastic money-value figure was applied to the kite balloon, and Frank heard someone say, "I don't care how much they cost, or how important they are, I'm not going down that low to shoot one down. I'm staying upstairs where it's reasonably safe!"

Luke is reported to have made a snide remark and stated that he could shoot down a balloon any time he wished. Whether or not he said that, he certainly set out to prove it—with Joe Wehner to help him. These two went up to attack a kite balloon near Buzy on September 14, and Frank sent it down in flames while Joe fought off a formation of eight Fokkers. When these intruders had been driven away, Frank went off on his own and knocked down another over Boinville.

The next day the two pilots went aloft again, but became separated. Luke destroyed another balloon near Boinville, and while still at very low altitude turned and attacked a second over Bois d'Hingry. He was successful again, but on turning away was attacked by seven Fokkers. Fortunately Wehner, who had downed a balloon himself near Verdun, spotted the action and went in like a dervish and shot two Germans off Frank's tail. Both went down completely out of control. That same afternoon Luke went up alone and downed another *Drachen*—six balloons in three days! On the evening of September 16 three more kites fell before the guns of Luke and Wehner.

On September 18 Luke and Wehner spotted two balloons near

Labeuville, and going down, with Joe protecting his tail, Frank destroyed both observation bags. Zooming away from these, Frank saw Joe engaged with a flight of six Fokkers, and joined this fray. Luke shot down two of the enemy aircraft, then suddenly lost his pal. Assuming that Wehner had escaped, he turned back deeper into the German lines and saw a flight of Spads attacking a Halberstadt. Moving in fast, Luke went through the French formation like a rocket and sent the two-seater down in flames. He had destroyed two balloons and three aircraft in the space of ten minutes, but his satisfaction was turned into deep gloom when he landed and learned that Wehner had been shot down and killed.

Colonel Hartney, now a Group commander, conferred with Colonel Mitchell, and it was decided to send Luke to Paris for a fourteen-day furlough. In fact, Colonel Hartney himself saw Frank on the train and gave him orders to have a good time and forget the war and his deep despond over Joe's death. "You have enough money. Go see what Paris has to offer a war hero!" his C.O. advised.

But Luke was back within a few days complaining that there was nothing to do in Paris. Colonel Hartney was too bewildered by this explanation to do anything about it, and Luke began his balloon-busting once more. On September 26 Luke went out on a *Drachen* show with Lieutenant Ivan Roberts, and although Frank scored again, Lieutenant Roberts was shot down. Depressed over this loss, Luke was absent without leave and was ordered to stay on the ground, but he disobeyed and took off to destroy a kite over Bantheville. Then, instead of returning to his own field, he landed on one of the Cigognes strips and did not show up until the next morning.

Captain Alfred Grant, Luke's squadron commander, again grounded the Arizona youth, but Luke took off in his Spad in defiance of orders, landed at a forward emergency field to refuel, and headed for German territory. Captain Grant ordered his immediate arrest, but in the meantime Luke had dropped a note over the American balloon headquarters at Souilly that read: "Watch those three Hun balloons along the Meuse. LUKE."

It was an amazing exhibition that brought out everyone on the 27th's field, including Colonel Hartney and General Mitchell, who watched through binoculars. One by one, at five-minute intervals, the three German balloons went up in flames. Luke was severely wounded while attacking one of them, but he continued on and finished his task. From this time on, legend again takes over. Some say he next strafed German troops in the streets of Murvaux, then had to land in an open field near the edge of the village. Wounded and groggy, he climbed out of his cockpit and attempted to make a stand in a small cemetery. A platoon of German infantrymen gave him a chance to surrender, but the wild Arizona youth refused and tried to shoot it out with a .45 automatic. It was a hopeless gesture. Luke went down with a dozen bullets in his chest.

Frank Luke was awarded the Medal of Honor posthumously and credited officially with twenty-one victories, although some records differ, giving him but eighteen. But no matter what his score, Frank Luke's career was tragic, and he died needlessly five weeks before the Armistice.

Reed McKinley Chambers was born in Onaga, Kansas, August 18, 1894, and after his family moved to Memphis, Tennessee, he served with the Tennessee National Guard on the Mexican border. In 1917 at the outbreak of war, he enlisted in the Aviation Section, Signal Corps, and after completing his training went on March 1, 1918, to France, where he was assigned to the 94th Pursuit. He is credited officially with six enemy aircraft and one balloon.

DAVE PUTNAM, ALL-AMERICAN BOY

David Endicott Putnam, a descendant of General Israel Putnam of Revolutionary fame, was born at Jamaica Plain, Massachusetts, was educated in Newton, then entered Harvard, where he starred in all sports and became president of his class. Frankly an extrovert, David was a handsome boy with a sterling background. He was not yet nineteen when his country entered the war, and although he passed his examinations for the new Aviation Service, he was not accepted because of his age. Being determined to get into action, Dave worked his way to France on a cattle boat and was accepted by the French and completed his training by October 17, 1917. He was never a member of the Lafayette Escadrille, but was posted to Spa.94, with which he served from December 12, 1917, to January 1, 1918. He was then assigned to Spa.156 and fought with them between February 7 and June 1. He was with Spa.38 until June 8, 1918, when he was transferred and commissioned with the U.S. Aviation, serving with the 139th Pursuit Squadron. He was killed in combat September 13, 1918.

Dave Putnam was a young whirlwind, aggressive, and a skilled pilot who gave his commanders many worries trying to keep him under control. While serving with Spa.156, which was operating on a quiet front where there were few enemy planes, he thought nothing of flying twenty miles inside the enemy lines looking for targets. When Spa.156 relinquished their Spad-7's for Morane Parasols in the early spring of 1918, Dave seemed to delight in the change, flying these tricky monoplanes with great skill. On one occasion he singlehandedly attacked eighteen German single-seaters, shot down the leader, and escaped before the enemy knew he was in their area.

Spa.38 was commanded by Georges Madon, and the French ace had a high regard for Putnam and taught him many tricks. It was with Spa.38 that Putnam reached the zenith of his skill, developing a style of his own that combined wild aggressiveness, shooting skill, and cleverness in combat maneuvers.

On June 5, 1918, during the Second Battle of the Marne, Putnam claimed to have shot down five enemy planes in as many minutes. Complete confirmation was difficult to obtain, however, and he was credited with only one. On another occasion he engaged four enemy two-seaters in a thirty-five-minute running battle and finally downed one of them. The next day he tackled eight Fokkers and destroyed two of them. On still another day he shot down three without receiving a bullet in return.

When he was transferred to the U.S. Air Service, David Putnam had to change his tactics. In the first place, he was made a flight commander and was responsible for five other pilots every time he went into the air. America had adopted Britain's flight-formation system, and there was little chance for anyone to become a lone-wolf airman. This constricted Putnam's style considerably, but he accepted it with good grace, and led many attacks against German infantry all through July and August, carrying out dozens of low-altitude strafes and light-bombing missions.

On September 12, David decided to try his old style and with Lieutenant Wendel A. Robertson went over the line, where fifteen enemy planes trapped them. Dave managed to shoot one down before they escaped. On their way back to their own lines Dave saw an Allied observation plane being attacked by eight enemy single-seaters, and as he nosed down to intercept he was himself brought down with two bullets that passed through his heart. He fell near Limey and was buried outside Toul near Raoul Lufbery. He destroyed twelve enemy planes. Although some historians credit him with thirty-four, the first figure is probably closer to the mark.

John Charles Biddle was a reputable lawyer with a scholastic background that encompassed Princeton and Harvard universities before he was admitted to the Pennsylvania Bar in 1914. Two days after America entered the war, Biddle joined the French Aviation and, after completing his course in July of that year, was assigned to Spa.73 as a fighter pilot.

He did not run up a startling record there, scoring only one victory over a German two-seater on December 5, 1917. He was then commissioned in the American Air Service—transfer papers had been cleared and signed—but since there was nowhere to go, he stayed with Spa.73, flying routine patrols and awaiting the call. Finally, in January, 1918, he joined the motley group of unemployed Lafayette Flying Corps pilots who were sent eventually to the new 103rd Pursuit Squadron. These men were eager to prove their worth and went full out to show the other American squadrons how it should be done. It was Paul Baer, as a matter of fact, who possibly should be credited with the first victory of the American Air Service, when he downed an Albatros near Rheims on March 11, 1918. The first victory scored by a so-called all-American squadron—composed of men who had been trained by American instructors—was credited to Alan Winslow of the 94th Pursuit.

During these delays and waits, Biddle put in his time writing a monograph on aerial fighting, which was to be adopted for the training of American pilots. It was a thoroughly readable work, an interesting as well as a practical study, and was one of Biddle's many contributions to his service. He also worked on the problem of destroying kite balloons and at one time made a long study of the types of incendiary bullets available, but when he went to the U.S. Air Service this project had to be dropped.

On May 15, 1918, Biddle was shot down in no man's land after he had spotted an enemy plane at 1,800 feet between Ypres and Langemarck. He saw that it was flying at a very slow speed, and determined to make short work of this apparent cripple, he nosed down and started to fire; but before he could put in a telling burst he was stopped cold by a very alert gunner. Biddle realized that in all probability he had attacked an armored plane, but before he could make further investigation he was wounded; his engine was out of action; and he had to make the best of it and land in a patch of shell holes and barbed wire. He pancaked in, then had to run, crawl, and clamber several hundred yards under heavy shellfire until he reached a British trench. He never learned what type of aircraft had shot him down, but it probably was a Junkers J-1, known popularly as the Flying Tank.

Charles Biddle was in a hospital for about a month, then was made C.O. of the 13th Pursuit Squadron, where he began his run of victories. He downed two Albatros single-seaters on August 1 at a point north of Pont-à-Mousson. Two weeks later he caught up with a Rumpler two-seater, killed the enemy observer, and forced the pilot to land the aircraft intact inside the French lines not far from Nancy. His sixth official victory was a Fokker over Verdun, and before September ended, Charles had rung up his eighth. He was named commanding officer of the new 4th Pursuit Group but the war ended before this force, as such, could resume operations. After the war Biddle wrote a book entitled *Way of the Eagle,* the story of his war experiences.

An American ace who is seldom mentioned is John W. F. M. Huffer, who is credited with seven victories. He was the first commanding officer of the 94th Pursuit Squadron, and had a distinguished career. Huffer, who was born in Paris of American parents, enlisted in the French Foreign Legion in September, 1915, and transferred to aviation early in 1916, earning his wings by June of that year. He was assigned to N.65, and later to N.62, with which he served until March, 1917. From July to September of that year he piloted two-seater Farmans on dangerous reconnaissance work, but then returned to N.62, which had been equipped with Spads to become Spa.62. He remained there until February, 1918, having served both in France and Italy. He was commissioned a major in the U.S. Air Service, and after two months of combat service was sent to Colombey-les-Belles, where he was assistant operations officer of the 1st Air Depot. On July 15 Huffer returned to the front to command the 93rd Aero Squadron, a post he held until shortly after the Armistice.

BOLD FRANK BAYLIES

Another New England youth who served with the French and died before he could transfer to the American service was Frank Leaman Baylies of New Bedford, Massachusetts, where he received his early schooling, which was continued at the Moses Brown Preparatory School in Providence, Rhode Island. He did not go on to college but returned home to enter his father's business. He was fortunate in that his family owned an automobile and he became an expert driver and mechanic, which skill enabled him to join the American Field Service to drive an ambulance in the Verdun and Argonne sectors for months. He was awarded the Croix de Guerre for his courage under fire, and when he applied later to serve with the French Aviation, he was quickly accepted.

On November 17, 1917, he was sent to Spa.73, but after a month with them was transferred to Spa.3 of the Cigognes, and served with this escadrille until he was killed on June 17, 1918.

Frank started slowly, determined to learn the ropes, and he did not have victory until February 19, 1918, and another month passed before he repeated it. By the latter part of April he was getting the feel of things and knocked down two Fokkers, bringing his score to four. Throughout May he had engagements almost every day, and in that month seven more enemy planes fell before his guns. He recorded his twelfth victory on June 2. Like Dave Putnam, Baylies found it necessary to go deep into enemy territory to find any action; many of his combats could not be verified, and he may have scored many more times. Whatever he started he was determined to finish, a quality that may have been the cause of his death.

Late in the afternoon of June 17 he was flying a two-ship patrol with Edwin Parsons, who had decided to ignore an invitation to join the U.S. Air Service and to stay with the French. On this occasion Baylies' Spad was an especially fast mount and he flew far ahead of Parsons in his anxiety to get at a formation of Fokker triplanes. Believing that Parsons was still near at hand, Frank attacked immediately. Before Parsons could get close enough to help, another triplane snapped out of a cloud above and latched onto Baylies' tail. The first enemy burst caught the Spad cold, and it rolled over on its back, dragging a long plume of smoke. Parsons saw it gliding into the enemy area, but could not escort it for any distance, since the Fokkers had turned to attack him. He barely escaped into his own lines.

A few days later a German pilot roared across the Storks' field and dropped a message that stated that Baylies had been killed and had been buried with full military honors.

AMERICAN ACES OF WORLD WAR I

Score	Rank and Name
26	Captain E. V. Rickenbacker
21	Lieutenant Frank Luke, Jr.
17	Major Raoul Lufbery
13	Lieutenant George A. Vaughn, Jr.
12	Captain Field E. Kindley
12	Lieutenant David E. Putnam
12	Captain Elliott W. Springs
10	Major Reed G. Landis
10	Captain Jacques M. Swaab
9	Lieutenant Paul F. Baer
9	Captain T. G. Cassady
9	Captain Frank O'D. Hunter
9	Lieutenant Chester E. Wright
8	Lieutenant James D. Beane
8	Lieutenant Henry R. Clay, Jr.
8	Captain Hamilton Coolidge
8	Lieutenant Jesse O. Creech
8	Lieutenant Wm. P. Erwin
8	Lieutenant L. A. Hamilton
8	Lieutenant Clinton Jones
8	Major James A. Meissner
8	Lieutenant Joseph F. Wehner
8	Lieutenant Wilbur W. White
7	Major Charles J. Biddle
7	Lieutenant Howard Burdick
7	Major Reed M. Chambers
7	Captain Harvey W. Cook
7	Lieutenant Lansing C. Holden
7	Major John Huffer
7	Captain De Freest G. Larner
7	Lieutenant Wendel A. Robertson
7	Lieutenant Leslie J. Rummel
7	Lieutenant Karl J. Schoen
7	Captain Sumner Sewall
7	Lieutenant Wm. H. Stovall
7	Captain Jerry C. Vasconelles
6	Lieutenant Byrne V. Baucom
6	Captain Arthur R. Brooks

AMERICAN ACES OF WORLD WAR I (cont.)

Score	Rank and Name
6	Captain Douglas Campbell
6	Captain Edward P. Curtiss
6	Lieutenant Arthur E. Esterbrook
6	Lieutenant Murray K. Guthrie
6	Captain James Norman Hall
6	Captain Leonard C. Hammond
6	Lieut. Col. Harold E. Hartney
6	Lieutenant Frank K. Hayes
6	Lieutenant Donald Hudson
6	Major James A. Keating
6	Lieutenant Howard C. Knotts
6	Lieutenant Robert O. Lindsay
6	Lieutenant John K. McArthur
6	Lieutenant David M. McClure
6	Lieutenant Ralph A. O'Neil
6	Lieutenant William T. Ponder
6	Lieutenant Kenneth L. Porter
6	Captain Martinus Stenseth
6	Captain Edgar G. Tobin
6	Lieutenant R. D. Vernam
5	Lieutenant Wm. T. Badham
5	Lieutenant Herbert L. Baer
5	Captain Clayton Bissell
5	Captain Harold R. Buckley
5	Lieutenant L. R. Calahan
5	Captain Everett R. Cook
5	Lieutenant George W. Furlow
5	Lieutenant Harold H. George
5	Captain Charles G. Gray
5	Lieutenant Edw. M. Haight
5	Captain James A. Healy
5	Ensign David S. Ingalls
5	Lieutenant James Knowles
5	Lieutenant Frederick E. Luff
5	Lieutenant Zenos R. Miller
5	Lieutenant J. Sidney Owens
5	Captain David McK. Peterson
5	Lieutenant Orville A. Ralston

Score	Rank and Name
5	Lieutenant John J. Seerley, Jr.
5	Major Victor H. Strahm
5	Lieutenant Francis M. Simonds
5	Lieut. Col. William Thaw
5	Lieutenant Robert M. Todd
5	Lieutenant Rodney D. Williams

AMERICAN ACES WHO SERVED WITH THE FRENCH
(Did not transfer to U.S. Service)

Score	Rank and Name
12	Lieutenant Frank L. Baylies
8	Lieutenant Edwin C. Parsons
8	Lieutenant James J. Connelly
5	Lieutenant Ewart S. Miller
5	Lieutenant Charles H. Vail
3	Lieutenant Norman Prince

AMERICAN ACES WHO SERVED WITH THE BRITISH
(Did not transfer to U.S. Service)

Score	Rank and Name
20	Captain Warren Gillette
20	Captain John W. Malone
19	Captain Alan Wilkinson
18	Lieutenant Stanley Rosevar
18	Captain Frank R. Hale
18	Lieutenant Thayer Iaccaci
16	Captain Oren J. Rose
16	Lieutenant Howard Kolburg
15	Lieutenant Clive Warman
14	Lieutenant Frederick Libby
11	Lieutenant Paul Iaccaci
10	Lieutenant Lancelot L. Richardson
8	Lieutenant Dean I. Lamb
7	Lieutenant D. M. Longton
6	Lieutenant Frank A. Robertson
5	Lieutenant Francis Magoun
5	Lieutenant Alexander Matthews
5	Lieutenant William Pace
5	Captain David D. Tipton
5	Lieutenant Frederick Westing

CHAPTER **12**

Aces of the Empire

> *Unquestionably, the fighting airmen of the British Empire con-*
> *tributed to World War I more sound tactical and strategic*
> *effort than the flyers of any other service. Most seemed born*
> *to the cockpit, and their inherent spirit of sportsmanship pre-*
> *pared them for the deadly dueling in the skies. At the same*
> *time, British designers contributed the best in the program*
> *of military aircraft of that day, and their leaders who had*
> *come up from the 1914–15 squadrons understood the true*
> *application of the aircraft to the problems facing ground*
> *troops better than the staffs of any other nation involved.*
> *Great Britain's magnificent effort and sacrifice is probably the*
> *finest and most appealing story of that campaign.*

ACES OF THE EMPIRE

CANADIAN airmen performed an outstanding role in World War I
and many became ranking aces in the British list. As early as September 15, 1914, an organization known then as the Canadian Aviation Corps was established. This force was conceived by the Minister of Militia and Defence, Colonel Sir Sam Hughes, who at the
same time was assembling the First Canadian Contingent for service with the Motherland. It was his intention to provide the Canadian Expeditionary Force with its own Aviation Corps, although
at that time he had no real idea what the function of such a corps
would be.

A provisional commander, E. L. Janney, was commissioned a captain and authorized to spend $5,000 for an airplane, which was bought in the United States and flown to Valcartier, a military camp near Quebec. This airplane accompanied the Canadian First Division to Britain—in a crate—and was unloaded on Salisbury Plain. It never flew a real military mission and was sold eventually for scrap; upon which the provisional commander resigned his commission and returned to Canada.

In 1915 the Army Council in London suggested that complete units be raised in Canada for service with the Royal Flying Corps, but this idea was ignored for nearly three years, by which time the Armistice was just around the corner. In the meantime, the R.F.C. was enlisting young Canadians, and eventually set up a special establishment in Canada to recruit men for flight training in Canadian flying schools. In 1917 a reciprocal agreement was made with the United States whereby ten American squadrons were trained in Canada during the summer, and airfields in Texas were provided for R.F.C. winter training. During the last two years of the war 3,135 pilots and 137 observers were trained in Canada and Texas for the Royal Flying Corps and Royal Air Force in aircraft built in Canada and powered with American Curtiss engines. Before the Armistice 2,624 of these men went overseas, a majority of whom saw action, and many paid with their lives.

There is no reliable figure to indicate the number of Canadians who flew in World War I. One set of "official" figures discloses that at the close of hostilities 11,244 Canadian officers and cadets were serving overseas, while another figure indicates that a total of 15,359 Canadians served with the R.F.C., the R.N.A.S., and the R.A.F. A further 7,453 served as ground crew. Canadians are prone to point out that of the 7,589 flying men lost in the British air services, about one quarter were Canadians. Of the twenty-seven British flyers credited with thirty or more enemy kills, ten were Canadians, and as a group the Canucks accounted for 438 enemy aircraft.

These figures are often used by certain critics of the British effort to highlight their argument that Britain's war was fought chiefly by men of her colonies. This is unfair, of course, since it was fairly easy for Canadians—and Americans—to apply for and be accepted with the British service. It is easy to ignore the fact that British young men were just as eager to fly as any representative group, and that they volunteered in comparable numbers.

TRANSFERS WERE DIFFICULT

However, by mid-1916 the cream of Britain's youth already was in other arms of the military service, and had been trained for infantry, engineers, artillery, machine-gun sections, and even the new tank corps. It was most difficult for them to obtain transfers to the flying services, since they were most valuable to the ground or sea arms.

My own experience illustrates this point. I was a member of a mounted-infantry regiment, and by 1916 cavalry was of little use in France; we were therefore dismounted and equipped to fight as infantry. I was among the many who saw the advantage of flying compared to trench warfare, and made application for a transfer. Seven other members of my immediate group—all English youths—made the same applications, but I was the only one accepted. I can only assume that I was the one who would be least missed.

During the same time Canadians and Americans were volunteering for R.F.C. commissions and flight training in North America and, after reaching a certain point in their flight program, were commissioned, although none of them had heard a shot fired. Most of them became first lieutenants long before they reached Britain or France. We who were active-service volunteers started to fly as machine gunners on the Western Front with the same rank as we had held in our previous regiments. In my case I was a cavalry trooper (private) and flew as an observer-gunner for months before I was promoted to corporal, and put in many more months before I was commissioned and given a chance to become a pilot.

This was typical of the treatment afforded British volunteers who wished to fly. What openings were available in the training schools were filled by Canadian and American volunteers. By the time I had been wounded and decorated, and had flown several hundred hours of patrol time, these volunteers from overseas were filling the training camps in Britain, dressed in swish officers' uniforms, drawing commissioned rank *and* flight pay, and living in the best quarters available—although not one had experienced more than a few hours' solo on something they called a Jenny. In France, where the war was being fought, we had not heard of the Jenny, and when we went back to England still wearing our war-weary N.C.O. uniforms, to live on our N.C.O. pay until some variation of the flight cadet rank was devised, we were carefully segregated from the commissioned flight students, and when trainer aircraft were available we eventually were taught to fly.

This aside, of course, in no way detracts from the splendid records of the many Canadian airmen. They were honored with 495 British decorations, and other medals bestowed by Allied countries brought the total to more than 800; and among those who were never honored were the thousands of Canadian pilots and observers who served the work-horse roles in the air. They flew on every type of operation and in all theaters of war. They manned the day and night bombers and handled flying boats for the Royal Naval Air Service. Many were members of the Army co-operation crews who flew slow two-seaters at low altitudes at great risk to spot targets for the artillery. Some were observers perched in the wicker baskets of the captive balloons. Others were Zeppelin killers, among them Stuart D. Culley, who, after taking off in a Sopwith Camel from a towed lighter in the North Sea, went aloft and shot down the Zeppelin L.53, the first air hero to employ a version of the naval flight deck. The modern aircraft carrier was evolved from the success of that primitive platform.

Other Canadians flew the Western Approaches, the English Channel, and the North Sea. They braved the Adriatic and the Mediterranean, risked the mountain gorges over Italy, Macedonia, Thrace, and the Dardanelles. They flew and died in Egypt, Palestine, East Africa, and Mesopotamia, and one and all performed their day's work quietly and efficiently, writing many gallant actions into the history of Canadian aviation.

COLLISHAW'S BLACK TRIPLANES

A grim trick was played on the Imperial German Air Service on April 1, 1917, when a five-ship flight of jet-black triplanes began a murderous scourge that left the Ypres-area section of Baron von Richthofen's Circus decimated. Nothing had hit Germany's vaunted airmen so unmercifully since Oswald Boelcke had formed his elite fighter *Jasta* late in 1915. This quarrelsome quintet swept everything before it for eight blistering weeks; eighty-seven enemy aircraft were downed, with the loss of but one Sop triplane pilot.

This scourge had three incredible features:

1. The quintet had selected the Sopwith triplane as their mount, a plane that had been turned down by every crack British squadron because it was supposed to be fragile, sluggish, and most unwarlike. It was armed with only one machine gun and had several other mortifying characteristics.

2. The pilots of this belligerent group were led by an unknown whose previous flying experiences had been confined to flitting about the Belgian coast line aboard a Sopwith Pup, gathering no particular glory or reputation. He ended up, however, a lieutenant colonel with sixty-eight confirmed victories.

3. They brazenly shattered a very rigid British rule by daubing their aircraft with a distinctive color, and furthermore, each pilot had the audacity to select an individual insigne! Prior to this only Albert Ball had been permitted to identify his Nieuport scout with a red nose spinner—nothing else.

Admitted, there were aces with more victories than Ray Collishaw, and there were eighteen-ship squadrons that racked up remarkable scores; but there is no counterpart to the devastation wreaked by this five-plane flight that was part of Number 10 R.N.A.S. Squadron.

Here, then, is the story of this Canadian who packed more real adventure into his life than any ten men might experience. His career ranged all the way from the steppes of Russia to the Western Front, Mesopotamia, and the icy wastes of Antarctica. He served with the British Fleet Air Arm all through World War II and is now living in Canada.

Ray Collishaw could have been created by a writer named Dumas; his history reads like fiction, and it is incredible that one man could survive so many mixed adventures and not suffer more than a scratch! Billy Bishop is often held up as the flyer with a charmed life, but Bishop flew on the Western Front for only about six months. Collishaw tackled Germany's Flying Circus from October 12, 1916, until October 1, 1918.

Ray was born in 1893 in Nanaimo, British Columbia, a small seaport forty miles west of Vancouver. It is not surprising, therefore, that young Collishaw turned to the sea and the science of marine navigation. He must have been a reliable hand, for the ill-fated Captain Robert Falcon Scott selected Collishaw as his navigator aboard the *Nova Terra* that took the British party to Antarctica in 1911. When Scott made his heroic dash to the South Pole, Ray remained aboard the vessel and eventually brought the *Nova Terra* back safely to port.

At the outbreak of the war the young Canadian made his way across the continent and worked his passage to Britain. He intended to serve with the Royal Navy, but after some routine training with the British Fleet, he transferred to the Royal Naval Air Service, and by January, 1916, was a qualified pilot. He was assigned to patrolling the English Channel in search of enemy submarines, an important but dull, time-consuming task. Collishaw then transferred to the Third Wing of the R.N.A.S., a move that put him in the cockpit of a Sopwith Pup. This was a low-powered biplane with gnatlike maneuverability. It was light and could be landed almost anywhere, but more important, it could maintain its height after the most violent maneuvers. Ray loved this little gadfly and had his first success while learning the tricks of air combat.

About this time the Third Wing was moved into the Belgian battle line, and Ray was assigned, along with several other Pup

pilots, to bomber-escort duty. It was while carrying out this work
that he shot down a Fokker over Oberndorf. On October 25 he
racked up a "double" when he shot down two of Von Richthofen's
Circus pilots over Lunéville, for which the French awarded him the
Croix de Guerre.

Collishaw next joined Number 3 Squadron, R.N.A.S., on the red-
hot Somme front. This unit was headed by another Canadian,
Squadron Commander R. H. Mulock, who already was an ace and
in addition had been credited with the sinking of a submarine.
Number 3 Squadron scored eighty victories in just over four
months and lost only eight pilots in that same period of time.

Ray added little to Number 3's history, except to get himself
shot down by a Fokker on December 27, but he was not injured.
He sensed that he was playing in the wrong league and contrived
a switch to Number 10 Squadron on the Belgian front. This transfer
carried an automatic promotion to flight commander, and it was
then that Collishaw conceived the idea of a 100 per cent Canadian
flight of his own.

The Pup was becoming obsolete, but there was little to chose
from until Ray learned that a number of R.F.C. squadrons had
been offered the new Sopwith triplane but for some strange reason
preferred the new French Spad. After a few trial flights with the
Sop Tripe, he found that it handled even better than the Pup; it
climbed like a banshee and was delightful on the controls. He
agreed that it was not as husky as it might be, but in proper hands
would more than fill the bill. "If we can outclimb them, we have
them cold. We won't ever need to dive to escape," he concluded.

Ray hand-picked a quartet of Canadians who were keen for action but would bow to a reasonable amount of teamwork and discipline. He selected Ellis Reid of Toronto, J. E. Sharman of Winnipeg, J. E. Nash of Hamilton, and Mark Alexander of Montreal. All
were under twenty and bubbling with enthusiasm. Every one of
them felt the same about the triplane as did their leader, and when
he suggested that they have their own flight insignia they all
agreed.

"Any ideas, anyone?" their flight commander queried.

Reid said, "The German Circus idea of painting their star-turn ships red is wonderful, but they might say we were copying."

Sharman, the Winnipeg boy, argued, "We don't have to copy them. Let's paint our Tripes black. You know—*Black Death* rides the skies!"

Everyone roared, but admitted it was a wonderful idea.

Collishaw chipped in, "You know, those Sops would look murderous painted black. Yours is *Black Death*, Sharman. My bus will be *Black Maria*. The rest of you can select your own names."

Before the day ended the five Tripes in the hangar at Droglandt had been daubed midnight black and carried gaudy golden names, *Black Maria, Black Death, Black Roger, Black Sheep,* and *Black Prince.* Thus arrayed for battle, they took to the skies early in April, 1917.

THE SCOURGE OF THE WESTERN FRONT

The initial appearance of the Black Flight caused a mild sensation, but it did not exactly end the war then and there. For a time the flight was assigned to the Home Fleet, where they saw few enemy planes, but on April 28 Collishaw caught a venturesome Roland scout over the town of Ostend; that was the end of the Roland, and Ray joined the honorable company of aces.

During the first twelve days of May, with full confidence that his black pack would support him, Collishaw began to scrawl a searing record across the Western Front skies. An Albatros D.3, a Halberstadt D.2, and a German seaplane that piled up in the Ostend Basin went down before his Vickers. On May 15 the British transferred the Black Flight to the Ypres area and assigned them to the Eleventh Wing of the Royal Flying Corps.

All this took time and Collishaw did not score again until May 30, when an Albatros scout plunged down over Messines Ridge. The little-known Albatros triplane had made its appearance on the Western Front, and Collishaw did his best to write it off the German books. On June 1 he downed one over Saint-Julien, and two days later clobbered a second in the same area. His third and fourth of this type plunged down on June 7 and 8, and it must be admitted that the Albatros *Dreidekker* was seldom heard of again.

But Ray was not alone in the glory; his pals were getting their share of hits, and before the summer was half over they had to prowl deep in enemy territory to get any action. On June 5 Ray took on one of the toughest of the enemy two-seaters, the Albatros C.3, but the story was the same. The biplane could not get a bead on the darting British triplane and fell in flames over Mervic.

The next day Collishaw set something of a record when, seeking out the Von Richthofen Circus, his Black Flight trapped a large formation over Messines. One went down in the battered village; a second fell in Ploegsteert Wood; and the third wound up in the shell-torn sector east of Messines. They all were the latest D.3's. Collishaw was honored with the Royal Naval Air Service's Distinguished Service Cross for that lively afternoon.

Black Flight was now in full cry. As stated above, an Albatros plunged down on June 7, and on June 10 Ray got an Albatros D.3 east of Menin and an A.E.G. bomber over Ypres. In one patrol on June 15 he shot down four in a row, three Halberstadts and an Aviatik two-seater. Another D.3 fell before his single Vickers gun on June 24. It will be seen that Black Flight was not picking on sitting ducks or the old artillery-observation types. They were selecting the cream of the crop.

But the men under Collishaw's command did not have it all their own way. They were over the village of Le Bizet on June 24 when they saw a British R.E.8 being harassed by a formation of German Circus fighters. The old artillery bus was having a bad time and Lieutenant Nash went to cover its tail. While Collishaw and the others fought to divert the main Albatros force, Nash apparently got into trouble under the guns of a green-striped scout. He probably had some kind of engine failure, for the Sop Tripe could not climb to safety. The green-striped Albatros bore in again and again, following Nash down and sending him crashing into the trenches below.

Meanwhile Von Richthofen in his blood-red plane flew through the swirling pack and shot off the wings of the R.E.8, which fell near Le Bizet. With that "kill" the Red Knight hurried away, apparently deciding not to argue with Collishaw and company. Later Von Richthofen claimed the R.E.8 as his 56th victory.

This was the Black Flight's first setback, and Collishaw swore to exact full revenge. On June 27 he took his flight, filled out with another Canadian, to hunt the Circus, and met Von Richthofen's group over Courtrai, where Collishaw's training and discipline met the supreme test. The Sop Tripes darted in and out but did not fire a shot until Ray cut a green-striped Albatros out of the pack. While this was going on, the others noticed a blood-red D.3 that remained high upstairs, carefully guarded by four other German scouts.

Collishaw attacked like a black hawk of eternity and drove the marked Albatros into the open. The red plane above did not make a move while the black Tripe and the green-striped Albatros fought it out. The fight raged high over the industrial town of Lille for more than ten minutes. They were evenly matched, but Greenstripe finally made his first mistake; Collishaw hissed in like a black blade and the German fell in flames on the fortifications of the old city. One sharp pass, one short but deadly burst, and it was all over. Not only had Collishaw avenged Nash, but he had killed in fair combat the great Lieutenant Karl Allmenröder, victor over thirty Allied airmen and said to be Von Richthofen's friend!

When it was all over, Collishaw and his Black Flight found that the prevailing wind had carried them deep into enemy territory. Three other members of the Circus had gone down and its formation was scattered widely. But did the Red Knight in the all-red Albatros come down and take issue with the five Sop triplanes that were miles inside the German lines? He did not.

But it mattered not to Collishaw and his Black Flight whether the enemy flew all-red fighters or were young newcomers aloft for glory. They took them on anywhere, on their own terms, in any numbers—and Ray's score rose accordingly. During the first twelve

302   Decisive Air Battles of the First World War

days of July he added eight more Germans to his list, all but one of them first-line fighting scouts.

On July 15 he encountered a new German machine that he was to remember for many a day. His Black Flight was jumped suddenly by a formation of Pfalz scouts, and Collishaw immediately turned and accepted the challenge without noticing that they were engaging a new type. He went into his anti-Albatros routine. This meant you let the nose-heavy D.3 dive past and you got him while the pilot struggled to haul her back into a zoom. It had worked a dozen times, but this time Ray got the surprise of his life.

This was not an Albatros! It was a new Pfalz D.3, a type that was being filtered into a few Albatros *Staffeln* because of its marked ability to climb out of a sharp dive. It was fitted with a concave tail plane, and was becoming a menace in Allied balloon circles. It was not quite as fast as the Albatros, but was much more maneuverable.

The first thing Collishaw knew, his Sop Tripe was riddled with Spandau lead, the joystick started to wobble in his hand, and it was plain that most of the controls had been shot away. This could be the long, last dive.

It was now that the much-maligned triplane produced a quality of stability that had not been realized. After a short dive it began to spin, but then came out of it in two revolutions and started a smooth dive toward the Allied trenches. It continued the recovery and by the time it was over the British rear area, it actually was trying to level off. It hit rough ground fairly hard and rolled itself into a ball, but Collishaw stepped out with only a few minor cuts and bruises.

Another man might have "swung the lead," as the British say, and requested a reasonable period of rest and diversion, but not Collishaw. He went aloft the next day, as soon as a new Tripe was blacked up.

But this was the period for getting his bumps. On July 17, two days after losing his battle with the Pfalz, Ray was caught off base by a flock of Albatros scouts. This affray took place over the famous

Polygon Wood when thirty D.3's of the Circus poured down and cut off the five Sop triplanes. Collishaw received the first blast and his Le Rhône was shot to junk, and there he was again aloft with little to employ in his own behalf but the law of gravity. He decided to make the most of Sir Isaac Newton's discovery, and was able to escape with fifty to sixty slugs in his brand-new machine. This time he piled up beyond the trenches outside Saint-Julien. It was another matchwood and old-iron conclusion, but again Ray walked away.

Collishaw had an explanation for his good fortune. "Sailors are born to die at sea," he always said.

Ray went back into the sky on July 20, and now it was his turn to play rough. An Albatros D.3 went down minus its wings just west of Menin; the next day another piled into Passchendaele; and on the 27th he hung up a double kill when he nailed a Pfalz and an Albatros.

Three days later he left his Black Flight and accepted a leave to Canada. It was a wise move, for in the period of about two months, through June and July, 1917, Black Flight had shot down eighty-seven German aircraft with the loss of only one pilot. Collishaw himself had downed twenty-nine enemy planes in that short time. When the offer of a leave was made, Collishaw did not stage an unreasonable scene and refuse to go, as had a number of ranking aces. He accepted gratefully and went to Nanaimo to enjoy himself. He had the D.S.O., the D.S.C., the Croix de Guerre, and had done more than his share, if he never fired another shot. This was the end of Black Flight, for no one else attempted to take over and compete with the record made by Ray Collishaw.

AND NOW THE DEADLY CAMEL

Ray was returned to action late in November of 1917 and assigned as commander of Number 13 R.N.A.S. Squadron, located at Dunkirk. He was now flying Sopwith Camels, the most maneuverable of them all, and had two Vickers guns under his cowling. Again he took his time to learn the tricks of the Sopwith and did not score until December 1, when he tangled with a German sea-plane and splathered it all over the mole at Zeebrugge. On December 9 he trapped an L.V.G. two-seater over Middelkerke, and another seaplane folded under his fire above Ostend. It will be seen that Collishaw was beginning his second spell at the front in much the same manner as he had started his first, taking it easy, picking his shots, not rushing the glory hunt.

Ray was made squadron commander of Number 3 Squadron, R.N.A.S., on January 3, 1918, which became Number 203 Squadron, R.A.F., when the Royal Air Force was organized. He was given the new R.A.F. title of squadron leader on April 1, 1918, and apparently was occupied with administrative duties arising from the amalgamation of the R.F.C. and R.N.A.S., for he did not get into action again until June 8, when he torched an L.V.G. over Wancourt.

That victory marked the beginning of a new Collishaw scourge. By this time the Pfalz D.12 was in the air and was assumed to be the nemesis of the Allies, but Ray knocked them down every time he encountered them in the same sky. In midsummer the famed Fokker D.7 appeared, and Collishaw almost put Tony Fokker out of business. Between June 15 and September 25 he accounted for ten D.7's, scoring "doubles" on four occasions. He was awarded the Distinguished Flying Cross on July 6, and a Bar was added to his D.S.O. on August 3.

Ray's contempt for the newest Fokker D.7 can be appreciated best from his record through part of August and September when the D.7 was supposed to be at its zenith. On August 10 two fell before his guns over the village of Bray-sur-Somme, and the wings of two more were neatly clipped on September 5 over Bourlon Wood. He scored another "double" on September 24, sending them down into Bourlon Wood, and on September 26 downed two more in a scrap over Saint-Amand.

By this time British officials wisely decided that enough was enough—a profitable decision as it turned out. Collishaw was promoted to lieutenant colonel and returned to Britain on October 1,

1918, to help form what was to become the Royal Canadian Air Force.

Like so many more when the war ended, Ray was at loose ends; so he teamed up with his former commander, R. H. Mulock, who had closed out his war developing a new long-range Handley Page bomber group. Collishaw and Mulock tried to get into the trans-atlantic air race and were ready to take off from Canada on a west-to-east crossing when Collishaw was recalled by the British Air Ministry. Once in London, he learned that a British force was being raised to support the "White" troops of the old czarist regime, then commanded by General Anton Denikin, who was attempting to oust the Bolsheviki government that had seized control of Russia. Collishaw was asked to command a Royal Air Force Russian expedition. Anything was better than the horrors of peace, and Ray jumped at the opportunity, and with sixty-two flying officers, fifty-three of them Canadians, he took a force of Camels and D.H.9 bombers to the new Russian front.

Two days after his arrival Ray had his first combat with a brand-new German Albatros D.5 that was flown beautifully by an unknown adventurer. He shot it down, then discovered that the dead pilot was wearing the uniform of the old German Air Service. The war may have been over for most, but Ray Collishaw was still fighting Germans in new German aircraft—and registering victories.

His command remained in Russia for nearly a year and during that time he was credited with more than twenty "enemy" planes; but since he was an official member of the British forces, this feature was played down by the Royal Air Force, and there is no accepted list of these victories.

The Russian venture collapsed in the spring of 1920, but Ray remained in the Air Force and the following fall was sent to Egypt, where he was in command of the 84th Squadron. While there he was given orders to take his pilots and old Sopwith Camels to Persia, where the Bolsheviki were menacing a British protectorate. In Persia he was in full command of the R.A.F., still flying Camels and D.H.9's. His headquarters were set up at Kalvine on the

Caspian Sea. While serving there Colonel Collishaw was honored with the Order of Commander of the British Empire, and was next sent to Mesopotamia to fly against the insurgent Arabs.

Promotion continued through the years and at the outbreak of World War II Collishaw was a wing commander and later an air commodore in command of a fighter group based aboard one of Britain's aircraft carriers. He served with distinction through the whole campaign and remained in the British service until his retirement to Nanaimo shortly after the war ended.

BOUNCING BILLY BISHOP

Heading the list of Canadian air fighters was Lieutenant Colonel William A. Bishop, who scored seventy-two victories and was awarded every British decoration from the Victoria Cross to the Military Cross. Major Donald MacLaren was credited with fifty-four, Major William Barker with fifty-three, Captain W. G. Claxton downed thirty-nine, Captain F. R. McCall was credited with thirty-seven, Captain F. G. Quigley thirty-four, Major A. D. Carter thirty-one, Captain J. L. M. White thirty-one, and Captain Andrew E. McKeever thirty.

Colonel Bishop, who was the outstanding figure in this gallant company, started his war as a cavalryman and was given a chance to transfer to the R.F.C., where he was an observer. After a crash accident, he was sent back to England to receive pilot training. Once he returned to the front and was flying Nieuport single-seaters, he became a real menace. He was a deadly marksman and at times a lone eagle. While flying with Number 60 Squadron he had a reputation for attacking from great heights any number of enemy machines. He then topped off his early career by attacking singlehanded an enemy airdrome early one morning and destroying a number of aircraft that were sent up to drive him off. It was this attack that brought him the Victoria Cross, although he had destroyed nearly fifty planes by the time the award was gazetted.

He was sent back to Canada for a rest, and on his return to Britain was ordered to form what became known as Number 85

Squadron, equipped with S.E.5's. Bishop selected a number of outstanding pilots, including Elliott White Springs, and took this squadron out to the front. Bishop had been given strict orders to command, not fly, war patrols, but he soon ignored them and ran up another long score. Officialdom finally clamped down and ordered him back to headquarters in London. On his last day at the front he flew from dawn to dusk and shot down five more airplanes, making twenty-five in twelve days and bringing his total to seventy-two.

GALLANT ALAN McLEOD

Only nineteen Victoria Crosses were awarded to members of Britain's air services during the four long years of the war. Three of these were won by Canadians Bishop, Barker, and a fresh-faced youth named Alan A. McLeod. McLeod was not rewarded for his ability to shoot down Fokkers; he never flew a multi-gun Camel, an S.E.5, or a Snipe. He was the pilot of an Armstrong-Whitworth F.K.8, a most ungainly artillery-spotting aircraft, and took great pleasure in carrying out self-appointed kite-balloon strafes.

Had this V.C. adventurer been conceived by a writer of the old pulp school, his story would have been rejected by any self-respecting editor. After all, there are limits to what a war hero is expected to perform; but when Alan A. McLeod's Victoria Cross citation was read out at Buckingham Palace, even King George V, who had heard nearly everything, stood transfixed with amazement as he listened to the details of the fantastic adventure.

Unquestionably, Alan McLeod was destined to become a military hero. As a youngster he had gloried in the classroom epics of King Arthur, the Light Brigade, and General Baden Powell, who wrote the original handbook for the Boy Scouts of the world. His father, one of the hardy Scots who helped to conquer the Canadian wilderness, was a country doctor who blazed the trail of Empire under the banner of the Hudson's Bay Company. Alan was born in Stonewall, Manitoba, and much of his early life was influenced by fre-

quent contact with members of the Royal North-West Mounted
Police.

In the summer of 1913, when Alan McLeod was just over fourteen years old, the Fort Garry Horse, a Canadian territorial regiment based at Fort Sewell, sent out a call for volunteers. Alan
signed up, although he was nowhere near eighteen, but he had a
persuasive manner. As he was *almost* big enough and had a way
with fractious horses, his age was overlooked. For two glorious
weeks, looking more like an angelic choirboy than a swaggering
cavalryman, Alan plodded about in oversized boots, baggy breeches,
and a bandolier of rifle ammunition. He was Trooper A. A. McLeod!

When the Kaiser sent his armies swarming across Belgium,
Alan was only fifteen. The summer maneuvers of the Fort Garry
Horse suddenly took on the grim realities of war. Canada immediately threw in her lot with the Mother Country, and her First
Division was to be the pick of the Dominion. A call went out for
tough men who had grown up in the Far North or in the timber
country. Ex-Mounties, or veterans of the Boer War, were selected
and the Canadian First was officered by the cream of the crop from
the finest military schools. There was no place for a fifteen-year-old
boy, so young McLeod stiffened his upper lip and stepped aside.

Within two months of the start of the war Canada had sent the
largest body of soldiers overseas that had crossed the Atlantic at
one time. It consisted of 33,000 men—a complete division and half
of a reserve division. They sloshed through their final training in
the muck and mire of Salisbury Plain and in March, 1915, were
blooded in the attack against Neuve-Chapelle, and that April held
the line through the first poison-gas attack at Ypres.

Alan McLeod read every word about it in the newspapers but
stuck manfully to his schoolbooks, and waited. In the spring of
1916, after his seventeenth birthday party, he applied for enroll-
ment in the Royal Flying Corps. The R.F.C. officials in Toronto
were very courteous but explained that Alan would have to wait
another year. Three days after his eighteenth birthday he arrived

at the Toronto depot again, took his physical examination, and the next day donned the uniform and began his cadet course.

He made exemplary progress and his instructors pushed him along, and he started his dual-control instruction by July 4. After three short training flights he was ready for his first solo aboard an Avro trainer. Ten days later he was sent to Camp Borden, where he won his "wings." By August he was on board the S.S. *Metagama* headed for Britain, and got his first taste of war when the *Metagama* was chased all over the North Atlantic by a German submarine. The ship evaded the U-boat and Master McLeod was deposited in London just in time to experience a number of the heavy Gotha raids that battered England through the first four days of September.

McLeod was posted to Number 82 Squadron, which was being organized for service in Flanders. This squadron was equipped with Ack-W's, artillery-spotting machines, and when it was announced that the young Canadian would have to be dropped because he was not yet nineteen, Alan didn't fret too much. He had come over to fight, not flit around in an old artillery-observation bus.

To keep this young dynamo occupied, he was transferred to Number 51—Home Defence—Squadron that flew all-black F.E.2b's on anti-Zeppelin defense. For two dreary months of bad weather, Alan clawed his way up through the muck and murk over London to search for Gothas or gasbags, until his commanding officer sensed that this youngster really "liked to fly." On his observation that Alan had more spirit than all the rest of the pilots and gunners in that squadron and should be on the Western Front, instead of being wasted in England, Alan was sent to France late in November, but hardly as he had planned.

Impressed by numbers, Alan had reasoned that if Number 82 Squadron was flying old Armstrong-Whitworths, and Number 51 was equipped with pusher Fees, to get aboard a real fighter one should join a squadron with a much lower number. He discovered that Number 1 Squadron, R.F.C., had started out in 1914 as an airship squadron and only just now was considered capable of flying airplanes. In the light of that intelligence, Number 2 ought to be the next-best outfit, so he made a request to be posted there without finding out what that squadron was flying.

On his arrival at the R.F.C. pilots' pool at Saint-Omer he discovered that the official guides had been well greased for his assignment and, when it was too late, learned that Number 2 was flying Armstrong-Whitworths! But once he found the officers' mess he learned that a former Number 2 Squadron pilot, Lieutenant W. B. Rhodes-Moorhouse, had been awarded the Victoria Cross. True, he had died before it could be bestowed, but a V.C. was a V.C.

When the commanding officer of Number 2 saw what had been assigned him, he said, "What is this, a nursery for Mellin's Food toddlers? This urchin can't be more than fifteen!" And he ordered Alan to take up a senior observer to prove he could actually fly. "I don't care what he has in his logbook. I want to know whether he can really fly one of these machines."

There was nothing to it so far as McLeod was concerned. He made a clean take-off, put the bus through routine maneuvers, and brought her back to the field and put her down—just like that!

"He's not too bad," the senior observer admitted grudgingly.

A NEW BALLOON BUSTER

Lieutenant McLeod made his first flight over the line a few days later. It was just another artillery-observation mission in which the Ack-W fluttered about the back areas and observed the fire of the British guns. Although some enemy planes appeared now and then in the distance, nothing unusual occurred. When the task was finished, the observer tapped McLeod on the shoulder and they went home. Just a typical art-obs day.

But McLeod had imagination. He was willing to bide his time. He had learned patience by now, and since both he and the observer had a machine gun, something might get in front of him.

On a certain day he had a Lieutenant Comber in the rear seat. The sky was overcast and they were trying to carry out artillery shoots, but the weather was so bad that they could not find the target. Instead, they encountered a flight of eight Albatros single-seaters, beautifully painted in reds, yellows, and greens. It was a pleasing picture, except for the fact that these attractive biplanes were shooting at them. Comber yelled at McLeod, then fired at the Jerries. "Let's get out of here!" he pleaded.

The young Canadian pilot reacted immediately. He had been given definite orders what action to take in such circumstances, but another urge told him this was just what he had hoped for, for months. At that same instant a gaudy Albatros swept by and Mc-Leod took a shot for the old Fort Garry Horse.

The Ack-W reacted beautifully, as if she were a fighter, and went into a very sharp turn. This brought them into what was practically a tail spot of the Hun; there was a short burst from the front gun, and Comber quit his activity to stare amazed as a green-and-yellow Jerry went twinkling down in flames.

"Who did that?" he yelled.

McLeod turned and grinned. "I did," he answered, and wheeled the "art-obs" plane around to try again. The other Jerries went into a fine formation—and dived into a wad of cloud.

When they returned and ran up to the hangar apron, a group of officers and mechanics gazed at the damage that had been inflicted by the Albatros flight.

"What happened?" their flight commander demanded.

"Eight Huns jumped us," Comber explained. "Then Mac jumped a Hun and shot him down!"

"He tackled a Hun—with THAT?" The flight commander gasped. "He must be off his onion. No one *attacks* Huns with an Armstrong-Whitworth. You just pray and scuttle home."

"This kid does," Comber said mournfully.

McLeod won a certain amount of acclaim with that episode, and he continued to add to this renown with every patrol. He became so brazen, in fact, that the flight commander had to take Lieutenant Comber out of Alan's bus and assign another impetuous youth, Lieutenant Reginald Key, to the rear cockpit. In order to weld this new association he ordered them to go over the line and eliminate a particular enemy kite balloon. "No one else seems to be able to down it. Perhaps you two cuckoos can torch it."

McLeod and Key were delighted with such an assignment and, taking to the air, headed for Bouvines southeast of Lille. They sighted the *Drachen* swinging from its steel cable in the cold January wind. Going in from above, McLeod heeled his bus over as if he were flying a Camel or an S.E.5, and went roaring into a blizzard of antiaircraft fire.

This particular balloon was protected by a double battery of quick-firing guns, but the young Canadian had expected this and stirred his massive control stick as if he were mixing a gigantic Christmas pudding. When he was somewhere near the kite he triggered his Vickers.

While the pilot was thus enjoying himself, Key sat hunched over his rear gun watching for enemy scouts. One came up from below, but its pilot changed his mind and crossed their nose in such a way that McLeod could not get his sight on the attacker. Key waited until his pilot banked, then sent a long burst into the Fokker until it burst into flames. At the same time the balloon gasped, gushed flame, spiraled, and flopped across its own winch.

When this news was certified, the other pilots of Number 2 Squadron wailed, "Now that McLeod kid is attacking balloons. What next?"

The young Canadian was mentioned in dispatches—a British dodge to avoid more practical awards—and someone thought up another ridiculous assignment. If McLeod and Key could accomplish this one, there was a promise of two weeks' leave in London. There was an antiaircraft battery in the La Bassée sector that had annoyed Number 2's artillery spotters for weeks. If there wasn't anything special to do the next morning, why not dispose of this nuisance?

That night McLeod and Key figured out their problem, and made plans to invade London. They first borrowed a couple of 50-pound Cooper bombs from a near-by D.H.4 squadron, bolted on a temporary bomb rack, and awaited the dawn. After breakfast the next day they roared off for La Bassée, where antiaircraft and machine guns welcomed them. Key urged his pilot to go down to about fifty feet, reasoning: "We've got only two bombs and we can't waste time experimenting." McLeod obliged and Key put the Coopers where they would do the most good, after which they shot up the whole area until they had no more ammunition. It can only be assumed that the Western Front was reasonably quiet over the next fourteen days.

On his return from leave in England, Key was "borrowed" by another Ack-W squadron that sorely needed the kind of inspiration with which these young men were enlivening Number 2. His place was taken by an Englishman named A. W. Hammond, who had already won the Military Cross.

NOW HE'S A BOMBER!

Germany's great spring offensive was about to open and there was plenty of work for willing air crews. New German *Staffeln* had been sent to the British front, and the great Von Richthofen was back from a leave and a trip to the Russian front. His gaudy Circus was daily in the air, and other Fokker packs were making things hot all along the Belgian front. With the great attack of March 8–9 the Allies realized that the enemy was putting up a desperate stand, and desperate measures would be needed to counter the drive.

McLeod and Hammond were called into their squadron headquarters and told they might fly and fight as they pleased—*when not on their regular patrols.* Few airmen of that day would have considered this an honor, but McLeod and Hammond reacted as if they had been handed a birthday cake nine inches thick.

Number 2 Squadron stayed aloft and spotted for the guns through the German March push, putting in ungodly hours. Every man was worn to a frazzle, but they hung on somehow, because the German fighter squadrons made the mistake of engaging British fighters rather than carrrying on the more important tactical work that would have helped their ground troops. As a result, the art-obs squadrons stayed aloft and ranged the field artillery that finally decimated the onrushing German infantry. The enemy did not have the reserves to continue or to consolidate any gains—which is the final answer in any campaign.

McLeod and Hammond carried out their artillery-spotting task every day, then became self-appointed bombers and were so successful that other Ack-W's were equipped with Cooper bomb racks. It was difficult to determine whether Number 2 was an art-obs squadron or a contour-attack unit.

On the night of March 26 the two youths returned from their last patrol of the day and learned that they had been assigned to carry out a special raid the next morning along with six other Ack-W planes. They turned in early and by nine o'clock the next morning were in the air again, heading for Bray-sur-Somme, where the Germans were concentrating a strong force for a new attack toward Albert. The seven pilots were ordered to take any measures to stop this advance.

The weather was dreadful, as usual. Clouds hung low—the best ceiling was in the vicinity of 1,500 feet—and fog drifted in to add to their trials. The formation tried to fly a compass course but was widely separated in a short time. After twenty-five minutes of this Blind Man's Buff, McLeod took a chance and went down through the murk to pick out a landmark. They had no sooner broken through than enemy guns opened up and Mac had to zoom upstairs. A minute or so later he tried it again and received the same backhanded welcome.

Giving it up as a bad job, McLeod turned back to more friendly territory and landed on a field being used by Number 43—Camel—Squadron, where they invited themselves for lunch. The C.O. of Number 43 thought they were crazy to be knocking about over Albert in an old Ack-W, and suggested that they go home and let the fighters continue the war. He even sent up a couple of Camels to have another look around, but from all accounts the area was still socked in with fog.

Ignoring the reflection on their Ack-W and a warning that Von

Richthofen's Circus considered this area their especial beat, Mc-Leod and Hammond took off once more. They reached Albert with little trouble and continued east at about three thousand feet altitude in order to stay below the clouds. They headed for Bray, which at the time was about fifteen miles insides the enemy lines; as they circled this area Hammond spotted a kite balloon and its winch in action. The Englishman had never had a smack at a balloon, and he put the proposition to the Canadian. McLeod agreed that the winch was just the spot for their bombs and started down.

As the Ack-W creaked into its dive, Mac spotted a Fokker triplane just below and forgot all about the bombs, the winch, and the gasbag. The Fokker Tripe saw them coming and sideslipped out of McLeod's view. The Canadian tilted up on a wingtip; Hammond put three short bursts into the three-decker and it rolled over on its back. As they moved back to take on the balloon winch, they saw the Fokker spin down into the ground.

THE AIR FIGHT OF THE YEAR

At that minute the clouds parted and a formation of seven triplanes came down on a sunbeam. Whether Von Richthofen was leading this pack is a question, but they undoubtedly were members of the Red Knight's Circus. They swarmed about the old Ack-W, firing from all angles. Hammond had never been in a tighter spot but he performed like a professional. McLeod probably knew they had run into real trouble, but he kept cool and flew the machine as it had not been flown before. He nosed down under one gaudy triplane, giving Hammond a clean upward shot, and the Fokker burst into flames. Another triplane zoomed from below and raked the art-obs bus from prop to rudder, and both Hammond and McLeod were "pinked" by Spandau bullets.

A second enemy burst came in from a tight angle and Hammond was wounded again. Realizing that he had only two thousand feet to work in, McLeod nosed down and pointed the bus for the British lines. At that instant he was hit in the fleshy part of one leg. From that point on, a series of almost unbelievable events took place. Hammond, who already had been wounded three times, was bellowing his encouragement and firing short bursts at the six triplanes. McLeod had no idea what Hammond was screaming about, so he turned to make sure he still wanted to keep in the game. With that Hammond seemed to disappear. He dropped lower and lower in his cockpit until there was nothing but the tip of his helmet showing above the Scarff ring. The rear cockpit floor had been shot away and Hammond had just saved himself by grabbing the gun mounting.

McLeod could not figure what Hammond's carrying on meant; he turned to more realistic matters, and whenever a Fokker crossed his line of flight he fired his front gun, all the while trying to see how he could get to the British lines and make a getaway. The next time he looked around Hammond had hauled himself up and was sitting on the base ring of his gun mounting and firing at their tormentors from that cramped, illogical position.

Then a long burst from below ruptured their gas tank, sending a stream of flaming liquid swirling through McLeod's cockpit and coursing on down the framework of the fuselage. There was nothing the young pilot could do but get out of the cockpit because the first gush of flame had burned his flying boots and the lower half of his leather jacket. Hammond was still sitting above a long jet of flame that was eating the rubber soles from his flying boots.

McLeod climbed out on the lower left wing and with one leather-clad arm inside the blazing cockpit somehow maneuvered the bus into a sideslip. This carried the flame from Hammond and the tail surfaces, giving them two questionable chances: one, to make a landing of some sort; the other to permit Hammond to hold off their attackers.

The sideslip and McLeod's courage in staying with the controls were their salvation. Seeing the old Ack-W going down in flames, the Fokkers turned away, leaving one Jerry pilot to follow them down to get full details for the confirmation. Hammond allowed this Fokker to come in for a close look—then shot him down, his second Fokker in this particular fray.

Meanwhile McLeod was out on the wing root changing hands on the varnish-sizzling joystick. He kept the ship heading for the British lines, but still maintaining the sideslip—a miracle of flying under those conditions. When his altitude was giving out and the shell-hole area was coming into view, he had to level off and make plans for landing. He had little idea where he was or how far he had progressed from the Jerry back area; and the next thing he knew the blazing Ack-W plowed through some old barbed wire, bounced over water-filled shell holes, and finally nosed into an abandoned machine-gun pit.

It was a beautiful write-off!

McLeod tried to keep from being sliced in two by the flying wires as they came to their bouncy halt; then he remembered they were still carrying bombs. He fully expected them to go off, but luck was still with them. He turned to look for Hammond, who was nowhere to be seen, so he ripped the wreckage apart with his bare hands and pulled the Englishman clear. The Germans were already shelling the area from a short distance away; that at least told McLeod which way to head if he could get Hammond to his feet. McLeod had been wounded five times, but under the stress of the situation felt just weary—very weary.

Weak, dizzy, and frantic with concern, McLeod pulled Hammond by his collar and crawled from shell hole to shell hole while British voices cried caution and encouragement. The Tommies put down a curtain of rifle and machine-gun fire to keep enemy snipers from cutting off the airmen. McLeod crawled and hauled to within twenty yards . . . ten yards . . . five yards, until at last willing hands appeared over the revetment and pulled them in. It was then discovered that the gallant Hammond had been wounded six times, and now both of them fainted from loss of blood.

The Germans put down such a wicked box barrage of fire that it was hours before the two airmen could be moved out to an advanced dressing station. For weeks thereafter Alan McLeod lay between life and death, but Hammond, who had not been burned so seriously, seemed to recover faster.

On May 1, 1918, the London *Gazette* announced the award of the Victoria Cross to Alan A. McLeod for his gallant effort in getting his aircraft and observer back to their lines. Hammond was awarded a Bar to his Military Cross. On September 4 both appeared at Buckingham Palace to receive their honors from the king.

After the ceremony McLeod was sent back to Canada, to rest and recuperate; but instead, he contracted influenza, which was sweeping North America at the time, and he died five days before the Armistice was signed.

Canada will long be proud of her young V.C. who was but a few months over nineteen when taken from his family and native land.

MAJOR BARKER, ACE SUPREME

In the innumerable pages of history concerned with World War I, the lives and deeds of its pilots make up a considerable portion, and at one time claimed world-wide interest. This was a new art of destruction, carried out by young knights in full view of thousands of earth-bound observers. Their battles, victories, and defeats will never be seen again. The cast of characters in these daily dramas were household names for a time: Billy Bishop, Albert Ball, Eddie Rickenbacker, Georges Guynemer, Jimmy McCudden, Manfred von Richthofen, Max Immelmann, and half a dozen legendary heroes flaunting the title, The Mad Major.

Their names had a certain cadence, a certain tang, producing an immediate picture of spectacular war flying. Yet almost nothing has been written or said about one man who had no superior among air-war heroes. For deadly effectiveness, for sheer will to fight no matter what the odds, and for successful execution, Major —later Colonel—William George Barker of Dauphin, Manitoba, Canada, stands alone.

Baron von Richthofen, premier ace of the Imperial German Air Force, has been pictured as a serious, dedicated killer, fighting with what has been termed Teutonic ruthlessness. He had a most im-

pressive score, but there is no evidence that he enjoyed one minute
of his war career.

In comparison, Billy Barker seemed to find a natural joy in com-
bat. Von Richthofen was courageous but fought with caution.
Barker had no use for conservative tactics or foolproof maneuvers.
It was neck or nothing from the day he enlisted until he finished
victorious in his last air engagement, an epic fight in which single-
handed he engaged no fewer than sixty enemy fighter aircraft.
This, unquestionably, was the greatest aerial battle of World War
I. How Barker survived to receive Britain's highest award, the
Victoria Cross, only the sky gods can reveal.

On the morning of October 27, 1918, Major Billy Barker took on
sixty enemy aircraft and brought his total score to fifty-three before he was forced out of action and batted down inside his own
lines. It was the most dramatic air contest of the campaign, for it
pitted the finest single-seater fighter of the Allied services against a
complete *Jagdgeschwader* of Fokker D.7's and triplanes. With the
Armistice but two weeks away, it was a display of gallantry that
marked the peak of Allied courage and military aircraft design.

Major Barker had served for many months on several fronts and,
after receiving seven decorations, was given a supervisory post at an
air-fighter school in Britain. Just previous to this he had served on
the Italian Front, and before assuming this new assignment he
thought he should find out what conditions and enemy tactics his
pupils would be likely to encounter in Belgium and France. After
some argument, he was posted temporarily to Number 201 Squadron, R.A.F., a fighter unit equipped with the new Sopwith Snipe.
This machine was the ultimate development of the rotary-powered
fighter-scout of the period. It had a top speed of 123 miles per
hour, climbed to 10,000 feet in nine minutes, and had a service ceiling of 20,000 feet. It could stay in the air for three hours, and the
power plant was the Bentley BR1, which had a maximum output of
242 horsepower at sea level. As a fighting machine the Snipe was

far superior to anything produced previously by Allied or German aircraft manufacturers.

On this particular morning, October 27, having already delayed his departure to get in one more day's flying, he took off for Hounslow, England. The route took him along the hottest sector of the Western Front, where German Circus formations were still valiantly trying to halt the Allied onrush.

As he flew parallel to the battle front, Major Barker spotted a German two-seater well over on its own side of the line and flying at a very high altitude. German two-seaters of 1918 were especially efficient at these thin-air levels; but breaking the rule and ignoring his orders, Barker crossed over and attacked. The enemy gunner gave a good account of himself, but the two-seater went tumbling down minus its wings within a few minutes. At that same instant a Fokker triplane attacked Barker, and the first enemy burst hit his right thigh, but Barker immediately put the Snipe into a tight turn to attack and shot the triplane down in flames.

By the time this speedy action was over, a complete German Circus of well over fifty triplanes and a squadron of their new D.7 biplanes had boxed in the wounded Snipe pilot. Actually, Barker could have nosed down, fed the Bentley the sauce, and, because of the rugged design of the Sopwith, outdived the opposition. What had he to gain by staying at their level? He had a ticket in his pocket that meant he could relax in England with an easy school-command job. He was painfully wounded and had every excuse for pulling out. No one on the Western Front would have questioned such a decision.

THE CLASSIC AIR BATTLE

Barker decided to fight it out. For one thing, he had heard much about the comparatively new Fokker D.7 biplane. The Americans on the French Front had declared it to be the finest war machine in the German command. The British did not think too much of it, and Barker realized he never would have a better chance to find out. So he pulled his nose up, went into tight turns, and made the

Great Experiment. By the same token he may have sensed that he was on his last patrol, but he huddled down in his seat and decided to see it through. His stand proved to be the great classic of World War I fighting.

Pencil lines of tracer bullets converged on him from all directions. The air was pungent with gasoline fumes, the stench of burned oil, exploded cordite, and that indescribable odor of burned aircraft. The sturdy Snipe was spattered with lead again and again, but the amazing aircraft continued to zoom and twirl. Barker fought like a master, tripping off short, deadly bursts, holding his fire, making the most of his skill at deflection shots, and always slipping and swerving to avoid the enemy malevolence. A Fokker D.7 exploded before his guns and twisted earthward. Another followed it in short order, for Barker was turning inside every other plane, whipping in and out of the dogfight like an enraged hornet.

A new burst of Spandau fire pierced the thigh muscles of his other leg, but he still maintained control. Why he continued to fight no one knows; after another wild circuit he fainted from loss of blood, and without a controlling hand the Snipe went into a spin. The resultant rush of air revived the Canadian and he pulled out of the spiral to find another Fokker in front of him. There was no time for the niceties of bringing the German into the Aldis sight, nothing about cross hairs and allowance for the various factors of speed and direction; Billy just pressed the triggers on his spade grip and another enemy biplane screwed over and augered toward the ground.

But luck was running out for Barker. An incendiary bullet shattered his left elbow and he must have passed out again, but the Snipe continued to fly and stay inside the wreckage-strewn orbit of action. As he came to, Barker realized that he would have to make one final effort to cut his way clear. Painfully he eased the rudder bar off center and charged his assailants. A Fokker D.7 burst into flames, but a score of enemy bullets closed the Snipe's fighting career, and it began to fall in pathetic sideslips and helpless flutters.

The enemy *Jagdgeschwader* made one last try to finish this redoubtable flyer; in the exchange Barker's fuel tank was punctured, but he managed to switch to the reserve container and head for his own lines. How he got there he could never explain, but fortunately he fought his way to a British rear area without knowing exactly where he was. With the last drain of consciousness he pulled out of another spin and held her in a westward glide until the gallant little machine plunked down in an area befouled with rusty swatches of old entanglements. The Sopwith biplane tore its wheels clear, bounced over a number of shell holes, and finally nosed over on her back. A group of Scottish Highlanders rushed from their dugouts and rescued Barker. The only injury he had received in the crash was a broken nose.

The brave Canadian lay unconscious for days in a military hospital at Rouen, and when he finally came to, he was told that he had accounted for at least six German planes and had been awarded the Victoria Cross.

CLARK'S ADVENTURE WITH "'ARRY TATE"

But not all Canadian heroes were fighter pilots. Joseph Clark of Toronto went to glory as an observer aboard a British "'Arry Tate," the affectionate term for the R.E.8. (Harry Tate was an English music-hall comedian of the period who told fantastic stories of his adventures in motorcars and flying machines.) Joe Clark, who had been a newspaperman like his father, Gregory Clark, first served as an officer with a Canadian infantry regiment. Later, when he transferred to the R.F.C., he had to settle for duty in an art-obs machine.

During the hundred days when the Allied advance of 1918 was in full swing, Clark and his pilot flew constantly to maintain close touch with the ground forces. This was unenviable work, for the R.E.8, although providing a splendid platform for observation, was almost helpless to defend itself against enemy fighters. However, a number of stalwarts of the Joe Clark stripe gave the lie to this and at times created news of the man-bites-dog type by shooting down Fokkers when the exact opposite situation should have prevailed.

On September 13, 1918, Clark and his pilot were directing an artillery shoot on three long-range enemy guns mounted on railroad flatcars well behind the lines. In this mission the observing aircraft crossed the trenches, flying low, and circled over the target while the Allied gunners fired a number of shots. As these shells exploded the points of impact were noted and the R.E.8 observer would send back the information and suggested corrections while his pilot flew a low figure-8 course between the targets and the front lines.

Communication from the battery to the aircraft was not always of the best, and it often was necessary for the ground gunners to lay out strips of cloth into single letters of the alphabet which represented coded sentences or messages.

Clark and his pilot flew back and forth until they had put the artillery gunners dead on the target. Once the big railroad guns had been eliminated, the R.E.8 crew had to fight its way back through a swarm of enemy fighters. On another occasion, a few days later, Clark spotted a new German battery and quickly ranged a British artillery force so well that the German guns were soon eliminated. The next day, finding the 57th Division held up in its advance toward the Schelde Canal, Clark and his pilot flew ahead at an altitude of 400 feet, studied the situation, and dropped messages to the infantry commander that enabled the division to continue its advance.

On discovering later that the Germans had destroyed some bridges, Clark reported the move, took photographs that showed not only the extent of damage but the location of dumps of material from which equipment for quick repair could be found. With men like Clark in the air, the enemy was never able to reorganize and make any sort of stand. Clark carried out another successful artillery shoot on October 5 while a patrol of eight Fokkers constantly harassed the lumbering R.E.8. Joe took a minute to shoot down one, and the others decided suddenly that they were running out of fuel.

Another Canadian observer hero was Lieutenant Blayney Scott

of Victoria, British Columbia. Scott had been awarded the Military Cross while serving with the Canadian artillery before he switched to the Royal Flying Corps. His most exciting adventure befell him on July 5, 1918, when the fuel tank of his R.E.8 was hit by machine-gun fire from the ground during a low-level counter-battery reconnaissance. When the tank went up in flames Scott coolly stepped out on the lower wing, stuffed his cap into the tank fracture, thus dousing the flames, and ordered his pilot to complete the mission. They destroyed an enemy battery, then returned to their base. Shortly after he returned to Canada, Scott was stricken with influenza and died, as did Alan McLeod.

THE TWO-SEATER ACES

Canadians will be found high in the lists of two-seater fighter squadrons, particularly those who flew the Bristol Fighter. They were fortunate in that they entered the British service when such equipment was available. Others who had joined earlier had to be content to fly and fight aboard more primitive mounts—proving that a man's time brackets are as important as his favor with Lady Luck.

There were a great number of Bristol Fighter pilots who have been listed as aces in some R.F.C. records. They were all commissioned officers, and there is no reference to any N.C.O. aerial gunners, although it is known that dozens of these volunteers ran up remarkable scores. In some cases, of course, they were commissioned and trained as pilots, at which time their victories gained as aerial gunners might or might not be included in their eventual scores. American records in recent years have presented the victories of "observers," as they were known, in the lists of U.S. Air Service aces. Generally speaking, however, aerial gunners or observers are not included in "official" ace lists, a point that leaves many readers somewhat bewildered, since any enemy aircraft shot down, whether by a single-seater pilot or an aerial gunner private, is just as much a loss to the opposing force, and if its crew is killed, it dies just as dead.

Major Andrew McKeever of Number 11 Squadron is credited with thirty enemy aircraft, but McKeever came to a tragic end, after returning to Canada, when an automobile he was driving on Christmas Day of 1919 skidded on an icy road and he was killed in the accident—an especially sad death for a man who had fought the best of the German Air Force without suffering a scratch.

A short list of Bristol Fighter pilots who ran up lengthy scores includes—

	Squadron	Victories
Maj. Andrew E. McKeever	11	30
Captain Edward McKelvie	22	29
Captain H. G. Luchford	20	29
Captain J. E. Gurdon	22	27
Lieut. W. McK. Thomson	20	22
Captain D. Latimer	20	22
Maj. A. M. Wilkinson	48	20
Captain Wilfred Beaver	20	19
Lieut. A. Thayer Iaccaci *	22	18
Captain T. P. Middleton	20	16
Lieut. Clive T. Warman *	22	15
Captain Fred Libby *	48	14
Lieut. Paul Iaccaci *	20	11

* Americans serving with the British.

Other Canadians who attained high standards in Bristol Fighter squadrons were Captain Alfred C. Atkey of Toronto; Captain Eugene Coler and Lieutenant Kenneth Conn of Almonte, Ontario; Captain Robert E. Dodds of Hamilton; Captain Dave McGoun of Montreal; Captain Ernest Morrow of Toronto; and George Thomson of Celista, British Columbia.

Many Canadians also ran up splendid records in the two-seater squadrons while working on tactical missions. John F. Chisholm of Montreal started his air career with the Royal Naval Air Service and, when the R.A.F. was formed, became a member of 218 Squadron, flying D.H.9's against all German naval establishments. He was particularly good on photographic missions, and later concentrated on German U-boats and submarine pens, and during the summer of 1918 led twenty-five raids against German strongholds in thirty days. On his final flight he disabled a Fokker fighter, but was then hit by antiaircraft fire and had to land in Holland, where he was interned for the remaining days of the war.

Captain William B. Elliott of Saint Catharines took part in more than one hundred bombing raids. Bill Cleghorn of Toronto participated in fifty-nine, then was killed in action while dropping food and supplies to a group of encircled infantry near Houthulst Fôret. There were dozens more, the records of whom are not always available, but there is sufficient evidence to show that Canadians performed their share of two-seater work, as well as the more glamorous fighter missions.

THE ZEPPELIN HUNTERS

One of the outstanding airmen wearing the Canadian insignia was Flight Lieutenant Robert Leckie, who by 1944 had become Canada's Chief of Air Staff. Leckie was born in Glasgow but went to Ontario while a schoolboy. When the war began, he bought his own flight training at the Curtiss Flying School in Toronto. With ticket in hand he gained a commission in the R.N.A.S. and flew from the Great Yarmouth air station on North Sea patrols for more than two years, during which time he won three important decorations.

On May 14, 1917, while flying off Texel, one of the West Frisian Islands, Leckie, who was piloting a flying boat, attacked a German Zeppelin and brought it down. Flight Lieutenant C. J. Galpin, listed as the commander of the flying boat, was awarded the D.S.O. and Leckie the D.S.C. How the authorities were able to differentiate between the efforts of these two airmen in this particular action is something of a mystery.

Later Leckie had another encounter with a Zeppelin, this time from the observer's cockpit of a two-seater landplane. The Great Yarmouth station was warned on the night of August 5, 1918, that five enemy airships were approaching the east coast of Britain.

Leckie was C.O. of the station that night and he sent out a hurried call for pilots. The first to turn up was Major George Cadbury and the only bus available was an ancient D.H.4. Cadbury beat Leckie into the pilot's seat, and they took off at 9:45 P.M. After climbing to nearly 17,000 feet they sighted three of the Zeppelins. Cadbury moved into a position below what proved to be L.70. Leckie had brought along a drum of incendiary ammunition and his first burst set the big airship on fire, and it fell a helpless torch near Wells in Norfolk.

The remaining two Zeppelins dumped ballast and turned for home with Cadbury and Leckie in wild pursuit; but the altitude was too much for the war-weary D.H.4, and although Leckie fired several long-range rounds, the raiders escaped.

L.70 was the latest addition to Germany's lighter-than-air fleet, and the famous Peter Strasser, head of the German Airship Service, whom many considered "the life and soul" of the Zeppelin fleet, was aboard. His loss saw the end of Germany's airship raids on Britain. Both Leckie and Cadbury were honored with the new Distinguished Flying Cross.

Leckie had made more than one hundred important raids on enemy territory, chiefly over the Bight of Helgoland. He made the first night flight across the North Sea from Yarmouth to Borkum and return by flying boat. He led flights over German waters, taunting enemy seaplanes into action, and on one occasion spent three days on a rough sea after landing beside a disabled D.H.4 to pick up its crew, although he knew that he would be unable to take off again because one of his own engines was giving trouble.

Canadian flying-boat men played an important role in Britain's air effort, but their heroic actions have received little attention. Shortly after Leckie and Cadbury had downed L.70, Flight Sub-Lieutenant Basil Hobbs of Sault Sainte Marie, bagged L.43, which was making a naval patrol. Hobbs previously had sunk an enemy submarine and had damaged several others. On October 1, 1917, while he was flying with the famed Flight Commander Sholto

Douglas, their twin-engined flying boat was forced down far out at sea but they taxied all the way back to Felixstowe on one laboring engine.

It was from a nucleus of such men that Canada eventually created her Royal Canadian Air Force, which took an important part in World War II. There is a general misunderstanding concerning this, for many believe that Canada had its own air force late in World War I. An attempt was made to set up such an organization, but beyond selecting a fighter and a bomber squadron to form a cadre, little was done beyond the routine of service organization. A headquarters was set up and a few officer appointments made, but the Canadian Air Force, as it was called, never flew in action. The service was disbanded early in 1920, and it was not until late that year that the Canadian Air Force actually came into being, and later was awarded the right to place "Royal" before its service name.

They had in truth well earned the honor.

THE ANZAC ACES

Australia, New Zealand and South Africa also contributed their share to Britain's war in the air, as can be noted if one studies the ace lists that have been drawn up by various semi-official authorities. However, these groups were not important numerically, and few of their representatives reached the Western Front.

Although a number of her sons served in Royal Flying Corps squadrons, Australia did not produce a recognized force in France until the middle of 1917, when Number 3 Squadron was put into the Cambrai front. Numbers 2 and 4 arrived later. Previously, several Australian squadrons had performed well in what in those days were considered "sideshows"—the actions in Mesopotamia, the Sinai Desert, and against various forces of Turkey. All these campaigns, while not comparable to the battles along the Western Front, produced many interesting stories, but there is not room to present them here.

However, high-ranking aces from the Anzac forces include—

	Victories
Captain R. A. Little	47
Captain A. H. Cobby	29
Captain E. J. K. McLoughry	23
Captain R. King	22
Captain F. R. Smith	13
Major R. C. Phillips	12
Lieutenant L. T. E. Taplin	12
Lieutenant H. G. Watson	10
Captain Ross M. Smith	9
Captain T. C. R. Baker	8
Captain A. T. Cole	7
Captain H. G. Forrest	7
Lieut. L. B. Jones	7
Captain G. F. Malley	6
Lieut. A. J. Palliser	6
Captain A. W. Allen	5
Major H. H. Balfour	5
Captain E. D. Cummings	5
Lieut. E. R. Jeffree	5

THE MAD MICKEY MANNOCK

A complete book on the records and accomplishments of British airmen who destroyed twenty or more enemy planes could be written with little trouble, but limitations of space prohibit such a presentation. Instead, the short histories of only a few of the outstanding can be offered.

Major Edward Corringham Mannock comes first to mind. This one-eyed airman with a consuming hatred of the enemy could have provided Hollywood or the thriller writers with a hundred plots, if they had only accepted his story without attempting to embellish the facts.

Although a few Americans who professed to know him referred to Mannock as "Mickey," and spoke rather flippantly of him as "Mick," this strange man was not an Irishman. He was born in a British military barracks, the son of a Scots Greys trooper from

Glasgow. Mrs. Mannock was a Lancashire girl whom Edward's father had met in Ireland when his regiment was stationed on the Curragh. Most of Edward's adult life was spent with friends in Wellingborough, Northamptonshire, England—a few miles from where the author was born.

When Edward was twelve his father deserted his family, and through weeks of destitution and later years of dreary toil, young Mannock somehow held the family together. Eventually he signed on as an apprentice lineman with a British telephone company. He worked hard, studied communications in his spare time, becoming an expert in that field.

He was installing a telephone system in Constantinople when the war broke out. Turkey joined the Central Powers, and he and the other Britishers in his group were interned. As the months wore on, it was discovered that Mannock was blind in one eye, and thinking this "old crock" could not give them any trouble, his captors repatriated him in an exchange of prisoners in April, 1915. Little did Turkey know that it was releasing a man who would become one of the greatest air fighters and would destroy the equivalent of several enemy squadrons.

On his arrival back in England, Mannock joined a Royal Army Medical Corps regiment, the best he could do at the time since he was considered a noncombatant. Later he was permitted to transfer to the Royal Engineers, presumably to string telephone wires; but after reading of the deeds of Major George Hawker, Mannock applied for admission to the Royal Flying Corps. When he took his physical examination, he worked out a tricky double shuffle to fool the eye doctor. When asked to read the chart one eye at a time, he raised his right hand and covered his blind eye and read clearly. Then changing hands, he covered the same eye, completely fooling the examiner. His transfer finally took place in August, 1916.

Mannock was an inept student, and for a time it was feared that he would have to be returned to the Engineers; fortunately he was placed in the hands of an instructor who diagnosed his trouble. This was the famous Jimmy McCudden, the son of another time-serving soldier. After many months on the front as an aerial gunner and a pilot, McCudden had been sent back to England for a "rest" period of instructing.

A NOT-SO-HOT PILOT

Edward Mannock was fairly good in the air, but his landings were dreadful. He could scarcely be called a stunt pilot—few great air fighters were. Von Richthofen admitted once that he had never looped in his life. Ball and Bishop were not skilled airmen, but one and all, they were great marksmen. It should be remembered, also, that Mannock was much older than the average school pupil, being twenty-nine at the time and very serious. He had set political opinions, leaning toward the tenets of socialism because of his early poverty. He was a persistent pupil and put himself through self-imposed drills in which he tried to perform every maneuver perfectly. He seemed a mixed bag of schoolboy impetuosity and veteran conservatism to his companions, but his logbook displayed more than his share of buckled undercarriages. Mannock finally reached France with Number 40 Squadron on March 31, 1917, and began his war career on Nieuport scouts.

At first Mannock showed little or nothing with Number 40; his shooting was just a waste of ammunition, and only by continual practice was he able to hold his place. Again, the fortunes of war moved him along. He was made a captain commanding a flight, and his determination to do well began to show dividends. He insisted on tight formations and refused to allow any of his pupils to leave the element except in case of engine trouble. He was never ashamed to admit that he experienced fear, but as the weeks went on, his hatred of the enemy became an obsession. His persistence paid off in time, for he was scoring at least once a week.

Mannock had no use for so-called chivalry, and when he heard of Von Richthofen's death in 1918, he refused to drink a toast to the dead baron, saying, "I hope he roasted all the way down."

After about a year at the front, Mannock went back to England for a period of instruction, but when Number 74 Squadron, R.F.C., was formed, he was made a flight commander under the famous New Zealander, Major Keith "Grid" Caldwell. By this time Mannock had won the Military Cross twice and was credited with twenty-four victories.

When the routine training of the new squadron was completed, it went to Ayr in Scotland for a course in fighter tactics, after which it took its S.E.5's to France. Over the next eight months Number 74 Squadron destroyed 140 enemy aircraft, with a loss of but fifteen pilots killed or taken prisoner. Mannock was then given command of Number 85 Squadron in June, 1918. This was the outfit Billy Bishop had taken out to the front, and when "Bish" was withdrawn to help organize a Canadian air force, Mannock was promoted and given his command.

A short time later, while he was escorting a young New Zealander, Second Lieutenant D. C. Inglis, on an offensive patrol with the promise of showing him how to get a Hun, Mannock met his finish. They had started out about five-thirty that morning and climbed to 5,000 feet over Merville, where Mannock spotted a two-seater and, after pointing it out to Inglis, led the way down for the attack. The major then went up from below, zooming and firing, and in a minute the enemy was spinning down in flames.

Then for some unknown reason Mannock continued to follow the burning hulk down as if he thought the German pilot were bluffing, and eventually he and Inglis were shooting at the wreck as it burned on the ground some two miles inside the enemy line.

Once he was satisfied that a real victory had been scored, Mannock led the way back, zigzagging at 200 feet, with every enemy gun below pounding up at them. Suddenly near Merville, Inglis saw the nose of his leader's S.E.5 tilt down. The left wing dropped gently away, and the plane gradually began to spin. "I could see a small flame and some smoke flicking out from the right side of the plane," Inglis explained later. "Round and round it went until it hit the ground near some trenches. On impact it burst into flames."

As if unable to comprehend that the great Mannock had really gone, Inglis continued to circle the burning wreckage until convinced that The Master would never emerge from that pyre. The youngster turned for home to tell the story, and on the way he too was hit and his engine disabled. A great gush of smoke enveloped him and a spray of gasoline slashed across his face. The Hisso stopped, and he stretched his glide as far as possible, piling up in no man's land, where he was rescued by a platoon of Welsh Guards. Inglis lived to end the war and had eight victories.

Major Edward C. Mannock was lost forever, and a short time later was honored with the Victoria Cross posthumously. In some records he is credited with seventy-three victories, leader of the British contingent, but because he always credited newcomers with "kills" he himself had made, simply to give them encouragement, it will never be known how many of the enemy this gallant man downed. At best, his victory record is quite sketchy, and it is impossible to state with authority how many Huns he actually destroyed. It is sufficient to add that he was possibly the greatest patrol leader on the Western Front.

ANOTHER "DUD" PILOT GOES TO GLORY

Another British ace, actually a South African, who is seldom mentioned in histories was A. Weatherby Beauchamp-Proctor. He was awarded the V.C., the D.S.O., the M.C., and the D.S.C. for his fifty-four victories. The author was fortunate to meet this great flyer shortly after he had been decorated by King George V at Buckingham Palace.

Beauchamp-Proctor was about five feet two inches tall and rather swarthy in complexion. Before joining up, he had studied law in South Africa and, while training at Lilbourne with Number 84 Squadron, used to spend his evenings reading massive law books. Despite his shyness, he was popular with his companions, but was a problem to his flight commander. Like so many who became great, he could do everything but make a clean landing, and used to wipe off a couple of undercarriages a week. Why he did not kill himself in his student days is a mystery.

When the famed Sholto Douglas took command of Number 84,

he wanted to dismiss the South African, but the young man was so likable and his size so suitable for the S.E.5 cockpit that he was permitted to stay on. However, when 84 Squadron flew across the Channel to take over a set of hangars at Estrée-Blanche, he was not allowed to go by air. He had to cross by boat and was grounded for a week after. He was very much humiliated by this, but when he was sent into the air in an S.E.5 he shot down two Huns in a few minutes. There was no holding him after that. He became the fireball of Number 84 and when he was awarded the V.C. the following citation was read out:

For conspicuous valour and devotion to duty between August 8 and October 8, 1918, this officer proved himself the victor in twenty-six decisive combats, destroying twelve enemy kite balloons, ten enemy aircraft and driving down four other enemy aircraft completely out of control.

Between October 1 and October 5, 1918, he destroyed two enemy scouts, burned three enemy kite balloons and drove one enemy scout completely out of control. On October 1, 1918, in a general engagement with about twenty-eight machines he charged one Fokker biplane near Fontaine and a second near Flamincourt; on October 2 he burned a hostile balloon near Selvigny; on October 3 he drove down completely out of control an enemy scout near Mont d'Origny, and also burned a hostile balloon; on October 5 he destroyed a third hostile balloon near Bohain. On October 8, 1918, while flying at a low altitude after destroying an enemy two-seater near Maretz, he was wounded painfully in the arm by machine-gun fire, but continuing on he landed safely at his aerodrome, and, after making his report, was admitted to hospital.

In all he proved himself conqueror over fifty-four foes, destroying twenty-two enemy machines, sixteen kite balloons and driving down sixteen enemy aircraft completely out of control. Besides these, his work in attacking enemy troops on the ground and in reconnaissance both during the withdrawal following the Battle of Saint-Quentin from March 21, 1918, and during the victorious advance of our armies commencing on August 8, has been almost unsurpassed in its brilliancy and as such has made an impression on those serving in his squadron and those around him, that will not be forgotten.

After the war Beauchamp-Proctor stayed on in the Royal Air Force, despite his devotion to the law, but tragically his old landing problem caught up with him. While practicing for an air demonstration at Upavon, England, in 1921 he apparently flew into the ground while landing an S.E.5. Some say he must have strained his eyes with his continued study of his law books, but this presumably is an opinion that could have been reached only by a nonreader.

McELROY, THE MYSTERY MAN

A mystery man of the British service was Captain George E. H. McElroy, who is credited with forty-nine enemy aircraft. For years this man was listed as a Canadian, but no one in Canada has any idea where he was born. It was also said that he was born in England and had been taken to Canada as a schoolboy, but how he got to Britain was never explained. It is also disclosed that he was born at Donnybrook, near Dublin, Ireland, on May 14, 1893. Wherever he came from, Captain McElroy began his career as the world's worst fighter pilot. He floundered through a dozen hours of dual-control instruction, making little headway; but being a happy-go-lucky type, he managed to scramble through flying school, leaving a carnage of broken undercarriages, wrecked wingtips, and shattered propellers. It was said that he put the Avro factory on three shifts a day turning out trainers. He had more lives than a two-headed cat, and was in and out of the hospital like a leather-covered bobbin.

On one occasion it was an Avro that almost saw his finish. His instructor pointed to a brand-new aircraft, one without a scratch, and said, "Don't think about anything. Just walk over to that bus, climb in, go through the engine-starting sequence—and take off. Don't worry about anything. Get into the air and throw her about. She's tough and you can fly hell out of her. I'll be watching you."

Mac did exactly as he was told. The Le Rhône started with a

bang. The mechanics stepped aside and withdrew the wheel chocks, then began some mysterious warning signals. Obeying orders, Mac took no notice and, having a clear field, opened the throttle. The Avro reacted like a quirted stallion and went off in a crazy circle. No matter what Mac did to the controls, the 504-K just ran amok.

All too late he discovered that he had taken off with the aileron, rudder, and elevator controls locked. Before he could diagnose the trouble fully, the Avro had turned enough to be headed for an open hangar. It smashed first through a set of trestles on which some wings were being doped. A reserve engine stood on a cradle —but not for long; it was flipped up with a prop blade and dropped neatly into the back seat of another trainer. Two spare machines were jacked up for service, but McElroy's bus charged through and cut off two sets of wings with neatness and dispatch. With one final lunge the 504-K crashed its way through a rear-wall bench and on through the elephant iron sheeting of the wall. Minus its wings, propeller, and nose skid, the juggernaut shot out the other side and scattered itself all over the parade ground.

"It was a rather interesting experience," Mac admitted later. "Also, it just goes to prove how tough these R.F.C. trainers really are."

Weeks went by; new classes came along and were graduated; but McElroy was still trying to tame the Avro. He tried his luck with B.E.'s and old Martinsydes. He switched from school to school, hoping that a change of climate might help. Once his superiors threatened to make a balloon observer of him, but Mac came through with two safe landings in a row and all was forgiven. He got through almost a week without any damage, but on Saturday the field was strewn again with spruce splinters, hunks of laminated props, and long strips of doped canvas. The gravediggers on the hill would await the red Very signal, but McElroy always foxed them somehow, and tottered off to meet the meat wagon for another first-aid treatment.

Then came Bloody April of 1917, when Britain desperately needed pilots and any Quirk who could get off the ground was sent out to the front . . . *but not McElroy.* Instead, he was kept in Britain on what was explained as Zeppelin patrol. However, during that desultory duty he did fly for nearly a month without breaking up a machine. On the strength of that superb effort, he was tabbed for a spell overseas and sent to the famed Number 40 Squadron located at Bruay and given a Nieuport scout. Thus, after eighteen months of learning to fly McElroy finally went to war, but he always said, "Never mind how long it took me to learn to fly; I sure was a finished pilot when they finally sent me out, and I knew how to crash without killing myself."

Within a week McElroy had bundled up two brand-new Nieuports and seemed on his way back to London for Zeppelin patrol, but he made such an appeal to his C.O. he was allowed to stay. He was not let loose on the front for nearly eight weeks, however, and by that time Number 40 had turned in their Nieuports for S.E.5's. Dame Fortune relented at last, for not even McElroy could bust up an S.E.5.

McElroy started active-service flying early in October, 1917, but did not register a victory until after Christmas, when he took on a new German L.V.G. which he encountered by accident. Not knowing that this was supposed to be one of the enemy's finest two-seater fighters, Mac attacked and, after a lengthy tussle with the rear gunner, on whom he expended most of his ammunition, finally sent the L.V.G. down. This victory worked like a charm, and three days later McElroy downed two more. These engagements taught him that it wasn't necessary to load an enemy aircraft with lead; if it was hit in the right place a mere handful was sufficient.

WHERE GUNNERY COUNTS

Mac now became a new person. He took great interest in his guns and worked on precision marksmanship. He refused to allow any of the armament-shed staff to service his weapons, but took care of them himself, as did Billy Bishop.

The new year saw McElroy at his best. He seemed to concentrate on two-seaters, contour chasers, and any German aircraft that hindered Allied infantry. The two-seaters of that time were not "cold meat," for they had speed and maneuverability and were well armed. The Hannoveraner, popularly known as the Flying Whale, commanded considerable respect, but McElroy shot down twelve of these biplane-tailed fighters before he checked out.

On January 16 Mac destroyed two D.W.F. two-seaters and one of six Pfalz fighters that were furnishing the escort. Two days later he caught a Hannoveraner cold by sneaking below its blind spot and raking it with his top-wing Lewis. In an effort to gain some command of the situation the German pilot overcontrolled and ripped off his own wings.

Mac seemed to go wild through the first two weeks of February, destroying seven enemy aircraft. He was awarded the Military Cross and promoted to captain. With that promotion McElroy was transferred to Number 24, also equipped with the S.E.5. As a flight commander he no longer could act as a lone wolf, but had to lead offensive patrols and engage in routine fights with the enemy. This responsibility seemed to have little effect, however, for in the next few weeks he shot down thirteen single-seater scouts and one Rumpler. When he wasn't leading his own flight, Captain McElroy went out on self-appointed ground-strafing expeditions. His energy seemed boundless, and for weeks he carried out an average of five patrols a day.

By the time the Germans were well into their March, 1918, push, McElroy had run his score up to twenty-eight. The enemy squadrons that tried to afford cover for their advancing infantry seemed to encounter Mac everywhere. On one occasion while engrossed with a German A7V tank—one of those schnapps cases on wheels—three Albatros fighters arrived to make things difficult. In less than five minutes two went down completely out of control, and the third nosed straight in with a dead pilot at the stick. Unfortunately for Mac, the British infantry was retiring too fast and there were no friendly observation balloons up in the area, so he received credit for only one. Later that day he downed an

L.V.G., and closed out the afternoon with an attack on an enemy machine-gun nest.

During the height of the enemy push throughout the next three weeks, McElroy was in the air practically every minute of daylight, fighting in his unorthodox manner like a man inspired. He ran his score up to thirty-four; then the inevitable happened. Like so many of his type, he had burned himself out and was ordered back to England for a long furlough. He did not put on a childish scene, but said instead, "Thanks, Skipper. I'm really looking forward to a bloody good rest."

In his absence Germany made her final bid to gain control of the air by sending the new Fokker D.7 into the battle—an aircraft that was to play an interesting role in McElroy's career. The chief feature of this Fokker mount was its ability to retain sensitive control at slow flying speeds and at high altitudes, where most Allied types were prone to become somewhat logy. It also climbed well, and its lightning recovery from a dive made it quite formidable in combat; but it was not the premier air fighter of the war, as so many aviation writers have tried to prove.

McElroy in England heard various stories concerning this new German mount, and although most of the yarns were exaggerations, he wanted to get back to look it over. He became irritable and restless—the charm and laughter of a leave had been dispelled—and he made several pleas to return to the front. But he was held back for eleven weeks to get him in physical shape once more, and late in June was reassigned to his first love, Number 40 Squadron.

Mac scored twelve times in the next six weeks, but he sensed that the long rest had slowed him somewhat. "My reflexes are slack," he complained. "I wish I had stayed away from London and its wild life. I should have stayed out here and tapered off slowly, instead of dropping the job. It happens to all of us."

How right he was. Baron von Richthofen was lost after he had been out of action for some time. Raoul Lufbery was killed during his first air fight after his "rest" at Issoudun. The list is long, including McCudden, Ball, Guynemer, and a dozen others. All came to the ends of their careers after long pauses for rest when they did not enjoy real relaxation.

But McElroy carried on and kept up his reputation. He turned his attention to enemy kite balloons but, although he risked everything low down, could never get a confirmation. He led a three-ship element against four Fokker D.7's on July 1 and forced one to crash in the battered city of Lens. His two companions accounted for one in flames and sent down the others out of control. From that day on, McElroy had nothing but contempt for the D.7.

WHY GREAT AIRMEN CRACK UP

For a week he had no luck at all and swore that the enemy airmen were avoiding him. He was unreasonable in all his viewpoints, although his friends tried to calm him and encourage him to take a less serious view of the situation.

"I know. I know. I'm losing my touch. How can a man stay razor-keen if those Hun devils stay out of the air? That's what they are doing, you know. They're staying out of the air when we go on patrol. I don't know how they do it, but they seem to know."

McElroy tried lone patrols late in the afternoon. He also arose before dawn and worked on enemy airdromes over the lines, but the Jerries did not respond. This psychological rebuff was more destructive than a swarm of Fokkers. Without firing a shot they were consuming every volt of Mac's energy, and with that went his timing and confidence.

On July 10 a small sample of his old activity returned when he began a period of triumphs that resulted in the destruction of seven Hannoveraners in twelve days. He sent them down with ridiculous ease and a frugal expenditure of ammunition.

While he was attacking one of these two-seaters near La Bassée on July 20, Death made a wild snatch at him. A loose connecting rod of the engine in a borrowed S.E.5 gave way, ripped the Hisso to junk, and the whole mess caught fire. Mac, however, had learned to cope with all such situations and immediately went into a steep sideslip that kept the flames from devouring the longerons, and he reached the ground safely. He clambered out of the hulk with nothing more serious than a few scorches and a bruised knee.

Five days later, while returning from an attack on a munitions convoy, McElroy met two more Hannoveraners, and the fracas that ensued was a classic of snap-shooting and one of the fastest "doubles" of the war. The two German planes apparently were making a low reconnaissance, one carrying a camera while the other acted as escort. Mac went in, firing short bursts from an abnormally long range, but one must have killed the pilot of the camera airplane. The observer in the second "Hannah" turned to fire at the intruding Britisher, but before he could take aim, a string of Kynochs ammo stitched his fuselage, knocked him away from his gun, and passed on to kill the pilot in the front cockpit.

July 31, 1918, saw the last of this hero who began his flying career so inauspiciously. It was a misty morning, a scene that might have been staged by a morbid dramatist. As the S.E.5 rumbled out for a take-off, its prop swirled up ghostly forms that held their funereal shapes until McElroy had passed into the heavier mists above. No one had any idea what happened. His end was as mysterious as his beginning. His wrecked plane was found hours later near Laventie, which then was just inside the British lines. There was no answer in the bullet-pocked cockpit.

Was McElroy killed while contour chasing along the German front-line trenches? Or did he fall before the gun of some vengeful Hannoveraner gunner? He may have been downed by some novice flying the D.7 he so despised. One thing *is* certain; Lothar von Richthofen, who usually claimed every noted British ace lost in action, made no bid for this gallant gentleman.

Conclusion

IT WILL BE noted that throughout this book much space has been given to the heroics and careers of many single-seater pilots, although the author's personal affection has rested always with the air crews of the two-seater squadrons. However, no matter how deep we delve in our continued research, how much we try to raise observers and gunners to their rightful position in air history, the efforts, successes, and sacrifices of the fighter pilots outnumber the pages of gallantry displayed by the multi-seat airmen. The situation is quite understandable, since in the routine record of daily flights and combats the single-seat airman has an unquestioned advantage. It is simple to tot up his efforts through the number of victories credited to him. It is more difficult to dramatize a pilot or an observer on the strength of the number of bombing raids he has carried out, the stack of aerial photographs he has taken, or the success of the art-obs shoots he has completed.

Recording officers who daily jotted down the patrols, combats, and over-all accomplishments of their squadrons found it simpler to present the efforts of individuals, as compared to those of air crews. If an enemy plane was shot down by a single-seater fighter, it could be credited to the pilot, and his terse explanation of the fight was easy to embellish into a dramatic narration. Not so the work of the two-seater squadrons. A pilot and air gunner might be attacked by an enemy machine and each would take his turn in returning the fire. If the attacker was shot down eventually, it was almost impossible in most instances to credit the victory to either

342

member of the team. In some squadrons all victories were credited
to the pilot, particularly if the aerial gunner was a noncommissioned member of the unit. At times the pilot would insist that his
gunner be credited with some particular kill, but these instances
were few and far between. I, for one, was fortunate to have one
or two such pilots, but even then was seldom credited with all I
had earned rightfully.

It will be noted, too, that I have included a list of American
air aces, but have refrained from offering such lists for other par-
ticipants. I have a reason for this. I have yet to see anything resembling an official list of British aces. Lists have been compiled by
diligent historians, but in very many instances diverse figures are
noted, and those who claim to be "in the know" argue that the
scores of certain leading aces have been padded. After the war,
practically no one accepted the German scores, pointing out that
"truth was not in them," and historians produced point after point to
show that Germany throughout the war had distorted all records
for her own benefit. But as the bitterness of battle died down and
ex-enemies met once more under more comradely conditions, the
propaganda arguments tapered off, and for some strange reason
the histories of the German airmen became more popular than
those of any of the Allies. The Von Richthofen story was printed in
a dozen languages and appeared on bookstalls all over the world.
His Fokker triplane was for years the most popular with the model
makers and his claims of having destroyed eighty British aircraft
were accepted as gospel, despite the fact that British authorities
proved again and again that twenty-one of the Red Knight's victories could not be confirmed in any documents available in the
Berlin archives.

French records may be as reliable as any, but again there are
strange variations in many of the scores offered. Some say that
the French were most demanding in their requirements for a victory, whereas others point out that the French airmen preferred to
fly lone-wolf patrols, and once they had reached a certain level in
the ace list, their claims were never questioned, although many of

their combats were fought well over the enemy lines. What is one to believe?

Some German authorities have questioned Billy Bishop's record, particularly in reference to his claim of having shot down three of their planes and damaged three others during his famous attack on a German airfield on June 2, 1917. They have long insisted that Bishop made only one quick pass at a number of planes on the ground, and when their scouts went aloft to intercept him, he hurried home.

These differences of claims are to be expected, but they give credence to the belief that most ace lists are not too trustworthy, and it was to illustrate this that I have presented the most recent list of American airmen credited with five or more victories. It must be emphasized that this list is not official. An "official" list was made up during the early 1920's, when it would seem all combat reports had finally been checked, clarified, and accepted. But in many cases this list is at odds with more recent compilations.

As an instance, in the 1920's Eddie Rickenbacker was credited with twenty-five victories; today his score is twenty-six. Frank Luke was given eighteen in the early list; now his score is nineteen or even twenty-one. After the war Lufbery had seventeen to his credit, and in recent lists his score remains the same; but Bill Thaw, who was given three in the early records, is now an "ace" with six. In the 1920's America claimed only sixty-nine aces; in recent compilations the number is eighty-two.

It was for this reason, and several other factors, that the scores of German, French, British, Italian, and Russian airmen who served in World War I have been dispensed with. I started out to compile my own list; but in attempting to track down reliable figures for the leading representatives of that campaign, I realized that there was not enough time—and that if the task were ever completed, I would leave myself open to the criticisms of the purists, each of whom would demand that his particular hero should have been credited with what each considers his rightful score.

It should be pointed out that it is almost impossible to know who shot down any particular enemy. In aerial combat in which any number of aircraft are involved, so many bursts of fire are triggered off that it is difficult to say who destroyed any one machine in the mêlée. Pilot A might dive on a plane he saw moving out of the main fray and might spatter it with a telling burst, but for all he knows the enemy pilot may have been killed some minutes before.

By the same token, what about the pilot who is hit during a fight, as was Billy Barker? Suppose he manages to stay with his formation long enough to have it escort him into his own lines. The opposition can have no idea he has been wounded, and although he may have landed safely, he may be out of action for months in a hospital. Who is to be credited with his removal from the campaign?

Then there is the well-known story of the British art-obs machine that was fired on by a German Fokker pilot. Both the pilot and the observer were hit, but the enemy pilot could not know this since the R.E.8 continued on—flying toward its own lines—and finally made a perfect landing along the furrows of a plowed field a few hundred yards from its own airdrome. When the maintenance men went out to give aid they were astonished to find that both men were dead, and that the old 'Arry Tate had flown herself. What German lost his chance for a credit in that case?

Which country downed the most aircraft is an academic question, since the one fighting over its own territory has a great advantage. Once she was stopped on the Marne, Germany settled for a defensive role, and Great Britain and France had to carry the war to her. As pointed out before, German airmen had little trouble obtaining credits for their successes. There they were, all wrapped up in their own back yard, including those who had flown too far over and had run out of fuel, or had encountered prevailing head winds that forced them down unharmed in enemy territory.

While the ace list was inevitable, it does not necessarily indicate which individual flyer or which service was superior. An airman who became an ace in the first eighteen months of the war had a tougher task than one who flew during the last year and a half. Allied airmen who flew through 1916 and 1917 faced tougher opposition than those in 1914 or the closing months of 1918. British airmen, in particular, ran up some amazing scores in the late summer and fall of 1918. German flyers had a short period of superiority in the early part of 1918 and should have racked up some reputable figures, but again it must be admitted that their best weapon was the fact that they usually could select the battleground. But whether or not the top scorers are to be given the bulk of the credit for their side's eventual victory raises many a question. And they always will be raised, because it was a most unusual war and our prejudices still rule our reasoning.

Glossary

Ace—Term originally applied to any fighter pilot who had been credited with five aerial victories. Universal usage has turned it into a generic term for any skilled pilot. The "ace" category was never accepted by the British.

Ack-ack—Front-line term for antiaircraft. The letter *a* was pronounced "ack" by signalmen to avoid mistakes in transmission. Thus, *a-a* was pronounced "ack-ack."

Archie—A derisive term for antiaircraft fire, originated by the British. It was derived from a music-hall ditty which ended with "Archibald, certainly not!" With use it was pared to "Archie."

Art-obs—Vernacular for artillery observation.

Apron—Concrete area laid down in front of hangars, used generally for a work area.

Balloon—An inflated gasbag used for various military purposes. Tethered by a steel cable, it could be sent to any altitude up to about 4,000 feet. When equipped with a basket and telephonic communication, it could be employed as an observation platform. Smaller types, put up for area defense, could be linked together to form a "balloon barrage" with the idea of entangling invading aircraft.

Barrel (v.)—Rolling the aircraft over and over, like rolling a barrel.

Besseneau—A wartime canvas-covered hangar usually large enough to accommodate six aircraft. It could be erected or dismantled in a very short time.

Biplace—Franco-American term for a two-seater aircraft.

Blériot—Generic term applied to most early monoplanes, named after Louis Blériot, the first man to fly the English Channel, in a monoplane of his own design.

Brevet—Originally referred to a commissioned rank in which an officer was given a grade higher than that for which he received pay. Later it was taken to mean that a student had received his wings and commission at the same time. Thus brevet (v.) was understood generally to mean that a man had been awarded his flying certificate.

Blimp—Small, nonrigid airship employed on naval patrols during World War I.

Breeze up—One has a breeze up when one is frightened. A *gust up* indicates that he is practically scared to death.

Brisfit—An affectionate term for the Bristol Fighter.

Brolly—British slang for umbrella. During World War I it was applied to the parachute used by balloon observers. "I went over the side and took to my brolly."

Bung off (v.)—Professional parlance meaning to get going, clear off, mooch or vamoose.

Cabrank—The line where planes are ranked after a patrol.

Camber—The curvature of a wing or airfoil.

Caudron—A French aircraft manufactured by the René Caudron Co.

Chandelle (v.)—To go into a corkscrew climb. Often talked about but seldom performed.

Ceiling—The limit of an aircraft's altitude. When it won't climb any higher, it has reached its ceiling.

Chasse—French for "chaser." All scouts were assumed to chase the enemy. After using the chasse term for a few months, the Americans switched to the term "pursuit."

Chocks—Triangular blocks placed before the landing wheels to prevent the aircraft from moving forward while the engine was being tested.

Contour chasing—Flying low, using the contour of the area as cover while attacking enemy troops and defenses low down. A contour fighter was one specially designed for this purpose and usually was lightly armed below.

Coupez (v.)—To "cut" or switch off the ignition after landing. Many of these French terms were adopted by American pilots early in the war because they had French mechanics to service their planes.

Center section—A small airfoil set above the fuselage to which the outer wing panels are bolted.

Glossary

Cowling—The metal cover enclosing the engine.

Dawn patrol—The first scheduled duty flight of the day. Usually the least active, since the Germans were notoriously late risers, and it was not nearly so dangerous as movie writers have depicted.

Dogfight—A wild aerial mêlée in which dozens of aircraft participate and fight at very close quarters; engagements in which more planes are lost in midair crashes than by the exchange of gunfire.

Dud—Anything that doesn't work: a shell that doesn't explode; a pilot who cannot stay in formation; an engine that won't start.

Dump—An open area used for storing military supplies.

Drachen—German word for kite balloon.

Elevator—The horizontal control surface set on the tail assembly to control the up-and-down movements of the nose of the aircraft. Also known as flippers or horizontal stabilizers.

Empennage—The complete tail assembly of any aircraft.

Epaulet—The shoulder strap of a military jacket to which a man's rank or regimental insignia is affixed.

Essence—French term for gasoline. The British called gasoline "petrol" since it is a product of petroleum. The Americans called their fuel "juice" or "sauce."

Fee—Slang term for British F.E.2b pusher plane.

Fish-tailing—Swinging the tail of the machine from one side to the other to help shorten the landing glide.

Fitter—*See* Rigger.

Flight—A unit of six planes. A squadron generally was composed of three flights, A, B, and C.

Flechettes—Small steel darts designed to be dropped on massed troops.

Fourragère—A braided cord decoration worn by members of a group after their organization has been awarded that honor. Sometimes called an aiguillette.

Free lance—A pilot who elects to fly lone patrols after his regular missions have been accomplished.

Funk hole—Any handy shelter used to avoid enemy fire; also, an unpleasant duty.

Fuselage—The part of the airplane that forms the main body to which the main planes, tail, and undercarriage are attached.

Gazette—The official journal of the British government. All commissions, decorations, and awards are "gazetted," or officially announced, in its columns. For instance, "He was gazetted a major."

G.S.—General Service. Anything belonging to the British military forces. There were G.S. tunics and G.S. wagons. The American version is G.I.—General Issue.

Glide angle—The shallowest angle a plane will glide in safety after the engine has been switched off.

Gravel crushers—A slang expression for the infantry.

Ground strips—Colored cloths laid out on the ground for signaling purposes. White strips were used at airfields to warn incoming aircraft of certain ground conditions or emergencies.

Hauptmann—German military rank equivalent to captain.

Haversack—Bag of heavy web or canvas fitted with a shoulder strap used by British soldiers for personal gear or rations Comparable to French *musette*.

Hisso—Simplification of Hispano-Suiza engine, a vee-type, water-cooled power plant.

Hoick (v.)—To pull up sharply from level flight. To zoom.

Horsepower—The unit of power equaling 33,000 foot-pounds, that is, capable of raising 33,000 pounds one foot in one minute. *Brake horsepower* is the horsepower developed by an engine at the propeller shaft.

Hun—A term of contempt for German soldiers or airmen, used chiefly by the British. It was used also in British flying schools to mark heavy-handed students who broke up more than their share of training aircraft.

Immelmann turn—A sharp maneuver in which a plane changes direction by zooming, turning on its side so that the controls are reversed (the rudder becomes the elevator, etc.) and the elevators whip the aircraft around very fast. Incorrectly credited to Max Immelmann, it was in general use as a stunt or exhibition maneuver before the start of World War I.

Incidence—Angle at which the wings are set to the line of flight. The angle of incidence determines the aircraft's ability to climb or produce lift.

Jagdgeschwader—A German fighter command. Generally five squadrons.

Jagdstaffel—A German fighter squadron, usually made up of ten planes.

Jasta—Hunter-fighter group.

Jastaschule—German school of air fighting.

Joy rags—Your best uniform, reserved for furlough or special occasions.

Joystick—Slang for control column. Believed to have been originated by the simple stick control devised by an Englishman named Joyce.

Kanone—German title for a fighter pilot who has destroyed ten enemy aircraft.

Keel surface—All the airplane seen when viewed from either side.

Kiwi—Royal Flying Corps vernacular for any nonflying officer. Name of a flightless New Zealand bird.

Lager or *Laager*—German term for prison-camp area.

Landing lights—In World War I night landings had to be made with the aid of primitive flares set out along the available landing strip. They were usually discarded oil drums filled with oil-saturated rags that were lighted when a friendly plane signaled its return.

Leading edge—The front edge of a wing or airfoil. The edge that strikes the air first. The rear edge is known as the trailing edge.

Liberty engine—A twelve-cylindered, water-cooled engine developed in the United States after the declaration of war against Germany in 1917.

Logbook—History of an air pilot's training and war flights.

Longerons—The main structural members running the length of the body or fuselage.

Main spar—Chief structural member of a wing, to which all ribs and bracings are attached.

Melinite—A picric powder about two and one half times as powerful as ordinary gunpowder.

Monocoque—A type of fuselage or airplane body in which the main loads in the structure are taken by the skin covering.

Nacelle—A body that enclosed either the crew or the engine.

Oleo—The shock-absorbing portion of an undercarriage leg.

Pancaking—Landing the airplane so slowly that it drops hard and flat—like a pancake.

Parachute flare—Pyrotechnic flare attached to a parachute to provide illumination. It is dropped from an aircraft or fired from a gun, chiefly to observe military movements and targets.

352

Performance—Flying characteristics of an aircraft, such as its speed, rate of climb, and ceiling.

Pitot tube—An air-inlet tube set outside the cockpit and connected to the air-speed indicator. The pressure from this tube actuates a diaphragm and indicating needle.

Prototype—The first machine of a new style to be built.

Pocket—There is no such thing as an air pocket. Aircraft in flight may experience violent upward or downward lurches, but these are caused by turbulent air rising or falling. There are no "holes" or vacuum spaces in the atmosphere.

Quirk—British slang term for the B.E. aircraft; also, a new and very clumsy flight student.

Radial engine—An aviation engine with its cylinders arranged radially around a master crankshaft. In this, the cylinders are stationary and the crankshaft revolves.

Rotary engine—An aviation engine in which cylinders are also set radially around its crankshaft, but which revolve around the master crankshaft.

Rigger—One employed in assembling or servicing the body of the airplane. The *fitter* takes care of the engine.

Sausage—A conical tube of fabric flown over an airfield to indicate the direction of the wind.

Scarff ring—A machine-gun mounting used on most Allied two-seaters. It was invented by a Warrant Officer Scarff of the Royal Naval Air Service.

Slipstream—The zone of disturbed air noted behind a whirling propeller.

Tarmac—Permanent artificial paving made of tar and macadam. Generally laid down in front of British hangars overseas.

Tractor airplane—A plane in which the propeller or propellers are mounted in front of the main support planes.

Zoom—A sudden change of direction upwards.

Bibliography

Barnett, Lieutenant Gilbert. *V.C.'s of the Air.* J. Burrow & Co., Ltd.

Barron, Elwyn A. *Deeds of Heroism and Bravery.* Harper & Brothers.

Biddle, Major Charles. *Way of the Eagle.* Charles Scribner's Sons.

Bishop, Major William. *Winged Warfare.* George H. Doran Co.

Bordeaux, Henry. *Georges Guynemer, Knight of the Air.* Yale University Press.

Bott, Captain Alan. *Cavalry of the Clouds.* Doubleday, Page & Co.

Coppens, Willy. *Days on the Wing.* John Hamilton, Ltd.

Cutlack, F. M. *Australian Flying Corps.* Angus & Robertson, Ltd.

Fokker, A. H. G., and Bruce Gould. *The Flying Dutchman.* Henry Holt & Co.

Gibbons, Floyd. *The Red Knight of Germany.* Garden City Publishing Co.

Gibbs, Phillip. *Now It Can Be Told.* Harper & Brothers.

Golding, Harry. *The Wonder Book of Aircraft.* Ward, Lock & Co., Ltd.

Hall, James Norman. *High Adventure.* Houghton Mifflin Co.

Hartney, Harold. *Up and at 'Em.* Stackpole Sons.

Heydemarck, Hauptman. *Double-Decker C.666.* John Hamilton, Ltd.

Johns, W. E. *Fighting Planes and Aces.* John Hamilton, Ltd.

Jones, Wing Commander Ira. *King of Air Fighters.* Ivor Nicholson & Watson.

Lewis, Cecil. *Sagittarius Rising.* Harcourt, Brace & Co.

Liddell Hart, B. H. *The Real War.* Faber & Faber.

McConnell, James R. *Flying for France.* Doubleday, Page & Co.

McCudden, James T. B. *Five Years in the Royal Flying Corps.* Aeroplane & General Publishing Co.

MacMillan, Norman. *Great Airmen.* G. Bell & Sons.

Middleton, Edgar. *Glorious Exploits of the Air.* D. Appleton & Co.

Miller, Frances Trevelyan. *The World in the Air.* G. P. Putnam's Sons.

Monk and Winter. *Great Exploits in the Air.* Blackie & Son, Ltd.

Nordhoff and Hall. *The Lafayette Flying Corps.* Houghton Mifflin Co.

Parsons, Edwin C. *The Great Adventure.* Doubleday, Doran Co.

Raleigh and Jones. *The War in the Air.* Oxford University Press.

Rickenbacker, Edward V. *Fighting the Flying Circus.* Frederick A. Stokes & Co.

Roberts, Leslie. *There Shall Be Wings.* Clark, Irwin Co., Ltd.

Robertson, Bruce. *Air Aces of the 1914–1918 War.* Harborough Publishing Co., Ltd.

Rockwell, Paul Ayres. *American Fighters in the Foreign Legion.* Houghton Mifflin Co.

Saunders, Hilary St. George. *Per Ardua.* Oxford University Press.

Strange, L. A. *Recollections of an Airman.* John Hamilton, Ltd.

Sutton, H. T. *Raiders Approach!* Gale & Polden, Ltd.

Thetford and Riding. *Aircraft of the 1914–1918 War.* Harborough Publishing Co., Ltd.

Ticknor, Caroline. *New England Aviators.* Houghton Mifflin Co.

Toulmin, H. A. *The Air Service.* D. van Nostrand Co.

"Vigilant." *German War Birds.* John Hamilton, Ltd.

Whitehouse, Arch. *Hell in the Heavens.* W. & R. Chambers, Ltd.

———. *Legion of the Lafayette.* Doubleday & Co., Inc.

———. *The Years of the Sky Kings.* Doubleday & Co., Inc.

Index

Ace appellative, 86
Aces, American, list of, 289–91
Aero Club of France, 15
Aircraft
  American: Curtiss flying boat, 25; Curtiss-J (Jenny), 27, 240, 295; Wright biplane, 15
  British: Armstrong-Whitworth, 310–15; B.E., 8, 33; Bristol Fighter, xii, 155, 196, 324, 325; D.H.2, 89, 133, 134, 146; D.H.4, xiii, xvi; D.H.9, 28, 208, 305; Farman, Henri, 15, 17; Farman, Maurice, 8, 17; Handley Page, 28, 121; Martinsyde, 8; R.E.2, 33; R.E.8, 322; S.E.5, xv, xviii, 155; Short seaplane, 8; Sopwith Camel, xv, 12, 155, 196, 208, 240; Sopwith Dolphin, 196; Sopwith 1½-Strutter, 89; Sopwith Pup, 135; Sopwith seaplane, 8; Sopwith Snipe, 319; Sopwith Tabloid, 38; Sopwith triplane, 296; "The Quirk," 56, 57; Vickers Gunbus, F.B., 5, 18
  French: Blériot monoplane, 15, 17; Bréguet, 17; Caudron, 17; Deperdussin, 17; Hanriot, 20, 69, 151; Morane Bullet, 77; Morane Parasol, 214; Morane-Saulnier, 17, 18, 61; Nieuport Scout, xv, 17, 137; R.E.P., 17; Salmson, 28; Spad, xv, 239; Voisin, 17, 132, 133
  German: A.E.G., 11; A.G.O., 11, 185; Albatros D.1, xvii, 28, 78, 135; Albatros D.3, 149, 154; Aviatik, 13, 14, 159, 201; Brandenburg seaplane, 197, 198; Dornier Do.X., 198; D.W.F., 11; Etrich, 4; Euhler, 11; Fokker D.7, 150, 239, 320; Fokker Eindekker, 91, 128, 129; Fokker triplane, xviii, 189; Friedrichshafen G.3, 176; Gotha, 28, 121, 176; Halberstadt, 28,

151; Junkers J.1, 176, 286; L.V.G., 11, 150, 174; Pfalz scout, 150, 304; Roland, 173, 174, 185; Siemens D.3, 184; Taube, 10
  Italian: F.B.A. Flying boat, 20; Nieuport-Macchi, 19; S.A.M.L., 20; Savoia-Farman, 19
Aldershof field, Germany, 192
Alexander, Mark, 298
Alkan, Sgt. Mechanic, 89
Allard, Professor Émile, 20
Allmenroeder, Karl, 155, 301
America's entry, 260–63
Ammunition, 44–47
Annoeulin, France, 180, 181
Anzac aces, 328, 329
Auger, Capt. Alfred, 251

Babbington, Flt. Com., 39
Bach, James, 50, 60–66
Ball, Capt. Albert, 50, 138, 166–81
Ball, Lieut. Cyril, 181
Balsley, Clyde, 137, 161, 162
Baracca, Maj. Francesco, 67, 68, 164
Baracchini, Flavio Torello, 163, 164
Barker, Maj. W. G., 69, 177, 306, 318–22, 345
Barlow, Air Mechanic R. K., 32
Barron, Bombardier R. H., 156
Battle, Capt., 245
Baylies, Frank L., 287, 288
Beauchamp-Proctor, A. Weatherby, 333–35
Beaulieu-Marconnay, Oliver von, 184
Bernert, Lieut. Fritz, 153
Bettington, Maj. A. V., 89
Biddle, John Charles, 285–87
Bishop, Maj. William A., 49, 138, 172, 306, 344
Black Flight, 299
Blume, Walter, 194, 195

355

Index